Syria: From National Independence to Proxy War

Linda Matar • Ali Kadri
Editors

Syria: From National Independence to Proxy War

palgrave
macmillan

Editors
Linda Matar
National University of Singapore
Singapore, Singapore

Ali Kadri
London School of Economics (LSE)
London, UK

National University of Singapore
Singapore, Singapore

ISBN 978-3-319-98457-5   ISBN 978-3-319-98458-2 (eBook)
https://doi.org/10.1007/978-3-319-98458-2

Library of Congress Control Number: 2018954733

© The Editor(s) (if applicable) and The Author(s) 2019
This work is subject to copyright. All rights are solely and exclusively licensed by the Publisher, whether the whole or part of the material is concerned, specifically the rights of translation, reprinting, reuse of illustrations, recitation, broadcasting, reproduction on microfilms or in any other physical way, and transmission or information storage and retrieval, electronic adaptation, computer software, or by similar or dissimilar methodology now known or hereafter developed.
The use of general descriptive names, registered names, trademarks, service marks, etc. in this publication does not imply, even in the absence of a specific statement, that such names are exempt from the relevant protective laws and regulations and therefore free for general use.
The publisher, the authors and the editors are safe to assume that the advice and information in this book are believed to be true and accurate at the date of publication. Neither the publisher nor the authors or the editors give a warranty, express or implied, with respect to the material contained herein or for any errors or omissions that may have been made. The publisher remains neutral with regard to jurisdictional claims in published maps and institutional affiliations.

Cover illustration: Photo of Baghdad Gate, Raqqa Syria by John Wreford / Alamy Stock Photo
Cover design by Tom Howey

This Palgrave Macmillan imprint is published by the registered company Springer Nature Switzerland AG
The registered company address is: Gewerbestrasse 11, 6330 Cham, Switzerland

Contents

1 Introduction: Syria in the Imperialist Cyclone   1
  Ali Kadri and Linda Matar

Part I   A Historical Perspective of the Syrian Conflict   27

2 What Went Wrong: Understanding the Trajectory of
  Syria's Conflict   29
  Raymond Hinnebusch

3 The New Struggle for Syria and the Nature of the Syrian
  State   53
  Eberhard Kienle

4 Syria: Strong State Versus Social Cleavages   71
  Hiroyuki Aoyama

Part II   Macroeconomy and Society   93

5 Macroeconomic Framework in Pre-conflict Syria   95
  Linda Matar

6   The Syrian Conflict: Selective Socioeconomic Indicators   115
    Nabil Marzouk

7   Lebanon Can't Give Him a Future: Revolutionary
    Subjectivity and Syrian Rebel-Workers in Beirut   133
    Philip Proudfoot

Part III   The Politics of the Syrian Conflict   159

8   Syria in the 'Resistance Front': Persistence Through
    Reconfiguration?   161
    Aurora Sottimano

Part IV   Sectoral Analysis   183

9   The Political Economy of Public Health in Syria: Some
    Global and Regional Considerations   185
    Kasturi Sen

10 The Political Economy of Thermidor in Syria: National
    and International Dimensions   209
    Max Ajl

11 Syria's Food Security: From Self-Sufficiency to Hunger
    as a Weapon   247
    Myriam Ababsa

12 Conclusion: China's Role in Syria's National Security   269
    Linda Matar and Ali Kadri

Index   289

NOTES ON CONTRIBUTORS

Myriam Ababsa is a Social Geographer based in Jordan since 2000. Former student of ENS Fontenay-Saint Cloud, she is an Associate Researcher at the French Institute of the Near East (Institut Français du Proche-Orient (IFPO)) and a consultant. Her work focuses on the impact of public policies on regional and urban development in Jordan and Syria.

Max Ajl is a Development Sociologist at Cornell University. He is based in Tunis, where he is researching state agricultural development policy during the era of state-directed development. His fields of expertise include comparative international development, world-systems theory, Middle East political economy and rural political economy. He has published in *The Journal of Peasant Studies* and *Review of African Political Economy* and edits *Jadaliyya*'s Palestine and Political Economy pages.

Hiroyuki Aoyama is a Professor at Tokyo University of Foreign Studies. His specialty is political thought in Syria and Lebanon. He also runs the site "Facts on the Arab Spring in Syria" (http://syriaarabspring.info).

Raymond Hinnebusch is a Professor of International Relations and Middle East Politics at the University of St Andrews, Fife, Scotland. He is the Founder and Director of the Centre for Syrian Studies. He is the author of numerous articles and books on Syria.

Ali Kadri teaches at the National University of Singapore (NUS) and is a Visiting Fellow at the London School of Economics (LSE) Centre for Human Rights—Laboratory for Advanced Research on the Global

Economy. His most recent publication is *The Cordon Sanitaire. A Single Law Governing Development in East Asia and the Arab World* (Palgrave Macmillan, 2018).

Eberhard Kienle is a Research Professor at the National Center for Scientific Research in Paris and teaches politics at Sciences-Po, Paris. Previously he was a Director of the French Institute of the Near East (IFPO) in Beirut. He also taught at St. Antony's College, Oxford, and the School of Oriental and African Studies (SOAS), University of London.

Nabil Marzouk is a Researcher at the Syrian Center for Policy Research in Damascus. He was a National Strategic Planning Specialist for the 11th five-year plan in Syria (2011–2015) and team leader for the 10th five-year plan (2006–2010), as well as consultant for the State Planning Commission (2004–2007).

Linda Matar is a Senior Research Fellow at the Middle East Institute in NUS. She is also a Lecturer at NUS's College of Alice and Peter Tan. Her research and teaching involve the political economy and economic development of the Arab Near East and Southeast Asia.

Philip Proudfoot is Visiting Research Fellow at the Center for Middle East Studies, Lund and British Academy Post Doctoral Fellow at University of Bath. Philip was the Assistant Director of the Council for British Research in the Levant's British Institute in Amman. His research focuses on the relationship between labour migration and the revolution in Syria.

Kasturi Sen is a Social Scientist working on the political economy of Public Health. She is based at Wolfson College (CR), University of Oxford. Her research interests include health systems in conflict-affected regions, the health impact of sanctions and on the political economy of health and development. She has taught at London, Oxford and Cambridge Universities.

Aurora Sottimano is a Lecturer at Leiden University, a Visiting Researcher at the Center for International Studies (ISCTE-IUL) Lisbon and a Senior Fellow at the Centre for Syrian Studies, St Andrews University (UK). Her research and expertise lie in the politics, political economy and international relations of the Middle East, with focus on Syria.

Abbreviations

ACB	Agricultural Cooperative Bank
ACU	Assistance Coordination Unit
AIIB	Asian Infrastructure Investment Bank
AQI	al-Qaeda in Iraq
ASP	Arab Socialist Party
BIS	Bank for International Settlements
BRI	Belt and Road Initiative
CFSAM	Crop and Food Security Assessment Mission
EIU	Economist Intelligence Unit
ENS	Environment News Service
EU	European Union
FAO	Food and Agriculture Organization
FIRE	Finance, Insurance and Real Estate sectors
FSA	Free Syrian Army
FYP	Five-Year Plan
GAFTA	Great Arab Free Trade Agreement
GCC	Gulf Cooperation Council
GCM	General Company for Mills
GDP	Gross Domestic Product
GFCF	Gross Fixed Capital Formation
GIZ	Deutsche Gesellschaft für Internationale Zusammenarbeit (German Development Agency)
GPs	General Practitioners
GTZ	Deutsche Gesellschaft für Technische Zusammenarbeit (German Technical Cooperation)
HDI	Human Development Index
HOBOOB	General Establishment for Cereal Processing and Trade

HS	Historical Sociology
HSMP	Health Sector Modernisation Programme
ICARDA	International Centre for Agricultural Research in Dry Areas
ICC	International Criminal Court
IDPs	Internally Displaced Persons
IFAD	International Fund for Agricultural Development
IFIs	International Financial Institutions
ILO	International Labour Organization
ILOSTAT	International Labour Organization Database
IMF	International Monetary Fund
IMR	Infant mortality Rate
IR	International Relations
IRIN	(formerly) Integrated Regional Information Networks
IS/ISIS/ISIL	Islamic State/Islamic State of Iraq and Syria or Islamic State of Iraq and al-Sham/Islamic State of Iraq and Levant
ISI	Import-Substitution Industrialisation
IT	Information Technology
LMICs	Low- and Middle-Income Countries
MAAR	Ministry of Agriculture and Agrarian Reform
MDGs	Millennium Development Goals
MENA	Middle East and North Africa
MLA	Ministry of Local Administration
MMR	Maternal Mortality Rate
MOH	Ministry of Health
MSA	Mother Syria Assembly
NAPC	National Agricultural Policy Center
NCC	National Coordination Committee
NGOs	Non-Governmental Organisations
NUS	National University of Singapore
OBOR	One Belt One Road
OCHA	United Nations Office for the Coordination of Humanitarian Affairs
OPE	Out-of-Pocket Expenditure/Expenses
OPTs	Occupied Palestinian Territories
PA	Populist Authoritarianism
PCCW	Pacific Century CyberWorks
PHC	Primary Healthcare
PKK	Partiya Karkerên Kurdistanê (Kurdistan Workers' Party)
PLAN	People's Liberation Army Navy
PPA	Post-Populist Authoritarianism
PPPs	Public-Private Partnerships
PYD	Partiya Yekîtiya Demokrat (Democratic Union Party)

RMB	Renminbi
R&D	Research and Development
R2P	Responsibility to Protect
SANA	Syrian Arab News Agency
SCMP	South China Morning Post
SCPR	Syrian Center for Policy Research
SHI	Social Health Insurance
SYP/SP	Syrian Pound
TBEA	Tebian Electric Apparatus
UAR	United Arab Republic
UN	United Nations
UNDP	United Nations Development Programme
UNGA	United Nations General Assembly
UNHCR	United Nations High Commissioner for Refugees
UNICEF	United Nations Children's Fund
UNSCR	United Nations Security Council Resolution
US	The United States of America
USSR	Union of Soviet Socialist Republics (The Soviet Union)
WB	World Bank
WDI	World Development Indicators
WFP	World Food Programme
WHO	World Health Organization
WWI	World War I
WTO	World Trade Organization
YPG	Yekîneyên Parastina Gel (People's Protection Units)

List of Figures

Fig. 2.1	Junctures in the Syrian conflict's trajectory	31
Fig. 4.1	Population ratios based on religious/sect groups and national/ethnic groups (estimated). Source: Author's computations based on Collelo (1988: 63) and Middle East Watch (1991: 90)	74
Fig. 4.2	Distribution of resident areas based on religious/sect groups and national/ethnic groups. Source: Author's computations based on Boustani and Fargues (1991: 29), Collelo (1988: 62–67), and Commins (1996: 47–48, 70)	75
Fig. 4.3	Relation between politics and social cleavages under parliamentary democracy. Source: Author's analysis	79
Fig. 4.4	Relationship between power struggles and social cleavages under the one-party rule authoritarianism. Source: Author's analysis	81
Fig. 4.5	Use/manipulation of social cleavages under the "two-tier power structure". Source: Author's analysis	86
Fig. 9.1	Health expenditure trends: government health expenditure vs out-of-pocket expenditure. Source: compiled from National Health Accounts (2010), Ministry of Health, Syria, by C Van der Veer (IM), Belgium	199

LIST OF TABLES

Table 4.1	Major social cleavages in Syria	75
Table 9.1	Health indicators in Syria, 1970–2010	193
Table 9.2	MMR per 100,000 live births in Egypt, Jordan, and the Syrian Arab Republic	194
Table 9.3	Public spending on health care in Syria in 2003	195
Table 10.1	Successive changes in the land laws, 1958–1963	215
Table 10.2	The distribution of land in the countryside in 1970 and 1981	222
Table 10.3	The distribution of land in the countryside in 1981 and 1994	225
Table 10.4	Production expenses, procurement prices, and profit margins for selected crops	229
Table 11.1	Wheat and Barley production, surface and yield (1970–2011)	250
Table 11.2	The evolution of cereals and legumes production 2004–2008	255
Table 11.3	Syria wheat, barley, and maize production (2010–2014)	260
Table 11.4	Bread prices by province in August 2015	262

CHAPTER 1

Introduction: Syria in the Imperialist Cyclone

Ali Kadri and Linda Matar

In 1946, Syria's anti-colonial war ended in victory. The post-colonial government's task of building development through self-reliance or socialism during the 1950s and 1960s was followed by the easing of the socialist stance under Hafez al-Asad and ended with the introduction of fully fledged neoliberal reforms in the 2000s. These three periods—socialist developmentalism, its easing, and its termination—are the three main stages of Syria's recent economic history, until the breakout of the conflict.

Since independence, Syria has struggled to fend off imperialist aggression. Throughout its age of progressive reforms, beginning with its first national parliament in 1954, and during its era of socialist dirigisme, Syria became a relatively prosperous and economically self-contained nation (Hemesh 2014; Chouman 2005). Starting from a colonially induced low developmental base in the post-independence era,[1] it registered significant advances against illiteracy and in improving healthcare and other human development indicators. Most significant among its socialist policies were

A. Kadri (✉)
London School of Economics (LSE), London, UK

National University of Singapore, Singapore, Singapore
e-mail: a.kadri@lse.ac.uk

L. Matar (✉)
National University of Singapore, Singapore, Singapore
e-mail: linda@nus.edu.sg

© The Author(s) 2019
L. Matar, A. Kadri (eds.), *Syria: From National Independence to Proxy War*, https://doi.org/10.1007/978-3-319-98458-2_1

land reform and redistribution measures. These righted the wrongs of centuries of inequality and harmonised the pace of economic development for years to come.

Swept by the global momentum of neoliberalism after the fall of the Soviet Union, Syria loosened its socialist dirigisme and opted to enter the world of free markets. By late 2010, the economic model that had previously ensured the basic needs of society through local capacities and resources came apart. Inevitably, economic fragility slipped into political fragility.

Syria exists in a war zone. It has been and remains officially at war with Israel. Given its level of underdevelopment, its security is not only a matter of its national defences—it does not enjoy the high-tech military capabilities to ensure it a self-defence capacity through technological parity and instead must rely on peoples' war. For that, Syria first depends on the unity of its people, their anti-imperialist forms of consciousness, and the security of the livelihoods of its working masses. Security for Syria is a holistic affair: it is the synergy between the primacy of national security and communal and individual securities. Such a security dynamic encompasses all the sub-components of security: security of health, education, shelter, and so on and the economic and social policies that cement industrial production and the public sector of the economy. Obviously, neoliberalism is an ideology that favours private over the public concerns. It quintessentially de-securitises Syria.

By embarking on the neoliberal road, Syria followed the mantra that the private sector is the true leader of development. It acceded to the delusion that a momentarily diluted sovereignty is a small price to pay for long-term economic success. However, just as every other state falling outside the cordon sanitaire of imperialism failed the task of development under the diktat of neoliberalism, Syria succumbed. By 2010, its social and economic indicators, the true gauges of value transfer to the working class, plummeted.

Development has its rules. No state can develop if it does not emplace the necessary institutional safeguards to subordinate economic to social goals. Syria's old, new, and state bourgeoisie were in control of the levers of state power. They were eager to expand and dollarise their private concerns and/or to recapture the lost properties confiscated under the Arab socialism of the 1960s. The institutions tasked with development lacked a working-class component. As such, they aligned development with private, as opposed to social, ends. And above all, they compromised national security. The resultant disaster is strictly the responsibility of the neoliberal class, which is the cross-border class relationship that extends to but is not limited to Syria. This relationship takes institutional form and power in the political sphere and its accompanying policies of dollarised finance that continue to grab public wealth via Syrian holding companies and offer their services as border guards for the Israeli state. This layer of the Syrian bourgeoisie, the "holding company layer," is the subordinate partner of financial imperialism. It assists in setting ablaze the Syrian social formation at the behest of its more senior partners abroad who, in turn, at the behest of capital incarnate in history, effect the accumulation side of growth by waste, setting aside excess capacity, or the destruction of underutilised capacity in a world of overproduction.

In Syria's race for American-style "modernity"—the ostentatious consumption signifying status and the Veblenian emulation of the richer imperialist masters—much was lost. The state, the organ that organises the expansion of national capital, capitulated to the competing interests of comprador-merchants willing to dismantle the country and sell it as scrap metal. An international financial class devoured its Syrian offspring, growing as it does by the destruction of value.

Although market reforms began in the late 1980s as soon as the USSR fell, it was not until the mid-2000s that the state started to seriously ration its public and welfare provisioning. By the late 2000s, it had laid most of its financial and real wealth at the feet of the private sector. Resource allocation mechanisms followed personal interests and whims. Peculiarly, the wide-ranging liberal economic reforms introduced by Bashar al-Asad eroded the income share of labour in the GDP (Matar 2016). In 2006–2007, his government introduced such a tremendous and rapid raft of liberal reforms that their impact resembled, to a certain degree, the "shock therapy" experienced by Russia after the fall of the Soviet Union. The government removed the price caps on necessities, withdrew subsidies that supported the basic consumption bundle, and retrenched the credit and trade facilitation that backed nationalist industrial production. Although the rate of new entrants into the labour market continued to rise at a diminishing rate, the neoliberally designed rate of "decent" job creation declined at a much faster rate. What could have been a boon amidst lower long-term fertility rates, which lowered the rate of new entrants into the job market, became a bane because of fiscal and monetary contraction, combined with the deregulation of the external channels of value flows—namely, the capital and trade accounts (Kadri 2016). In response to lower investment and consumption demand, labour demand plummeted. Yet in official figures, the unemployment rate declined. As occurred elsewhere, an immense pool of redundant labour, which eked out a living in informal poverty employment, was now counted as employed. However, the real unemployment rate, the one associated with "decent" living standards, rose.

Whether by repression or by ideologically alienating measures, liberal economic reforms crowd out the public or labour-related concerns. They exert downwards pressure on an otherwise well-deserved income share of the working class. Rising inflation dampening labour's purchasing power, widening economic and social polarisation, neglect of rural areas, and increasing rural-urban migration contributed to the *objective conditions* of social unrest in Syria. The *subjective conditions*, the perception that there is a crisis of rule within the ruling class (Lenin 1917), arose as reactionary media fanned the flames of sectarianism and as other Arab regimes appeared vulnerable and easy to topple early in the Arab Spring.

A caveat may be called for here. These subjective and objective circumstances prevail in all societies, including the advanced ones. However, they interact to dis-equilibrate an order only under specific historical contingencies or when the organisational and ideological balances of the class struggle reach a threshold requiring realignment. For instance, one can think of the American two-party system, be it Trump's or Hillary's popular support during the 2017 election campaign, to appreciate that an indoctrinated and alienated working class can inflict upon itself significant harm without exhibiting the slightest signs of awareness. Working classes are internationalised social and historical relations whose dividedness is the manifestation of capital. And to be sure, for any working class to segment along identitarian and sectarian lines is a self-defeating course of action.

Leading Indicators of Syria's Descent

Prior to the Arab Spring, there were several indications that reforms were headed in an anti-worker direction. Principally, investment moved away from industry into commercial types of activities to ensure quick returns to the reconstituted post-liberalisation comprador-merchant class. Our meetings with the Chambers of Commerce and Industry, prior to the Arab Spring, revealed the exuberance of the former group and the dismay of the latter. Naturally, no changes to the production base go unanswered by changes in production relations. The shift away from industry to commerce, declining productivity followed by falling wages and rising income inequality, was mirrored by an ideological shift away from nationalism, the Ba'ath party, and pan-Arab politics.

The downside risk of such a model came into evidence as the hegemony of the state over civil society shrunk and the hidden ferment of popular discontent with the declining standards of living escalated. Although the dichotomy internal-external is analytical, let us say for the sake of expository clarity that the poor interface of neoliberal policies with society impacting the working class is the internal component. Put differently, the Syrian working class is the internal or national side. Internal and external in terms of value relations cannot be associated with the construct of identity or nationality. After all, the dollar is the world's currency and an international wealth-holding medium. As such, it unites ruling classes across national borders. Internal and external are defined according to class, not nation.

However, neoliberalism is a worldwide dominant ideology—the ideology of the global ruling class. It is an external ideological doctrine forced down the throats of the Third World. Just as it was imposed on weak states everywhere to usurp their surpluses, it was also forced upon Syria. In our conversation with Syrian official figures in different ministries, between 2007 and 2008, we were repeatedly informed that Syria wanted to satisfy the International Monetary Fund (IMF) and the World Bank (WB), institutions from which it took advice.

Syria even sought to join the World Trade Organization (WTO). With respect to this institution, we asked the official in charge of reforming trade: Why are you removing the trade barriers that protect your fragile industries, and abide by WTO rules when the US would veto your accession to the said organisation? He facetiously answered that we are turning economically to the right in the hope that in the future we can turn politically to the right. These measures were grave miscalculations everywhere. In the case of Syria, a country situated in a region moulded and riven with oil and war, the results are self-evident. War is a much bigger business to imperialism than trading in Syrian cotton and textiles.

Classes co-integrate by the medium of abstract value, the money form, and increased dollarisation. They are cross-border relationships within a hierarchical order of determination. They can be of the same genre—a bourgeoisie—but with certain subordinate classes of lesser weight involved in the more grotesque forms of violence, repression, and exploitation. The reforming class in Syria was Syrian by passport. But passports are not determinants of class. As makers of history, classes are the concomitant of history, principally impersonal and objective. Peoples belong to classes and they mediate *immediacy* (current conditions)—that is, they manage or change current conditions (immediacy) in line with historical necessity or, as is the case currently, by the degree of retreat of revolutionary ideology.

Syrian reforms occurred in a moment of socialist ideological defeat. During our visits to Syria in 2008 prior to the Arab uprising, the phrases "reforms are inexorable, the president is Western oriented and married to a British person, and that the old socialist Ba'ath remains an impediment for development" echoed everywhere. The Syrians who were letting down the nation's political and economic safeguards belonged above all to the class of imperialism. They were not Syrians in working class or national terms. They were bourgeois subordinates within the same imperialist class, headed by US-led financial capital. True, they were in terms of geography and physical being internally based. But ideologically they were external forces assaulting Syria. The same US-led imperialism that has been committing wanton aggression against regional states in the service of their deconstruction was the overdetermining historical force aggressing Syria.

Our hypothesis was, and remains, that Syria—the real home of culturally diverse working people—underwent an imperialist assault before and during the Arab Spring to tear it asunder. In standard political economy parlance, US-led imperialism breaks down geographic barriers to subvert and re-articulate less developed modes of production, to un-weave their social fabric and re-weave them into the social fabric of US capitalism. In political calculus, Syria is a country whose obliteration would leverage US–Israeli power over the region. Bringing democracy to Syria or anywhere else via US imperialism is not a serious proposition. Imperialism cannot impart a democracy which it does not enjoy—neither now nor in its own history. The notion that the Western formation, whose class rule has annihilated hundreds of millions since the long sixteenth century, is democratic because it votes is an even less serious proposition. Just as Bertrand Russell was struck with the fact that a man as intelligent as Aristotle never realised that he lived in a slave society, so too should everyone regard the claim that the West is a democracy.

Capital reproduces by war. If, for a fleeting moment, the voting system, the alienation, and the stultification of the Western working classes do not deliver the desired capital-oriented results, violent repression would ensue. That is not a hypothetical statement—rather it is empirically and historically substantiated by the annals of European/American labour history which are written in the crimson of capital's victims.

At the time of writing, the Syrian conflict is still ongoing. Because the conflict is internationalised and mediates outstanding global imbalances, only the historically contingent rise of China augurs hope. Those who thought of Syria and its conflict in terms of sectarian barbarians confined to their own national boundary ought to be soberly reminded that the neoliberal assault, just as the ongoing war, are proxies for imperialism within the international class struggle—conversely also, the struggle against imperialism. Neglect and contempt for geopolitics, the personalisation of class, its reduction to the person of Asad, and parochialism, which are the mainstay of "the elitist intellectualist circles, mainly those of the cosmopolitan anti-national leftist type," reduce the impact of anti-imperialist struggle upon the unfolding of social dialectics in each separate case/region/and so on to nothing (Abdel-Malek 1977). The Western left obviates two principal currents of history: wars of imperialist aggression and the necessity to combat imperialism.

The politics of capital are the precursor for war-related expansion. Ranked geo-strategically, Syria preoccupies a significant chunk of international relations debate. The US imperialist resources allotted to finance its war in Syria, and its associated ideology, are almost unlimited. Many are unaware that US-led capital earns what it spends. Vulgar discussions speak of rising war cost or debt thwarting imperialist expansion. These miss the point and purpose of such purchases. War spending absorbs the surplus and acts countercyclically in favour of capital. War reshapes value relations for profit making as well. The American war effort requires bond issuance, which absorbs excess dollars created in the frenzy of financialisation and that would otherwise form bubbles or precipitate another financial or demand-led crisis. Imperialist war is a win-win game for the US-led financial class. Many social scientists bobbling around in search of grants after the commercialisation of education may not be able to resist the lure of US financing, which is really the credit of the financial class. Consequently, it cannot surprise that they reproduce the dominant ideology. Resultantly, the mainstream is awash with the cliché that al-Asad is a demon. Many already adhere to the faux ethic of regime change in Syria. Judging by Iraq and Libya, for instance, regime change does not end the war. What it does is strengthen the most obscurantist armed groups. For capital, a religious order which disparages women and rights in general resonates nicely with its inner drive. One ought to recall that legalised segregation was still the norm in the US only five decades ago. If the US-sponsored jihadists win in Syria, slavery might just slip back into the capitalist world by their spiritual élan. To be sure, all is unethical under capitalism. The calculus of the contribution of class struggle to the defeat of US-led imperialism, especially the effort of the Syrian Arab Army in defeating the US and its allies in Syria, is essentially the only *just* anti-imperialist tactic and strategy.

Neoliberal bourgeois elements in the Syrian government still fail to see that this war cannot be outmanoeuvred with merchant bargaining. They also fail to see that US-led imperialism may hang them as a show of force even if they prostrate at its feet. Even their attempt to introduce modifications to Decree Number 66 of 2012 through Law Number 10 of 2016, which organises housing ownership and reconstruction in two areas of greater Damascus, came to be another platform from which to commit aggression against the Syrian state. The plan addresses shanty town-like structures built over the decades preceding the war, without permits or safety standards. The Western sectors attentive to regional events, left and right, were up in arms accusing the government of sectarianism. The purpose of the Law is to formalise the ownership of the original residents, yet Deutsche Welle headlined its dispatch on the Law with the title, "Syria: Expropriation is 'punishment for those who protested'," and Counterpunch stated, "Syria's New 'Law Number Ten' Devastates Sunni Refugees" (Deutsche Welle 2018; Lamb 2018). The moment one hears a Western body bugle Sunnism-Shiism, suspicion should be aroused. Why would a progressive say Sunnis instead of immiserated working people? The bourgeoisie, busy accumulating, does not identify with any working group by its sectional denomination. The irregular housing in these two areas, the problems associated therewith, and the government efforts at dealing with them have been in the news for years before the war. It is clear the new Law aims to protect the original people living in these two areas while dealing with organising the reconstruction. The worrisome part of the Law is its allowances for privately owned holding companies which intend to grab peoples' property for pittances or less.

To be specific, the Law gives one-month notice to property owners (Syrian Prime Ministry 2018). But it allows for anyone who has any relation, personally, or by proxy or power of attorney, to apply within this one-month grace period and indicate his or her place of residence, attaching pertinent documents, if available, or *just indicating* without documentation in their application the locations, shares, lines, and kind of property or rights one claims and any legal action related to the property. Furthermore, the Law allows for relatives of the applicants, to the fourth degree, to make the application (Syrian Prime Ministry 2018). The Western interlocutors have taken no effort to read the Law before passing judgement. If some want to read Sunni into words they have not read, they are clearly engaged in sectarian incitement.

One should be critical of the Law because it aims to revive real estate and tourism as opposed to popular housing. Furthermore, one should be critical of the holding companies, which would own part of the rebuilt structures and which belong to the same class that had undermined Syria's national security in the past. Their plan is to mimic the failed Lebanese Solidere model. Syria is still at war, and an emphasis on reconstructing for tourism, while neglecting national industry and social infrastructure, is a repeat of the blunders of the past. For any ruler, the undermining of sovereignty remains the only legitimate reason for toppling the reigning government.

It took the USSR's end to tamp down the intensity of the Lebanese war—which is not to say that it totally ended. The thinness of such thinking about the tenacity of US imperialist aggression, a state whose macroeconomy expands by spending on war and the credit to support the war, is what prevailed prior to the Arab uprising amongst too many official Syrian circles. It lingers until the present. There are limitless possibilities of how the future will unfold, but a war of this calibre is a testing ground for international power displays.

It is a mistake to read recent Syrian history like the mainstream media and academia's bedtime story: repressed people non-violently rose, but the regime forced them into a violent posture that led to the militarisation of the conflict and the involvement of imperialism. Such a narrative is selectively biased and indeed incoherent. Time, or Western historical time, the tempo and chronology of history as it unfolds within a capitalist-dominated social order, prostrates at the feet of US-led imperialism. The US chooses the time to inflict the damage. Moreover, the story-telling approach presumes that there are inherent virtues in Western democracy. It presupposes that at one point or another, primitive people rise to the ideal, which is Tocquevillian democracy—without the slaughter of colonised Algerians, of course. The mainstream has a god, which is the goodness of the democracy in Western formations. Its imperialism is not really, truly nasty. It is a laid-back mission civilisatrice. The US is forced to expand and engage abroad at a cost to itself. They really cannot imagine that these costs are the profits of the financial class, without which the global economy would sputter and spin from its smooth whirring. We think it is because they presume that the macroeconomy of the US suffers just like any individual when it incurs debts. There is no other way to explain this penchant and permissiveness vis-à-vis US imperialism but utter ignorance. The US-European mission is to impart "good," while its depopulation, its reduction of life before the historically determined expectancy, occurring as we speak, is just an unintended consequence.

Global Imbalances and Syria

Just as the US and Israel backed the secessionist Kurdish forces in Northern Iraq, they also backed the Northern pro-US Kurdish forces in Northern Syria. These conjoint imperialist/Kurdish forces have weakened the central states in Iraq and Syria. In Iraq, the combined imperialist/Kurdish assault, which dates back to 1959, along with the prolonged UN-imposed embargo (1991–2003) resulted in the massacre of hundreds of thousands of people (Gordon 2010). In Syria too, the imperialist/Kurdish alliance eviscerated the state as it confronted hordes of mercenaries. The imperialist forces engage an already much weaker Syria, and, by implication, the position of US-led imperialism as it strengthens its grip over a strategic region further cements its hegemony over the globe. To see the salience of imperialist aggression as policy and as the mode by which the grounds for the expansion of capital are practised from the very onset of the conflict is what thinking historically or in abstract/social time means. The balance of forces that existed then—early in the conflict or before Russian intervention—was characterised by a prevalence of Gulf-funded Islamists alongside a weak international socialist movement. US imperialism decided the pace with which it deconstructed Syria. Before Russian intervention, the US could dictate the way war resources were harnessed to compress or lengthen the social time required to meet the demands of accumulation by militarism. To even entertain the thought that "Western democracy" will lay back and let Syria develop into some prosperous state is either credulity or complicity. Moreover, from the outset, the Syrian opposition was ideologically in cahoots with imperialism through its liberalism—the ideological expression of capitalism.

To date, the geostrategic position of Syria has proven to be more complex and intractable than imagined. Regional and international players have continued to reinforce their intervention, frustrating any resolution. Syria has become the grounds for settling regional and international scores. The assault on Syria is in part an assault on its long-standing ally, Russia. Backed by the consent of an ascending China, Russia's move reasserts and circularly if partially contributes to the integrity of the Syrian state. This has enabled the Syrian government to break the political and military stalemate in 2017, as it reclaimed control of lost territories. The display of Russian power in Syria undermines the image of the US as the hegemonic empire in a time of delicate global transitions. Disagreements are acute and notable scholars warn that a nearly unthinkable World War Three has become a possibility (Chossudovsky 2018).

To further complicate matters, the conflict has dragged in a plethora of state and non-state actors (such as ISIS), providing the alibi for US-sponsored mass murder/destruction of the major cities surrounding the Mesopotamian desert, such as Raqqa, Ramadi, Mosul, and so on. The elimination of living people and assets is elimination of value. The elimination of historical landmarks is also elimination of value as conventionally understood as well as cultural value. Both destructive processes are industries of war, which realise the military commodity by the consumption of assets and human lives, and laterally dehumanise the subject or masses of the region. Imperialism, like colonialism, needs to bestow a-less-than-human status on their subjects, as part and parcel of the rationale for their eradication. Capital, the social relationship, is still with us; why should its tested methods ever change? The US-led assault attempts to transform the most historical people of the planet into a people without history.

Beyond its humanitarian character, for instance, the Syrian refugee problem exerts global downwards pressure on wages. It is just another outstanding problem under capitalism that fuels xenophobic politics in nations most capable of providing the required humanitarian assistance. Back in 1976, Garrett Hardin pondered the possibility that Europe might shoot refugees on the high sea (Hardin 1976). With the rise of a populist-rightist belt in East and South Europe, France and Germany have delegated the regulation of refugee/labour flows to their lesser partners in the EU periphery. Refugees both produce and boost the capital relation. Beyond the charity and the humanitarian fanfare, the creation of refugees significantly bears upon the sphere of production.

THE SYRIA DEBATE

Although a Russian or an American retreat in Syria would signal significant shifts in the tectonic plates of geopolitics, the mainstream debate is more about pseudo-moral condemnation of crimes during times of inter-communal proxy wars. Gowan (2018) attributes such de-prioritisation of imperialism on the part of the liberals to "philanthropic fantasies and sentimental phrases about fraternity," upon which Engels once remarked. They advocate "edifying humanism" and "generic, vague, moral appeals" not "concrete political action" to challenge "a specific social system." Western academics escape from the clash of real social forces into an amorphous humanity, and as such they are certainly air on the side of imperialism and not the Syrian people (Gowan 2018). What is less widely debated is that war is constant under capitalism and its humanitarian crisis is part of the imperialist industry.

So far, the struggle against US imperialism in the centre has borne little fruit. During the latest tripartite US-led assault on Syria, in April 2018, the Western anti-war movement was absent. Its agenda centres on the environmental message that seeks to save some animal species for viewing by richer children at a future date, while the poor Third Worlders sink in the Mediterranean. The Western anti-war movement has never been historically significant, and to assume that the Western working classes will lead world revolution was and remains quite misleading. In the main, the Western working classes are financially integrated with capital, which is why significant numbers are proponent of fascism. That is also true of the petty bourgeoisie in the South. But what distinguishes the North is its political concentration of power. The Western working classes' contribution to capital, via their political participation through the "democratic" ballot box, buttresses capital's ideology and its daily crimes. While ISIS has its crimes produced Hollywood-style on YouTube videos, for the Western society of the spectacle (to borrow from Debord 1994 [1967]), the death of thousands from hunger daily and the fast-eroding capacity of the planet to sustain life cannot be seen nor thought.

War as a Value Relationship

In a world where the value of the commodity in price form overweighs the value of human lives, the process of accumulation with which war is bound is not necessarily visible on the surface. As the war ravages Syrians, destroys economic and social infrastructures, levels a significant part of humanity's shared historical heritage and nature, and reconstructs psychological and identity cleavages between working people, it also contributes to global accumulation. Militarism and its wars are an auto-contained domain of accumulation and a system that requires feedback to regulate efficiency and functionality. The US-led capital class, whose sources of growth through finance have grown alongside financialisaton, is the main beneficiary of global militarism. Treasury bills financing wars, the expansion of the dollar money supply, are the source of finance and financial expansion. Such fictitious dollar-denominated debt does not have any real corresponding value in the economy. This debt is also the moneyed wealth of the financial sector—every credit is also debit. These monetary expansions are in constant search of collateral. And apart from the taxing of the working class, war is the best means to underwrite the expansion of financial wealth. The debts, which are also credits, incentivise more imperialist wars. The expansion of the money supply that eggs on further wars is the *differentia specifica* of US-led imperialism. That is why in Syria, the US-led class is the only imperialist class, not Russia nor China.

The system's feedback loop for Syria, the corrective measures that would redress the fault in its development, is or is not its own by the degree Syria opposes imperialism. The real but abstract social relationship or the class exerting power over the Syrian course of events was the imperialist class prior to the conflict and continued to be the imperialist class since the conflict started—albeit to a lesser degree as a result of Russian intervention. At any rate, the corrective and feedback loop for Syria, what it would take to set it on a sounder course of development, principally lies in the domain of international relations and the politics of superpowers—hence, the bottleneck.

In value terms, war efficiency may be said to be the rate of consumption of living and dead labour and assets per unit of additional value produced. Because war is production by destruction, it follows that the more it destroys, the more it produces. In the same production process, which is war, there are Syrians serving as inputs to production with their lives, as well as workers associated with imperialism. In a commodified, hence moneyed process, the imperialist heartland, the creator of finance for the expansion of production, is the power that also applies the Law of value in militarism, which is concomitantly the recipient of a greater share of value in money form. War profit, manifest as the appearance of war-generated value, is a significant proportion of the world's product. Such a high profit area draws in variety of capitals in search of higher returns and hence the reduction of a normal life's chronological time into abstract time, or the social time that compresses the normal lengths of lives to the demands of the socially necessary labour required for production as war. However, the real reason for depopulation in and through war exceeds simply the demands of war profits. Crises of overproduction forcing underutilisation find in wars the most valuable contribution in the measures that deepen an already constant state of depopulation.

It is not solely the intensity of the consumption of life in a short time span with the use of quality war machinery which constitutes value; it is also the subject in the value relation, its identity. Thus, within the category of value, there are the value shares of the working class and the value shares of imperialism whose determination hinges on revolutionary consciousness and forms of working class organisation within the class struggle—here of course we mean the global class struggle. Thus, the value share of imperialism rises by the departure of war and other profits from the share of working people enduring the treachery of war and the synergy by which the process of war boosts or diminishes revolutionary consciousness. Alongside the real war, there is another war ongoing that lays the social foundation for the production of future surplus value: the war to reconstruct a state, which continuously divides working people.

The mainstream suggests replicating the Iraq-Bremer sectarian constitution to end the war in Syria. Such model is a modified version of the Lebanese Taif Accord, a sectarian arrangement that has its origin in the 1926 French-designed constitution for Lebanon. A state as a means to further the interests of the bourgeois layers in each sect is always and will always be in a state at war with itself. The conflicts in Iraq and in Lebanon are far from being over. These divisive constitutional measures deepen the chasms upon which imperialist-sponsored wars endure. They culminate intense phases of conflict and endow what imperialism has gained by genocide and ethnic cleansing, the new facts on the grounds established by the use of force, with legal status. The dispossession of the working class, the counter land and asset reforms inflate social inequality to the point of persistent social violence. The war combines with the low shares of working class incomes devolved by the sectarian state to supplant working class unity and further de-subjectify labour in the value relationship. The working class loses the power to negotiate its living wage and the thrust of commodification transmutes resources untouched by capital into the legal property of comprador capitalists.

Other than the prolonged debilitation of the region, what purpose does it serve to erect a state governed by sects that reproduce by snatching rents from and destroying their own social formations while each of them is subordinated/integrated vertically with imperialism? Mainstream proposals to mimic the Bremer plan for Iraq in Syria are a statement of intention to surrender, or forced submission, to imperialism. They are also the juridical fodder for future wars. However, that is not to say that the vicious circle lasts forever. Just as constructed-divisive identities were erected in a state of defeatism, they can be deconstructed in the practice of anti-imperialist struggle.

Syria is now divided between the government and imperialist-controlled regions. Its dismemberment is continuously redesigned by the degree of external support and funding to the warring parties. Furthermore, over the last seven years, a war economy has developed—paired with its by-product, a war bourgeois. No amount of US financing is too costly for

Syria's war. Syria is in the spotlight, and a shift in the international power balance achieved on its territory favouring the US will redeem any future costs the empire may incur. Such is the enormity of the problematic that work which criticises US intervention into Syria faces. Salient mainstream positioning on Syria, which is more about the personal love-hate relationships with presidents, corroborates Bertrand Russell's view that very little of the books goes into politics. Taking positions on Syria is assuming a class position at the heart of the international class struggle—history, but history shorn of the fables and tall tales which cover it and conceal its truth. Progressive forces have always been perfectly aware of the shortcomings of the Syrian ruling class. They have also been perfectly aware that nothing justifies siding with US-led imperialism in a war of national liberation led by the Syrian Arab Army.

Purpose and Structure of This Endeavour

This edited volume attempts to explore the causes and complexities of the Syrian conflict. More pertinently, it examines the historical background that has laid the objective conditions for Syria to end up in its current disaster. The compilation is an interdisciplinary effort with viewpoints and positions from different angles of the political spectrum. The initial papers for this volume were presented at the annual Middle East Institute conference at the National University of Singapore (NUS) on 1st and 2nd of September 2016. The editors were only part of a team that selected the papers to be included in this volume. The objective is to provide a broad-scope analysis of what went wrong in Syria. We hope that the work at hand illuminates our understanding of what has become an almost intractable Syrian crisis.

Much of the recent literature on Syria has focused on the proceedings and course of the conflict itself. It has addressed internal and/or external dynamics of the conflict, rebel militarisation and fragmentation, and the foreign policy implications of the more powerful international and regional players. Just as with any other social situation, the Syrian conflict is governed by multifarious and interconnected elements, such that no amount of theoretical literature can adequately explain them. This volume examines several dimensions in the development of state, society, and politics in Syria. In particular it addresses issues of power, neoliberal reform, and management of regional and international challenges and assesses the food security question and the government's social service provisioning. It also touches upon the underlying implications of various policy and strategic measures that had driven Syria into war. Furthermore, the work investigates Syria's political reconfiguration—a process whose drivers are both regional and international, threat and opportunity.

The chapters presented herein draw on a broad range of disciplines and expertise, which highlight the more obscure factors that have shaped the baleful events. It also delves further into history, rather than opting for the myopic and self-blinding obsession with the current government of Bashar al-Asad. It partially covers the post-independence period, looking into the Ba'athist rule (1964–1970), the Hafez al-Asad government (1970–2000), and Bashar al-Asad government (2000–2010), and touches upon the recent conflict. While the contributors to this collection do not overindulge in speculation around conflict resolution, they explore some of the contemporary events in ways that can inform current debate.

One addendum or framing comment is worth articulating here. The mainstream literature has exonerated colonialism and, with it, imperialism of any wrongdoing by trivialising the Sykes-Picot Treaty. It may be worthwhile to note that reductionism in history, which is after all a continuum of events shaped by social action, is inappropriate. Facts on the ground, like the Sykes-Picot, are created and reared. Some develop, and some do not. It is not just the Sykes-Picot Treaty of 1917 which determines the burdens that have weighed on post-colonial Syria or lack thereof afterwards, as the pro-imperialist interlocutors would like us to believe. Sykes-Picot matters but it is not the only thing which matters. Capital is a constant. Through colonialism and imperialism, it has aggressed the nation, remoulded national class structures, and obliterated resources as part and parcel of the accumulation process. The belligerence of imperialism, which is the rule rather than the exception, also determines the forms of realisation of citizenry in the state, the form of the national political process. The debate around the impact of a purposively analytically "isolated" Sykes-Picot is a malign diversion. It is ideologically useful to create a mini-industry wondering whether one of the imperialist treaties was consequential to future development, and to wonder this in isolation from all the surrounding facts, in order to inculpate the national forces.

The volume is divided into four parts. Each part elaborates on the origins and the dynamics of today's crisis from a specific disciplinary angle. Put together, they provide a basically holistic picture of Syria's developmental trajectory starting in the mid-twentieth century up until the present day. Part I presents a historical reading of modern Syria since its political independence in 1946 up until the contemporary period. Part II discusses macroeconomics and social conditions before and during the conflict. Part III focuses on the politics of the conflict. The volume also brings into perspective sectoral analysis, mainly the health and agricultural sectors, which are presented in Part IV.

Altogether, the edited volume consists of 12 chapters in total, which scholars from a variety of disciplinary backgrounds submitted. We have tried to channel this multidisciplinary research, as much as we could in this space, towards explaining how Syria went from tenuous stability into a war-torn society. The views and arguments presented in the chapters are, of course, those of the authors. As mentioned earlier, the chapters were presented at a conference held at NUS. At the time of the conference, the late Professor Peter Sluglett was head of the Middle East Institute at NUS. A conference on Syria was his idea. He extended his utmost support and made available needed resources to make the conference the success it was. It is unfortunate that he passed away before seeing the result of the work in this collected volume.

The chapter breakdown is as follows. Raymond Hinnebusch's incisive chapter examines the trajectory of the Syrian conflict by laying bare the points of inflexion that have pushed the mass protests in 2011 to end up in their current proxy war form. Chapter 2 by Hinnebusch is the first chapter in the historical section. His presentation writes in the vein of the path-dependency concept that highlights the over-determinacy of structure over agency. The analysis is traced back to the post-WWI period when Western imperial intervention imposed the flawed regional state system. According to Hinnebusch, this ironbound structure has sharply constrained the options of agents—national leaders—in their pursuit of state-building and power consolidation. Thus, Hinnebusch traces the conflict's origins to the contradictions that existed during the pre-uprising phase. Moving forward, structural over-determinacy can also explain why Syria became vulnerable to the bursting Arab Spring in 2011 and why and how the initial protests turned into a violent and intractable armed conflict. He argues that the Syrian conflict has passed through several junctures at which alternative choices were available to actors. Every time actors chose to tread a certain route, the structural context within which subsequent actors had to operate was altered. Hinnebusch concludes that competitive external intervention for and against the Syrian government has prolonged the conflict and obstructed various attempts to enforce a compromised political settlement. His comprehensive contribution has bearing on a wide range of fields of study, including authoritarian resilience, democratisation, social movement theory, sectarianism, and civil and proxy war.

In Chaps. 3 and 4, both Eberhard Kienle and Hiroyuki Aoyama provide a reading of the political history in Syria from independence until the present. They both bring into critical perspective Patrick Seale's seminal work, *The Struggle for Syria*, published in 1965. They remind the readers that post-independence Syria faced more or less similar internal and external challenges when it sought to ensure some semblance of stability in a territory bracketed by borders initially carved by external powers. The authors' analysis however presents different conclusions. Kienle argues that Syria's current challenges are not new, especially since the Syrian conflict has boiled down to actors in a politically divided state who have enjoyed privileged alliance with external actors—an alliance that is stronger than their solidarity with fellow Syrians (Chap. 3). Kienle stresses that the new struggle for Syria, like the old one, is premised on identity politics or, more precisely, societal cleavages. The country's deep divisions pushed various actors vying for territorial control to enter strong cross-border alliances. Such alliances were initiated without reference to the judgement, wishes, or wills of all Syrians who were forced to witness such cooperation and endure its consequences. Kienle concludes, given that cross-border ties are stronger than in-country ties, Syria then can be considered a "territorial" rather than a "nation" state.

In contrast to Kienle's conclusion, Hiroyuki Aoyama argues Syria managed to consolidate itself into a strong state despite societal divisions, especially during the reign of Hafez al-Asad (1970–2000). Aoyama deploys identity and social cleavage when examining the political underpinnings of the Syrian conflict. He contends that the strength of the Syrian state has varied across time depending on the balance of forces that prevailed during the specific historical phase (Chap. 4). More explicitly, he stresses that national cohesiveness is commensurate with the weakness of colonial or imperialist forces. He reminds us that struggle for independence in Syria in the Mandate period attested to national unity among intra-social formations and intra-racial groups. It was a period when the Syrian people transcended colonially constructed religious and cultural differences and defined their identity based on national unity and language-based and territorial community. Moving forward, Aoyama reveals how social cleavages played a role in politics under the authoritarian rule of Hafez al-Asad, which, according to him, relied on the "two-tier power structure" (the "visible" and the "hidden" powers). Hafez al-Asad managed to strengthen his social base of support by building alliances based on social classes. He thereby drew close with the big capitalists—the old bourgeois class. This, in turn, widened the gap between the capital city (Damascus) and other cities (Homs and Hama), thereby decreasing the power of the traditional governing classes. The Hafez al-Asad administration, through social cleavages based on region, split the traditional governing classes into a pro-government group and an anti-government group. It also used the pro-government group to act as a conduit for the anti-government group. In doing so, the government mitigated the build-up of resentment on the part of either group. Aoyama concludes that the relationship between social cleavages and politics in Syria has faced an eminent pitfall—"confusing political pluralism with cultural pluralism." He stresses that the intermediation of the cultural identity in politics assumes pro- or anti-imperialist valency depending on the balance of power with imperialism. As Syria liberalised its economy and shifted towards the West, it became self-evident that imperialist ideology would extend to it and more thoroughly permeate it in the form of more acute sectarian politics, thereby inhibiting national integration.

In Part II, which focuses on the Syrian economy and society, Linda Matar examines the macroeconomic strategies and the main adjustments that took place in the period between 2000 and 2010 (Chap. 5). Her work employs data taken from primary and secondary sources. Matar argues that the interrelated workings of fiscal, monetary, and exchange rate policies channelled resources in a socially inefficient way. Unrestrained liberalisation distorted the path of capital accumulation and generated price shifts that resulted in an inequitable form of income distribution. The fiscal regime, which targeted the necessary consumption bundle via indirect taxation and subsidy removal, pushed the people's purchasing power onto a lower path. The neoliberal monetary regime and pegged exchange rate measures broadened money creation to inflate the assets of the holders of capital while the working population faced inflation. In view of risk and the small market size, the dollar-pegged exchange rate regime, along with a relaxation of capital account controls, drew financial resources away from the national economy. Similarly, in trade, unconditional openness undermined key components of the manufacturing sector. Over the three decades that preceded the uprising, the share and productivity of the manufacturing sector in Syria had consistently declined despite several measures of economic liberalisation targeting an improvement in its performance. The mantra of liberalisation that advocated short-term stabilisation undercut the basis for long-term growth and resulted in a crisis like the shock therapy experienced by post-Soviet economies—but with worse results, given the militarised conflict. Matar also examines the macro reform measures during times of conflict. She concludes that the government during times of conflict continues to employ laissez faire tools to facilitate various economic activities to the private sector who can sidestep the penalising Western-imposed sanctions. However, loosening of state control has increased capital flight and opened the space for war traders to control supply and distribution, increasing profit margins, pillage, and market chaos.

In Chap. 6, Nabil Marzouk presents key indicators and estimations taken from published projects that he has been involved in while working with the Syrian Center for Policy Research. In doing so, he emphasises Syria's geostrategic position and its impact—namely, the political instability that has characterised Syrian history since its 1946 independence. He argues that shifts in state policies since the 1980s have debilitated development. He also focuses on the 2001–2010 period during which the government expanded neoliberal economic policies, without attending to social safety nets, and which in turn weakened the social contract. As a result, the level of human development in its various dimensions did not meet expectations. Marzouk points out that the Syrian people's spontaneity in the 2011 protests has thus far borne heavy costs. Marzouk concludes that as an observer from the inside, the principal blame lies squarely upon the external forces that took opportunity of Syria's weakness to destroy Syrian society and productive capacity.

Philip Proudfoot focuses on the social aspect of the Syrian crisis by tracing it through the lives of Syrian migrant workers in Lebanon (Chap. 7). More specifically, he provides an ethnographic perspective on the Syrian crisis. Based on several months of field research in Lebanon, Proudfoot describes how, when the uprising erupted in 2011, some migrant workers in Lebanon expressed support for what they called "the revolution." He also summarises the material conditions that pushed such labourers to migrate in the first place, including daily economic hardships and survival difficulties which manifested in mass pauperisation. Proudfoot illustrates how some of these labourers who settled in Lebanon indirectly participated in the uprising through new communication technology. He shows how the uprising was experienced and lived-out at a distance by these migrant workers. The often-neglected perspective of Syria's labouring diaspora that Proudfoot reveals is important because for these men the same socioeconomic pressures that structured their initial decisions to migrate from the countryside to sell their labour power in the city resembles what many have identified as the material foundations for the uprising itself.

In Chap. 8, Aurora Sottimano discusses the politics that surround the Syrian conflict. Sottimano focuses on the "resistance front," comprising Syria, Iran, and Hezbollah, and traces the change in the government's political discourse—from the initial anti-imperialist narrative to the recent reconfiguration into a counter-insurgency stance since the start of the Syrian conflict. She argues the resistance discourse has influenced Syria's domestic and foreign policies and partly shaped the trajectory of the Syrian uprising. She also reminds us that Syria during Hafez al-Asad's rule struggled to establish its strength and stability in a turbulent region buffeted by constant regional and international intervention. This, in turn, impacted Syria's foreign policy and pushed Syria to form a political alliance with the revolutionary Islamic Republic of Iran. She then illustrates how Bashar al-Asad embraced the discourse of the "resistance front" with its anti-imperialist stance against regional (Israel) and international (US) interference. Sottimano shows how such a stance was key for Syria's authoritarian upgrading and regional strategies. She concludes that the West's adoption of the "War on Terror" prompted Syria to re-articulate its nationalist discourse and foreign policy. As a result, the politics of resistance transformed into the politics of resistance partners and the front has turned into a transnational counter-insurgency coalition. Sottimano concludes that such developments require a reconsideration of the ideological assumptions, capabilities, and persistence of the "resistance front."

The last part of the volume focuses on the health and food security questions. Kasturi Sen examines the health sector and situates her analysis within the broader context of the political economy of neoliberalism in Syria (Chap. 9). She argues that the health sector in Syria was a key part of neoliberal reforms that were initiated after 2003. Until the enactment of the "modernisation" programme (HSMP) in 2003, Syria provided free healthcare to its citizens. Sen reminds us of the achievements of health services during Syria's dirigiste experience, when health services were centrally organised by the state under a command-and-control structure. At that time, there was strong emphasis on primary care and health promotion. Data pertaining to the health indicators reveals that Syria witnessed positive health figures, as witnessed by its declining infant mortality rate (IMR) and maternal mortality rate (MMR). At a later stage, Sen argues that the health sector in Syria, like other low- and middle-income countries (LMICs), faced ensuing challenges as part of the global restructuring of the health sector in the Global South. As such, the EU-led HSMP in Syria aimed at reducing public expenditure in health services, charging user fees, and supporting autonomous hospitals through PPPs. The EU-led HSMP had serious social implications, particularly for the poorest segments of the population, who could not afford the fees for medicines and other user fees and charges for hospital and health services. Sen concludes that the health sector in Syria has worsened during the conflict. Learning from the post-conflict experience of other countries such as Lebanon, she emphasises the importance of reinstating an integrated publicly led healthcare system. Given the current critical conditions, only the state can rehabilitate the health infrastructure and alleviate the consequences of human capital devastation.

Max Ajl and Myriam Ababsa tackle the food security questions. Ajl in Chap. 10 offers a sociological perspective of the Ba'ath pact with Syria's peasantry, situating the analysis within a global historical context. He highlights Arab nationalism, the global rise of anti-systemic movements from 1917 onwards, and mass local mobilisation. He explains how the post-1958 Syrian state was the product of local anti-systemic movements as well as the ideological Syrian manifestation of a global movement and argues that it is only by inserting the rise of the Syrian developmental state and its radical agrarian policies in world-systemic perspective that we can properly understand the original state-society pact. He also posits that such a social pact allowed for a stable if politically repressive developmental compact. Ajl proceeds to trace the course of developmental decay, identifying the policy changes and the political ecology through which the Ba'ath party gradually broke its alliance with the peasantry and the urban working class, as well as the social effects of those changes. He terms the gradual rolling back of social policies which the Ba'ath initially emplaced as a gradual process of Thermidor—passive-revolution-in-reverse. As such, Ajl does not limit the study of the passive Syrian "revolution" to the national plane—a methodological nationalism—but situates the analysis in a wider and longer historical trajectory within which the gains of the Arab nationalist movements all slowly faded in sync and in synergy. Included amongst the causal vectors which pushed the Syrian social formation along trajectory are not merely the breakdown of the Bretton Woods system of fixed currencies and the gold standard, leading to petrodollar flows, but also the social solvent of war and preparation for war, a crucial mechanism of developmental decay, particularly in states sharing an armistice line with Israel, as well as anthropogenic climate change, a world-ecological process, rooted in core-state consumption patterns. Ajl concludes that one can comprehensively understand the roots of the Syrian crisis if one situates the analysis within and against the tableau of global North-induced anthropogenic climate change and world-systemic shifts and pressures more broadly.

In Chap. 11, Myriam Ababsa reviews the history of agriculture in Syria from the late 1950s until the end of 2016. She shows how Syria was self-sufficient in food production until the neoliberal economic opening in the 2000s. Syria, after Turkey, had the most productive agricultural sector in the Middle East. During most of Syria's development trajectory until the drought years (2006–2010), agricultural production accounted for no less than 25 per cent of GDP. Ababsa highlights that due to the severe drought implications, Syria had to rely on international aid and food supplies for the first time in its history. However, she adds that agricultural production was at risk before 2006 because of the government's enactment of agrarian counter-reform. An example includes Law 56 of 2004, which allowed landowners to terminate farming contracts. In addition to that, the government's mismanagement of water and land resources forced the agricultural sector to lose more than 40 per cent of its workforce between 2002 and 2008. Since the war started in 2011, especially after the emergence of the Islamic State in 2013, Ababsa illuminates how Syria's food production has faced serious challenges in terms of farmers' weak access to seeds and fertilisers. Additionally, food and water have been used as weapons and leverages to political change by all warring parties. Ababsa concludes that access to food has become the main preoccupation for most Syrians, both in the state-controlled areas and in besieged areas. People living in areas controlled by the Islamic State have lived under critical conditions given the lack of supply of basic food necessitates and the inability of the smugglers to enter either Raqqa or Deir Ezzor.

In the concluding chapter (Chap. 12), Linda Matar and Ali Kadri address China's role in Syria's national security. Talk about reconstruction in Syria have been afoot for a while, especially after the Syrian government with the help of its allies Russia, Iran, and, more discreetly, China started to retrieve more of the lost territories from the other warring parties. China has expressed interest in contributing to Syria's reconstruction. This can be verified from Chinese sources that we accessed. With the help of colleagues at the National University of Singapore who read Mandarin and who have researched Chinese sources, we demonstrate the willingness of China to assist in the reconstruction of Syria. Obviously, China has strategic interests in furthering its Belt and Road plan in the Arab region. In this final chapter, we address this topical issue and we stress that any reconstruction effort in Syria must boost the national security effort, evade the past blunders of Iraq and Lebanon, and most importantly rebuild the social infrastructure.

Note

1. The qualifier colonial may admit little differentiation between places like India and Syria, where the Mandate or the French presence on Syrian soil was actually short. Judging what is and is not colonial by the presence of boots on the grounds leaves out the structural impact of power that shapes development and resource extraction without colonising troops landing on the shores of the colonies. Such boots on the grounds criterion of what constitutes colonialism is narrowly empirical. An assessment of colonialism, the act of reformulating social production processes with the aim of resource usurpation, should also consider the fact that the Western colonial powers have dictated the changes to modes of production in the Southern Mediterranean way before they invaded the Southern Ottoman Vilayets. The impact of structures of powers in terms of colonisation is at times more potent than the actual act of colonising a nation.

Bibliography

Abdel-Malek, A. (1977). Geopolitics and National Movements: An Essay on the Dialectics of Imperialism. *Antipode, 9*(1), 28–35.

Chossudovsky, M. (2018, May 8). Global Warfare. Preparing for World War III? Targeting Iran. *Global Research*.

Chouman, A. (2005). *The Socialist Experience in Syria, the Consequences of Its Movement Towards the Market Economy, and the Impact of Restructuring and Globalization*. Unpublished Paper.

Debord, G. (1994 [1967]). *The Society of the Spectacle*. New York: Zone Books.

Deutsche Welle. (2018, April 28). Syria: Expropriation is 'Punishment for Those who Protested. *Deutsche Welle*. Retrieved May 12, 2018, from http://www.dw.com/en/syria-expropriation-is-punishment-for-those-who-protested/a-43572305

Gordon, J. (2010). *Invisible War: The United States and the Iraq Sanctions*. Cambridge, MA: Harvard University Press.

Gowan, S. (2018, April 25). Another Beautiful Soul: Counterpunching the Global Assault on Dissent. *What's Left*. Retrieved April 17, 2018, from https://gowans.wordpress.com/2018/04/24/another-beautiful-soul-counterpunching-the-global-assault-on-dissent/

Hardin, G. (1976). Lifeboat Ethics. In G. R. Lucas Jr. & T. W. Ogletree (Eds.), *Lifeboat Ethics: The Moral Dilemmas of World Hunger*. New York: Harper & Row.

Hemesh, M. (2014). A National Model for Development and Reconstruction. *Economic Files*. Damascus: Syrian Economic Society. Retrieved from http://www.mafhoum.com/syr/articles_14/2014-6.pdf

Kadri, A. (2016). *The Unmaking of Arab Socialism*. London: Anthem Press.

Lamb, F. (2018, May 4). Syria's New "Law Number Ten" Devastates Sunni Refugees. *Counterpunch*. Retrieved May 12, 2018, from https://www.counterpunch.org/2018/05/04/syrias-new-law-number-ten-devastates-sunni-refugees/

Lenin, V. (1917). The State and Revolution. In *Collected Works* (Vol. 25, pp. 381–492). Moscow: Progress Publishers.

Matar, L. (2016). *The Political Economy of Investment in Syria*. Basingstoke: Palgrave Macmillan.

Syrian Prime Ministry. (2018). Law Number 10, *Syrian Prime Ministry*. Retrieved from http://www.pministry.gov.sy/contents/13502/القانون-رقم-/10/-لعام-2018-القاضي-بجواز-إحداث-منطقة-تنظيمية-أو-أكثر-ضمن-المخطط-التنظيمي-العام-للوحدات-الإدارية-وذلك-بمرسوم-بناء-على-اقتراح-وزير-الإدارة-المحلية-والبيئة-وتعديل-بعض-مواد-المرسوم-التشريعي-رقم-66-لعام

PART I

A Historical Perspective of the Syrian Conflict

CHAPTER 2

What Went Wrong: Understanding the Trajectory of Syria's Conflict

Raymond Hinnebusch

INTRODUCTION

The Syrian conflict raises numerous puzzles and theoretical issues bearing on traditions of MENA (Middle East and North Africa) politics and IR, such as authoritarian resilience, democratisation, social movement theory, sectarianism, and civil wars. This chapter addresses key questions, contextualised within these wider bodies of literature, regarding the origins of the uprising and its subsequent trajectory: (1) what were the causes of the conflict, both in terms of structure (crisis and contradictions within the pre-uprising order) and agency (choices of the actors)? and (2) why did the uprising lead to neither democratisation nor revolution from below and instead descend into violent semi-sectarian civil war and a failed state?

A HISTORICAL SOCIOLOGY LENS FOR UNDERSTANDING THE SYRIAN CONFLICT

As a lens for taking this macro and long-term view of the crisis, *Historical Sociology* (thereafter, HS) has several advantageous points of departure (Hobden and Hobson 2002: 3–59).

R. Hinnebusch (✉)
University of St Andrews, St Andrews, Scotland

1. *Path dependency*: much of the analysis of the Syrian conflict is afflicted by "presentism" and an over-stress on agency—usually framed as the "good guys" (peaceful protestors) versus the "bad guys" (the dictator, jihadists). By contrast, HS warns us that history matters: specifically, the historical evolution of structures sharply constrains the options of agents that tend to reproduce power practices that have historically "worked." These notably include those identified by the father of sociology, Ibn Khaldun, and systemised by Max Weber.
2. *Co-constitution of states and states systems*: while some of the analyses of the Syrian conflict often see external factors as secondary, HS tells us that states and states systems co-constitute each other; by extension, *state failure* is also co-constituted by the interaction of the "international" and "domestic" (or internal) forces.
3. *Agency and structure's* interaction explains Syria's trajectory. Path dependency narrowed options but the choices among these, that is to say the road taken by agents at several key junctures, led to quite different outcomes than those that would likely have followed from other choices; these altered, in turn, the structural context within which subsequent actors had to operate. To paraphrase Marx, men make their own history, not in conditions of their own choosing, but in circumstances transmitted from the past (Marx 1852).

The Junctures of the Syrian Conflict's Trajectory

Syria's vulnerability to the spread of the "Arab Spring" was in good part owing to the flaws built into the structures of rule that Bashar al-Asad inherited, exacerbated by his own neo-liberal reform project. If Bashar's choices were importantly shaped by the state-building undertaken by his father, so the challenges faced by Hafez and the solutions he found for consolidating his government can, in turn, only be understood in context. This means, above all, the unfavourable conditions bequeathed to Syrian state-builders in the post-WWI imposition by the Western great powers of the regional states system—an episode popularly, if somewhat historically inaccurately, known as "Sykes-Picot".

Once the Syrian uprising began, several key junctures—points at which several alternative roads were possible—shaped the conflict's trajectory, as summarised in Fig. 2.1. The onset of the uprising, via the successful

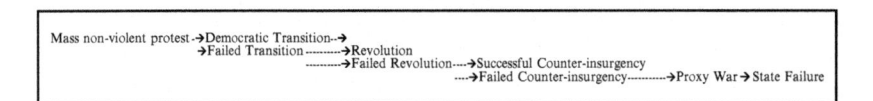

```
Mass non-violent protest →Democratic Transition→
              →Failed Transition--------→Revolution
                         --------→Failed Revolution----→Successful Counter-insurgency
                                       ----→Failed Counter-insurgency--------→Proxy War→ State Failure
```

Fig. 2.1 Junctures in the Syrian conflict's trajectory

mobilisation of mass protests in spite of an unfavourable opportunity structure, initially appeared to be a triumph of agency by thousands of ordinary citizens. At this juncture, several of the conditions under which non-violent protest might have led to democratisation were present; but owing to the choices of hardliners in both government and opposition, and among external powers, this window of opportunity was missed. At the second juncture, the failure of democratic transition and the militarisation of the opposition might have led to revolution from below, but Syria's social structure was biased against this and government strategies (agency) obstructed it. With the failure of revolution, government "counter-insurgency" might have prevailed, but external intervention on behalf of the opposition cost the government its monopoly of violence and territorial control. This, together with tit-for-tat violence (agency of government, opposition, and external interveners), tipped Syria into a failed state. Balanced intervention for and against the government kept a compromise political settlement off the agenda. Finally, the structural conditions created by state failure and the fragmentation of governance in this vacuum, in turn, shaped agency, namely, "competitive regime remaking" and a cross-border spillover which could remake "Sykes-Picot" itself—a return to the starting point of the Syrian tragedy.

Historical Context

The Syrian crisis cannot be understood in isolation from state formation across the Levant in which the states created after WWI have been in recurring crisis since their birth; not only Syria but Iraq, Lebanon, and Jordan have all experienced regular combinations of domestic revolution, civil war, and external intervention.

Thus, an essential context for understanding the Syrian crisis is the Western imperial imposition of the regional states system in what Fromkin called a "peace to end all peace" (Fromkin 1989). This created a set of profoundly flawed states in some ways "set up to fail": identity was fragmented, with powerful sub- and supra-state identities competing with state identity for the loyalty of populations. Irredentism was thus pervasive, giving rise to successive radical trans-state movements against what were seen as "artificial" states. This so afflicted Levantine states with deep instability, that for a period they were considered nearly ungovernable. Of the several revisionist movements that mobilised in the 1950s and 1960s across the region, the Ba'ath party was the most successful, coming to power in Syria and Iraq.

Thereafter, the rise and decline of Ba'athist state-building set these two states on similar trajectories, the second context, for understanding the current crisis. After two decades of experience with various governance formulas from monarchy or liberal oligarchy to charismatic military dictatorship, Ba'athist state-builders in the two states, nearly simultaneously hit on a winning power building formula with patrimonial practices combined with Leninist party organisation, centralising bureaucratic practices, etatism, and populist distribution (Hinnebusch 1990). This appeared to stabilise robust regimes and strengthen state-centric identities in both Syria and Iraq; however, these regimes also had similar built-in vulnerabilities which came to the surface when, for various reasons, they passed their consolidation peaks, manifested in domestic grievances that intersected in varying ways with external intervention to produce profound crises in both states.

STATE FORMATION UNDER HAFEZ AL-ASAD: NEO-PATRIMONIAL REGIME CONSOLIDATION

Neo-patrimonial regimes—hybrids of personal and bureaucratic authority—are ubiquitous in the Middle East. Particularly in fragmented societies such as the Levant, the use of asabiyya (primordial ties) to construct cores of trusted followers around the patrimonial leader, is a historically reproduced technology of power. Thus, Hafez al-Asad constructed his "presidential monarchy" by inserting trusted men drawn from his family, tribe, and Alawi sect in the command posts of the state. In particular, trusted sectarians were appointed to the security apparatus charged with defence of his regime, hence with implementing hard repression against opposition and whose loyalty and stake in the regime was so strong they were unlikely to defect.

Yet, the patrimonial core of the state rested on a large bureaucratic apparatus that co-opted much wider social forces, indeed incorporated cross-sectarian, cross-class alliances into government institutions. Thus, co-optation to ministerial office took place via a sort of communal arithmetic in which each sectarian group was represented; semi-Leninist party organisation penetrated and recruited in all communities, paralleled with populist redistribution (land reform, state employment), giving wider strata stakes in the regime. Economic liberalisation was used to co-opt the Damascene merchant class. The availability of rent (oil revenues, foreign aid) provided patronage to incorporate key elite constituencies. Legitimacy was built around supra-state secular Arab nationalism (Hinnebusch 1990).

This state-building ended Syria's endemic instability and consolidated nearly a half-century of Ba'athist rule. The test of robustness of the al-Asad government was its survival of the Ikhwan's Islamist revolt of 1978–1982. This was a direct result of the particular hybrid construction of the regime, explained, on the one hand, by the loyalty of the Alawi-dominated security forces and, on the other, by the fragmentation of Sunnis, with those incorporated into government institutions (Sunni peasants) or co-opted (Damascene Sunni bourgeoisie), remaining loyal. Hence, Ba'athist state-building appeared quite robust, in combining patrimonial authority with bureaucratic capacities. This seemed to overcome the vulnerabilities of a fragmented society and allowed the Ba'athist government to survive repeated crises.

This regime had, however, special vulnerabilities that, in some respects, were the other side of the coin of its strengths. One was the dominance of the al-Asad administration by Alawi officers in a Sunni-majority society, which tended to alienate many Sunnis; another was the repression of the opposition, which stored up animosities. These flaws were initially overcome by populist measures such as land reform by which the government won over plebeian constituencies, notably Sunni peasants (Hinnebusch 1990). However, such inclusion of constituencies required governmental command of significant revenues; but the state, overdeveloped relative to its economic base, generated a frequent fiscal deficit that could only be sustained by external "rent." Hafez al-Asad deftly used his nationalist foreign policy, making Syria a front-line state with Israel, to access aid from the Arab Gulf states and Iran and cheap arms and protection from the Soviet Union; however, this also embroiled Syria in costly conflicts with Israel and in Lebanon and generated Western hostility—particularly dangerous after al-Asad lost his Cold War era Soviet patron. Moreover, in the 1990s economic aid declined, and while the gap was temporarily filled by Syria's own oil revenues, these were set to decline in the 2000s. The ruling formula was becoming unsustainable.

Syria Under Bashar al-Asad

The transformation of the Syrian regime under Bashar al-Asad has to be understood as an instance of a region-wide movement from populist ("PA") to post-populist ("PPA") forms of authoritarianism widely discussed in MENA literature on the 1990–2010 period (King 2009; Guazzone and Pioppi 2009). As a result of the vulnerabilities of populism, chiefly the exhaustion of statist development, the MENA state aimed to activate private and foreign investment as alternative engines of growth, a strategy pursued, however, at the cost of its sacrificing of the original popular support on which it had initially consolidated itself. This move was accompanied by what Heydemann (2007) called "authoritarian upgrading," on which there is also extensive literature, by which regimes supposedly adapted to the global hegemony of neo-liberal capitalism and tried to compensate for the loss of their populist constituencies by co-opting new more privileged business constituencies; yet for every vulnerability of the populist period supposedly "fixed" by this, such "upgrading" had negative side effects and produced new vulnerabilities.

Bashar al-Asad's immediate challenges on coming to power were twofold: he sought to adapt the economy to the decline in rent by accessing alternative new sources of revenues; since Syria was being isolated in the West because of nationalist foreign policies (e.g. opposition to the US invasion of Iraq), this focused notably on attracting expatriate and Gulf capital. This, it was thought, required such neo-liberal policies as tax cuts, tariff removals, cuts in welfare subsidies and in public services. Second, Asad sought to concentrate power in the presidency and to throw off the accountability, that existed at the time of succession, to his father's cronies—the "old guard" and to the Ba'ath party collegial leadership. After a long struggle with the old guard, Bashar successfully purged them at a 2005 party congress. In parallel, new elites were co-opted to power—the technocrats charged with implementing the economic reforms and new crony capitalists flourishing on them, notably his cousin, Rami Makhlouf (Hinnebusch and Zintl 2014).

One reason observers did not expect the uprising to spread to Syria was that "authoritarian upgrading" was perceived to be working, successfully compensating for risks of post-populism (Haddad 2011). The young president, having the image of a reformer and also of a nationalist due to his standing against Israel and also the US invasion of Iraq, seemed to enjoy considerable personal legitimacy. The co-optation of new constituents was making up for those being excluded—new businessmen, returning expatriates. Gulf investment was coming in, enabling a new life of consumption in the big cities for the upper middle class. Islamic charities were allowed to fill the gap in decline of state welfare services, appeasing Islamic opinion (Hinnebusch and Zintl 2014). Moreover, neo-liberal exclusion of the lower strata was recent and less advanced than, for example, in Egypt.

Yet, this disguised the vulnerabilities that these policies were aggravating. The purge of the old guard Sunni barons had narrowed the elite and cost the al-Asad government the support of their clientele networks in Sunni society. It made the regime over-dependent on the presidential family, Alawi security barons and technocrats lacking support bases. Bashar had debilitated the party apparatus and the worker and peasant unions, which he saw as resisting his reforms, but this also enervated his regime's connection to its rural Sunni constituency. Indeed, as the party and corporatist infrastructure of the administration contracted, the intrusive and arbitrary behaviour of the corrupt security forces that filled the vacuum became more intolerable, hence the ubiquitous demand for "dignity" during the protests. The structural balance in the regime was shifting toward patrimonial authority at the expense of bureaucratic and inclusionary capacity. Neo-patrimonial regimes, as the Arab uprisings show, are vulnerable to deconstruction as power shifts from the ruling party/bureaucracy to the presidential family. In Syria, this was exaggerated and made more salient by the sectarian cleavage between the al-Asad government's inner core and the Sunni majority and fed a perception of sectarian discrimination against the latter (Hinnebusch and Zintl 2014; Perthes 2004).

The costs of post-populist change can be seen in the neglect of the regime's former peasant constituency. Land reform and subsidisation of agriculture had established a rural base on which the regime had consolidated itself against its historically urban-centred rivals. This base was, however, being enervated by forces partly outside of the regime's control. Inexorable population growth on relatively fixed land resources meant that the typically multiple sons of the land reform peasants that had been the backbone of government support in villages were left landless, forced on to a shrinking job market, and therefore unincorporated into the government's rural base. At the same time, as Ba'athist ideology declined, the vacuum was gradually filled by the penetration of the countryside by Islamist discourse, where it hitherto had had little resonance. Then, in the later 2000s Syria was hit by a drought of unprecedented severity, causing thousands to desert the villages in the east of the country and crowd into suburbs of the main cities. Not only was the response of the government to their distress ineffectual but, at the same time, it was withdrawing rural subsidies, notably those on diesel fuel that peasants needed to power irrigation pumps (Hinnebusch et al. 2011). This was paralleled by a growing perception that, while the Sunni peasant majority was suffering, Alawis were given preferences for scarce jobs and Alawi crony capitalists enriching themselves on their insider connections. All of this was making the rural areas, small towns, and suburbs hotbeds of discontent that would be mobilised in the uprising.

The Ba'athist regime had, from its creation, built-in vulnerabilities that Hafez al-Asad had managed, aided by the right conditions—bipolarity, oil rent—to stay on top of. Bashar al-Asad tried to adapt to the less favourable environment of global neo-liberalism, by policies chiefly beneficial to crony capitalists and largely dependent on Gulf capital: even as the upper strata of society were acquiring a greater stake in the state, those at the bottom were being excluded and becoming more receptive to opposition discourse, whether liberal or Islamist.

In some respects, the deconstruction of Syria's ruling formula was an artefact of a new post-bipolar globalised world. Thus, even as the global convergence toward a homogeneous neo-liberalism was forcing MENA's rent-poor republics to renege on the populist "social contract" around which they had initially consolidated their power (and also as they lost former Soviet patron), globalisation was also diffusing new media and internet technology. These spread both West-centric democratisation and Islamist discourses that helped to delegitimise the post-populist ruling formulas of regimes such as Bashar al-Asad's in Syria.

THE SYRIAN UPRISING: FROM NON-VIOLENT PROTEST TO PROXY WAR

Syria's trajectory, starting with the beginning of the uprising, was defined by several junctures, where more than one turning point was possible, but the route taken then set up a path dependency that largely closed off many alternatives and set the country on a path to civil, and ultimately, proxy war.

Juncture 1: The Spread of the Arab Uprisings to Syria

Grievances might have been high among the many disadvantaged by Bashar al-Asad's post-populism, but the collective action problem seemed insurmountable and the opportunity structure for social movements in Syria unpromising. Civil society was too controlled and atomised to be a vehicle of mobilisation; for example, Syria had low and recent IT penetration compared to Egypt and Tunisia where it had been used to overcome atomisation and mobilise protest. There were no recognised nationwide charismatic leaders to mobilise protestors and no pre-existing organisation, although locally religious leaders sometimes made mosques available once the uprising got underway. However, insofar as leadership and organisation emerged they were the product of mobilisation, not the cause of it.

What explained what seemed then to be spontaneous individual decisions to join protests? The rational choice theory, often used to understand such decisions, cannot explain them in the Syrian context given the likely high costs for protestors: people knew the security forces were loyal and would not hesitate to use violence, as the repression of the 1982 Hama uprising had shown. There was also the fact that, in an authoritarian state intolerant of public dissent, oppositionists cannot know how many are with them and hence rational actors would be risk adverse and even if protests begin by the ideologically committed, the majority would be expected to "free ride", making the so-called collective action problem insurmountable. However, calculations of the likely success of protest are important and, as such, crucial to overcoming the collective action problem was the demonstration effect of the uprisings in other Arab states where in fact the security forces did turn against presidents; this, when combined with a wishful thinking that Syria was not that different from them (inaccurate analogies), changed calculations of dissidents as to their chances of success. There was also a certain loss of fear among the generation that did not experience Hama and spearheaded the uprising. Nevertheless, since individual self-interest would have deterred participation, some other powerful motivation must have driven mobilisation. Moral outrage at government killings seem to have motivated many. The role of tribal ties in overcoming atomisation in the rural suburbs, for example, in Dara'a where resistance to the regime first flared up before spreading elsewhere, was also important: when fellow tribesmen were killed by the security forces, honour required exacting revenge.

Mobilisation took place on two levels: at the local level, coordinating committees planned day-to-day protests, while cyber activists used the internet to share information, coordinate and publicise their protests, keep the momentum going, and convey a sense of national-level solidarity (Ghattas 2011). The result was that, with amazing rapidity, massive and unprecedented anti-regime mobilisation took place throughout 2011 and into 2012. Indeed, mass protests spread to most of Syria's towns and cities (if much less so in Damascus and Aleppo), with hundreds of thousands mobilising on successive Fridays. Whole quarters, suburbs, and towns fell out of government control. The protestors, although at first mostly unarmed, posed a serious threat to the regime's survival. Its security forces, lacking training and experience in crowd control, responded with excessive violence, multiplying its enemies and making funerals occasions for more confrontation. Government mismanagement of protests sparked the uprising and the internet, despite its relatively low penetration, provided enough connectivity to spread it countrywide (ICG 2011).

Juncture 2: The Failure of Non-violent Protest to Enable Democratic Transition

Two theories on transition explain how this mass non-violent protest might have led to a democratic transition in Syria. According to the non-violent resistance paradigm, mass protest on the scale that Syria experienced was more than sufficient to set entrain a destabilisation of the government. Moreover, as the paradigm predicts, repressive violence by the government only furthered resistance and could provoke foreign intervention (Stephan and Chenoweth 2008). Indeed, this was the calculation of the protestors. However, the two other ingredients needed, fracture of the ruling elite and defection of the security forces, did not happen on a sufficient scale.

The theory of pacted transition suggests why the elite did not fracture (O'Donnell and Schmitter 1986). In the scenario of pacted transitions, an elite split takes the form of government soft-liners marginalising the hard-liners and linking up with moderates in the opposition to agree a move toward democratisation that would guarantee the vital interests of the incumbent elite. This is most likely where opposition can mobilise enough mass protest to empower soft-liners in the government, whilst at the same time moderates within the opposition keep control such that its goals are minimalist—reform, power-sharing rather than government overthrow. Its methods must be non-violent, allowing agreement on preserving the vital interests of government elites and the marginalisation of hardliners on both sides. Concretely, if the president is a hardliner, the military high command has to abandon him (as in Egypt and Tunisia, where presidential families and the military command were at odds).

However, in Syria, hardliners on both sides marginalised the soft-liners. Bashar al-Asad aligned with the hardline security chiefs and abandonment of the president was deterred by the shared interests and sectarian affiliations of political and military elites; pushed aside were regime soft-liners such as Vice President Farouk al-Sharaa, Republican Guard commander Manaf Tlass, and Chief of Staff Ali Habib, all of whom counselled against use of force against protestors (Lesch 2012: 99, 116).

Hardliners quickly assumed the upper hand within the opposition as well and the goals of at least key parts of the opposition were maximalist. Indeed, determined activists, many of them exiles, systematically set out to spread the Arab uprising to Syria, using the internet and promoting a discourse of democratisation meant to delegitimise the government. The role of the Muslim Brotherhood in inciting the insurrection (via the "Facebook page of the Syrian revolution") particularly raised alarm bells in a government that had fought the Brothers for 40 years. In some instances, the government was deliberately provoked, for example, an anti-Alawi incitement by Salafi shaykhs; attacks on party headquarters, the officers' club, and statues of Hafez al-Asad; and incidents of armed attacks on the government's security forces (Worth 2013; Joya 2012). This, together with a perception that making concessions had led to the fall of other presidents, led the regime progressively to increase the level of repression aimed at protestors which, in turn, turned the protesters to demand the fall of the regime.

As several analysts argued, the mistake of the Syrian protest movement was its "rush to confrontation" with the government while the latter still retained significant support (Mandour 2013). Even though the government conceded many reforms that the opposition had been demanding for decades, those committed to its removal dismissed them as inadequate and insincere. The spilling of blood happened so quickly on such a significant scale that compromise was soon rejected on both sides. Opposition activists were not only morally outraged at the regime's killings but also believed that they could only be safe if the al-Asad regime was totally destroyed since if it survived it would be certain to seek retribution. The opposition hardliners were also deluded by false analogies that the overthrow of presidents in Egypt or Tunisia would be replicated in Syria (Mandour 2013).

This led to the marginalisation of opposition moderates, the older generation of traditional opposition, often former Marxists or Nasserites, organised in the National Coordination Committee (NCC) that opposed foreign intervention and sought a compromise settlement (Lesch 2012: 170–174). They put forth such a proposal at the Samiramis conference in

June 2013, a last chance to engineer non-violent transition, but it was rejected by both regime and opposition. As the older generation moderate opposition leaders lost control of their erstwhile followers, the revolutionary youth, there was no credible soft-line opposition leaders able to bargain with the government.

Western response to the conflict also aggravated the hardline dispositions on both sides. The West's discourse of Responsibility to Protect (R2P) and of humanitarian intervention, combined with the Libya example, encouraged the opposition to expect foreign intervention and drove their continued rebellion. It led them to rebuff attempts by two UN mediators to broker a compromise settlement. It also enhanced regime cohesion since all knew that the fall of the al-Asad government would bring on the International Criminal Court (ICC). Thus, Western interference reinforced the hardliners on both sides (Lesch 2012: 164–165).

Did agency, therefore, defeat the potential for democratic transition? This assumes that had key actors made different choices, outcomes could have been different. Perhaps the one actor who could have made the biggest difference was the President. What if Bashar al-Asad led the soft-liners instead of the hardliners? Some think the outcome would have been different; he could have won a free election and led the process of reform. Unfortunately, his March 30, 2011, speech at the beginning of the protests, in which he deprecated popular grievances, disillusioned the many who wanted him to use the crisis to advance reform (Lesch 2012; Wieland 2012).

Yet, it could well be that the regime was not at the time reformable, at least not without what might have been considered to its upholders to be excessive risks. The toxic combination of sect and crony capitalism on which the regime had come to be based was arguably incompatible with a liberal transition. Bringing in majoritarian democracy, particularly at a time when the decline of the Ba'ath party had debilitated its capacity to deliver cross-sectarian electoral support, carried a high risk that voting would be along sectarian lines empowering Sunni politicians at the expense of the Alawis. Democratisation would also empower the disadvantaged masses to attack the policies that constituted the crony capitalism that had enriched the ruling elite.

Juncture 3: Failure of Revolution from Below

A second juncture in Syria's trajectory came once peaceful democratic transition had failed. Given the scale of resistance, it was always possible that mass mobilisation might lead to revolution from below. By 2012 many outsiders believed the regime was on the ropes. But they were wrong: why?

Revolution requires a split in the regime combined with bandwagoning of much of society against it, as happened in Tunisia and Egypt. However, neo-patrimonial states like Syria, where the elites are united by sectarian ties around a patrimonial leader, are less vulnerable to elite fracture and where the regime retains coercive and co-optative capabilities, it can contain anti-regime mobilisation.

Bandwagoning mobilisation against the regime requires a cross-class (middle-lower class) coalition; this takes a high and widely shared level of grievances. In Syria, while many were aggrieved by Bashar al-Asad's policies, others had welcomed them. Importantly, Syria's social structure was not favourable: anti-regime mobilisation on cross-class grounds was *crosscut* by communal and urban-rural cleavages. When cleavages are cross cut, mobilisation along the lines of *both* class (horizontal) and communal (vertical) cleavages is diluted.

Syria's uprising cleavages took a distinctive form that reflected both the success and the vulnerabilities of Bashar's post—populist authoritarian upgrading. Different from Egypt but somewhat similar to Libya, the uprising was geographically dispersed and away from the capital, beginning in the rural peripheries, then spreading to small towns, suburbs, and medium-sized cities, where its foot soldiers were unemployed youth, refugees from drought, and others among the "losers" of a decade of post-populist neo-liberalism. For a considerable period, protest was contained in the periphery, while the centres of power (Damascus) and business (Aleppo) stayed relatively immune. This corresponded precisely to the geographical distribution of benefits and costs of Bashar's post-populist upgrading. Different from other cases, also, was that the uprising had from the beginning a sectarian dimension, inevitable given the Alawi dominance of the regime and the concentration of the uprising among the majority Sunnis. The main occasion for mobilisation became Friday prayers, with imams, natural leaders of their neighbourhoods and, outside the main cities, mostly anti-regime, taking the lead. Saudi-financed Salafi and Muslim Brotherhood connected elements actively mobilised protestors. Initial centres of grievances were mixed areas where Alawis and Sunni lived together as in Latakia, Banias, and Homs. The uprising then spread to Hama and Deir Ez-Zor, traditional bastions of Sunni piety resentful of the secular regime. Tribes also played a role; the decline of the security forces' control of them through subsidies and exemptions and its replacement by Saudi money was important in the government's loss of control over the tribal periphery (Hinnebusch 2012).

Given this character of the opposition—pious lower class, rural, and Sunni—the social base on which the regime relied to survive had many of the opposite characteristics and was the product of a decade of "authoritarian upgrading." It comprised the crony capitalists, urban government employees, and the minorities, especially Alawis and to a lesser degree Christians who, not suffering from the restrictions on public religiosity and church building typical elsewhere in the Muslim world, were rallied by exploiting their fear of Salafi Islam. The main cities, Damascus and Aleppo, where the investment boom, the take-off of tourism, and the new consumption were concentrated remained largely quiescent months into the uprising, although their poor suburbs were often hotbeds of revolt. The regime was able to mobilise significant counter-demonstrations in these cities. The middle class of the two main cities originally saw Bashar as a reformer and, while they were disillusioned by his repression of the protestors, they preferred a peaceful democratisation and feared instability and loss of their secular modern lifestyle if traditional rural or Salafi insurgents took power. While exiled businessmen who had lost out to government-connected operators were big funders of the insurgency, much of the in-country business class saw no alternative to the regime and initially hoped it would end the disorder (Abbas 2011). The unevenness of the uprising, notably its inability to overcome the regime at the power centres, reflects the concentration of many winners of Bashar's post-populist strategy in the main cities; while the relocation of the (especially Islamist) opposition from the cities (its heartland in the 1980s rebellion) to the rural periphery in 2011 exactly mirrors the post-populist shift in the regime's base (Abboud 2016: 78–80).

The regime's survival strategy was also key to a partial sectarian polarisation that obstructed mass-based revolution. The regime sought to rally its minority base, particularly the Alawite-dominated security forces, which being implicated in violence, could expect retribution if the government fell; indeed, the security forces' use of violence against protestors did not cause big defections since the opposition was painted as a sectarian other (jihadi) among the government's constituency. The government also sought, by accusing the opposition of Islamist terrorism, to frame the alternatives for the middle class as the social peace it protected or else jihadi violence in order to deter many in the "middle"—other minorities, the Sunni upper middle class in Damascus and Aleppo—from bandwagoning with the opposition. Indeed, a significant portion of them acquiesced in the regime as the lesser of two evils; this was all the more the case once radical Islamists, and especially al-Qaida-linked jihadists, assumed a high profile within the opposition and as the opposition fragmented into warring camps (Lesch 2012: 51–52; Abboud 2016: 77–80). The opposition also started framing the conflict as sectarian in order to mobilise the Sunni majority. However, the Sunni community remained divided by urban-rural/class cleavages: much of the urban upper middle class refrained from bandwagoning against the government.

This scenario is quite at odds with the non-violent resistance or revolutionary scenarios in which the government is isolated from the vast majority of the population, precipitating its collapse, and it distinguishes Syria from Tunisia and Egypt where the incumbent presidents proved unable to rally sufficient support to survive. This exemplifies how differences in the social structures of societies make for important variations in the vulnerability of authoritarian regimes to revolt: in relatively homogeneous societies such as Egypt and Tunisia, mass anti-government mobilisation is likely to be much more thorough and decisive than in communally diverse ones like Syria.

Thus, there were enough grievances in Syria to produce an uprising among a big segment of the Syrian population but not enough to lead to the bandwagoning needed for revolution or regime collapse. The bottom line is: a revolutionary scenario requires a rather exceptional broad mobilisation by a united society against a divided state; in Syria, by contrast, a cohesive regime confronted a divided society.

Juncture 4: Toward Proxy War: Between Failed Revolution and Failed Counter-insurgency

Even as revolution was failing, government counter-insurgency might have been the alternative outcome. Once protests turned into armed insurgency, the government, with an organised army behind it, had a great advantage over fragmented, lightly armed insurgents. Yet, counter-insurgency failed, largely, as will be seen, owing to external intervention against the regime. Once that happened, civil war, morphing into proxy war, became the default mode.

Two dynamics drove toward civil war: escalation of violence, plus, territorial contestation. Escalation of tit-for-tat violence was inexorable. The opposition strategy depended on a level and scale of protests that the security services would be stretched thin and exhausted, perhaps so provoked they would increase violence that would turn a majority of the population against the regime, or split it internally and especially lead to such disaffection in the army that it would become an unreliable instrument of repression. Indeed, as the regime failed to contain the protests at one level of violence, it increased the level—killing many protesters, provoking the turn to armed resistance by the opposition.

The opposition also knew that it could not win without breaking the alignment between the regime and urban elites: it attempted via bombings and armed infiltrations of the cities to undermine the economy and security in pro-government areas. A further watershed in intensification of the conflict was its spread to Aleppo where the opposition escalated the fight, infiltrating and seizing half of the city, to demonstrate that the upper and middle classes would not remain immune to the violence. In the summer of 2012, battles in Aleppo drew in increasing numbers of jihadist fighters. There followed the destruction of large parts of Syrian's industrial base and looting on a massive scale as whole factories were dismantled and exported to Turkey.

The opposition also believed that the threat of external intervention would force the regime to refrain from bringing its full military advantage to bear—or if it did so, that such intervention would be provoked, as had happened with Qaddafi. Indeed, anti-regime activists, including Syrian expatriates who were instrumental in initiating and internationalising the uprising, understood that they could not succeed without external intervention, at least enough to restrain the regime's repressive options. External activists told those on the ground, pointing to the Libya no-fly zone, that "the international community won't sit and watch you be killed" (Seelye 2011). They claimed that another Hama was not possible because "Everything is being filmed on YouTube and there's a lot of international attention on the Middle East" (Seelye 2011). Although the regime did avoid the inflammatory use of violent rhetoric that had invited intervention against Qaddafi, it quietly and incrementally increased the use of violence from a "security solution" to a "military solution." The move toward a military solution in which heavy weapons were used in built-up urban areas appears partly to have been a response to the killing of over a hundred government soldiers and police in the Islamist stronghold of Jisr ash-Shughur in June 2011 and also a bid to prevent establishment of "liberated areas" that would facilitate Western intervention on behalf of the opposition, as had happened in Libya.

Increased government violence did stimulate increased military defections: not of whole units, hence not threatening the regime's core, but enough individual defections that, combined with the external provision of safe havens (in Turkey) and external arming, enabled the construction of the "Free Syrian Army." At the same time, the incremental depletion of the government's military manpower debilitated its capacity to secure territory. As the government lost its monopoly of violence, so did territorial contestation increase and it gradually withdrew from the far east of the country leaving much of the country's grain-growing areas and oil resources to opposition factions. In parallel, high levels of violence drove the jihadisation of the anti-government Sunni rural underclass, which, together with the trans-state movement of non-Syrian militants into Syria, empowered jihadist groups like Jabhat al-Nusra (now known as Hayat Tahrir Al-Sham) and Ahrar al-Sham. Their greater fighting prowess put the government on the defensive.

However, it is likely that without the external factor government counter-insurgency might have prevailed (Phillips 2016). It was, indeed, competitive external interference that *tipped* the country into a failed state. Opposition insurgency was enabled by the copious flows of arms and financing from the Arab Gulf to support fighters, by the safe haven provided by Turkey which also allowed the transit of foreign fighters and helped organise anti-government forces, and by game changing anti-tank weaponry that neutralised the government's counter-insurgency military advantage. Once the regime looked in danger of crumbling, counter-intervention by Iran, Hezbollah, and later Russia blocked an opposition victory, with the result being stalemate up until 2017. This "balanced intervention" was decisive in the prolongation of the conflict since it obstructed various attempts to broker a compromise settlement by UN mediators: each side believed that it could win if its external patrons increased support. Patrons did provide clients enough support to keep fighting, driving an inexorable increase in the *level* of violence, hence, state failure.

Features of State Failure

The idea of state failure implies that *either* government-guaranteed order exists or anarchy reigns; but there are *degrees* of state failure and forms of non-state governance. In Syria two opposite dynamics took place in parallel: the territorial fragmentation of authority and attempts to re-establish it over broader territories. As path dependency would suggest, in an authority vacuum, agents try to reproduce power building practices—charismatic movements, patrimonial governance—that had historically "worked" in the creation of MENA states.

Governance Fragmentation, Security Dilemma

One feature of state failure in Syria was the territorial fragmentation of governance as authority, particularly but not exclusively in opposition-controlled areas, was fragmented among local neighbourhoods and warlord fiefdoms. This was accompanied by a *security dilemma* (Posen 1993): the breakdown of order led to some high-profile sectarian massacres, like Ishtabraq and Houla, generating a fear of the "other" at the grassroots level; many people came to depend on their communal group and neighbourhoods for security as these formed local defence militias on both sides of the conflict. This tendency was accelerated by the breakdown, in many areas, of the normal economy by which the various parts of the country had been integrated; in its place, people, unable to make a normal living, sought survival through spoils or joined armed bands led by local warlords competing to tax economic flows and take cuts of external resources.

Competitive Regime Formation

Parallel to this, however, a counter-process was underway: "competitive regime formation" under which actors on both sides attempted to reconstitute or reconfigure authority over wider areas. Chiefly, the al-Asad government and the Islamist-led opposition competed to fill the Syrian space.

The al-Asad regime reconfigured itself to survive the conflict into a much more *coercive* and *exclusivist* but also *decentralised* form of neo-patrimonialism. The core of the regime, centred around the al-Asad family, security services, and elite army units, contracted as all those not committed to its hardline view of the opposition were marginalised and power re-centred on those in command of violence.

The core's main loyalist base was the Alawi sect, absorbed *en masse* into the army and security apparatus, living in uniformly Alawi suburbs. Implicated in regime crimes, suffering high casualties, facing existential threat if the government collapsed, it had no viable option to defect, even though there was a lot of resentment at the regime for its failure to defend the community and a growing unwillingness to fight outside Alawi areas. The regular army, on the other hand, had been downsized from manpower shortages and reconfigured for counter-insurgency; defections stopped but performance was highly variable, and, with some elite units aside, the army often appeared unable to stand up to jihadists. Notably, it still incorporated Sunnis who enjoyed upward mobility through military careers and identified with the army.

Parallel to the fragmentation in opposition territories, in the government areas, too, there was a decentralisation of power to locales; as the regular army contracted, pro-government communities assumed their own self-defence, in a process of "militia-isation." Some amounted to "weaponised" clientele networks headed by pro-government businessmen-patrons; some were self-financing through protection rackets and extortion. Although an effort was made to organise these local forces into a centrally directed National Defence Force, centre-periphery relations had changed: bureaucratic command gave way to the tissue of personal and clientele loyalties and bargaining (material incentives, threats) vis-à-vis armed "fiefdoms."

In parallel, however, the regime attempted to preserve the "state"—that is, the bureaucracy. Government-controlled areas included two-thirds of the population and, indicative of a still partly functioning public sector, were less afflicted by education and health deficits compared to opposition areas. Even in opposition areas, the government retained a shadow presence, with Damascus continuing to pay salaries of state employees in such areas. Services, such as provision of passports and educational exams, were still under state control, forcing people to travel from opposition-controlled countryside to government-controlled provincial capitals for such services; many also moved into government-controlled areas because of the greater security there, and since these migrants included many Sunnis, there was, ironically, a sectarian diversification in government-controlled areas, notably Damascus, but also minority-dominated areas such as Latakia and Tartous provinces. However, as, over time, resources at the command of the government became scarcer, benefits, such as state jobs, were increasingly confined to proven loyalists.[1]

In opposition-controlled territories, the most robust counter-regime builders have been the salafist-jihadist movements such as Jabhat al-Nusra (known today as Hayat Tahrir Al-Sham), Ahrar al-Sham, and ISIS. These took forms that would have been recognisable to Ibn Khaldun: charismatic leaders professing radical Islamist ideologies and leading armed movements with some bureaucratic capabilities. Their greater ideological self-discipline compared to corrupt Free Syrian Army (FSA) warlords enabled them to provide a more robust governance, although their attempts at state-building was obstructed by their frequent rivalry, often degenerating into armed conflict, notably between ISIS and other jihadists. They varied in how far they prioritised a trans-state caliphate, as did ISIS, or only the overthrow of al-Asad and Islamisation of the Syrian state, the goal of Ahrar al-Sham. But all were highly exclusionary of any who did not profess their fundamentalist version of Islam and in the areas they governed their harsh puritanical rule tended over time to alienate the population (Abboud 2016: 175–178; ICG 2013: 11–15; Lund 2013a).

Squeezed between the government and the jihadists were the remnants of the Local Coordinating Council activists, grouped with FSA elements and traditional notables, often governing through elected councils. Governance was highly fragmented, ineffectual, and marginalised by warlords or targeted by regime bombing and food sieges (Abboud 2016: 77; ICG 2013; Ali 2015).

Trans-state Spillover and State Remaking

The Syrian and Iraqi conflicts were, from the outset, intertwined and over time became increasingly so, symptomatic of shared trans-state identities. When the US destroyed the Iraqi state in its 2003 invasion, Syrian tribes crossed into Iraq to join their kin in resistance to the US occupation; when Syria self-destructed, Iraqi tribes joined those in Syria rebelling against the government. Eastern Syria and West Iraq, where central governments lost control, became breeding grounds of trans-state jihadists, intertwined with tribal fighters (who had always seen the borders as artificial). Sectarian militias, whether ISIS fighters or Shia militias, moved back and forth as the two states became a single arena of battle.

Although the majority of Iraqis and Syrians continued to support the integrity of their state borders, armed minorities took advantage of states' loss of territorial control to advance border remaking agendas. Kurds, denied a state at the foundation of the states system, gave rise in Syria to a movement, the PYD, that sought, at a minimum, federalisation and self-governance comparable to the Kurdish Regional Government in Iraq. Some aimed to forge a new Kurdistan via their trans-state links across Syria, Turkey, and Iraq (Stanfield 2013).

The spectacular rise of the most visible irredentist movement, ISIS, can only be understood as a function of the interaction of external intervention and state failure in the Levant space. It was the US invasion of Iraq, dismantling the Ba'athist state, that created the authority vacuum enabling the rise of al-Qaeda in Iraq ("AQI"). ISIS was born out of an amalgamation of AQI with ex-Iraqi Ba'athists (displaced by the US invasion) and tribal supporters (trained and armed by the US in the late 2000s but marginalised by the Shia-dominated Baghdad government). ISIS flourished in a vacuum of state failure: its financial and military resources were seized from the failing Iraqi and Syrian states. Its claim to protect Sunnis and to provide a modicum of order in place of these failed states was very plausible. Particularly attractive to its fighters was the idea of a revived caliphate in place of the Versailles-imposed Westphalian system: ISIS famously claimed to abolish Sykes-Picot, that is, the "artificial" Syrian-Iraqi border. Indeed, the undoing of "Sykes-Picot," in many ways the root origins of the region's intractable turmoil, is no longer unthinkable (Hassan 2014; Itani 2014).

Conclusion

External imposition of a flawed regional states system constituted a structure that narrowed options for state-building by indigenous leaders. Ba'athist state-builders in Syria and Iraq finally found what appeared to be a robust hybrid formula, a populist version of neo-patrimonialism that combined Khaldunian practices—asabiyya—with modern bureaucracy, semi-Leninist party organisation and revolution from above. But these states had built-in flaws that, in the right conditions—a combination of internal rebellion and external intervention—would lead to state deformation, beginning with the US invasion of Iraq and deepened by state failure in Syria.

It was never inevitable that the Syrian uprising would end in a failed state since agents had choices at each juncture, even though path dependency might have made it seem to them that none of their choices were good ones. In Syria, non-violent protest could have led to a compromise transition had hardliners not hijacked the leadership on both sides: for them compromise seemed more risky than pursuit of their zero-sum pathways. Although the opposition sought in the name of making a revolution from below, to match and overtake the government's violence, the social structure and regime survival strategies blocked the bandwagoning mobilisation against the government that this required. Neither could the government, once it lost its monopoly of violence, wage a successful counter-insurgency in the face of external backing for an increasingly effective jihadist opposition. War became the default mode: the outcome, a failed state, created a new structural situation—security dilemma, authority fragmentation—in which competitive state formation by regime and jihadists sought each to fill the Syrian space (or even to merge it in a larger arena of battle) but ended up locked into a stalemate up until 2017. The equilibrium point reached was at much higher levels of violence than hitherto in which any distinction between combatants and non-combatants melted away in a particularly pernicious version of the current era's "new wars."

Note

1. The analysis of the regime's adaptation is based on Khaddour (2015a, b), Lund (2013b, 2015), and Samaha (2017).

Bibliography

Abbas, H. (2011, October). *The Dynamics of the Uprising in Syria*. Arab Reform Brief, 51.

Abboud, S. (2016). *Syria*. Cambridge: Polity.

Ali, A. K. A. (2015). The Security Gap in Syria: Individual and Collective Security in 'Rebel-Held' Territories. *Stability: International Journal of Security & Development, 4*(1), 1–20.

Fromkin, D. (1989). *A Peace to End All Peace; The Fall of the Ottoman Empire and The Creation of the Modern Middle East*. New York: Avon Books.

Ghattas, K. (2011, April 22). Syria's Spontaneously Organised Protests. *BBC News*. Retrieved from www.bbc.co.uk/news/world-middle-east-13168276

Guazzone, L., & Pioppi, D. (2009). *The Arab State and Neo-liberal Globalization: The Restructuring of the State in the Middle East*. Reading: Ithaca Press.

Haddad, B. (2011). *Why Syria Is Not Next—So Far*. Retrieved from http://www.jadaliyya.com/pages/index/844/why-syria-is-not-next-.-.-.-sofar_with-arabic-translation-

Hassan, H. (2014, June). More than ISIS, Iraq's Sunni Insurgency. Carnegie Endowment for International Peace. *Sada*. Retrieved from http://carnegieendowment.org/sada/?fa=55930

Heydemann, S. (2007). *Upgrading Authoritarianism in the Arab World*. Analysis Paper No. 13. Washington, DC: The Saban Center for Middle East Policy at the Brookings Institution.

Hinnebusch, R. (1990). *Authoritarian Power and State Formation in Ba'thist Syria: Army, Party and Peasants*. San Francisco: Westview Press.

Hinnebusch, R. (2012). Syria: From Authoritarian Upgrading to Revolution? *International Affairs, 88*(1, January), 95–113.

Hinnebusch, R., & Zintl, T. (2014). *Syria: From Reform to Revolt: Politics and International Relations*. Syracuse, NY: Syracuse University Press.

Hinnebusch, R., et al. (Eds.). (2011). *Agriculture and Reform in Syria*. Boulder, CO: Lynne Rienner Publishers, Inc.

Hobden, S., & Hobson, J. (2002). *Historical Sociology of International Relations*. Cambridge: Cambridge University Press.

International Crisis Group (ICG). (2011). *The Syrian People's Slow Motion Revolution*. Brussels and Damascus, 6.

International Crisis Group (ICG). (2013, October). *Anything but Politics: The State of Syria's Political Opposition*. Middle East Report.

Itani, F. (2014). *Roots and Futures of al-Qaida Offshoots in Syria*. Knowledge Program Civil Society in West Asia, Special Bulletin 6, September.

Joya, A. (2012). Syria and the Arab Spring: The Evolution of the Conflict and the Role of Domestic and External and Factors. *Ortadoğu Etütleri*, 4(1, July), 40–43.

Khaddour, K. (2015a, July 8). *The Asad Regime's Hold on the Syrian State*. Carnegie Middle East Centre. Retrieved from http://carnegie-mec.org/2015/07/08/assad-regime-s-hold-on-syrian-state

Khaddour, K. (2015b). *Assad's Officer Ghetto: Why the Syrian Army Remains Loyal*. Retrieved from http://carnegie-mec.org/2015/09/30/assad-s-officer-ghetto-why-syrian-army-remains-loyal

King, S. (2009). *The New Authoritarianism in the Middle East and North Africa*. Bloomington: Indiana University Press.

Lesch, D. (2012). *The Fall of the House of Asad*. New Haven: Yale University Press.

Lund, A. (2013a, August 27). *The Non-State Militant Landscape in Syria*. Combating Terrorism Center at West Point. Retrieved from https://ctc.usma.edu/posts/the-non-state-militant-landscape-in-syria

Lund, A. (2013b, July 24). *Gangs of Latakia: The Militiafication of the Assad Regime*. Syria comment. Retrieved from http://www.joshualandis.com/blog/the-militiafication-of-the-assad-regime/

Lund, A. (2015, March 2). *Who Are the Pro-Asad Militias?* Carnegie Middle East Center. Retrieved from http://carnegie-mec.org/diwan/59215?lang=en

Mandour, M. (2013, October 26). Beyond Civil Resistance: The Case of Syria. *openDemocracy*. Retrieved from www.opendemocracy.net/arab-awakening/maged-mandour/beyond-civil-resistance-case-of-syria

Marx, K. (1852). *The Eighteenth Brumaire of Louis Bonaparte*. Marxists Internet Archive.

O'Donnell, G., & Schmitter, P. (1986). *Transitions from Authoritarian Rule: Tentative Conclusions About Uncertain Democracies, Part 4*. Baltimore, MD: Johns Hopkins University Press.

Perthes, V. (2004). *Syria Under Bashar al-Asad: Modernisation and the Limits of Change*. Adelphi Papers. London: Oxford University Press for IISS.

Phillips, C. (2016). *The Battle for Syria. International Rivalry in the New Middle East*. New Haven: Yale University Press.
Posen, B. (1993). The Security Dilemma and Ethnic Conflict. *Survival, 35*(1, Spring), 27–47.
Samaha, N. (2017, February 8). *Survival Is Syria's Strategy*. Report Syria, The Century Foundation. Retrieved from https://tcf.org/content/report/survival-syrias-strategy/
Seelye, K. (2011, March 28). Syria Unrest 'Cannot Be Contained'. *The Daily Beast*. Retrieved from www.thedailybeast.com/articles/2011/03/28/syria-unrest-cannot-be-contained-dissidents-say.html
Stanfield, G. (2013, July). *The Remaking of Syria, Iraq and the Wider Middle East*. RUSI Briefing Paper.
Stephan, M. J., & Chenoweth, E. (2008). Why Civil Resistance Works: The Strategic Logic of Nonviolent Conflict. *International Security, 33*(1), 7–44.
Wieland, C. (2012). *Syria – A Decade of Lost Chances: Repression and Revolution from Damascus Spring to Arab Spring*. Seattle: Cune Press.
Worth, R. (2013, June 19). The Price of Loyalty in Syria. *New York Times*. Retrieved from http://www.nytimes.com/2013/06/23/magazine/the-price-of-loyalty-in-syria.html?partner=rss&emc=rss&_r=2&pagewanted=all&

CHAPTER 3

The New Struggle for Syria and the Nature of the Syrian State

Eberhard Kienle

THE OLD STRUGGLE FOR SYRIA

In his seminal *The Struggle for Syria* published in 1965, Patrick Seale dwells extensively on the role that external powers and actors played in the politics of the country after independence (Seale 1965, 1986). Covering the period from 1945, when the departure of the last French troops transformed virtual into actual political independence, to 1958, when Syria and Egypt temporarily merged to form the United Arab Republic (UAR), Seale's classic shows in great detail how various Arab and non-Arab states, some of them neighbours, others further afield, vied for influence in the newly decolonised republic. Saudi Arabia, Egypt and Iraq, even (Trans) Jordan, all sought to bring Syria into their own orbit by supporting 'friendly' domestic forces, helping them to gain power or to consolidate their generally precarious grip on the country. Turkey, Israel, France and the United Kingdom pursued similar aims, but obviously were unable to underpin their efforts with Arab nationalist rhetoric. As Middle Eastern politics were increasingly influenced by the superpower rivalry that marked the post-Yalta world order, the United States and the Soviet Union became

E. Kienle (✉)
National Center for Scientific Research, Paris, France

major players in the Syrian pitch. This is the story of Malcolm Kerr's *Arab Cold War*, another seminal study of the politics of the Middle East that focuses on the 1960s and 1970s (Kerr 1972). To quote Seale,

> ...it is as a mirror of rival interests on an international scale that she [Syria] deserves special attention. Indeed, her internal affairs are almost meaningless unless related to the wider context, first of her Arab neighbours and then of other interested powers. It is no accident that Syria should reflect in her internal political structure the rivalries of her neighbours since, as I hope to show, whoever would lead the Middle East must control her. There are many reasons for this view: one is the strategic position of Syria, guarding the north-eastern approaches to Egypt, the overland route to Iraq from the Mediterranean, the head of the Arabian peninsula and the northern frontier of the Arab world. Another is that Syria can claim to have been both the head and the heart of the Arab national movement since its beginnings at the turn of the century, both the generator of political ideas and the focus of countless dreams and patriotic fantasies. Part, at least, of this heritage falls to whoever rules her. (Seale, 1965, 1f)

However, political forces and actors in Syria were not simply the pawns of sinister and power-hungry foreign powers. Frequently, Syrians took the initiative and actively sought external support in order to contain their domestic rivals or to prevail over them. The author of *The Struggle for Syria* adds:

> Syria's internal politics were unusually complex and her indigenous contribution to the guiding ideas of Arab politics particularly rich. She must not, then, be thought of as the passive victim of other people's quarrels. At times, indeed, the reverse is the case: discord in Syria is exported to her neighbours and beyond ... It is this two-way traffic in and out of Syria that forms the subject of this study. (Seale 1965: 3)

Ultimately, the struggle for Syria boils down to actors in a politically divided state entertaining privileged relationships with external actors, sometimes responding to their solicitations, sometimes courting them. Both external attempts to find Syrian allies and Syrian attempts to find external allies reflected the political opportunities and constraints that characterise a country whose population is deeply divided—to the extent that Michel Seurat, one of the most astute students of post-independence Syria, openly wondered whether this population formed a 'society' (Seurat

1980: 89). Frequently Syrian actors were closer to actors who were not Syrian citizens and who acted from outside Syrian territory than they were to other Syrians. Such closeness could be considered as 'merely' strategic or even tactical, had it not involved a considerable amount of mutual trust—trust to work together against other Syrians.

Thus, after overthrowing President Shukri al-Quwatli in 1949, Syria's first military ruler, Husni al-Za'im, quickly sought Iraqi support to contain potential Egyptian interference in favour of his elected predecessor. While al-Za'im soon reverted to the Egyptian option, his co-conspirator Sami al-Hinnawi who toppled him after only a few months once more sought Iraqi support to consolidate his position in Syria. The most vivid illustration remains of course the establishment of the United Arab Republic (UAR) in 1958, which, contrary to popular belief, was not initially advocated by President Gamal Abdel Nasser. In February of that year, a delegation of Syrian military officers and members of the Ba'ath Party travelled to Cairo to ask the Egyptian president to agree to the merger of the two states. Presented as the first step towards the political unity of all Arabs, the request was largely motivated by the Ba'ath's fear of being sidelined by the rise of the Syrian communists and persecuted after a possible right-wing coup to stop the advance of the left (Seale 1965; Kerr 1972).

Parallels with Today

Seale's account depicts a situation that very much resembles the one that prevailed soon after the beginning of the current Syrian war in March 2011. No doubt, initial contestation by and large divided the population in supporters and opponents of the regime (and, of course, bystanders). However, with the passage of time, additional cleavages became apparent (and possibly emerged) between the various opponents, in particular after the summer of 2011 when armed resistance turned from a sporadic into a permanent and finally dominant feature of the conflict. Each of the armed groups pursued its own agenda with little or merely tactical coordination with other such groups. Differences were sometimes political and ideological, but more often derived from their competition for power and influence. No doubt because armed groups more than peaceful protesters depend on supplies of resources from outside—most crucially weapons and ammunition—they also need to establish closer relations with external actors, who in turn seek to instrumentalise them for their own objectives

(Pierret 2013; Phillips 2016). The same logic applies to the rulers of Syria who started the cycle of violence and counter-violence. As the various armed groups managed to establish their control over specific parts of the territory, political fragmentation *ipso facto* took on a geographical and demographic dimension.

The need for resources felt by contending actors inside Syria combined with the calculations of their external suppliers led to a variety of alliances (of sorts) that enabled the former to obtain material support and the latter to influence events or at least to believe that they did. While the regime increasingly relied on its ties with Hezbollah, Iran and Russia, the various armed opposition groups received material support from Turkey, Jordan, the countries of the Gulf Cooperation Council (GCC) and the West. It is also worth noting that part of the support from the GCC came from non-governmental sources. The armed groups sided with one or several external actors, simultaneously or successively, and so did the external actors themselves. For instance, this kind of special relationship tied the governments of Turkey, Qatar and Saudi Arabia to the Free Syrian Army, which roughly became the armed wing of the Syrian National Council, the main representative body of the opposition in exile. Other such relationships tied Turkey to *Ahrar al-Sham*; the (largely but not exclusively Kurdish) Democratic Union Party and its People's Protection Units to Russia and the United States (who nonetheless disagreed about almost every other aspect of the Syrian conflict); and the Islamic State to private donor networks in the Gulf States and to its sympathisers and supporters around the world, including Europe and North America (Pierret 2013; Phillips 2016). In some cases the external actors called the shots, on other occasions domestic actors refused to comply. Without much success, the United States (US) and its allies made their support conditional on greater coordination among the opposition groups; on other occasions the United States brought their Kurdish allies to respect Turkish interests in its fight against ISIS (Islamic State of Iraq and Syria). Saudi Arabia managed to influence, reshape and broaden the major representative body of the Syrian opposition in exile, though without enhancing its effectiveness (Phillips 2016).

As in the early years after independence, Syria today is an internally divided country where competing actors entertain privileged relationships with external actors and indeed pursue their own foreign policies. Though (still) a state in terms of international law and formally recognised as such, it is failing once again to act as a unified actor on the international scene and indeed as a state as far as a variety of internal matters are concerned. The obvious difference between the 'old' and the 'new' struggle for Syria resides in the means that are employed by the contenders. In the 1940s and 1950s, they largely mounted intrigues, plotted military coups and sought to buy political support (cash in hand), while in the current conflict, they resort to open military conflict and armed (surprise) attacks against each other and against civilians thought to be supporters of their adversaries.

Contrast with the Reign of Hafez al-Asad

Both the old and the new struggle for Syria sharply contrast with the reign of Hafez al-Asad who managed to transform Syria from a passive object of competing neighbourly desires into an active historical subject pursuing its own coherent interests and policies. No longer did Syria's environment shape Syria, but Syria now shaped its environment. More precisely, it was al-Asad and his ruling group who transformed Syria into a strong actor on the international scene as they progressively crushed competing power centres in the country. But, rather than reflecting the 'national interest', their policies at home and abroad merely reflected the interests of this group that had successfully managed to impose itself.

After staging two successive—and successful—coups, first discreetly in 1969, then openly in 1970, and ditching his former allies, Hafez al-Asad managed to provide his government with sufficient domestic support to stay in power and to project this power beyond the country's borders (Batatu 1981; van Dam 2011; Seale 1988). In 1973 Syria and Egypt launched the October (or Ramadan) war to break the stalemate that had prevailed since the 1967 war and thus prevented a negotiated settlement of the conflict with Israel. Although the Israeli army could reverse initial Syrian and Egyptian gains, the war led to disengagement agreements on the Golan and the Sinai in 1974. In the end Syria refused to sign a peace treaty with Israel which might have enabled it to regain control of the Golan. However, Sadat's visit to Jerusalem in 1977, the Camp David Accords of 1978, the peace treaty between Israel and Egypt of 1979 and the return of Sinai to Egypt were the direct results of the military effort jointly prepared with Syria (Quandt 2005).

In 1976 Syria intervened militarily in the Lebanese Civil War, imposed its will on the warring factions, permanently stationed its troops and secret services in the country and thereby dominated its politics for the next

29 years. The intervention illustrated Syria's strength all the more as it first stopped the advance of Palestinian forces and their Lebanese allies who were opposed to the political status quo in the country and later prevented the largely Christian advocates of this same status quo from imposing their agenda with strong Israeli support. Yasser Arafat and his supporters were expelled twice from Lebanon during the presence of the Syrian troops, first in 1982 and then in 1983 (Petran 1987; Traboulsi 2012; O'balance 1998). In fact, military action against the Palestinians was taken even though it threatened to shake the very legitimacy of the al-Asad regime, which rested on Ba'athism as an Arab nationalist ideology and thus by extension on the defence of the Palestinian cause. Not much later, in the war between Iraq and Iran that raged from 1980 to 1988, Damascus supported the latter, while all other Arab capitals supported the former. Primarily determined by the conflict with its Iraqi counterpart, the position of the al-Asad regime was remarkable as it put Syria at odds with the rest of the 'Arab world' whose wider interests, like the more specific ones of the Palestinians, officially formed the backbone of al-Asad's legitimacy (Kienle 1990). Syria stuck to its decision throughout the war, even though it lost the financial and material support hitherto granted by the wealthy oil-producing states in the Arab peninsula. Partly motivated by the continued *mésentente* with Saddam Hussein, Syria condemned the Iraqi invasion of Kuwait in 1990 and participated in the international coalition to liberate the country in 1991. More generally, this policy reflected al-Asad's acute awareness of the end of the Cold War that not only deprived Saddam Hussein of Soviet support but also forced—and enabled—Syria to embrace the 'New World Order' as defined by the then US President George H.W. Bush. After condemning Hussein's move in Kuwait, al-Asad quickly defeated General Aoun who had been challenging the authority of Syria and its allies in Lebanon with Iraqi support and then tightened his own grip on the country. The liberation of Kuwait initiated the demise of the Iraqi rulers and even the Iraqi state, drove a nail into Saddam Hussein's future coffin and thus strengthened Syria. Last but not least, al-Asad and his supporters managed to keep Turkey on its toes by providing a rear base to the Kurdistan Workers' Party (PKK) and hosting its leader Abdullah Öcalan from 1979 to 1998 (Kienle 1990; Hinnebusch 2015).

The survival of the al-Asad regime, its rapid consolidation and its resilience against challenges such as the Hama uprising in 1982 and the coup attempted by Hafez's own brother Rifat a year later may be explained as a result of an efficient strategy combing repression, co-optation and legitimation (Merkel and Gerschewski 2011). The extent and severity of repression has been amply documented by human rights observers such as Amnesty International and Human Rights Watch, testimonies like those by Yassin al-Haj Saleh (Haj Saleh 2012) and of course the massacre of some 10–30,000 people during the shelling of Hama. Strategies of co-optation aimed not only at the Ba'ath's traditional constituencies of small-scale owners of capital, middling peasants, public sector workers and civil servants but increasingly at a new category of entrepreneurs who were benefitting from the controlled policies of economic liberalisation known as the (first) *infitah*. Reinforced by the effects of co-optation, its legitimacy was based on its constant rhetorical defence of the Palestinian and Arab cause and more generally the embrace of anti-imperialism and social justice defined as an 'Arab version of socialism' that became sufficiently elastic to accommodate the rising new entrepreneurs. However, the flexibility of the legitimation strategy and the underlying attempts to simultaneously co-opt employees and employers, and thus labour and capital, also sowed the seeds of social conflict and contestation that culminated in the 2011 uprising.[1]

Ultimately, however, the presumed strength of the al-Asad regime—more apparent than—and by implication that of Syria was the result of favourable external and indeed global conditions, at least from the moment al-Asad appeared to external actors as a convincing ally. External moral and material support facilitated repression as well as co-optation, even though it also allowed the regime to pursue policies like the containment of Palestinian forces in Lebanon that could be seen as contradictory to its official legitimation strategy. Thus the Soviet Union staunchly supported Syria throughout the Cold War, providing significant development aid, including building the Tabqa dam on the Euphrates, weapons, markets and political support. The USSR also sought a window into the Mediterranean and an Arab ally with a common border with Israel (even though such proximity also entailed risks).

This support only weakened towards the end of the Cold War when the new Secretary General of the Communist Party, Mikhail Gorbachev, asked al-Asad to pay for weapons in cash. It is no doubt the decline in Soviet support, prompted by the growing exhaustion of the USSR, that heightened al-Asad's awareness of global changes and led him to move closer to the West. In 1979 Syria also entered into an alliance with the new Islamic Republic that had replaced the monarchy in Iran. However, the benefits of this alliance became manifest only after the end of the Iraq-Iran War in

1988. During the war, they were more than offset by the loss of support from the other Arab states that all sided with Iraq, as did the Soviet Union. Although on a far more moderate scale than generally assumed, Iran provided military aid and economic support in the form of tourists, oil, trade and investment (Kienle 1990). Thanks to its however limited participation in the liberation of Kuwait in 1991, Syria found itself on the right side not only of the declining USSR but also of the United States and the rest of the West.

Prompted by the collapse of the Soviet Union and consistent with overtures to the West, the new wave of economic liberalisation in the 1990s known as the second *infitah* in spite of its limited and selective nature further convinced the winners of the Cold War that Syria was open for business and ready to enter the era of globalisation that was supposed to consecrate the worldwide victory of capitalism. Domestically it led to considerable expectations and indeed first arrested the decline in economic growth perceptible since the mid-1980s and then led to its increase in the 1990s, the latter also boosted by the production and export of oil. By favouring and tying parts of the private sector closer to the regime, it temporarily stabilised the position of the latter before alienating its less well-off constituencies. Strengthening crony capitalism on the one hand and economic marginalisation on the other in the longer run, the second *infitah* initiated a trend towards growing material inequality, eroded the social fabric of the country and thus contributed to the contestation that began in 2011. Moreover, the regime implemented a degree of political window-dressing such as slightly less controlled parliamentary elections and some human rights improvements that somewhat enhanced its international reputation. Finally, the now merely rhetorical nature of its hostility towards Israel further contributed to the overall impression of a regime on the mend.

However, even under Hafez al-Asad, Syria's strength had been apparent rather than real. Cracks were visible to whoever wanted to see them under the polished surface of a regional power increasingly embracing what is commonly referred to as modernity. In Nazih Ayubi's terms, Syria was a fierce rather than a strong state (Ayubi 1996): its strength resided in hard talk and in heavy-handed repression rather than in economic performance and social, or rather societal, cohesion. Syria indeed remained socially as divided as it had been in the days of the old struggle for Syria. The Ba'athist rhetoric of Arab nationalism papered over but failed to lessen divisions that separated geographical regions of the country, town and countryside and, in spite of its socialist colouring, social groups based on criteria such as income, wealth and status. More importantly, it failed to unite its initial and traditional constituency of small-scale owners of capital, peasants, civil servants and army officers (the latter two frequently hailing from the first two) that formed the backbone of al-Asad's regime. Rather, the political ascendancy of these 'intermediary classes' prompted and exacerbated the competition for power and resources among their members in which loyalties based on regional, family and religious (sometimes also linguistic) ties were heavily mobilised. The increasing emphasis on Arab nationalism and unity thus coincided with deepening societal divisions that have been analysed by numerous authors including Nikolaos van Dam, Raymond Hinnebusch, Hanna Batatu, Alasdair Drysdale, Michel Seurat and Elizabeth Picard.[2] Most strikingly, these cleavages appeared in the struggle for power in Syria (i.e. the theme of the monograph of the same name published by Nikolaos van Dam) that pitted Sunni, Druze, Isma'ili and Alawite officers against each other throughout the 1960s. Identity-based dynamics of solidarity and exclusion led to the successive purge of the Sunnis, Druze and Isma'ilis from most important positions in the armed forces. Important as they have been, such cleavages based on regional, religious and family ties do not account for all the forms of factionalism in Syrian politics, which had become awash with examples of disagreements among family members and alliances across religious divides.

Marked throughout its history by changing but ever-present societal divisions, the Syrian state was further weakened by the longer-term effects of the second *infitah* already referred to. Initially, the additional measures of economic liberalisation adopted in the 1990s no doubt increased economic growth and thus directly and indirectly enabled the regime to draw on additional resources to pursue its interests both domestically and abroad. The combination of partial economic liberalisation and crony capitalism allowed the regime to direct material benefits towards its supporters and broaden the circle of beneficiaries who remained indebted to it and under continued authoritarian rule frequently continued to depend on it. Co-optation and its trickle-down effects strengthened a regime that continued to have the means to repress dissent if necessary and to prop up its legitimacy. However, the combination of selective economic liberalisation and crony capitalism gradually proved to be detrimental to the material conditions of growing parts of the population, dashing the hopes of many who (unreasonably perhaps) had hoped to be among the winners.

The co-optation of some increasingly led to the 'de-optation' of others; support from the beneficiaries of these policies was matched by defections from among the regime's old support basis of small-scale owners of capital and peasants left out from the windfalls, as well as civil servants and public sector workers. While the loyalty of the latter two categories could in part be bought through salary rises, workers in the informal sector that was naturally boosted by economic liberalisation fell through the cracks. The inflow of capital and investments also strengthened the position of entrepreneurs vis-à-vis that of the regime. At the same time, increasing economic exchanges with the outside world increased the exchange of ideas, in some quarters weakened officially defended values and norms, and thereby increased the diversity of thought as well as of social and cultural practices. Official statements, including the foundations of regime legitimacy, were challenged, and these challenges resulted in a Huntingtonian dilemma in which the rulers had increasing difficulty in reconciling competing and contradicting demands for material and symbolical resources emanating from different parts of the population (Huntington 1968). Finally, attempts to guarantee Syria's position in a world marked by global exchanges, the search for foreign investment and international recognition put limits on the overt recourse to repression. As a result, the Syrian regime increasingly faced diverse internal challenges that illustrated the Potemkinian nature of its apparent strength.

The Struggle as a Mirror of the State

Like the old one, the new struggle for Syria is closely related, indeed premised, on the societal cleavages that divide Syria. The fact that domestic actors enter into alliances with external ones to contain or even defeat other domestic actors is proof of cross-border links that are stronger than solidarity with fellow Syrians. Such cross-border ties are no doubt a common phenomenon in the politics and international relations of numerous countries. For instance, competing parties in democratic elections frequently get symbolical or rhetorical support from like-minded parties in neighbouring countries. In contemporary Europe the parties of the extreme right, in spite of their nationalist agendas, have been supporting each other in the run up to parliamentary and presidential elections. Similarly, most of the rest of the European Union supported the Remain camp in the 2016 Brexit referendum in the United Kingdom. Conversely, Donald Trump advocated Brexit in the 2016 presidential campaign, while

European leaders sided with his competitor, Hillary Clinton. However, in these cases external support for domestic actors is ultimately mediated by the electorate as a whole and thus, except for the case of monarchies, by the sovereign. In contrast, Syrian actors allied themselves with external actors without referring the case to the ultimate judgement of all Syrians and preferred to impose these alliances on fellow Syrians. The strength of cross-border ties with external actors compared to cross-country solidarity with other Syrians shows that Syria is a 'territorial' rather than a 'nation' state, in Bahgat Korany's terms (Korany 1987). More precisely, it is a state in the sense of a territory defined by borders, a population and a polity claiming legitimacy and attempting to rule this territory and population. However, unlike in a nation state, the population does not form a—however imagined—community of solidarity including all and only the inhabitants of the territory, a community that is stronger than any other community at infra-state level (Anderson 2006).

It is certainly true that in part the new struggle for Syria has been waged by armed groups that have established themselves by force in various parts of the country and which do not necessarily represent either the local population or its interests. Some of them reach out to the local inhabitants, attempt to co-opt them or include them in asymmetrical alliances. Others act like occupation forces in a foreign country. However, the current conflict(s) cannot be reduced to struggles among groups without any social base in the areas from where they act. Loyalist forces have enjoyed popular support in significant swathes of the country, including the North-West, parts of Aleppo and Damascus. Conversely, the People's Protection Units clearly recruit (though not only) from the Kurdish-speaking population in the North of the country where they fight ISIS and the al-Asad government. However, the issue is not whether or not the armed groups represent the local population. The important fact is that the armed groups operate from areas where they are able to claim some kind of connection with the local population that they can instrumentalise: for instance, there are no armed rebel Sunni groups in non-Sunni areas, and there are no armed Kurdish groups in non-Kurdish areas.

Syria remained a territorial state during the reign of Hafez al-Asad. The skilful recourse to repression, co-optation and legitimation facilitated by an international climate favourable to his administration strengthened Syria in appearance rather than in reality. As they failed to mitigate the societal divisions among Syrians and to promote an imagined community encompassing all Syrians, Hafez al-Asad's policies also failed to transform

Syria into a nation state that might have been more stable. Continued authoritarian rule moreover prevented the territorial state from gaining additional legitimacy that it could have gained through more participatory decision-making procedures. Devoid of overarching bonds of loyalty and democratic procedures, Syria remained a weak state.

Differences Between the Old and the New Struggle for Syria

In spite of their similarities, the old and the new struggle for Syria differ in four major respects. The first difference pertains to the importance of identity politics in the sense of solidarities based on cultural markers such as religion, language and the representation of family ties (which, even if real, need to be subjectively felt to provide the foundations of commonalities). In the new struggle for Syria, ties between internal and external actors frequently build on subjectively shared cultural markers. The most notable exceptions are ties with major global actors in America and Europe. Thus Sunni Muslim groups in the country receive support from Sunni Muslim governments and non-governmental actors in other Arab countries (with the notable exception of the Egyptian government), Turkey and further afield. The largely Alawite rulers receive support from Shi'ite actors such as Iran and Hezbollah, even though the effort to redefine the Alawites as 'Shi'ites' remains a precarious project of uncertain outcome. In contrast, in the old struggle for Syria, cross-border ties between internal and external actors hardly ever built on such sectarian similarities or considerations. At the time competing political actors in Syria mainly hailed from its Sunni Muslim majority whose allies in other Arab countries and in Turkey by and large also belonged to their respective Sunni Muslim majorities. Iran was not yet part of the game, and neither Hezbollah nor other major Shi'ite forces in Lebanon had yet come into existence.

Second, the new struggle is far more violent than the old struggle. In the latter, apart from the occasional assassination and execution, competitors mainly bought support, plotted conspiracies and intrigues and staged *coups d'état*. In the former, the parties to the conflict openly fight each other in what amounts to a fully fledged war, and they deliberately inflict suffering on civilians thought to support the other side. Most likely, the large-scale violence that marks the new struggle flows from the perception of the actors that the matter at stake is the defence not simply of interests but of identities and therefore of one's very existence.

Third, the old and the new struggle differ as to their impact on borders. In the old struggle, the external borders of Syria were either respected or attempts were made to unite Syria with other states. From the 1940s onwards, the Hashemite court in Amman lobbied for its Greater Syria scheme that aimed at the creation of a single state encompassing Transjordan, Palestine, Lebanon and Syria (and a close alliance, even federation, with Iraq), while its counterpart in Baghdad advocated its Fertile Crescent scheme that sought to unite these countries and Iraq in an 'Arab League' (to be distinguished from the Egyptian rival project that gave rise to the Arab League as we know it today). The latter project especially was popular in Syrian quarters that sought to check the influence of other Arab states (Kienle 1995). In 1958 the rulers of Syria persuaded the president of Egypt, Gamal Abdel Nasser, to establish the UAR already referred to above. Designed to ward off threats from the imperialist West and its alleged regional stooges (and even communism), it broke apart three years later. In 1963, an unsuccessful attempt was made to unite Syria, Egypt and Iraq and thus to strengthen the 'revolutionary' camp in the Arab East; following on its heels a plan to unite only Syria and Iraq also failed. In 1970 the al-Asad regime, still weak, joined a rather lose Federation of Arab Republics established by Egypt, Libya and Sudan that also floundered. Syria once more embarked on a tentative merger with Iraq in 1978 when the Camp David Accords threatened to arrest or even reverse the emergence of Syria as a strong regional actor. Faced with Egypt's 'defection' that tipped the balance of power further in favour of Israel, al-Asad cautiously sought a rapprochement with the Iraqi regime. The attempt ended in failure less than a year later when Saddam Hussein managed to concentrate all powers in Iraq in his own hands and visibly became a big threat like that of Israel. This being said, the al-Asad regime simultaneously expanded its jurisdiction 'informally', without redrawing interstate borders: illustrating its growing strength, its troops entered Lebanon in 1976 and according to its own account for almost 30 years attempted to end the civil war and prevent its resurgence (Seale 1965; Kerr 1972; Kienle 1990).

In contrast, the impact of the new struggle for Syria is messier, along the country's borders as well as within them. Something like a complete merger with a neighbouring country was envisaged by only one actor, ISIS, which considered Iraq as a part of its future realm and accepted the allegiance of like-minded groups in other parts of the Middle East such as Libya and the Egyptian Sinai. Such ambitions are reflected in its official name—the 'Islamic State in Iraq and Sham', the latter term referring to a geographical area larger than the current Syrian state (in the competing acronym, 'ISIL' is rendered by the term 'Levant'). In actual fact of course, ISIS has only dominated some of the Northern parts of the two countries, even though it tried to abolish the border between them and paid roughly equal attention to its two major strongholds, Mosul in Iraq and Raqqa in Syria.

At the same time, however, the new struggle for Syria entailed the internal fragmentation of the country into areas more or less dominated by the regime and competing political powers. Based on their own forces of coercion, the latter occasionally provided services ranging from education and health to the administration of justice and here and there allowed participatory institutions to emerge. Sometimes these services coexisted alongside those provided by the central government or relied on personnel that officially continued to receive their salaries from the latter. Permanently shifting in response to military defeats and victories, the boundaries of these areas have gradually settled around larger zones of domination and influence such as the government-controlled Damascus-Latakia corridor and Hama and Homs in the Western part of the country, the areas under the control of opposition forces including the environs of Dara'a in the South and Idlib in the North, the mainly Kurdish areas in the North that the Democratic Union Party (YPG) intends to unite under the name of Rojava and of course the North-Eastern parts of the country ruled by ISIS. The increasing territorial fragmentation that only mirrors the political division of the country may entail lasting divisions and may limit the future reach of central government even after an end of open conflict, possibly giving way to decentralised structures of sorts (Yazigi 2016). Considering the general reluctance of the 'international community' to endorse permanent changes to international borders, fragmentation is however likely to stop short of the replacement of the Syrian state with a variety of smaller states (that would all be recognised internationally).

Fourth, the new struggle for Syria is also fuelled by the rise of identity politics in the rest of the world, in particular in Europe and other parts of the West. In the recent past, the classic nation states of Europe where states as legal and political entities coincided more than in many other cases (though often imperfectly) with nations as communities of solidarity and loyalty have lost their appeal to increasing numbers of their inhabitants, even citizens, who consider themselves marginalised and excluded and thus identify with other actors that claim to defend them. The erosion of the nation state in Europe as the main focus of loyalty and solidarity pushes those who consider themselves excluded to migrate to lands where they expect to meet respect or even dominate. Disenchanted Muslims 'radicalise' into what is commonly called jihadists and are pulled into areas controlled by the 'truly' Muslim ISIS, while some disenchanted non-Muslims see in the ISIS the most radical challenger to the existing order and therefore 'Islamise' to join it.[3]

Concluding Remarks: From Old to New

Any explanation of the differences between the old and the new struggle for Syria seems to hinge on the growing importance of identity politics. Although they often divided populations (rather than 'societies') into mutually distrustful groups, societal cleavages based on religion and other cultural markers seem to have deepened under conditions of increasing insecurity and competition. Individuals who feel insecure seek security in communities based on shared cultural features such as religion that subjectively strengthen and protect them in the struggle for resources and power.

The creation of independent states in the process of decolonisation after World War II was one such moment in which competition exacerbated such societal divides; the inhabitants of these states could neither appeal to umpires nor rely on mutually accepted institutions which yet had to be built or at least endorsed. In Syria, but also in other countries of the Middle East, state power was definitely devolved from foreigners to locals, along with the power to allocate material and symbolical resources, even the power to define citizenship (Hourani 2002; Owen 2004). The political arena delineated by the borders of the new Syrian state, formerly mandatory Syria, was no longer manipulated or policed by France. Societal and political cleavages defined by cultural markers were exacerbated as the stakes increased; independence reinforced fragmentation all the more as neither foreign domination nor the struggle against it had produced an imagined community or a nation strong enough to neutralise infra-state loyalties and solidarities (Anderson 2006; Kienle 2016).

The other crucial moment coincided with the beginning of the current period of globalisation in the late 1980s. The end of the Cold War threw the countries of the old 'Eastern bloc' and their allies like Syria into the global arena of competition for investment, markets and other resources, an arena much larger than that of the Syrian state within which Syrians had been obliged to compete since independence. Domestic and foreign policies had to be adapted for the Syrian state and thus for Syrians to participate successfully in the new global game. Selective economic liberalisation to attract capital increased at least the perception of growing material inequality. It also led to greater social and cultural diversity, in particular between the internationalised beneficiaries of globalisation who tended to embrace 'foreign' practices and the others. Losers easily identified loss with identity, and cleavages based on cultural markers deepened and multiplied. No doubt, the interest-based alliance between Alawite officers and non-Alawite, largely Sunni, owners of capital and its ramifications cushioned both groups against the transformation of a societal division marked by religion into a fully fledged open conflict between Alawites and Sunnis. However, once the regime was openly contested, support and opposition for the conflict parties was increasingly framed in terms of cultural markers, either explicitly or implicitly. Even though the early contestation beginning in Dara'a was fuelled by social concerns and by repression, the fact that protesters were Sunnis raised the spectre of all Sunnis rallying in protest and thus of a Sunni-Alawite showdown. From the point of view of the regime therefore, protests had to be repressed fiercely, at the risk of further alienating the majority of Sunnis and in the hope of persuading all others who shared their economic interests with the regime into compliance.

Notes

1. For the history and political economy of Syria under the al-Asads, see, for instance, Perthes (1995), Matar (2016), Haddad (2012), and Belhadj (2013).
2. van Dam (2011), Batatu (1981), Seurat (1980), Drysdale (1981), Devlin (1976), Hinnebusch (2001), Picard (1980), Wieland (2012).
3. Roy (2016), Kepel (2016), Dumas et al. (2016).

Bibliography

Anderson, B. (2006). *Imagined Communities: Reflections on the Origin and Spread of Nationalism* (Rev. ed.). London: Verso.

Ayubi, N. N. (1996). *Over-Stating the Arab State: Politics and Society in the Middle East*. London: I.B. Tauris.

Batatu, H. (1981). Some Observations on the Social Roots of Syria's Ruling Military Group and the Causes for Its Dominance. *Middle East Journal, XXXV*(3), 331–334.

Belhadj, S. (2013). *La Syrie de Bashar al-Asad: anatomie d'un régime autoritaire*. Paris: Belin.

Devlin, J. F. (1976). *The Ba'th Party: A History from Its Origins to 1966*. Stanford, CA: Stanford University Press.
Drysdale, A. (1981). The Syrian Political Elite, 1966–1976: A Spatial and Social Analysis. *Middle Eastern Studies, XVII*(1), 3–30.
Dumas, C., Roy, O., & Kepel, G. (2016, April 14). querelle française sur le djihadisme. *Libération*.
Haddad, B. (2012). *Business Networks in Syria: The Political Economy of Authoritarian Resilience*. Stanford, CA: Stanford University Press.
al-Haj Saleh, Y. (2012). *Salvation O Boys: 16 Years in Syrian Prisons*. Beirut: Dar al-Saqi.
Hinnebusch, R. (2001). *Syria: Revolution from Above*. London: Routledge.
Hinnebusch, R. (2015). *The International Politics of the Middle East* (2nd ed.). Manchester: Manchester University Press.
Hourani, A. (2002). *A History of the Arab Peoples* (New ed., Part V). Cambridge, MA: The Belknap Press of Harvard University Press.
Huntington, S. P. (1968). *Political Order in Changing Societies*. New Haven, CT: Yale University Press.
Kepel, G. (2016). *La fracture: chroniques 2015–16*. Paris: Gallimard.
Kerr, M. H. (1972). *The Arab Cold War: Gamal Abd al-Nasir and his Rivals, 1958–1970* (3rd ed.). London: Oxford University Press.
Kienle, E. (1990). *Ba'th v. Ba'th: The Conflict Between Syria and Iraq 1968–89*. London: I.B. Tauris.
Kienle, E. (1995). Arab Unity Schemes Revisited: Interest, Identity, and Politics in Syria and Egypt. *International Journal of Middle East Studies, 27*(1), 53–71.
Kienle, E. (2016). Popular Contestation, Regime Transformation and State Formation. In E. Kienle & N. Sika (Eds.), *The Arab Uprisings: Transforming and Challenging State Power*. London: I.B. Tauris.
Korany, B. (1987). Alien and Besieged, Yet Here to Stay: The Contradictions of the Arab Territorial State. In G. Salamé (Ed.), *The Foundations of the Arab State*. London: Croom Helm.
Matar, L. (2016). *The Political Economy of Investment in Syria*. London: Palgrave Macmillan.
Merkel, W., & Gerschewski, J. (2011). Autocracies at Critical Junctures: A Model for the Study of Dictatorial Regimes. *Schlossplatz, 3*, 14–17.
O'balance, E. (1998). *Civil War in Lebanon, 1975–92*. Basingstoke: Palgrave Macmillan.
Owen, R. (2004). *State, Power and Politics in the Making of the Modern Middle East* (3rd ed.). Abingdon: Routledge.
Perthes, V. (1995). *The Political Economy of Syria Under Asad*. London: I.B. Tauris.
Petran, T. (1987). *The Struggle for Lebanon*. New York: Monthly Review Press.
Phillips, C. (2016). *The Battle for Syria: International Rivalry in the New Middle East*. New Haven, CT: Yale University Press.

Picard, E. (1980). La Syrie de 1946 à 1979. In A. Raymond (Ed.), *La Syrie d'aujourd'hui*. Paris: Editions du CNRS.

Pierret, T. (2013, August 9). External Support and the Syrian Insurgency. *Foreign Policy*. Retrieved October 19, 2017, from foreignpolicy.com/2013/08/09/external-support-and-the-Syrian-insurgency

Quandt, W. B. (2005). *Peace Process: American Diplomacy and the Arab-Israeli Conflict* (3rd ed.). Berkeley, CA: University of California Press.

Roy, O. (2016). *Le djihad et la mort*. Paris: Seuil.

Seale, P. (1965). *The Struggle for Syria: A Study of Post-war Arab Politics, 1945–1958* (1st ed.). London: Oxford University Press.

Seale, P. (1986). *The Struggle for Syria: A Study of Post-war Arab Politics, 1945–1958* (2nd ed.). London: I.B. Tauris.

Seale, P. (1988). *Asad: The Struggle for the Middle East*. London: I.B. Tauris.

Seurat, M. (1980). Les populations, l'Etat et la société. In A. Raymond (Ed.), *La Syrie d'aujourd'hui*. Paris: Editions du CNRS.

Traboulsi, F. (2012). *A History of Modern Lebanon*. London: Pluto Press.

Van Dam, N. (2011). *The Struggle for Power in Syria: Politics and Society Under Asad and the Ba'th Party* (4th ed.). London: I.B. Tauris.

Wieland, C. (2012). *Syria-A Decade of Lost Chances: Repression and Revolution from Damascus Spring to Arab Spring*. Seattle, WA: Cune Press.

Yazigi, J. (2016). *No Going Back: Why Decentralization Is the Future of Syria*. European Council on Foreign Relations, Policy Brief.

CHAPTER 4

Syria: Strong State Versus Social Cleavages

Hiroyuki Aoyama

INTRODUCTION

The books, *The Struggle for Syria* and *Asad: The Struggle for the Middle East*, written by Patrick Seale, provide reasonable hints for understanding the process of political development of Syria after independence (Seale 1958, 1988). These illuminate the historical background of Syria. Frequent coups and unstable domestic politics coupled with interferences by neighbouring countries became a normal and acceptable practice. Despite all of that, Syria developed into a stable and strong state under the administration of the ex-president, Hafez al-Asad, from 1970 onwards.

While Syria under the rule of Hafez al-Asad increased its involvement in the politics of the Arab Near East, including Lebanon and Palestine, as well as conducting sound domestic politics, it struggled with its geopolitical rival Israel for hegemony over the region. After the death of Hafez al-Asad in 2000, his administration was handed over to Bashar al-Asad, his second son. The rule of the latter, cynically branded as "*jumlūkīya*" (coined word made from "*jumhūrīya*" and "*malakīya*", "republicanism" and "monarchy" respectively in English) or "hereditary republicanism" (*jumhūrīya wirāthīya*), sporadically enhanced the pro-reformist movement represented by the "Damascus Spring" from 2000 to 2001.

H. Aoyama (✉)
Tokyo University of Foreign Studies, Fuchu, Japan
e-mail: aljabal@tufs.ac.jp

Bashar's rule also confronted regional and international pressure. In 2005, after Rafiq al-Ḥarīrī, the former prime minister of Lebanon, was assassinated, the Bashar al-Asad administration was suspected of involvement in the killing and faced hostility from Western countries. Despite its withdrawal from Lebanon, Syria remained more or less a stable political entity. It was the advent of the "Arab Spring" in 2011 that triggered the turmoil in Syria. It is then that the definition of the stability and even the very basis for the existence of a Syrian state came into question.

It is not easy to find the remnants of a strong state in Syria post-2011. The country has become a major battlefield in which domestic and foreign parties fight, as though reverting to Seale's *The Struggle for Syria*. At present, the Bashar al-Asad administration does not control the entire country; some territories are held with the so-called opposition (including Hai'at Tahrir al-Sham, formerly known as Jabhat Fateh al-Sham/the al-Nusra Front), Kurdish nationalists (Democratic Union Party (PYD) and Islamic State (IS)). All these factions struggle with each other, along with Russia, Iran, Turkey, and the US-led coalition against Islamic State, in addition to Israel occupying the Golan Heights and supporting opposition/terrorist groups in and around that area.

The Syrian conflict which produced the worst humanitarian crisis in the twenty-first century seems to end in terms of its fighting phase with the government reclaiming the lost territories starting in 2017. Recently, reconstruction and reconciliation have been the main agendas in Syria. The horizon, however, remains full of dark clouds given that Syria has been reduced into a "weak state". In spite of this, Syria has a history in transforming itself from a "weak state" into a "strong state". Examining the political history of Syria's transformation may provide hints for Syria's future.

This chapter analyses the process through which post-independent Syria enjoyed political stability as a "strong state" with a focus on the notion of social cleavages. The first section provides a reading of the historical formation of social cleavages in Syria since the French Mandate (1920–1946). I argue that social cleavages were established and firmly solidified by the French authorities. The second section reveals how social cleavages and politics were interrelated under the post-independence Syrian polity. The final section highlights the challenges that Syria faces given the current conflict. The chapter concludes that Syria can learn from its past in terms of bridging its social cleavages through integrative and participatory politics.

The Generation of Social Cleavages

Social cleavages are axes of polarisation in domestic political confrontation. According to Seymour Martin Lipset and Stein Rokkan who coined the concept, Western European countries faced social cleavages in terms of centre-periphery, state-church, urban-rural, and owner-worker amid the formation of nation-states and the Industrial Revolution, which were reflected in the political party systems in those countries (Lipset and Rokkan 1967).

There are two ambiguous views on how social cleavages affect politics in countries outside Western Europe, that is, countries that do not satisfy the requirements of institutional democracy. The first view is that the demise of a political party system due to the establishment of an authoritarian regime destroys the connection between social cleavages and politics (Hazama 2006: 7–10; Geddes 2003). This viewpoint is dominant in studies on Eastern European countries where authoritarian regimes were established through the formation of communist regimes that followed or overthrew parliamentary democracies. The second view is that an authoritarian state uses or manipulates social cleavages in order to maintain and strengthen its governance. This view is common in studies of African countries with an emphasis on politicising social cleavages on the basis of differences in religion, ethnicities, languages, and so on (Hazama 2006: 10–11; Laitin 1986).

In the case of Syria, its society exhibits cultural, regional, and religious diversity sufficient to create social cleavages, and its populace is conscious of the diversity. Syria's society can be characterised as "mosaic" or "*nasīj*" ("textile" in English) where various religious, sectarian, and ethnic groups coexist. Looking at the religious or sectarian groups, Syria has Sunni, Shia, Alawi, Ismaili, and Druze Muslims, Christians, and even a small Jewish community. As for national and ethnic groups, Syria has an Arab majority, Kurds, and Armenians (Armenian Orthodox Christians and Armenian Catholics). Emphasising the distribution of religious, sectarian, and ethnic groups in the Middle East needs careful deliberation, since it may easily promote the disintegration of countries in the region under the pretext of "democratisation" or "minority protection". Having said that, Figs. 4.1 and 4.2 show the (estimated) population ratios and the main resident areas based on religious/sectarian groups on the one hand and ethnic groups on the other, revealing the "*nasīj*" characteristic of Syrian society.

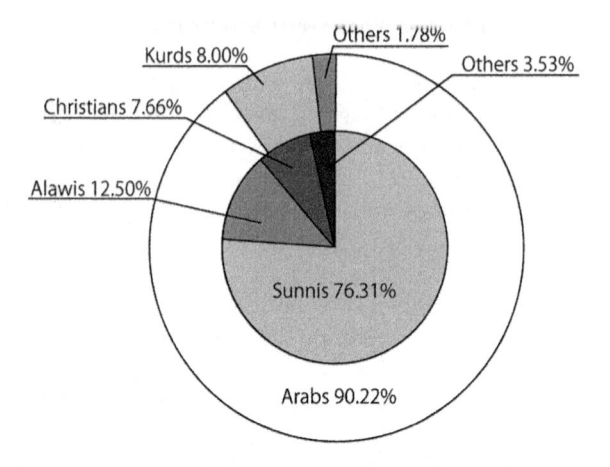

Others 1.78%
Kurds 8.00%
Others 3.53%
Christians 7.66%
Alawis 12.50%
Sunnis 76.31%
Arabs 90.22%

Fig. 4.1 Population ratios based on religious/sect groups and national/ethnic groups (estimated). Source: Author's computations based on Collelo (1988: 63) and Middle East Watch (1991: 90)

I argue that Syria's social cleavages are prominent at five main levels. As shown in Table 4.1, the first is based on differences between sects (Sunnis versus Alawis, Sunnis versus Druzes, etc.), while the second between ethnicities (Arabs versus Kurds, Arabs versus Armenians, etc.). The third social cleavage is marked by regional diversity or by differences in culture, custom, and economic life among "*bilād*" (the plural form of "*balad*" referring to "country" in English), that is among the large cities (Damascus versus Aleppo, Homs versus Hama, etc.). The fourth is the contrast between urban and rural areas, largely underpinned by differences in respective economic functions. The fifth is that of social class difference, that is, landowners and farmers in the traditional or feudalistic (*iqṭāʿī*) mode of production and capitalists and labourers under capitalism.

A historical reading of the origins of the social cleavages in Syria takes us back to the French Mandate (1920–1946). Syria's social cleavages were firstly generated under the French mandatory governance that dominated Syria's political and social framework. As is the case with France's establishment of a sectarian system (*al-niẓām al-ṭāʾifī*) in Lebanon, France focused on Syria's social diversity in an attempt to split Syria and maintain its rule (Aoyama 2006: 162). The French governance aimed at supressing the independence movement led by Arab nationalists. France's objective

SYRIA: STRONG STATE VERSUS SOCIAL CLEAVAGES   75

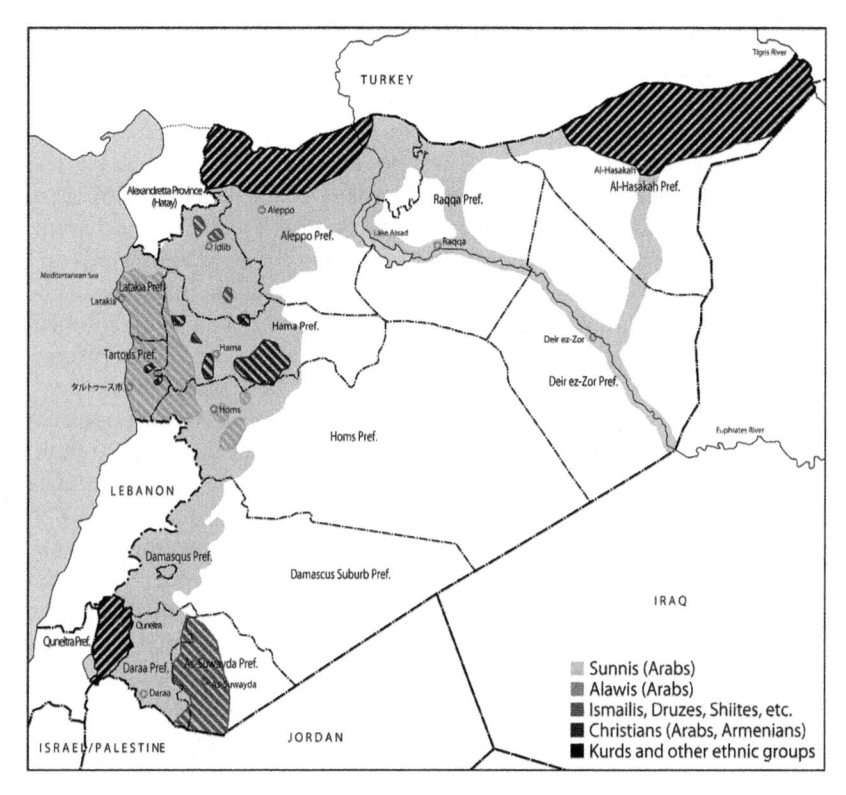

Fig. 4.2 Distribution of resident areas based on religious/sect groups and national/ethnic groups. Source: Author's computations based on Boustani and Fargues (1991: 29), Collelo (1988: 62–67), and Commins (1996: 47–48, 70)

Table 4.1 Major social cleavages in Syria

Factors of social cleavages	
Religions/sects	Sunnis vs. Alawis; Sunnis vs. Druzes; etc.
Nationalities/ethnicities	Arabs vs. Kurds; Arabs vs. Armenians; etc.
Regions	Damascus vs. Aleppo; Homs vs. Hama; etc.
Economic functions	Cities vs. rural areas
Classes	Landowners vs. farmers; capitalist vs. working class

Source: Author's analysis

was to quash the rise of any political power that threatened its mandate. France's governance was mainly enforced through two measures. The first was to give preferential treatment to minority groups in the Special Troops of the Levant (les Troupes Spéciales du Levant), the predecessor of the Syrian Arab Army (van Dam 1979: 39; Khoury 1987: 533–534). The French authorities actively recruited Alawis, Druzes, Ismailis, Christians, Caucasians, Kurds, and Armenians to the Special Troops of the Levant. This is because whereas Sunni Arabs, especially the rich landowners and merchants living in urban areas, were unwilling to allow their sons to be military personnel, the minority groups intended to obtain social advancement through the military which operated a performance-based promotion system (van Dam 1979: 39–40; McDowall 2000: 468).

The second measure was to give autonomy to areas largely populated with minorities. During the French mandate, the reorganisation of administrative districts was conducted frequently. In 1920 when the mandate administration started, Syria was divided into zones: Damascus, Aleppo (both of which had a Sunni Arab majority), and Latakia (Alawite majority). In addition, Alexandretta Province (*liwā'*), in which many Turks and Armenians resided, was designated as an autonomous district within Aleppo. In 1922, while Damascus, Aleppo, and Latakia formed the Syrian Federation, the whole area of Jabal al-Druze, which had a majority Druze, was detached from Damascus and given status as its own autonomous district. Furthermore, in 1924, Damascus and Aleppo constituted Syria, with the exclusion of Alexandretta, Latakia, and Jabal al-Druze. Later, in 1936, Latakia and Jabal al-Druze were incorporated into Syria, joining Damascus and Aleppo, but detached again from 1939 to 1942. In the meantime, Alexandretta became independent as the Hatay Republic in 1938 and was subsequently absorbed by Turkey in the following year (Khoury 1987: 58–59, 533–534; van Dam 1979: 39). The Syrian people were thus forced to be members of ephemeral states due to France's reorganisation. They were therefore prevented from having a firm national awareness, a factor which limited national mobilisation.

These French governance policies expressed in legal and political forms the already existing social and cultural diversity in Syria. Syria was made up of a mosaic of different people (with diversity, as mentioned, based on religion, sect, nationality, ethnicity, region, economic function, social class, and subjective allegiance). Thus, social cleavages were established and firmly solidified by the French authorities.

During the French Mandate, Arab nationalism, Syrian nationalism (*al-qawmīya al-sūrīya*), Marxism, and Islamism, represented forms of resistance to the Western powers' arbitrary border demarcation and its associated social cleavages generation (Aoyama 2006: 164). However, these ideologies were not universal enough in their reach to overcome all the divides created by social cleavages. As mentioned earlier, the concept of the nation for the Syrians did not correspond to that of the state given in the territory known as Syria. However, these ideologies did serve as principle for fostering national integration. Above all, Arab nationalism, Syrian nationalism (*al-qawmīya al-sūrīya*), and Marxism assumed a substantial role in supporting national integration in Syria. As a measure for resisting external intervention and social segregation, criticised as "sectarianism (*ṭā'ifyīya*)", the Syrian people sought to overcome their colonially constructed religious and other differences by defining their identity on the basis of historical unity, a language-based community, and a territorial community.

The History of the Relationship Between Politics and Social Cleavages

After attaining independence, in April 1946, Syria experienced three political regimes: parliamentary democracy, one-party rule authoritarianism, and authoritarianism based on a "two-tier power structure". Under each regime, social cleavages and politics have connected to each other in a unique form.

Parliamentary Democracy (April 1946–March 1963)

In the 17 years from its independence to March 1963, Syria had a politically unstable system due to successive coups (March, August, and December 1949, November 1951, and February 1954), military regimes (March to August 1949 and November 1951 to February 1954), and the union with Egypt (United Arab Republic, February 1958 to September 1961). Throughout this period, however, Syria had a parliamentary democracy, where social cleavages were reflected in tension among political parties.

In post-independence Syria, parliamentary elections were carried out respectively in 1947, 1949, 1953, 1954, and 1961. In the election of 1947, out of 114 seats, the National Party acquired 24 seats, the People's

Party obtained 20 seats, and the remaining 70 seats were occupied by independents. In the 1949 election, out of 114 seats again, the People's Party gained 63 seats, the National Party 13 seats, Islamic Socialist Front (an electoral alliance led by the Syrian Muslim Brotherhood) 4 seats, the Ba'ath Party 1 seat, the Syrian Social Nationalist Party 1 seat, and 31 seats went to independents. In the election of 1954, out of 142 seats, 30 seats were secured by the People's Party, 22 seats by the Ba'ath Party, 19 seats by the National Party, 4 seats by the Syrian Muslim Brotherhood, 2 seats by the Socialist Cooperation Party, 2 seats by the Syrian Social Nationalist Party, 2 seats by Arab Liberation Movement, 1 seat by the Syrian Communist Party, and 60 seats went to independents. In the 1961 election, for a total 172 seats, the People's Party won 33 seats, the National Party 21 seats, the Ba'ath Party 20 seats, the Syrian Muslim Brotherhood 10 seats, the Arab Liberation Movement 4 seats, and 84 seats went to independents. It should be noted that the 1953 election was implemented under the military regime, which therefore cannot be regarded as a free election. In that election, the Arab Liberation Movement overwhelmed other parties by winning 72 seats out of 82 seats (Deiter et al. 2001: 221).

In the period under the parliamentary democracy, the political community of Syria, including the political parties that obtained seat(s) at elections, was roughly classified into two political factions that confronted one another. The first one was conservatives that hoped for the maintenance of existing social and economic systems and their own political advantage. This faction was led by the leaders of the National Party and the People's Party that took the reins of government. The second political faction consisted of reformists who pursued social and economic reforms (especially agricultural reform). This faction comprised, among others, the Ba'ath Party and the Syrian Communist Party (see Fig. 4.3).

The confrontation between these two factions evolved in a manner that encompassed not only difference in political orientation, that is to say conservatives versus reformists, but also due to social cleavages in terms of religion, sect, region, economic function, and class. That is to say, while the conservative faction was considered to represent the interests of the traditional governing classes (big landowners and merchants) comprised of urban Sunnis and capitalists, the reformist faction was considered to speak for the subordinate classes (farmers and labourers) from rural areas, a high percentage of whom were from minority religious/sectarian groups (see Fig. 4.3).

```
                         Social cleavages
┌─────────────────────────┐     ¦     ┌─────────────────────────┐
│      Conservatives      │     ¦     │       Reformists        │     ┌──────────┐
│ (National Party and     │     ¦     │ (Ba'ath Party and Syrian│─────│ Military │
│   People's Party)       │     ¦     │    Communist Party)     │     └──────────┘
└─────────────────────────┘     ¦     └─────────────────────────┘

         Cities          Regions/economic       Rural areas
                            functions

  big landowners/merchants and      Classes      Farmers and laborers
         capitalists
       Sunni Muslims         Religions/sects   Minority religions/sects
```

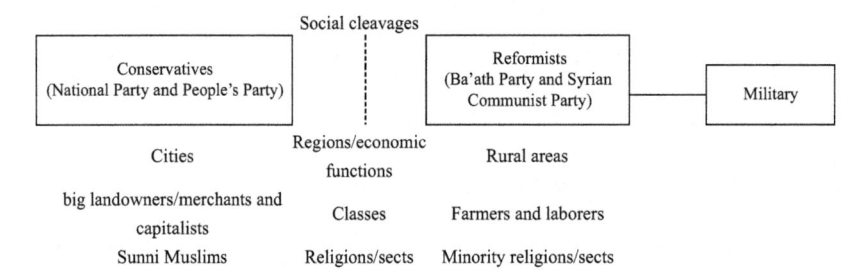

Fig. 4.3 Relation between politics and social cleavages under parliamentary democracy. Source: Author's analysis

Difference also existed within the political factions. Both the conservative faction and the reformist faction were not monolithic. For the conservatives, the National Party's base was located in Damascus, and the People's Party was based in Aleppo and Hama: the two conflicted with each other over regional interests. As for the reformist faction, the Ba'ath Party tried to prioritise the unification of the Arab nations, and the Syrian Communist Party prioritised Marxian internationalism and the uncompromising principle of class conflict. These two positions collided. Meanwhile, the Syrian Muslim Brotherhood also began to emerge as a political organisation; it can be regarded to be positioned in between the conservatives and reformist camps. Although the Syrian Muslim Brotherhood and the conservatives came from the same traditional class, the political orientation of the former at this period was closer to the reformist faction (Aoyama 1995: 51–55).

Furthermore, in analysing this period, it is impossible to ignore the role of the military as a political actor. The military had reformist tendencies in terms of its political orientation and social origin (see Fig. 4.3). They conducted repeated coups from the end of the 1940s to the early 1950s to break the political advantage of the conservative faction and to achieve social and economic reform. For instance, the coups carried out by Adīb al-Shīshaklī in 1949 and 1951 exhibited a reformist characteristic (Seale 1958: 120).

From the middle of the 1950s onwards, the Ba'ath Party increased its integration with the military, which led the so-called Ba'athist Revolution on 8 March 1963. After winning its first seat at the national election of 1949, the Ba'ath Party became the second largest party and played a leading role in the establishment of United Arab Republic in 1958. In the election of 1961, held immediately after the break-up of the United Arab Republic, the Ba'ath Party was the third largest party. It should be recalled, however, that what ultimately brought the Ba'ath Party to power in 1963 was not an election, but a coup carried out by young officers embracing the Arab Ba'ath ideology. That integration of the military in the Ba'ath Party, culminating in the 1963 coup, resolved the conflict between the conservative and reformist factions: the reformist faction emerged victorious. The involvement of the military also severed the relationship between the social cleavages and the party system by destroying the representative parliamentary democracy (Aoyama 1995: 51–55; Be'eri 1970: 336–337; Seale 1958: 28–31, 37, 39–41, 77–79, 158–159, 176–178; Torrey 1975: 157; van Dam 1979: 40–41).

One-Party Authoritarian Rule (March 1963–November 1970)

In the five decades following the "Ba'ath Revolution", Syria had an authoritarian regime. The period 1963 to 1970 is characterised by the Ba'ath Party running the country under their substantive one-party system. The social cleavages observed in this period became obvious amid a power struggle within the party.

The power struggle under the ruling of Ba'ath Party became evident at first between the two factions: *Qawmīyūn* ("nationalists" in English) on the one hand and *Quṭrīyūn* ("regionalists" in English) and Military Committee on the other. *Qawmīyūn* was a faction dominated by senior leaders from the establishment of the party, such as Mīshīl 'Aflaq and Ṣalāḥ al-Dīn al-Bīṭār. This faction's prestige had decreased due to its strategic errors including a short-sighted policy for unification with Egypt and the subsequent disintegration of the party immediately after the union (President Nasser insisted on the dissolution of all political parties in Syria as a precondition to the United Arab Republic). However, *Qawmīyūn* represented the front of the party and pursued the social and economic reforms while maintaining its traditional policy of prioritising Arab unity.

Quṭrīyūn was a faction of young second-ranked party members from rural areas in Syria, which independently continued to engage in party activities even after the National Command (*al-qiyāda al-qawmīya*) led by Mīshīl 'Aflaq (its Secretary-General) had determined to dissolve the Ba'ath Party upon union with Egypt. Its representative members included Yūsuf Zu'ayyin, Nūr al-Dīn al-Atāsī, Munīr 'Abd Allāh, Sulaymān al-Khashsh, Ibrāhīm Mākhūs, and Sa'd 'Abd Allāh. They sought radical reforms, setting

Marxist-branded socialism as the faction's top priority. The Military Committee was formed in Cairo in the summer of 1959 by 13 young officers including Amīn al-Ḥāfiẓ, Muḥammad 'Umrān, Ṣalāḥ Jadīd, Hafez al-Asad, and 'Abd al-Karīm al-Jundī, with further officers joining later. Similar to the members of the *Quṭrīyūn*, the young officers originated from rural areas, continued to conduct activities even during the time Ba'ath Party was dissolved, and had critical opinions regarding the leadership of Mīshīl 'Aflaq and Ṣalāḥ al-Dīn al-Bīṭār due to their ideology that paralysed the Ba'ath Party's activities at the beginning of the 1960s (Institute of Developing Economies 1983: 85–88).

The power struggle between *Qawmīyūn* on the one hand and *Quṭrīyūn* and the Military Committee on the other hand ended in a victory for the latter faction, but also highlighted the superiority within that group of the Military Committee, the chief force behind the "Ba'ath Revolution" and the real power broker behind the regime. The ideological struggle then was about the value to be prioritised out of the Ba'ath Party's three principles, "Unity, Freedom, Socialism", or whether priority should be given to Arab unity or socialism. Meanwhile, it is also worth reflecting upon the social cleavages that cut through both factions; these were demarked along economic function, with *Qawmīyūn* representing large cities and urban areas, while *Quṭrīyūn* and Military Committee leaning towards rural areas and local cities (see Fig. 4.4).

As mentioned earlier, the power struggle was finally settled with the *Qawmīyūn* on the losing side. During the ensuing fallout, the leading role of the military became more prominent, while the socialisation of the economy followed an Arabised model of Marxism-Leninism—the revision

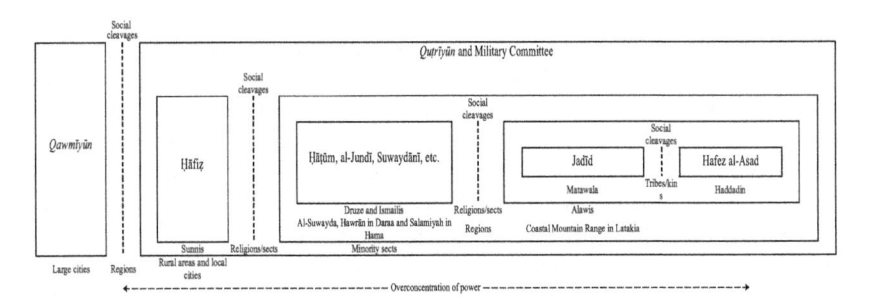

Fig. 4.4 Relationship between power struggles and social cleavages under the one-party rule authoritarianism. Source: Author's analysis

of Arab socialist ideology was referred to as "Arabization of Marxism (*taʿrīb al-mārkisīya*)" (al-Ḥāfiẓ 1997). At the party congress held in April 1965 (The Eighth National Congress), Mīshīl ʿAflaq stepped down from the post of Secretary-General of the National Command, which was a defining and tangible symbol of his and his faction's waning influence and authority.

However, a confrontation followed among the members of Military Committee, which reflected a social cleavage rooted in religious sect. The power struggle was between Amīn al-Ḥāfiẓ (a Sunni from Aleppo), Secretary-General of the Syrian Regional Command (*al-qiyāda al-qūṭrīya al-sūrīya*) of the Baʾath Party, and Ṣalāḥ Jadīd (an Alawi from Duwayr Baʾbda Village, Latakia), Vice Secretary-General of Syrian Regional Command. Furthermore, after Ṣalāḥ Jadīd completely excluded Secretary-General Amīn al-Ḥāfiẓ and other Sunni influential figures (and *Qawmīyūn*) such as Ṣalāḥ al-Dīn al-Bīṭār (a Sunni from Damascus, then-Prime Minister and Foreign Minister) and Munīf al-Razzāz (a Sunni from Damascus, then-Secretary-General of the National Command of the Baʾath Party) in the coup of February 1966, a confrontation between the minority sects came to the surface. This struggle resulted in Druzes from Al-Suwayda (including Salīm Ḥāṭūm, a member of the Syrian Regional Command) and Ismailis from Salamiyah (Hama) (including ʿAbd al-Karīm al-Jundī, Director General of the National Security Bureau of the Regional Command), and those from Hauran District (Daraʾa), including Aḥmad Suwaydānī, Chief of General Staff, were considered to be purged one after another between the middle of 1967 and the beginning of 1969 (see Fig. 4.4).

These successive purges increased the presence of Alawis at the top of the Baʾath Party. In the late 1960s, Vice Secretary-General Ṣalāḥ Jadīd and then-Minister of Defence Hafez al-Asad became opposed to each other over the relationships with the Baʾath administration established in Iraq in July 1968 and other military matters, including personnel. The confrontation ended in November 1970 when Hafez al-Asad defeated his rival. This power struggle evolved as a policy confrontation between Ṣalāḥ Jadīd who tried to force through rigid socialisation policies and Hafez al-Asad who aimed at easing of political and economic regulations. At the same time, this power struggle was explained as reflecting social cleavages among Alawi tribes, that is, the confrontation between the Haddadin and the Matawira, the former was regarded as Hafez al-Asad's faction and the latter as Ṣalāḥ Jadīd's faction (Institute of Developing Economies 1983: 91–94, 114–123, 136–146; van Dam 1979: 52–56, 83–94).

During this period, influential leaders made use of "old cleavages" (Barakat 1993: 48) to mobilise their religious/sectarian groups and tribal/kinsman to eliminate political enemies and strengthen their own power (see Fig. 4.4).

Authoritarianism Based on "Two-Tier Power Structure" (November 1970 Onwards)

From November 1970 onwards, Syria had a political regime essentially based on "populist authoritarianism" (Hinnebusch 2001; Heydemann 1999) or "neopatrimonial authoritarianism" (Aoyama and Suechika 2009: 10) under the direction of ex-President Hafez al-Asad. President al-Asad consistently showed his excellent political ability in both domestic and foreign politics, which transformed Syria from a "weak state" that had suffered from political instability into a "strong state" in the Middle East. What Hafez al-Asad established for smooth governance in Syria as a "strong state" was a political structure that I term as "two-tier power structure". The two-tier power structure is organised in a way to enable the "two powers", in the words of Maḥmūd Ṣādiq, to be exercised: "visible power" (*al-sulṭa al-ẓāhirīya*) and "hidden power" (*al-sulṭa al-khafīya*) (Ṣādiq 1993: 71–72).

"Visible power" is formal power to be exercised legally in Syria's political system. This "visible power" maintains the appearance that Syria is a law-governed state, with separation of powers, and with the machinery of state supervised by formal power apparatuses, including the People's Assembly, the Cabinet, and the President.

The People's Assembly as the legislature has 250 seats for assembly members, each with four-year terms, and who are elected under the large-constituency full multiple-entry system. Since the establishment of People's Assembly in 1971, the Ba'ath Party has occupied a majority of the seats, and the National Progressive Front, a political party alliance operating under the instruction of Ba'ath Party, has supported it as a coalition partner, together occupying more than two thirds of the seats. The remaining seats have been occupied by independents. Furthermore, almost all ministers in the cabinet have been the members of the Ba'ath Party; however, the cabinet has also had a certain number of independents and members of parties belonging to the National Progressive Front. The President as the head of state with a seven-year term is supposed to be first nominated as the candidate for the Presidency at the People's Assembly based on a proposal made by the Syrian Regional Command of the Ba'ath Party and then confirmed by a national referendum (Article 84 of Constitution of 1973). The office of President that Hafez al-Asad assumed was authorised under the Constitution of 1973 to exercise influence over all three pillars of the government, including legislative power when the People's Assembly is out of session, appointing and dismissing ministers including the prime minister, appointing and dismissing judges, and concurrently serving as the supreme military commander.

Although "nominal" power apparatuses are legally responsible for the preparation and implementation of policies as is the case with the legislature and executive of other countries, it was certainly not "nominal" power apparatuses that took decisions on crucial matters in the government and the state in Syria.

Meanwhile, "hidden power" is the informal power and the "sole and true power", which "quietly penetrates into every corner of all social and, political situations behind the back of public lives and public activities" (Ṣādiq 1993: 72). This power was exercised by "real" power apparatuses such as the *Mukhābarāt*, the military, and the Ba'ath Party.

Mukhābarāt is a general term for intelligence agencies, security agencies, and armed security forces involved in the monitoring and suppression of both internal and external governmental opponents. With Syria's *Mukhābarāt* holding 65,000 of full-time officers, and several hundred thousand part-timers, occasional collaborators, and informers, about 1 out of every 300 people in Syria—its total population as of 2011 was about 20 million—would be full-time officials of the *Mukhābarāt* (Perthes 1995: 193). This organisation consisted of many agencies, including Military Intelligence, General Intelligence, Air Force Intelligence, Political Security, the National Security Bureau, and the Republican Guard. While variously overseen by the military, the Interior Ministry, the Ba'ath Party, and other organisations and not institutionally connected with each other, these agencies operated by ensuring a certain order that serves the goals of safeguarding the government as well as the provision of favours to its supporters. President Hafez al-Asad existed as the keystone of this order and senior members of *Mukhābarāt* are tied to him based on not only kinship and fellowship but also on trust and, further, the mixed consciousness of awe and fear of the President.

It should be noted that the power of the President was enhanced by the *Mukhābarāt*, with its monitoring of society as well as mutual monitoring so that no agency or senior official would be a threat to the regime. Such a system for preventing the emergence of a faction in the regime capable of single-handedly posing a threat to the President was often sarcastically referred to as "the School of al-Asad" (*madrasa al-asad*) in Syria (*al-Wasaṭ* 1999: 10).

The military was actually the only political entity in modern Syrian history capable of overthrowing the government. After the establishment of Hafez al-Asad administration, the military was "personalised" by the exclusion of potential political rivals against the regime and the concomitant promotion of loyal officers. Its manpower was estimated to be about 300,000 active soldiers (excluding about 100,000 militias) and about 350,000 reserve soldiers (Cordesman 2005; GFP 2009; IISS 2010).

The intervention in politics by the *Mukhābarāt* and the military was exceptionally authorised by the President under the state of emergency (for more details of laws and regulations related to the state of emergency in Syria, see Mumtāz 2006). However, the Ba'ath Party, which is different from *Mukhābarāt* and the military in that it is part of both the "nominal" power apparatus and the "real" power apparatus, was authorised to achieve its political purposes through extra-legal measures. For instance, Article 8 of Constitution of 1973 stipulated that "the Ba'ath Party is the party to lead the societies and the state". Individual members of the military and *Mukhābarāt* have therefore tried to justify their political interventions by becoming Ba'ath members (Aoyama 2001: 5–23).

In Syria, as a result of building such power architecture, the multiparty system, which included the Ba'ath Party and the satellite parties of the National Progressive Front, was a front that did not conceal the real power brokers operating behind the scenes. In circumstances where the old legal provisions allowed real opposition to register (e.g., Political Party Law), these were regarded as "unauthorised" bodies and had restrictions imposed on their activities. As such, the multiparty system re-generated under the Hafez al-Asad administration was not in any way a real "democracy".

This did not necessarily mean that relations between social cleavages and politics were disconnected. Social cleavages played two important roles in this "two-tier power structure". The first role is in giving a government based on authoritarianism a democratic and pluralistic appearance. For example, this was carried out in such a manner that the posts of Prime Minister, Foreign Minister, and Defence Minister were assigned to

Sunnis, the posts of the Interior Minister and the Information Minister assigned to Alawis, with Ismailis from Salamiyah and Christians also joining the Cabinet (Ṣādiq 1993: 97–98). Sometimes, such arrangements were criticised as "sectarian" (see Aoyama 2006: 169). At the same time, however, they brought recognition that comprehensive personnel distribution was carried out. Through this method then, the Hafez al-Asad administration tried to exhibit that it was "democratic" and "pluralistic" and that it had an existence beyond major social cleavages.

The second role was the regime's use of social cleavages based on social classes to build social base of support. For example, the Hafez al-Asad administration forged strong alliances with big landowners and merchants (old bourgeoisie) in Damascus, the traditional governing classes that had been alienated politically and economically after the "Ba'ath Revolution". He cooperated with the old bourgeoisie when implementing his programme of cautious economic "*infitāḥ*" ("open door" in English) which widened the gap between Damascus and other cities (regions), among which are Aleppo, Homs, and Hama. Such a measure to overcome social cleavages and classes with those based on regions decreased the power of the traditional governing classes, those whose power stemmed from the more or less equal status of their outlying region. The Hafez al-Asad administration thereby split the traditional governing classes into a pro-government group and an anti-government group (see Fig. 4.5). This allowed the government to use the pro-government group to act as a

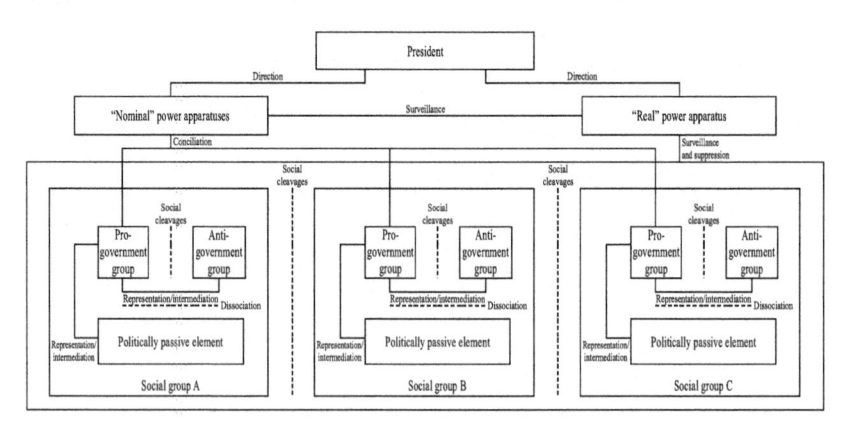

Fig. 4.5 Use/manipulation of social cleavages under the "two-tier power structure". Source: Author's analysis

conduit for the anti-government group. In doing so, the government mitigated the building up of resentment on the part of either group: the pro-government group had their business interests looked after, and the anti-government group at least had a line of communication through which to make representations to the administration (Fig. 4.5).

Even after such attempts to expand and strengthen its power base, al-Asad's administration could not completely suppress dissent. This was also not irrelevant to social cleavages. For example, the main internal confrontation in Syria under the Hafez al-Asad administration was against the Syrian Muslim Brotherhood from the 1970s to the early 1980s. The "Declaration of the Islamic Revolution in Syria and Its Methods" and the "Charter of the Syrian Islamic Front" were announced in November 1980 and January 1981 respectively by the Syrian Islamic Front (formed in October 1980), an anti-government coalition organisation led by the Syrian Muslim Brotherhood. Initially, Islamic rhetoric was toned down slightly in the hope of wider appeal to the populace, but ultimately it simply became a vehicle for extremists led by the Fighting Vanguard who denounced Alawites and minorities. The Syrian Muslim Brotherhood also challenged the Ba'ath administration by billing themselves as the representative of farmers and labours and by advocating economic and political liberalisation (Aoyama 1994: 127–134; Lobmeyer 1991).

To sum, countries with authoritarian regimes (especially Eastern European countries where authoritarian regimes were established through the victories of communists over parliamentary democrats) tend to be considered to have lost the linkage between social cleavages and politics (Lawson et al. 1999; Kitschelt et al. 1999). In Syria, however, social cleavages had played a role in politics even under an authoritarian regime.

The Pitfall Surrounding Social Cleavages

The authoritarian regime based on a "two-tier power structure" in Syria, first established under the rule of Hafez al-Asad, was handed to his son Bashār al-Asad after the death of the former in 2000. Inspired by the "Arab Spring", protests erupted in Syria in March 2011 and the Bashar al-Asad administration cracked down demonstrations by mobilising its military and security forces. It also embarked upon a series of reforms known as the "Comprehensive Reform Program" (*barnāmaj al-iṣlāḥ al-shāmil*). This programme consisted of the following laws and regulations: a law for lifting the state of emergency (Law No. 161 of 2011; coming into force on 22 April 2011), a legislative decree on the abolition of the National Supreme Security Court (Legislative Decree No. 53 of 2011; coming into force on 22 April 2011), the Demonstration Law (Legislative Decree No. 54 of 2011; coming into force on 22 April 2011), a Political Party Law (Legislative Decree No. 100 of 2011; coming into force on 4 August 2011), the General Election Law (Legislative Decree No. 101 of 2011; coming into force on 4 August 2011), the Amended Local Administration Law (Legislative Decree No. 107 of 2011; coming into force on 23 August 2011), and the New Information Law (Legislative Decree No. 108 of 2011; coming into force on 28 August 2011). By implementing such "reforms from above", the Bashar al-Asad administration tried to compete with the opposition and beat it at its own game.

Furthermore, the Bashar al-Asad government also promulgated a new Constitution on 27 February 2012 in a referendum in which 89.4 per cent of votes were cast in favour of the new Constitution (Aoyama 2012: 91–92). Article 8 of the former Constitution that had stipulated that the Ba'ath Party was the leading party was amended in the new Constitution to the following:

> The political system of the state shall be based on the principle of political pluralism, and exercising power democratically through the ballot box… Licensed political parties and constituencies shall contribute to the national political life, and shall respect the principles of national sovereignty and democracy. (Constitution of the Syrian Arab Republic 2012)

In addition, Article 9 of the new Constitution made explicit mention of Syria's diversity as follows:

> As a national heritage that promotes national unity in the framework of territorial integrity of the Syrian Arab Republic, the Constitution shall guarantee the protection of cultural diversity of the Syrian society with all its components and the multiplicity of its tributaries. (Constitution of the Syrian Arab Republic 2012)

Still no one can speculate on the kind of political order that might emerge out of the conflict and whether it might necessarily bring stability to the country. Moreover, nobody can tell if political transformation through the peace process between the Syrian government and the opposition, referred to as "Geneva Process" which has been advanced by the initiative of the US and Russia under the auspices of UN will achieve its goal. The only thing which can be said at the moment is that due to the turmoil over the last six and a half years, Syria has faced a situation that may endanger its very survival as a state. For instance, changes in demographics, economy, and social relations due to physical destruction, an outflow of refugees, the rise of militant jihadist groups, the expansion of Kurdish control, and continued apparent interference by foreign countries all endangered Syrian sovereignty. These issues must have no small effect on the connection between social cleavages and politics, whether or not instability continues or order is restored. It is premature to make an assessment at this stage, but it is safe to assume that Syria faces a long and difficult road.

Looking back into the history of the relationship between social cleavages and politics in Syria, we are reminded that there is a well-known pitfall when considering the pros and cons of political change, that is, confusing political pluralism with social/cultural pluralism. Syria's social cleavages are based on factors that are characteristic to societies such as religion, sect, nationality, and ethnicity. When these are associated with politics, social/cultural pluralism is emphasised rather than political pluralism. The under-emphasis of political pluralism promotes the so-called religious/sectarian conflict, which inhibits national integration, and impairs national function.

In order to avoid this pitfall, post-independence Syria held out an ultra-nationalist ideology: Arab nationalism. However, the reality on the ground was not that cultural pluralism was overcome, but that it was simply excluded from national dialogue. In the 1960s under one-party rule authoritarianism, leaders of the Ba'ath Party excluded rivals as part of their ideological and political fights. As a result, many social groups were robbed of the opportunity to participate in politics. But one is reminded that the intermediation of the cultural identity in politics assumes pro- or anti-imperialist pungency by the degree of balance of forces with imperialism. So, as the world shifted towards the West and neoliberalism, it became self-evident that imperialist ideology will extend to Syria in forms of more acute sectarian politics. Sectarianism as such is an extension of imperialist hegemony.

It may be possible to evaluate the use/manipulation of social cleavages under the "two-tier power structure" established by the Hafez al-Asad administration to "remedy" the process of exclusion. Meanwhile, it can hardly be said that such use/manipulation of social cleavages surpasses the precedents set in Western Europe where social cleavages and politics have been related to each other under the party political system. It is also possible to state that such use/manipulation of social cleavages in Syria is essentially no more than one-party rule authoritarianism in the 1960s.

The issue to be solved in the Syrian conflict, whether related to armed struggles or political processes, is to seek a new connection between social cleavages and politics while avoiding national disintegration, overconcentration of power, and exclusion. The Syrian government's urgent task is to overcome the difficult challenge, which is securing an integrative political participation by all Syrians.

Bibliography

Aoyama, H. (1994). The Propaganda of the Syrian Muslim Brotherhood: In the Anti-Regime Movement from 1976 to 1982. *AJAMES, 9*, 117–141, (in Japanese).

Aoyama, H. (1995). The Political Ideas and Policies of the Syrian Muslim Brotherhood in the Late 1940s and the Early 1950s: The Political Path of "the Islamic Socialism". *The Developing Economies, 36*(11), 47–68, (in Japanese).

Aoyama, H. (2001). *History Does Not Repeat Itself (Or Does It?!): The Political Changes in Syria after Ḥāfiẓ al-Asad's Death* (M.E.S. Series No. 50). Chiba: Institute of Developing Economies, JETRO.

Aoyama, H. (2006). Syria: Kurdish Nationalists' Challenge Against Authoritarianism. In Y. Hazama (Ed.), *Cleavage Structures and Political Systems in West and Central Asia* (pp. 159–209). Chiba: Institute of Developing Economies, JETRO, (in Japanese).

Aoyama, H. (2012). *Syria in Turmoil*. Tokyo: Iwanami Shoten, (in Japanese).

Aoyama, H., & Suechika, K. (2009). *The Political Structure in Syria and Lebanon*. Tokyo: Iwanami Shoten, (in Japanese).

Barakat, H. (1993). *The Arab World: Society, Culture, and State*. Berkeley: University of California Press.

Be'eri, E. (1970). *Army Officers in Arab Politics and Society*. New York: Praeger.

Boustani, R., & Fargues, P. (Eds.). (1991). *The Atlas of the Arab World: Geopolitics and Society*. New York and Oxford. Fact on File.

Collelo, T. (Ed.). (1988). *Syria: A Country Study*. Area Handbook Series. Washington, DC: U.S. Government Printing Office.

Commins, D. (1996). *Historical Dictionary of Syria*. Arab Historical Dictionaries, No. 22. Lanham and London: Scarecrow Press.

Constitution of the Syrian Arab Republic. (2012). Retrieved from http://www.voltairenet.org/article173033.html

Cordesman, A. H. (with the assistance of K. Al-Rodhan). (2005). *The Middle East Military Balance: Definition, Regional Developments and Trends.* Working Draft. Revised March 23, Washington, DC: CSIS (Center for Strategic and International Studies). Retrieved from http://csis.org/files/media/csis/pubs/050323_memilbaldefine%5b1%5d.pdf

van Dam, N. (1979). *The Struggle for Power in Syria: Sectarianism, Regionalism and Tribalism in Politics, 1961–1980.* London: Croom Helm.

Deiter, N., Grotz, F., & Hartmann, C. (Eds.). (2001). *Elections in Asia and the Pacific: A Data Handbook* (Vol. 1). Oxford and News York: Oxford University Press.

Geddes, B. (2003). *Paradigms and Sand Castles: Theory Building and Research Design in Comparative Politics.* Ann Arbor: University of Michigan Press.

GFP (GlobalFirePower.com). (2009). *Syria Military Strength.* Last updated June 11. Retrieved from http://globalfirepower.com/country-military-strength-detail.asp?country_id=Syria

al-Ḥāfiẓ, Yāsīn. (1997). *Ḥawla Baʿḍ Qaḍāyā al-Thawra al-ʿArabīya: al-Aʿmāl al-Kāmila* (Vol. 1, 2nd ed.). Damascus: Dār al-Ḥaṣād.

Hazama, Y. (Ed.). (2006). *Cleavage Structures and Political Systems in West and Central Asia.* Chiba: Institute of Developing Economies, JETRO, (in Japanese).

Heydemann, S. (1999). *Authoritarianism in Syria: Institutions and Social Conflict 1946–1970.* Ithaca and London: Cornell University Press.

Hinnebusch, R. A. (2001). *Syria: Revolution from Above.* Routledge.

IISS (International Institute for Strategic Studies). (2010). *The Military Balance 2010.* London: IISS.

Institute of Developing Economies (Ed.). (1983). *The Political Structure in Contemporary Arab East.* Tokyo: Institute of Developing Economies, (in Japanese).

Khoury, P. S. (1987). *Syria and the French Mandate: The Politics of Arab Nationalism 1920–1945.* Princeton: Princeton University Press.

Kitschelt, H., et al. (1999). *Post-Communist Party System: Competition, Representation, and Inter-Party Cooperation.* Cambridge: Cambridge University Press.

Laitin, D. D. (1986). *Hegemony and Culture: Politics and Religious Change Among the Yoruba.* Chicago: University of Chicago Press.

Lawson, K., Römmele, A., & Karasimeonov, G. (Eds.). (1999). *Cleavages, Parties, and Voters: Studies from Bulgaria, the Czech Republic, Hungary, Poland, and Romania.* Westport: Praeger.

Lipset, S. M., & Rokkan, S. (Eds.). (1967). *Party Systems and Voter Alignments.* New York: Free Press.

Lobmeyer, H. G. (1991). Islamic Ideology and Secular Discourse: The Islamists of Syria. *Orient, 32*(3), 395–418.

McDowall, D. (2000). *A Modern History of the Kurds*. 2nd Rev. and Updated ed. London and New York: I.B. Tauris.

Middle East Watch. (1991). *Syria Unmasked: The Suppression of Human Rights by the Asad Regime*. New Haven and London: Yale University Press.

Mumtāz, al-Ḥasan. (2006, June 14). al-Taʻrīf bi-Ḥala al-Tawāri'. *Niqābat al-Muḥāmīn - FarʻDimashq*. Retrieved from http://damascusbar.org/AlMuntada/showpost.php?p=7307&postcount=1

Perthes, V. (1995). *The Political Economy of Syria Under Asad*. London: I.B. Tauris.

Ṣādiq, M. (1993). *Ḥiwār ḥalwa Sūrīya*. London: Dār ʻAkkār.

Seale, P. (1958). *The Struggle for Syria: A Study of a Post-War Arab Politics 1945–1958*. London: Oxford University Press.

Seale, P. (1988). *Asad of Syria: The Struggle for the Middle East*. London: I.B. Tauris.

Torrey, G. H. (1975). Aspects of the Political Elite in Syria. In G. Lenczowski (Ed.), *Political Elites in the Middle East* (pp. 151–161). Washington, DC: American Enterprise Institute.

al-Wasaṭ. (1999). Fī Ḥiwār Shāmil maʻa al-Ḥayāt, Bashshār al-Asad: Al-Tafāʻul bi-al-Salām lā Yaʻnī al-Harwala. *395*(August), 10–17.

PART II

Macroeconomy and Society

CHAPTER 5

Macroeconomic Framework in Pre-conflict Syria

Linda Matar

Introduction

This chapter analyses Syria's macroeconomic framework in the ten years that preceded the Syrian uprising (2000–2010). I examine the functionalities of various policy tools and show how each alone, and all of them in synergy, contributed to resource misallocation. As a consequence, the capitalist class has gained enormously, while the majority of Syrians have seen their life conditions eroded.[1]

Furthermore, I argue that although the Syrian government during that period acknowledged that there were serious social problems that it needs to address, it could not escape the Western hegemonic neoliberal agenda that advises developing countries to endorse the mainstream economic conventions. This is not to say that Syria's ruling elites capitulated to undue pressure to accept the neoliberal medicine. They were keen to join the international financial order. Linking up to the international financial circuits ensures the growth of their nationally produced wealth in dollar-denominated terms (Kadri 2012). After 2005, they kicked off wide-ranging market-led economic reforms that enabled them to pursue this

---

L. Matar (✉)
National University of Singapore, Singapore, Singapore
e-mail: linda@nus.edu.sg

and other class-biased economic initiatives. When the Syrian authorities reformed their technical policy instruments, they prioritised growth, macroeconomic stabilisation and trade and capital account liberalisation, at the expense of equity, social development and income distribution. More specifically, the interworking of fiscal, monetary and balance of payment tools distributed the economy's wealth to a small segment of the country's population. The proof for the futility of the austerity package is ex-post facto evident in the destruction wrought upon Syria. On a relative scale, the prolonged Syrian crisis has proven much more severe than the "shock therapy" in the post-Soviet republics (Kadri 2016: 149).

When Syrians revolted in 2011, they struggled to reclaim part of the national income that was ripped off due to the repressive resource allocation mechanism. However, due to the over-determination of the crisis by external forces, it was not long before they realised that they had crossed a point of no return. A review of the macroeconomic performance prior to the conflict is useful because it reveals that macroeconomic strategies were misguided. Yet, current policies during critical times of conflict and those proposed for post-conflict Syria still embrace the mainstream orthodoxy (Hemesh 2015: 12). It may be important to note that the putting forward of progressive economic strategies may undercut the grounds upon which warlordism has recently emerged, because it disincentives the growth of the war economy.

The first section succinctly looks at the macroeconomy during 2000–2010. Each macro policy instrument and its respective reform is then analysed separately in the following sections. In much of my analysis, I employ macro data from official and secondary sources to construct quantitative measures and analyse social and economic trends. Since these instruments do not operate in isolation from one another, the final section will synthesise the effects of their interlocking relationships on the distribution mechanism.

A Snapshot of Syria's Macroeconomy During 2000–2010

In pursuing its 2000–2010 economic reforms, Syria much like other developing countries embraced mainstream economic strategies, generally in line with the agenda of the international financial institutions (IFIs) such as the IMF and the World Bank. By 2010, the private sector constituted almost 66 per cent of GDP (Seifan 2013: 110). However, that was not then the official narrative. In 2005, the Syrian government recognised the "social market economy" paradigm[2] as its new model for economic development. As such, it aimed at combining market mechanisms with social objectives (Hemesh 2015). Additionally, the *Tenth Five-Year Plan* (2006–2010) (10th FYP) alleged that the combination of economic development and social development was one of its basic principles (State Planning Commission 2007: Chap. 1). However, the government deployed "social market economy" cant to cement market liberalisation. It increased the scope by which market mechanisms were allowed to determine the allocation of resources, undermining the pro-equity growth model. The 10th FYP, one of the main remnants of Syria's centrally planned economic dirigisme, was socialist in principle, but capitalist in practice, since its programme adhered to the conventional wisdom.

In 2010, the government pointed out in its evaluation report of the 10th FYP that plan's main achievement was to foster a structural transformation of the economy from a state-led to a market-led "to a point of no return".[3] This transformation enabled Syria to integrate with the global economy (Hemesh 2015: 2). From a developmental point of view, the 10th FYP led to the abyss.

GDP and GDP per capita grew at 5 per cent and 2 per cent, respectively, in the period between 2000 and 2007. However, these rates were far less than what was achieved in the 1960s and 1970s (World Bank WDI 2016). The literature on Arab development reveals that the golden age of development in Syria as well as other Arab countries was in the 1960s and early 1970s (Kadri 2016). The Syrian government relied on semi-centralised economic planning. Through centralised bureaucracy and Soviet-style five-year plans, the government decided on resource allocation and distribution (Matar 2016). It endorsed a progressive tax system and imposed high tariff rates that ranged between 50 and 200 per cent, guiding resources within the economy (Seifan 2013: 98). The government also absorbed additional workers in the public sector, achieving social efficiency. Because of the lingering effect of the employment policy during the socialist period, 28 per cent of the labour force was employed in the public sector prior to the conflict (Seifan 2013: 100). In the words of Kadri (2016: 140): "This epoch constituted the heyday of security and post-independence achievements".

Until 2007, agriculture was the economy's backbone and contributed 20 to 25 per cent of GDP during the 1990s and early 2000s (Central Bureau of Statistics, various issues). As a minor oil-producing country,

Syria also relied on oil rents whose average share of GDP stood at 22.6 per cent during the 2000 period (World Bank WDI 2016). Oil production, however, witnessed a downward trend following the slow depletion of Syria's oil reserves during the 2000s. Overreliance on oil rents and failure to develop the productive sectors kept the economic foundation weak and susceptible to external disturbances. Rent-based economic growth did not generate productive employment or wage increases (Matar 2016).

Macroeconomic reforms shrank the middle class, the government's traditional social base of support, and widened the income gap between rich and poor. The government reduced its education and health spending and lifted the social safety nets that initially prevented individuals from falling into poverty. Very few had the privilege to enjoy wealth, education and health. The majority struggled to make a decent living on daily basis. Independent researchers estimated that the unemployment rate ranged between 15 and 20 per cent in 2010 (Seifan 2013: 127). In 2007, the poverty rate was 33.5 per cent. And in rural areas, it reached 62 per cent (UNDP 2010; Hemesh 2015: 9). The total number of people who were under the upper poverty line (90 Syrian pounds per individual per day) was more than six million in 2007 (UNDP 2010).

In the following sections, I expose the workings of fiscal, monetary and trade policies, demonstrating the influence of the structural adjustment programme on Syria's macroeconomic reforms between 2005 and 2010.

Fiscal Policy

By definition, fiscal policy refers to government spending, taxing and borrowing policies that are usually conducted by the Ministry of Finance or other specialist agencies to achieve certain macroeconomic goals. Expansionary fiscal policy features increase government spending and/or decrease tax rates. It aims to grow the economy, while contractionary policy is the opposite—lower government spending and/or higher tax rates. It is aimed at slowing economic growth (Fine and Dimakou 2016).

Although there is no conclusive evidence of an existing stable trade-off between inflation and growth, mainstream economists frequently support fiscal contraction as a means to stabilise prices in order to avoid price increases that allegedly can dampen growth. These economists argue that the size of public investment should be reduced to a minimum because it allegedly will crowd out private investment that is needed to lead the growth process, which it does more efficiently than the public sector.

As per the mainstream purported sequence of events, the orthodoxy favours low corporate taxation, limited government intervention and less government spending, a bundle of policies whose benefits allegedly trickle down to the majority of the people (Fine and Dimakou 2016). Nevertheless, experience shows that Arab economies underwent a de-development trajectory. After they adopted mainstream economic strategies around the late 1980s, their societies did not witness welfare gains (Kadri 2016: Chap. 1).

The alternative pro-poor economic approach subordinates deficit reduction to achieving growth induced by increased public investment. It argues that moderate levels of inflation and fiscal deficit are acceptable as long as the economy is operating below full capacity (not fully utilising resources). This approach recognises the powerful role that fiscal policy can play in enhancing the economy's productive resources by targeting and focusing resources on priority sectors (Roy and Weeks 2003). From a radical policy perspective, the government identifies the sectors essential to productive, employment-generating and sustained growth and prioritises them in terms of financial incentives, thereby facilitating the expansion of their capacity and output. According to MacEwan (2003: 13), "In shaping an alternative economic development strategy, a government does not simply want more investment; it wants more investment of a certain kind. *This requires that incentives be focused*".

In Syria, the government relied on contractionary fiscal policy in the mid-2000s to achieve "fiscal consolidation". According to the IMF's 2009 Article IV Consultation Report, "the authorities' medium-term fiscal strategy aims to contain the overall deficit below 5 per cent of GDP. The key pillars of this strategy are the introduction of a VAT in 2011, a further deepening of subsidies reform, and expenditure restraint" (IMF 2009: 7). As a result, total government expenditure, both current and development, as a percentage of GDP fell from 33 per cent in 2003 to 22 per cent in 2008 (Central Bank 2011). The government also streamlined its spending on social services as it intensified the market-friendly reforms. Public expenditure on health as a percentage of GDP fell from 7 per cent in 2005 to 5 per cent in 2010 (World Bank WDI 2016).

The government allowed the private sector to lead the growth process and liberalised investment laws to foster private investment and promote public-private partnerships. Data on private and public investment shows that public investment in the early 2000s superseded private investment. The average share of public investment out of total gross fixed capital formation (GFCF) during 2000–2005 stood at 58 per cent, while that of private investment was 42 per cent (Central Bureau of Statistics 2011). Following the government's acceleration of laissez faire reforms in the mid-2000s, public investment share shrank to 46 per cent, while the share of private investment rose to 54 per cent during 2006–2010 (Central Bureau of Statistics 2011).

The mandate of the structural adjustment programme was at odds with the socioeconomic realities of Syria. As a developing economy, Syria needed to promote its weak productive resources and ensure job creation for its youth. With a contractionary fiscal policy, the promotion of productive and employment-intensive economic growth was unattainable. The overall fiscal balance was not excessive in early 2000s as the fiscal deficit as a percentage of GDP did not exceed negative 5 per cent (State Planning Commission 2007: 74). As the IMF pointed out, "In recent years, the fiscal deficit has been smaller than what was envisaged in the original state budget" (IMF 2009: 7). Additionally debt service did not shackle state finances nor impose a burden on the balance of payment. The economy operated below full capacity, and its balance of payment was not binding, so the government could have opted to expand its expenditure and prioritise its incentives in order to promote productive types of investment, but instead endorsed restrictive fiscal measures. There was a rift between what the government announced as its priorities in endorsing the "social market economy" model and the stated goals in its 10th FYP.

Syria did not build on its import-substitution industrialisation (ISI) experience of the 1960s and early 1970s, but prematurely embarked on market-driven reforms without protecting the local production. Instead of installing an interventionist and targeted industrial policy that would prioritise the productive sectors in terms of incentives—credit, tax holidays and special subsidies—the government liberalised investment and treated all economic sectors equally. This pushed investors to seek ventures in fast-earning types of projects in the tertiary sector (Matar 2016). As public investment receded after 2005, the nationwide investment rate followed suit. GFCF as a percentage of GDP dropped from 27 per cent in 2005 to 23 per cent in 2007 and down to 21 per cent in 2009 (Central Bureau of Statistics, various issues). Concurrently, agricultural investment as a percentage of GFCF dropped from 15 per cent in 2005 down to 9 per cent in 2009 (Central Bureau of Statistics, various issues). Investment in manufacturing also witnessed a systematic decline. The imports of dies and moulds as percentage of total imports witnessed a decreasing trend during

2000–2010. It peaked in 2003 and reached its lowest in 2007 (UN Comtrade). This implies that the tools needed for the production of the equipment and for the internalisation of industrial know-how (investment in science and technology) had deteriorated. Manufacturing production did not exceed 3 per cent of GDP during 2000s (State Planning Commission 2007: 21) and consisted mainly of food and beverage products and textiles (Marzouk 2013: 42). The transition to a market economy had also led to a productivity decrease. Output per worker witnessed an average annual growth rate of 1.4 per cent after 1990. Compare this to a rate of 3.7 per cent during the 1960s and early 1970s, when the government relied on state-interventionist and import-substituting measures.[4]

Pre-conflict Syria relied on oil revenues. The decline in oil reserves has in turn led to reduced oil production and revenues. Oil-related revenues out of total government revenues declined from 58 per cent in 2001 to 48 per cent in 2003, further down to 22 per cent in 2007 (Central Bank Quarterly Bulletin 2006 and 2008). Additionally, total tax revenues averaged 8.5 per cent of GDP between 2000 and 2005 (State Planning Commission 2007: 72), much lower than the share of some developing economies, which is up to 20 per cent. This is due to widespread tax evasion[5] and corporate tax reduction that followed market liberalisation with the aim of stimulating private sector activities. The tax on profits declined from 63 per cent in 2003 to 35 per cent in 2004 and descended further to what is considered to be among the lowest globally—15 to 27 per cent in 2005 (Seifan 2013: 109). As a result, low tax revenues and declining oil revenues constrained the budget, giving the government the excuse to "rationalise" its spending.

As mentioned earlier, the 10th FYP followed the economic orthodoxy, whose principal recommendations emphasised macroeconomic stabilisation, low taxation, streamline of budget expenditure, inflation targeting and rationalisation of subsidies. According to the Syria Report (2006): "The new nature of the plan is seen by many in Syria as an important step towards embodying market rules into the economy and doing away once and for all with statist and centrally planned structure of the past". All this worked hand in glove with the mandates of the IFIs. Instead of pushing for direct and progressive taxation, the plan recommended the introduction of indirect taxes (State Planning Commission 2007: 79 and 85). Indirect taxation only helped to consolidate income inequality that already widened in the years that preceded the uprising. In contrast, progressive taxation constitutes the core of pro-poor fiscal policy. It plays a crucial role in guiding resources within the economy by restraining luxury consumption—which has a high import content—and encouraging investment. It can also help to attain a more equitable redistribution of income. Adhering to conventional wisdom that lower taxation will presumably induce private sector activity, the Syrian authorities reduced taxes. In retrospect, the drop in corporate tax rates did not induce private investment, especially in manufacturing (Seifan 2013), marking the failure of the mainstream economic strategy in achieving pro-poor and employment-intensive growth prior to the conflict.

Additionally, the government accelerated the promulgation of socially deficient economic measures and phased out subsidies on essential commodities and on gas and fuel in 2007–2008. Although it promised to dispense cash handouts in lieu of subsidies, the citizenry remained sceptical that such financial compensations would be delivered. In May 2008, the price of one litre of diesel oil increased by 275 per cent from 7 to 25 Syrian pounds and the price of a litre of fuel rose from 20 to 40 Syrian pounds (Seifan 2013: 135). In the absence of institutional safeguards that can protect citizens against price increases, the lifting of subsidies had a detrimental impact on a working class suddenly exposed to price increases on a variety of products.

Income Disparity Between Wage Earners

Between 2000 and 2010, the labour force participation rate for people aged 15 years and above fell from 51 per cent to 43 per cent (ILOSTAT database n.d.). The drop indicates the failure of state policies to create jobs for the growing labour force. It also signifies the high despondency rate among the population, who due to their demoralisation became convinced that it was better to remain jobless or get involved in unregistered informal activities. Those who dropped out from the labour force were not accounted for when computing the unemployment rate, because they had surrendered to their despicable situations or joined the informal sector.[6] Indeed, employment in the informal sector amounted to 30.7 per cent of total non-agricultural employment between 2000 and 2007 (Jütting and de Laiglesia 2009).

The official monthly real wage in absolute value remained nearly steady during 2000–2010. Real wages' share in total GDP, however, witnessed a decelerating trend. My computations show the share of total real wages in GDP fell by 7 per cent over 11 years, decreasing from 32 per cent in 2000 to 25 per cent in 2010 just prior to the uprising (ILOSTAT database n.d.). This signifies that neoliberal reforms decreased labour's share of total income, widening social polarisation. Additionally, because the official labour force participation rate declined and many more people joined the ranks of the informal sector where poverty-level employment prevailed, income inequality with the working class also increased. Simply, the government's labour policies had accentuated intra-working-class wage differences. According to ILO statistics, the wage bill for the total number of employed persons aged 15 years and above in the formal sector increased marginally between 2000 and 2010. This, however, was accompanied by a drop in the participation rate, signifying that workers in the formal sector were receiving higher wages at the expense of the mass of new poverty wage earners in the informal sector.

Monetary Policy

Monetary policy is the process by which the government regulates the money supply and the interest rate level through central bank operations, which involve open market operations—buying or selling government bonds—or the regulation of the financial sector. The mainstream economic approach advocates relatively high interest rates, to presumably raise domestic saving and attract foreign capital, which in turn can contribute to financing higher levels of investment (Sherman and Evans 1984). According to this orthodox perspective, high interest rates can avoid the balance of payment's slide into deficit and can control the rise in general prices. Nevertheless, evidence from some countries shows that high interest rates over the long term have been associated with regressive outcomes, such as economic slowdown, bubbles in the financial sector and balance of payment crisis (Chang and Grabel 2004). The pro-poor economic approach, however, recognises the key role that monetary policy can play in supporting the resource allocation mechanism. In this regard, monetary policy should be geared to accommodate fiscal policy (Fine and Dimakou 2016).

In Syria, monetary policy was a sovereign policy for more than 30 years. Around the mid-2000s, the government embraced the conventional doctrine when it reformed its monetary policy in order to pursue complete market openness. The stated goals of the 10th FYP focused on reforming monetary policy through undermining state control of monetary instruments and through promoting increased *independence* of monetary policy from fiscal policy. Decisions on the expansion of money supply, credit allocation and growth in credit were moved from the purview of the state to the private sector. The government gradually replaced administrative tools for conducting monetary policy with market-based tools (State Planning Commission 2007: 92–94 and 97). Such reforms blindly followed the conservative viewpoint and fully hewed to IMF dictates. In its 2009 Consultation Report on Syria, the IMF repeated its refrain: "[IMF] directors considered that a gradual move toward greater flexibility over the medium-term as the monetary policy framework develops would further increase monetary policy independence and maintain external stability" (IMF 2009: 38). The 10th FYP's word-for-word repetition of the IFIs' economic strategies is evidence that Syria had parted completely with its autonomous path. As such, the Syrian state had lost sovereignty over its macroeconomic strategies. In the words of Kadri (Kadri 2016: 100): "… under Arab socialism the economic policy was nationally controlled and served national social interests, as opposed to imperialistically controlled under neo-liberalism".

In this regard, there was no doubt that the interest rate policy after economic liberalisation would be directed towards easing the monetary stance. At that time, the claim was that high interest rates were impeding investment and that excess liquidity remained in the banking sector due to the high interest rate. Following IMF advice, the state lowered the interest rate for the first time in 2003, after holding it constant for 20 years. Interest rates on deposits and loans were reduced to stimulate investment. While the interest rates on deposits were reduced by 1 per cent, from 7–9 per cent to 6–8 per cent, those on loans were reduced by 1.5 per cent (Horani 2004: 5 and 6). Additionally, the authorities liberalised bank lending rates, allowing the private banks to set a margin of manoeuvre to lend at beneficial interest rates. The IMF commended these reforms because "It is important that interest rates are fully liberalised to allow for full transmission of policy signals" (IMF 2009: 12). However, reduction in interest rates did not transmit policy signals and stimulate investment, as avowed by the IMF. Instead, the private banks got involved in a *carry trade*-like strategy, whereby they borrowed money from the state at low real interest rates and invested in assets abroad with higher returns. There are no accurate figures as to how much money was transferred outside of the economy. One estimate of the capital leakage can be found in the data of the Bank for International Settlements, which reveals that net Syrian deposits in international banks averaged $24 billion in 2008 (BIS n.d., Table A6.1).

Up until 2003, credit issuance was under the authority of the state. In other words, the state rationed credit. No matter how low the real interest rate sunk, thereby improving borrowing terms for the private sector, the state still held back from issuing credit. This picture was to change later. The state relinquished its authority over credit and relegated this power to the private banking sector. Additionally, the private sector was allowed, through monetary policy reforms, to decide on money expansion and allocation. The private banks acted together and increased the supply of money to meet rising transaction demands. A cursory examination of the money supply reveals that the new monetary policy was class biased. In terms of broad money creation (M2), World Bank figures reveal that between 2000 and 2010, the Syrian government created the equivalent of $26.5 billion in additional money in national currency, which had a certain velocity—the number of times the money switches hand in the economy—and was exchangeable at a fixed dollar rate. Using ILO statistics, I estimated that the total amount of money needed to settle the wage bill for the period (2000–2010), as proxied by the sum of the first difference of the nominal wage bill, amounted to $4.9 billion. The remaining amount, $21.6 billion, was therefore made available to meet the business class' demand for money. One can discern the class nature of this policy in that only around a fifth of the additional money created went to the wage bill. The money created and destined for the capitalist class inflated their proportied assets, after which part of the additional wealth was exchanged to the dollar at a fixed rate. As such, the reformed monetary policy allowed for the creation of vast sums of money that was exchanged to the dollar at a fixed rate, strengthening the class divide in society.

Finally, although the 10th FYP stipulated that one of the aims of the monetary policy was to target inflation (State Planning Commission 2007: 98), it had a two-pronged policy. On the one hand, it shrunk the money supply destined to the working class. On the other, it expanded the money supply of the business class, inflating their assets. So the inflation of the goods that the poor consumed was somewhat restrained, whereas the inflated assets of the rich tripled in prices. This was evident in the real estate boom of the late 2000s, the fruit of speculative activities undertaken in the real estate market (Barout 2011).

Trade and Capital Account Policies

According to the mainstream economic approach advocates trade liberalisation allegedly promotes higher rates of output and increases efficiency and productivity, and free capital account attracts foreign inflows that in turn can finance current account deficit. Nevertheless, the alternative pro-poor economic approach argues that hasty trade liberalisation can have destabilising effects since the surge in imports harms the uncompetitive local industry (Chang and Grabel 2004). Furthermore, the opening up of the capital account fosters speculative capital inflows, impedes capital retention of national savings and facilitates capital flight and repatriation of profits (Palma 1998). This approach advises that vital industries be firmly protected before any trade openness is pursued. After all, the experience of the late industrialised economies shows that these economies managed to climb developmental ladder because their governments protected their manufacturing and agriculture industries (Chang 2003).

Syria hastily embarked on unbridled liberalisation of its trade and capital accounts. It opened up its markets to foreign competition without protecting and supporting its nascent industrial sectors. In relation to the support, the issue of targeted finance, R&D and access to technological know-how were all cited as sources of the collapse of many of the national firms. The government gradually reduced its monopoly on imports of a variety of products and authorised the private sector to import them instead (Matar 2016). It also substantially reduced customs on the blacklist of commodities that were vital to national production and security (Matar 2016: 115). Given the technological gap between foreign and Syrian products, it was quite ludicrous to even imagine that local industries would be able to cope with foreign competition. The dumping of Chinese imports created unfair competition that forced many local industrialists to close down their factories (Marzouk 2013). The closure of manufacturing firms led to the dislocation of economic resources from the manufacturing to the tertiary sector. As a result, imports surpassed exports in the last five years before the uprising. Exports increased by 34 per cent between 2005 and 2010, while imports increased by 62 per cent (Central Bureau of Statistics 2011).

In 2006, the government unified the multiple Syrian pound exchange rates against foreign currencies. By unifying the official budget exchange rate with the private sector exchange rate, the Central Bank placed all consumption items (necessity and luxury) under the same category.[7] Accordingly, exchange rate populism that offered immediate benefits to the poor through cheaper imports and lower inflation was abolished. Necessity goods, such as milk and sugar, were no longer exchanged at an overvalued rate against the dollar but placed in the same category as luxury items such as cars (Seifan 2013: 109).

To exacerbate the problems of the balance of payments arising from outright liberalisation, the government also lifted its control over the capital account, freeing capital movements in and out of the economy. This destabilised macroeconomic stability. On the one hand, the government facilitated resource drainage through capital flight. On the other, it also surrendered the regulation of its economy to the international market forces. With such openness, the government lost sovereignty over issuing credit substantiated by national means and relinquished its sovereignty to imperialism (Kadri 2016: 132).

A Synthesis of Macroeconomic Performance

I have so far examined each policy and its reforms separately. From a theoretical standpoint, these policies work together to either accelerate or retard the mode of development. Achieving egalitarian growth is dependent on the institutional framework of the society and the co-ordinated policies that accompany the process of growth (Rao 2002). In the Syrian case, it was obvious that both the institutional framework and the macroeconomic strategies were not conducive to promoting socially desirable goals. Pre-conflict Syria did not undergo the thorough institutional transformation needed to empower the incorporated institutions and the associated regulatory bodies, which in turn could have ensured the fulfilment of socially responsible outcomes and fundamental freedoms. Instead, the government set aside institutional transformation and pushed for an accelerated economic transition from state-led to market-led economic structure (Matar 2016: 100).

As has been seen in the implementation of similar neoliberal remedies elsewhere, a synthesis of the macroeconomic performance in Syria proves that the supposedly pristine theory of separate policy measures that allegedly can achieve economic efficiency generated anti-developmental outcomes when these policy instruments worked jointly together. The workings of the macroeconomic policies exhibited a class dimension. In retrospect, we can see that the government introduced a structural adjustment programme but failed to stimulate aggregate demand in the pro-poor vital sectors, causing a contraction in the real economy. As mentioned earlier, fiscal consolidation reduced the size of the public sector and cut down the public investment that could have generated new income-generating activities. The growth in the non-oil GDP declined by 3 per cent in 2009 as compared to 2005 (IMF 2009: 17), dragging with it economic and social dynamism. An inequitable tax system and an open capital account meant that the poor financed the process of growth through inflation and indirect taxation while the rich not only enjoyed luxury consumption but also invested their savings in higher-returning foreign assets.

In the absence of a national industrial plan, macroeconomic policies directed resources to non-productive sectors, which were insufficient to secure job creation and reduce poverty. Poorer productivity ensued, and a growing labour force found fewer jobs in an economy that needed high investment rates in order to escape the underdevelopment trap. This pushed workers to underemployment or to the less productive informal sector to make ends meet. Additionally, the phasing out of socialised health and education through the introduction of private-public partnerships led to a plunge in the quality of public health and education. The above points resulted in a shrinkage in the requisites of society and formed the objective conditions for the onset of the crisis (Matar 2016).

Through loose and market-based monetary policy instruments, the Central Bank created more cheap Syrian pounds to meet the demand of the private sector. The capitalist class, using the pegged exchange rate, converted their profits from Syrian pounds to the dollar and integrated part of its wealth into the global financial system through the open capital account. But the poor's wages were not inflation-indexed. They faced price inflation and contributed to capitalists' profits as they paid high prices for goods due to price increases (Kadri 2016: 138). The double impact of rising capital wealth and the decline in the share of real wages in national income reinforced social polarisation. This further suggests that macro policies were designed to favour capital and its holders.

To sum up, public policies in pre-conflict Syria influenced by the dictate of the neoliberal paradigm did not lift the economy out of its regressive state. They failed to create an enabling environment which could have generated employment, raised real income and enhanced human capabilities. The openness of the capital accounts facilitated capital flight and impeded the resource retention that is a crucial requisite for development. Additionally, the focus on growth and macroeconomic stabilisation meant that a broad spectrum of redistributive and welfare-enhancing measures, such as targeted credit to pro-poor sectors, subsidised health and education, vocational training, pensions and other entitlements, needed to be phased out. This resulted in a weaker redistribution of income and weaker human development. The government's decision to part with populism and move towards post-populism, by which the government abridged the social welfare provision, had sowed the "seeds of rebellion and of the protracted conflict" (Hinnebusch 2014).

Concluding Remarks: Syria in Conflict

This chapter demonstrated that pre-conflict macroeconomic strategies were anti-poor. A synergy between fiscal and monetary policies failed to materialise. Correspondingly, a synergy between the economic and the social dynamics did not take hold. Foremost, economic growth arose more on the basis of tertiary sectors than productive sectors. The same synergy also failed to enlarge economies of scale and productive capabilities that are key to sustained growth and rising incomes. Economic growth remained largely rent-based. It was unable to produce socially desired goals. Accordingly, this faulty economic path dependency added to the woes that deepened the crisis of capital accumulation.

Seven years have passed since the war in Syria has erupted. The economy has suffered from disintegration and the emergence of conflict economies and war trading. The severe destruction of public services, infrastructure, manufacturing firms and irrigation systems have hampered both industrial and agricultural production. The damaging of various water sources has also disrupted water supply to the densely populated cities of Damascus and Aleppo. Additionally, the seizing of oil wells by various Islamist armed groups has severely disrupted oil and gas production (IMF 2016). The government continues to deploy the same neoliberal approach that was endorsed during pre-conflict times. Instead of revising the ill-fated macroeconomic policy instruments that underpinned the social disaster, the government has relaxed state's control, weakening the state's grip over economy and society. Because of the Western-imposed economic sanctions, the government has introduced further liberalisation to facilitate various economic and investment activities to the private sector. However, market openness and the loosening of state control have increased capital flight and opened the space for war traders to control supply and distribution, increasing profit margins, pillage and market chaos (Hemesh 2015: 12). The state recently restored the Ministry of Supply and Internal Trade under a different name, which is a crucial step in times of conflict because it protects the basic consumption needs of the working strata. Although this is a positive step, it falls short of reversing the neoliberal strand that gripped the economic policies of the state (Hemesh 2015: 5).

The conflict has been internationalised and is not yet over. Naturally the solution to the conflict would involve an entente between the major international players. It is bewildering to think that the US wants to set up safety zones in order to pursue its narrow geostrategic interest, while the real safety zone should be for all Syrians all over Syria—free of foreign forces. Until we reach that point, emphasis should be placed on the state's economic resilience. I have argued elsewhere that the national struggle in Syria confronts not only the imperialist-sponsored Islamist reactionaries but also the hegemony of US empire. Consolidating the national front requires odd alliances and state-sponsored economic policies (Matar and Kadri 2015). Rebuilding economic strength begins with parting with the neoliberal doctrine that has weakened the national economy over the past two decades and fully submitted it to Western imperialism. Reconstruction policy for Syria must be guided first by an international commitment to end the financing of war. Although this is a tall order, the Syrian authorities can still, from an economic point of view, design a national economic plan that can set the process of accumulation on an autonomous path. The tenet of such a plan ought to be strengthening state sovereignty over Syria's territories.

There is no doubt that Syria faces financial hurdles in light of the acute fall in government revenues, Western-imposed sanctions and the draining of resources due to the war effort. Saving what remains of the state requires managing the allocation of resources in a productive and egalitarian manner. The strengthening of popular economic autonomy may gradually alleviate the power of the war bourgeoisie, which includes players from all sides of the conflict, who have wrung significant benefits from the continuation of the conflict.

Acknowledgements I am grateful to Umar Azmeh for his incisive comments on this chapter; all errors, however, are my own.

Notes

1. See, for instance, ACRPS (2013), Barout (2011), Haddad (2012), Hemesh (2015), Hinnebusch and Zintl (2015), Kadri (2012) and Matar (2016).
2. The "social market economy" paradigm advocates the engagement of both market forces and state intervention in the process of economic development. The private sector takes control of economic activities, and the state ensures that social and welfare benefits are delivered to the citizens. This new economic strategy is critically reviewed by Abboud (2015).

3. The evaluation report that assessed the performance of the *Tenth Five-Year Plan* (2006–2010) was prepared by the State Planning Commission, the Economic Technical Team and the Central Bureau of Statistics (Hemesh 2015). It was issued by the Economic Technical Team on 27 July 2010; however, it was not authorised to be fully published at that time (Hemesh 2015).
4. My computation based on data from World Bank WDI 2016 and Penn World Tables version 8.1 in Feenstra et al. (2015).
5. Samir Seifan estimated that tax evasion reached S£ 100 billion in 2009; see Seifan (2013: 109).
6. Job insecurity also pushed many to leave the country. Between 2005 and 2010, the total number of Syrians who immigrated is estimated to have reached to 10.2 per cent of total population (Marzouk 2013: 54).
7. Prior to the accelerated economic liberalisation, the government subsidised the import cost of the products that were not produced locally through a multiple exchange rate system. It treated public sector transactions (official budget exchange rate) separately from the private sector transactions (private sector exchange rate). The official budget exchange rate was overvalued. The usage of the overvalued exchange rate was undertaken for the purpose of subsidising the necessary consumption bundle of the working population. So in the case when foreign exchange rises, the overvalued official rate does not change, allowing the same amount of Syrian pounds to be exchanged for the foreign currency and, hence, buying the same amount for effectively fewer pounds (Kadri 2016: 141).

Bibliography

Abboud, S. (2015). Locating the "Social" in the Social Market Economy. In R. Hinnebusch & T. Zintl (Eds.), *Syria from Reform to Revolt: Volume 1: Political Economy and International Relations* (pp. 45–66). Syracuse, NY: Syracuse University Press.

Arab Center for Research and Policy Studies (ACRPS). (2013). *The Background of Revolution: Syrian Studies*. Doha: Arab Center for Research and Policy Studies.

Bank for International Settlement (BIS). (n.d.). *Locational Banking Statistics*. Retrieved from http://stats.bis.org/statx/toc/LBS.html

Barout, M. J. (2011). *The Last Decade in Syrian History*. Arab Centre for Research and Policy Studies. Doha: Arab Centre for Research and Policy Studies.

Central Bank, Monetary and Banking Statistics. (2011). Central Bank of Syria.

Central Bank of Syria. (2006 and 2008). *Quarterly Bulletin*. Damascus: Central Bank of Syria.

Central Bureau of Statistics. (2011). *Syrian Statistical Abstract*. Damascus: Central Bureau of Statistics.
Central Bureau of Statistics. (various issues). *Syrian Statistical Abstract*. Damascus: Central Bureau of Statistics.
Chang, H.-J. (2003). *Kicking Away the Ladder*. London: Anthem Press.
Chang, H.-J., & Grabel, I. (2004). *Reclaiming Development: An Alternative Economic Policy Manual*. London: Zed Books.
Feenstra, R. C., Inklaar, R., & Timmer, M. P. (2015). *The Next Generation of the Penn World Table*. Forthcoming in American Economic Review, Available for Download at www.ggdc.net/pwt
Fine and Dimakou. (2016). *Macroeconomics: A Critical Companion*. Chicago: University of Chicago Press Books.
Haddad, B. (2012). *Business Networks in Syria: The Political Economy of Authoritarian Resilience*. Stanford: Stanford University Press.
Hemesh, M. (2015). *Analytical Review of Macroeconomic Policies and Course Correction*. Economic Files. Damascus: Syrian Economic Society. Retrieved from http://www.mafhoum.com/syr/articles_15/2015-7.pdf
Hinnebusch, R. (2014, March 17). The Multiple Layers of the Syrian Crisis. *Political Insight*.
Hinnebusch, R., & Zintl, T. (Eds.). (2015). *Syria: From Reform to Revolt, Volume 1*. New York: Syracuse University Press.
Horani, A. (2004). *The Effects of Interest Rate Change in the Context of Economic Reforms*. Economic Files. Damascus: Syrian Economic Society. Retrieved from http://www.mafhoum.com/syr/articles_04/horani.htm
ILO, ILOSTAT database. (n.d.). Retrieved from http://www.ilo.org/ilostat
International Monetary Fund (IMF). (2009). *Syrian Arab Republic: 2008 Article IV Consultation*. IMF Country Report No.09/55, February 2009. Washington, DC: IMF.
International Monetary Fund (IMF). (2016). *Syria's Conflict Economy*. IMF Working Paper, WP/16/123.
Jütting, J., & de Laiglesia, J. (2009). *Is Informal Normal? Towards More and Better Jobs in Developing Countries*. Development Centre Studies, OECD (Organisation for Economic Co-operation and Development).
Kadri, A. (2012). *The Political Economy of the Syrian Crisis*. Working Papers in Technology Governance and Economic Dynamics (Number 46). The Other Canon Foundation, Norway.
Kadri, A. (2016). *The Unmaking of Arab Socialism*. London: Anthem Press.
MacEwan, A. (2003). Debt and Democracy: Can Heavily Indebted Countries Pursue Democratic Economic Programs? Paper presented at the symposium *Common Defense Against Neoliberalism*, Istanbul.
Marzouk, N. (2013). Lost Development in Syria. In Arab Center for Research and Policy Studies (ACRPS) (Ed.), *The Background of Revolution: Syrian Studies*. Doha: Arab Center for Research and Policy Studies.

Matar, L. (2016). *The Political Economy of Investment in Syria*. Basingstoke: Palgrave Macmillan.

Matar, L., & Kadri, A. (2015). Investment and Neoliberalism in Syria. In A. Kadri (Ed.), *Development Challenges and Solutions After the Arab Spring*. Basingstoke: Palgrave Macmillan.

Palma, G. (1998). Three and a Half Cycles of 'Mania, Panic and [Asymmetric] Crash': East Asia and Latin America Compared. *Cambridge Journal of Economics, 22*(6), 789–808.

Rao, J. M. (2002). *The Possibility of Pro-Poor Development: Distribution, Growth and Policy Interactions*. Unpublished manuscript.

Roy, R., & Weeks, J. (2003). *Thematic Summary Report: Fiscal Policy*. UNDP Asia-Pacific Regional Programme on the Macroeconomics of Poverty Reduction.

Seifan, S. (2013). Policies of Income Distribution and Its Role in Social Explosion. In Arab Center for Research and Policy Studies (ACRPS) (Ed.), *The Background of Revolution: Syrian Studies*. Doha: Arab Center for Research and Policy Studies.

Sherman, H., & Evans, G. (1984). *Macroeconomics: Keynesian, Monetarist, and Marxist Views*. New York: Harper & Row Publishers.

State Planning Commission. (2007). *The Tenth Five-Year Plan 2006–2010*. Damascus: Syria State Planning Commission.

The Syria Report. (2006, January 17). 5-Year Plan to Focus on Employment and Training. *The Syria Report*.

UNDP. (2010). *Third National MDGs Progress Report*. Damascus: State Planning Commission.

United Nations Comtrade Database. (n.d.). Retrieved from https://comtrade.un.org/

World Bank. (2016). *World Development Indicators*. Retrieved from http://databank.worldbank.org/data/reports.aspx?source=world-development-indicators

CHAPTER 6

The Syrian Conflict: Selective Socioeconomic Indicators

Nabil Marzouk

INTRODUCTION

This chapter provides an empirical snapshot of recent Syrian economic and social trends. The data presented herein draws on measurement projects that I have undertaken in an official capacity while working for the Syrian Planning Commission and, more recently, with the Syrian Center for Policy Research (SCPR). Since the 1980s, shifts in state policy have debilitated development. The gradual introduction of laissez-faire economic policies weakened the social contract and exacerbated socioeconomic unease. Still, the Syrian people were aware that violent confrontation would bring with it heavy costs. Just after the peaceful demonstrations began, external forces intervened to turn a peaceful protest into a militarised conflict.

The Syrian government in the decade prior to the 2011 uprising invested in anti-developmental projects instead of enhancing "state capacity," thereby seeding the objective conditions for the crisis. This was manifest in poor levels of intermediation of economic private gains with broader well-being of the working class, weak efficiency of institutions, and the low contribution of tax revenues to the budget. The neoliberal economic

N. Marzouk (✉)
Syrian Center for Policy Research, Damascus, Syria

reforms in the 2000s concurrently undermined the safety net of many, especially rural inhabitants.

More than six years of escalating conflict has had a catastrophic impact on people's lives, with hundreds of thousands of deaths, 6.36 million Syrians displaced internally, and more than 4 million external refugees. The Human Development Index (HDI) in 2015 had shrunk by 3.6 per cent from its level in 1990, placing Syria at the 149th place (out of 188 countries) in HDI ranking (UNDP 2016). Poverty has also risen to reach 85.2 per cent of the population, in addition to widespread multidimensional poverty (SCPR 2016a). During the conflict, the state has become weaker. Its sovereignty has shrunk with the expansion of regions dominated by armed groups, and it has been incapable of enforcing law or of generating revenues.

There has been massive destruction of productive sectors: infrastructure, roads, transport, houses, heritage, and natural resources. By the end of 2015, the total economic loss was estimated to have reached $254.7 billion (SCPR 2016a). The government's response to the crisis has been a further extension of neoliberal policies—although some key socialist policies have also been reinstated. This, in addition to the sanctions, has led to a worsening of national production and output, deepening recession, and a rise in the cost of living for most Syrians.

The first part of this chapter highlights some key features of the socioeconomic development of modern Syria. It is largely based on official data from the Central Bureau of Statistics, unless otherwise mentioned. The second part focuses on the impact of the crisis and uses data from *Confronting Fragmentation*, which SCPR published in 2016. I was involved in drafting the latter report, which focuses on the conflict's impact in the 2011–2015 period. The SCPR used a counterfactual methodology to estimate the economic losses which theretofore had occurred during the crisis. It compared the "crisis scenario," or the actual quantitative indicators that emerged because of the crisis, with a "continuing scenario" that presents figures based on projections of the past data, revealing what would have *likely* ensued had the crisis not taken place.

Socioeconomic Development in Modern Syria

Political instability has characterised the modern history of Syria since its 1946 independence. Factors which led to this instability include the foundation of Israel in 1948 and its later occupation of Syrian and Arab territories, the first military coup in 1949, and the later coups that followed until 1963. The Ba'ath government imposed a "state of emergency" and employed loyalists in key state functions regardless of their skills. Political instability has thus hindered development, since strengthening security had always been an absolute priority for the government, prevailing over and above the imperative to invest in "state capacity."

Until the late 1980s, the Ba'ath government maintained a populist discourse for the benefit of workers, peasants, and disadvantaged social groups. It emphasised providing free education and health services, subsidies to energy and basic food, inexpensive public services, and large public-sector employment.

During the 1970s, aid from Arab rich countries had ensured a good level of economic growth, a low unemployment rate, relative domestic price stability, and low public debt. With the economic crises in the mid-1980s and the confrontation with the Muslim Brotherhood, the government reinforced its grip on society by giving a larger role to the security forces. Since the late 1980s, the government began to shift to neoliberal policies, which it applied gradually and thereby widened the income gap between the rich and the poor.

During 2001–2010, the Syrian economy witnessed a relatively robust economic growth rate, mainly because of the production and export of oil. This growth failed to "trickle down" to the society. Under the guidance and advice of the International Financial Institutions, the government liberalised prices, reduced public investment, and lifted subsidies of all kinds, setting the economy on a path of de-development (SCPR 2013).

The 2001–2010 period witnessed a widespread loss of hope in the economic recovery that government had promised since the mid-1980s. In the new millennium, Syrians renewed their expectations to break through the developmental impasse, amidst the arrival of a young president promising reform, economic openness, and public freedom. Such discourse enhanced the aspirations of a wide variety of social sectors to move past the economic crisis, to rebuild weakened economic and social structures, and to create and widen opportunities for the younger generation to attain a dignified and productive life.

The instability in the region, caused by the US invasion of Iraq in 2003, had, however, been a real threat to Syria, one which reoriented government priorities. The government strengthened its security stance and its repressive orientation to social demands and obstructed political movements such as the "Damascus Spring." Moreover, the government overlooked or sidestepped long-promised human-centred reforms and instead accelerated neoliberal reforms that advocated macroeconomic stabilisation at the expense of social considerations.

Sectoral Development

Although the 2001–2010 period saw relatively robust economic growth rates, it also was marked by modest development. The average annual growth rate of real GDP at constant prices of 2000 was 4.5 per cent (SCPR 2016a: 19).[1] But the volatility of the growth rate was high, ranging between 0.4 per cent and 8 per cent, reflecting the impact of climate change and fluctuations in international oil prices. Moreover, Syria had a high population growth rate—about 3 per cent annually—putting its per capita GDP growth at around 1.5 per cent. The stagnation in per capita income widened the welfare gap between Syria and its neighbours. Amidst such stagnation, we can see that the socioeconomic trend during this period was one which failed to create the appropriate conditions for sustainable development.

The economy became more dependent on the rentier sector. The share of the primary sector—agriculture and mining—increased to more than 50 per cent of GDP in 2001 (Central Bureau of Statistics n.d., various years), while the share of the manufacturing sector was then merely 3.3 per cent. However, reductions in oil production accompanied several years of drought to reduce the GDP share of the agriculture and mining sectors to 36.7 per cent in 2010. The manufacturing sector's share remained 3.2 per cent in that year. The share of the service sector out of total GDP reached about 59.6 per cent in 2010, growing from 41.9 per cent in 2001 (Central Bureau of Statistics n.d., various years). These sectors contributed 84.4 per cent of economic growth during 2001–2010, while the contributions of the productive sectors reached 15.6 per cent in the same period (SCPR 2013: 19). Manifestly, GDP has witnessed structural changes over that period, as the services sectors increased markedly at the productive sectors' expense.

The Syrian economy depended on raw materials. Before the crisis, it had failed to achieve structural changes by shifting to an industrial economy—despite 50 years of planning for this change. The agricultural sector accounted for 25.6 per cent of GDP in 2001, but declined to 17.4 per cent in 2010 (Central Bureau of Statistics n.d., various years). Since the 1980s, the government has not established any large agricultural or irrigation projects. Its plan to shift to a modern irrigation system has been ineffective. The government's 2008 neoliberal policies liberalised the prices of oil derivatives and chemical fertilisers and reduced subsidies. Agriculture production costs increased, and some marginal producers became unwilling or incapable of sustaining production. The climate conditions and, to a greater extent, the government's policies severely damaged the agricultural sector during that decade, negatively affecting food sovereignty.

The mining sector witnessed a substantial decline in the production of oil—the main source of government revenues during the 1980s and 1990s and one which injected hard currency into the national economy. The sector's contribution to GDP decreased notably, and after 2006 Syria became a net importer of fuel, depriving Syria of a substantial source of foreign currency.

The development of the manufacturing sector was one of the goals which justified the adoption of market-friendly economic policies, starting in 1991. The aim was to encourage private investment in the manufacturing sector. The results, however, were modest, as the sector's contribution to GDP was only 3.3 per cent in 2001 and 3.2 per cent in 2010 (Central Bureau of Statistics n.d., various years). Minor progress had been made on infrastructural improvements and building industrial cities. The sector's growth scarcely reached 4 per cent on average during that decade (SCPR 2016a). Such statistics reflect the "reform illusion" that the government had advocated before the crisis.

The construction sector had witnessed ongoing poor performance. Many regulations and initiatives were issued to support private sector involvement in this sector. The introduction of neoliberal policies had facilitated the entry of some companies, particularly from the Gulf countries, to initiate tourism and real estate projects. This pattern of investment led to increased land speculation and rising prices, thereby preventing most people from owning their own homes. The share of the sector out of total GDP was 1.9 per cent in 2001 and increased to 3.8 per cent in 2010 (SCPR 2016a: 24).

The service sector witnessed rapid expansion during that decade. This growth was a result of the government imposing constraints on productive sectors, its introduction of communication services, the fast-growing cell phone markets, and establishing private banks and financial services. The increase in government services due to the shift of government activities from production to services led to an increase in public social services. In 2010, the service sectors became the economy's largest, with 59.6 per cent of total GDP (SCPR 2016a: 24).

That decade's economic performance revealed that Syrian economic policies had been unsuccessful. Growth was biased towards services, which thus deeply changed the national economy's structure. Manufacturing growth rate was 4 per cent during that decade, and agriculture experienced a severe crisis due to drought and mismanagement of water resources. The government decreased investment in the productive sectors, neglected agriculture, and abandoned state-owned enterprises. These policies were exacerbated following the opening to regional and international markets, price liberalisation, and decreasing subsidies for energy, seeds, and fertilisers. Facing high production costs, some producers stopped producing and moved to the informal sector, including especially the service sector. The primary consequence of these shifts in the productive sectors was an overall shift in the main sectors that contributed to GDP growth during 2001–2010, to wholesale and retail trade, and governmental services.

Syria's Labour Market

The Syrian population was estimated at 21.8 million in 2010. The population had grown between 2004 and 2010 at an average annual rate of 2.9 per cent.[2] Demographic changes accompanied the population increase, as people aged between 15 and 64 years—working-age people—increased from 50 per cent of the total population in 1994 to 54.4 per cent in 2004.[3]

The total number of labourers employed in 2001 tallied 5.1 million workers (Central Bureau of Statistics n.d., various years). In 2010, the total number of employed people had reached only 5.5 million. Labour force participation rate for people aged 15 years and above declined from 52.3 per cent in 2001 to 42.7 per cent in 2010,[4] reflecting chronic deficiencies in the national economy and its weak capacity to create job opportunities.

The unemployment rate was 10.3 per cent in 2001 and decreased to 8.6 per cent in 2010. The unemployment rate was higher among women (22 per cent) than for men (6.2 per cent) in 2010 (SCPR 2013). Nominal wages increased during the 2001–2010 period. However, real wages increased only from 2001 to 2006, after which they declined until 2010 (SCPR 2013).

Syria's Human Development Index

The Human Development Index (HDI), through its three components—income, education, and health—is in fact an indicator of the economic achievements and effectiveness and sustainability of the development process. Before the crisis, Syria saw a relative improvement in the value of its

HDI. Still, compared to other countries in the region such as Turkey and Jordan, HDI in Syria had increased very slowly. In fact, we suggest that the relative improvement in the value of HDI had been lower than what the Syrian people had expected. This raises questions about the nature and effectiveness of the development process during 2001–2010.

Syria had witnessed a notable drop in illiteracy rates among the portion of the population above 15 years of age. The illiteracy rate was 15.6 per cent in 2010. However the rate of illiteracy for women was 2.4 times that of men (SCPR 2013: 27). Some improvement occurred in indicators linked to basic education outcomes, but dropout rates increased in secondary and tertiary education, which had a negative impact on human capital.

Before the crisis, education in Syria faced several challenges. They included the poor quality of the educational system, weak financial resources—estimated expenditure on education for that decade averaged 4 per cent of GDP annually—imbalances in access to education between regions, and the large entry of the private sector into the educational system, which increased the cost of education without improving its efficiency.

The health system in Syria was based on free public services, and the government-linked institutions were that system's main components. In 2010, the public health sector included about 122 hospitals, with 71.8 per cent of hospital beds (Central Bureau of Statistics 2011), in addition to 1506 health centres, which provided free or semi-free services to all citizens. The quality of health services and health indicators deteriorated during 2001–2010, worsening most of all in rural areas. In 2010, the government reduced its health expenditure to less than 2 per cent of the budget, or about 0.33 per cent of GDP (Central Bureau of Statistics 2011).[5] Moreover, neoliberal policies transformed public hospitals into independent economic units, which were required to cover their costs. This deprived a large segment of society from health services, since they did not have the financial capability to pay for the treatment.

Enlarged Poverty

Income was the weakest component of Syria's Human Development Index. Many factors have led to poor incomes amongst Syrians, among which have been weak institutions, rising inequality, the rent-based structure of the economy, and the introduction of neoliberal economic policies (El-Laithy and Abu-Ismail 2010). It is worth noting that wages' share of net domestic product—in current prices—declined from 40.5 per cent in 2004 to about 33 per cent in 2010, at production factor cost.[6] If we compare the results of the household expenditure survey in 2009 with that of the labour survey in 2009, we see immediately that the average wage covered only 32 per cent of necessary family expenditures.

Greater Regional Disparities

Despite the overall secular improvement in Syria in terms of public utility provision, rural areas, especially the Northeast region, faced serious challenges. Data on illiteracy rates in 2009 shows marked differences between governorates. In Aleppo, the rate was 20.4 per cent, 15.4 per cent in Idlib, 25.7 per cent in Raqqa, 23.6 per cent in Deir Ezzor, and 21.3 per cent in Hasaka. At the national level, it was 14.2 per cent (SCPR 2013: 71). The Northeast region was Syria's poorest. Using the lower poverty line, the poverty rate was highest in that region's rural areas, reaching 17.9 per cent in 2010. Urban poverty was 11.2 per cent. The Aleppo governorate was the poorest, with a poverty rate of 19.8 per cent, followed by Sweida (17.7 per cent), Raqqa (17.5 per cent), and Daraa (15.4 per cent) (El-Laithy and Abu-Ismail 2010). In general, the urban-rural and inter-regional disparities continued during that decade with no indication towards any improvement.

THE SOCIAL AND ECONOMIC IMPACTS OF THE CRISIS

Over the past six years, the extended conflict has shattered the economy; created new war-related institutions, mechanisms, and markets; and divided the country into isolated regions. Subjugating powers have also diverted the country's economic resources to activities linked to the economy of violence; at the same time, the people's war against foreign invaders serves a broader anti-imperialist objective. Still, the government's neoliberal policies have re-directed resources away from the nationalist war effort at the expense of the people and what might have been a swifter victory.

Economic Loss

Economic losses have accumulated amidst the continuation of the crisis. In 2011, the loss was relatively limited. It increased significantly in the following years with the intensification of violence and ongoing military operations. The total loss in 2011 reached $12.1 billion (SCPR 2016a), comprising 44.6 per cent GDP loss, 47.1 per cent damages to capital stock, 7.4 per cent additional official government military expenditure, and 0.16 per cent armed groups' military expenditure (semi-public) (SCPR 2016a).[7] In terms of the "continuing scenario," if the crisis had not emerged, the Syrian economy would have experienced continued GDP growth, and in the counterfactual scenario, GDP in 2015 would have been 30.8 per cent higher than it was in 2010 (SCPR 2016a: 13).

The GDP loss has been projected to reach $163.3 billion by the end of 2015 (SCPR 2016a: 30). The increase in government military expenditure is estimated at $14.5 billion. The military expenditure of the armed groups is projected at $6 billion over the course of the crisis (SCPR 2016a: 30). The projected capital stock loss reached $137.8 billion in current prices by the end of 2015, with actual physical capital stock in 2015 accounting for 32.8 per cent of its projected counterfactual level at the same year. The loss in capital stock consists of three components, including (1) reduction in net investment of $47 billion (already accounted for in the estimate of GDP losses); (2) idle capital stock, as a result of physical capital ceasing to contribute to production, services, and value added, projected at $23.5 billion (also included in the calculation of GDP loss); and (3) partial or full damage to capital stock, estimated at $67.3 billion due to the damage incurred from the armed conflict that includes ruined public and private properties and other residential and non-residential buildings (SCPR 2016a: 30).

The estimate of the informal production of oil and gas by armed groups, which we consider a loss of the country's wealth, is projected to reach $5.2 billion by the end of 2015 (SCPR 2016a: 31). However, the portion of this loss that includes the black market price of oil has been already included in the armed groups' expenditures' contribution to GDP loss, leaving the net loss of $3.6 billion to be added to the total loss to the state. By the end of 2015, we estimate total economic loss at $254.7 billion in current prices. GDP loss accounts for 64.1 per cent of the total loss, damage to capital stock accounts for 26.4 per cent, while reallocation to increased military expenditures accounts for 8 per cent of total economic loss (SCPR 2016a: 31).

Structural Changes

By 2015, the unbalanced impact of the crisis on different sectors had led to serious changes in the structure of GDP. The agricultural sector accounted for an increasing share of GDP reaching 28.7 per cent in 2015 compared to 17.4 per cent in 2010. Internal trade was at 16.9 per cent, while the transport and communication sectors were at 14.9 per cent. The government services sector as a share of GDP witnessed a notable decline to reach 13.1 per cent in 2015 (SCPR 2016a: 24). During the crisis, the nature and structure of the economy continues to witness a generally adverse transformation compared to the pre-crisis period. Government policies, particularly since 2014, have prioritised military expenditure, thereby depriving service spending of state resources and reducing the space for commodity subsidies.

Demand Deterioration

Since the beginning of the crisis, the government applied partial counter-cyclical policies. It continued to pay wages, even in the areas outside its control. It also expended resources on subsidies until 2014, after which it adopted the so-called "rationalisation of subsidies" policies, which drastically reduced the subsidies bill, increased the prices of oil derivatives, and raised production costs. By giving priority to military expenditure, the government sharply reduced its expenditures on public investment and hence deepened an already deep economic recession caused primarily by sanctions and war devastation. Subsidy removal has also had a devastating social impact. In addition to that, supply bottlenecks have pushed prices up, further accentuating the devaluation of the Syrian pound.

Domestic price increases have driven the surge in the cost of living. By the end of 2015, the consumer price index was estimated to have witnessed an annual increase of 53.4 per cent compared to 25.8 per cent in 2014 (SCPR 2016a: 36). Meanwhile, the Syrian pound continued to collapse. It depreciated by 45.5 per cent to reach SYP 382 per dollar in the unofficial market by the end of 2015—in the official market, it dropped nearly as much, by 36.2 per cent, to reach SYP 279 per dollar (SCPR 2016a: 35).

The average level of household expenditure declined to an unprecedentedly low level. Inter-regional and intra-regional inequalities widened. Warlords have gained substantial profit through monopolies, pillage, and royalties, in addition to siphoning humanitarian and external aid, even while the poor have been unable to meet their basic needs. Furthermore, the escalation of conflict and additional neoliberal measures in 2015, such as furthermore subsidy removal, have added mounting pressure on households' purchasing powers, as they have been unable to procure the necessary goods and services for survival. As a result, public consumption as a share of GDP declined substantially by 33.1 per cent in 2015 as compared to 2014 (SCPR 2016a: 7).

Another type of demand that emerged during conflict is the "semi-public" consumption, a new expenditure category undertaken by different actors who have seized power in the areas outside the government control. These actors play the role of a public authority. They impose taxes and reallocate resources and external aid according to their interests. Semi-public consumption estimates, including military expenditure, reached 13.2 per cent of GDP in 2015, increasing from a very low 0.09 per cent of GDP in 2011 (SCPR 2016a: 27).

Exports have continued to depend on raw materials like sheep, phosphate, fruits, and vegetables. But the movement of such goods has been affected by border closures and the impact of ongoing battles. Indeed, the national economy has become increasingly dependent on imports due to the collapse of the productive sectors. Western sanctions have hindered Syria's ability to import basic goods, pharmaceuticals, and health commodities. External sanctions have induced significant rises in black market trading and allowed the subjugating powers to control and monopolise the trade in basic goods and services. In spite of all the restrictions, imports accounted for 39 per cent of GDP, while exports accounted for 11.4 per cent of GDP in 2015 (SCPR 2016a: 30).

Fiscal Policy

As mentioned earlier, during the war years the government has sustained military expenditure and shifted resources away from productive economic activities. Public expenditure accounted for 16.9 per cent of GDP in 2015, compared to 23.4 per cent in 2014. However, public expenditure, including the off-budget subsidies and the increase of military expenditure, dropped from 47.5 per cent of GDP in 2014 to 33.5 per cent in 2015 (SCPR 2016a: 32). This decrease was a result of the drop in the subsidy bill from 14 per cent of GDP in 2014 to 5.6 per cent in 2015, following the government's new policy of "rationalisation of subsidies" (SCPR 2016a: 32). However, expenditure on military remained the same, accounting for 13.2 per cent of GDP in both 2014 and 2015. The government's fiscal policies harmed the economy and contributed to a deeper recession.

Powerful actors in the areas outside government control have used force to reallocate resources and impose new forms of taxes and fees. The "semi-public" investment, which was implemented by these de facto actors in the areas outside the government control to ensure basic services, was estimated at 0.05 per cent of GDP in 2012 and increased to 0.41 per cent of GDP in 2015 (SCPR 2016a: 28). This investment, despite its increase, was considered low compared to the needs of the people inside the "opposition-controlled" regions, because the priority for these actors has always been on military expenditure.

On the revenue side, the government resorted to raising revenues by reducing the subsidy bill instead on imposing progressive tax system that attenuates from the war-related rent activities and can guide resource allocation within the economy. Consequently, the revenue ratio of GDP decreased from 6.2 per cent in 2014 to 5.4 per cent in 2015 (SCPR 2016a: 32). As a result, the budget deficit dropped from 17.2 per cent in 2014 to 11.5 per cent of GDP in 2015. The overall deficit decreased from 41.2 per cent of GDP in 2014 to 28.1 per cent in 2015 (SCPR 2016a: 33).

Collapse in Job Opportunities

The deterioration of all productive activities, destruction of productive assets, and the insecure environment have led to a sharp drop in job opportunities, resulting in an unemployment rate of 52.7 per cent by the end of 2015 (SCPR 2016a: 37). The only flourishing sectors were that of organised violence, through which the subjugating powers recruit people to be part of armed groups or through organising illegal activities such as smuggling, monopoly, theft, pillage, the weapons trade, and people trafficking. These illegal activities attracted around 17 per cent of Syria's active population in 2014 (SCPR 2016a).

When applying the counterfactual analysis and comparing the "continuing" and "crisis" scenarios, we estimate that the labour market lost 3.52 million job opportunities by the end of 2015. However, the actual loss compared to the 2010 pre-crisis employment status has been 2.69 million job opportunities (SCPR 2016a: 37).

Population Dispersion

The calamity in Syria involves all aspects of life—human, physical, spiritual, mental, and material, including environmental damage. The conflict has shattered Syrian society, through the enormous death toll, the displacement of millions, mostly children and women, in addition to millions of refugees and emigrants. These population shifts and displacements have had a drastic impact on Syrian demography, as hundreds of thousands of people, particularly male breadwinners, have been killed, injured, arrested, and kidnapped, enormously affecting their families' lives and living conditions. The loss of security in all of its many forms has compromised Syrians' human rights and dignity. After reviewing the population growth rates before 2010, the Syrian population was estimated at 21.80 million in 2010. By the middle of 2015, it is estimated to have declined to 20.44 million. If the conflict had not occurred, the population would have reached 25.59 million. Thus, counterfactually, the population figure has decreased by 21 per cent (SCPR 2016a: 40).

The total number of refugees was estimated at 3.11 million by the end of 2015. Turkey is the first and primary host of Syrian refugees, with 37.5 per cent of the refugees. Lebanon is the second and has hosted 35.6 per cent of Syrian refugees. The third is Jordan with 14.1 per cent. Egypt is the fourth (about 4.8 per cent), and Iraq is the fifth (4.6 per cent) (SCPR 2016a: 41).

Extended clashes, ongoing violence, and the lack of security have pushed hundreds of thousands of Syrians families to seek safer places inside the country. The number of internally displaced persons (IDPs) is estimated at 6.36 million in 2015, increasing from 5.65 million in 2014 (SCPR 2016a: 41).

Diminishing Human Development Dimensions

Apart from the hundreds of thousands of Syrians killed or disabled, the conflict has prevented people from acquiring appropriate health care, including child care and vaccinations. The Syrian health index had decreased by 30.3 per cent by the end of 2015 compared to 2010.[8] The ranking of the health index in Syria has dropped from 106th to 174th out of 195 countries, placing Syria among the worst countries in the world in terms of the HDI's health dimension (SCPR 2016a: 42).

Education has been the silent victim of the crisis. An enormous number of children have been displaced, some of them forced to work for family survival. Moreover, thousands of schools have been destroyed or damaged. The education index in 2015 fell by 34.3 per cent as compared to 2010 (SCPR 2016a: 43). It had been driven down by collapsing school attendance rates and a drop in the expected years of schooling. Unfortunately, almost half of the children of basic education age have been out of school since 2014. Students in higher education have dropped out as well, leading to a 24.6 per cent decrease in the average years of schooling when compared to the "continuing" scenario. This resulted in the drop of the education index in Syria from 124th to 173rd out of 187 countries in 2015.

The ongoing armed conflict has led to massive destruction of national assets and wealth. Capital stock, commercial and residential buildings, and natural resources have been destroyed. According to the "Population Status Survey 2014," the crisis has affected the property of 87 per cent of Syrian families, with varying levels of damage. Security conditions have forced about 57 per cent of industrial small workshops and about 60 per cent of large industrial plants to close. The degradation of productive activities has caused a huge reduction in revenues and purchasing powers of families. In 2015, the income index decreased by 24.3 per cent as compared to 2010 (SCPR 2016a: 44). Consequently, the ranking of Syria in the income index fell from 129th to 164th position out of 190 countries.

The overall effect of the crisis has precipitated a vast shrinking in the value of Syria's HDI. It has pushed the country into the "low human development" group, with a value index of 0.443 in 2015—the index value was 0.631 in 2010. The results, if events were to have proceeded in accordance with the projections of the "continuing scenario," show that Syrian HDI would have increased from 0.631 in 2010 to 0.653 by the end of 2015, putting Syria in the "medium human development" group. Consequently, the HDI of Syria has lost 29.8 per cent in 2015 compared with its value in 2010 and 32 per cent from its potential until the end of 2015 (SCPR 2016a: 45). The general HDI rank of Syria using the 2010 HDI results indicates a fall from 121st to 173rd place out of 187 countries.

Expanded Poverty

The economy's poor performance is a result of wide-ranging destruction of wealth, infrastructure, property, and natural resources. As mentioned earlier, reallocation of resources has taken place to cement a system of violence and disorder, all to the benefit of subjugating powers and rent-seeking actors. These factors, coupled with government policies which increased the price of basic goods and services, have forced most Syrian people into the poverty trap. Besides income poverty, the escalation of violence deprives a growing number of Syrian households from adequate and safe living conditions. According to the Population Status Survey 2014, about 30 per cent of houses had been destroyed by mid-2014. Additionally, thousands of health and educational facilities have been destroyed. This makes the poverty of Syrian families multidimensional and not just a question of access to or deprivation from cash incomes.

The burden of poverty is unbalanced among regions and governorates. The poverty rate increased in all Syrian governorates, but the highest overall poverty levels were registered in Al-Raqqa, Idlib, Deir Ezzor, Homs, and rural Damascus. The lowest rate was in Sweida at 77.2 per cent, followed by Latakia. The governorates suffering from extreme poverty were Deir Ezzor, Raqqa, Idlib, and Hasaka, whose rates reached 80.9, 80.3, 79.5, and 75.8 per cent, respectively (SCPR 2016a: 46).

Concluding Remarks: Towards an Alternative Scenario

In this chapter, I have surveyed the principal socioeconomic developments prior and post Syrian uprising. Syria's geostrategic position and its institutional bottleneck and lack of social participation were the root causes of the dire events. The absence of social dialogue is no less a factor of the problematic. Before the crisis, institutions were isolated and lacked popular trust. Syria witnessed a reverse development trajectory. The level of human development in its various dimensions did not meet expectations. In the 2001–2010 period, the government's extension of neoliberal economic policies devoid of social safety nets foregrounded the current crisis.

Over the last six years, the violence further alienated a weak state from society. However, as an observer from the inside, the principal blame lies squarely upon the shoulders of imperialist forces that took opportunity of Syria's weakness to destroy society. The Syrian people were aware that violence is risky. Meanwhile, the demands for social fairness and the weighing of ends and means in the course of the revolt were compromised. Although the regime took refuge in intensifying its state of siege and martial law, it was the externally financed groups that resorted to armed attacks that really undermined the aspirations of the Syrian people.

So far, the crisis has reduced the economy to one third of its 2010 level. It has destroyed a substantial part of national wealth, infrastructure, and heritage. The imperative is to end this crisis. This is beyond Syria's capacity. The efforts of the international community must be geared to impose effective pressure towards those who benefit from the war which now includes major international players. This is a tall order but launching dialogue amongst all involved may conclude an agreement. The SCPR has engaged in multiple pilot attempts at social dialogue in successive meetings that included persons from different backgrounds. They have agreed on key points regarding the future of Syria.

Syrians must design an alternative scenario for economic development. At any rate, forward-looking scenarios should attenuate the intensity of war and tyranny. In this regard, the alternative scenario should adopt a human-centred and rights-based approach that takes into account restoring lost capacity and allowing for popular participation. The prospects for future settlements and the attendant discussion should begin immediately. As a Syrian who has witnessed the catastrophe that has befallen my country, the time to design the future of Syria is now.

Notes

1. The SCPR adjusted the deflator for the manufacturing sector; consequently the overall GDP growth rate for the period between 2001 and 2010 changed accordingly; see SCPR (2016a).
2. See SCPR (2016b), *Forced Dispersion*.
3. Ibid.
4. Ibid.
5. Estimated expenditure in the general budget 2010, Central Bureau of Statistics 2011, Table 14/3.
6. Author's calculations based on data from Syria Statistical Abstracts, various years.
7. Part of the "semi-public" expenditure is allocated to military expenditure and the other part to services; see SCPR (2016a).
8. The estimation is based on the newly calculated life tables that estimated life expectancy at birth in 2010 at 70.5 years (SCPR 2016a).

Bibliography

Central Bureau of Statistics. (2011). *Syrian Statistical Abstract*. Damascus: Central Bureau of Statistics.

Central Bureau of Statistics. (n.d.). *Syrian Statistical Abstract*. Damascus: Central Bureau of Statistics, various years.

El Laithy, H., & Abu-Ismail, K. (2010). *Poverty and the Equitable Distribution in Syria*. Damascus: UNDP.

UNDP. (2016). *Human Development Report*. New York: UNDP.
Syrian Center for Policy Research (SCPR). (2013). *Socioeconomic Roots and Impacts of the Syrian Crisis*. Damascus: Syrian Centre for Policy Research.
Syrian Center for Policy Research (SCPR). (2016a). *Confronting Fragmentation: Impact of the Syrian Crisis Report*. Damascus: Syrian Centre for Policy Research.
Syrian Center for Policy Research (SCPR). (2016b). *Forced Dispersion: A Demographic Report on the Human Status in Syria*. Damascus: Syrian Centre for Policy Research.

CHAPTER 7

Lebanon Can't Give Him a Future: Revolutionary Subjectivity and Syrian Rebel-Workers in Beirut

Philip Proudfoot

INTRODUCTION

"I'm thinking about divorcing my wife," said Abdullah between gulps of Turkish beer, "are you shocked, Philip? I thought you'd have no idea ... but what can I do? She wants me to leave for Germany [on an 'illegal' boat] but I want to stay here—next to Syria. I love Syria. All I want is to return to my village someday. But Dala says she wants to live in the city ... she doesn't care about [tribal] tradition ... you know, I loved the revolution but she's not interested. When my friends come over she gets annoyed, especially if we eat on the floor ... she throws down forks at guests saying, 'don't eat with your hands because ... taṭawwarna hala' [we got developed now]".

It was December 2015 when the newly wed Abdullah decided to pass by my Beirut apartment for a drink. Abdullah is a 26-year-old Syrian construction worker from rural Eastern Syria and a former student of social science at the Lebanese University.[1] I met him in the summer of 2012, by which point he had participated both directly and indirectly in an uprising that had taken hold in Syria since March 2011.[2] I much admired his frankness and insight and, soon, Abdullah agreed to become my primary

P. Proudfoot (✉)
Center for Middle Eastern Studies, Lund, Sweden

© The Author(s) 2019
L. Matar, A. Kadri (eds.), *Syria: From National Independence to Proxy War*, https://doi.org/10.1007/978-3-319-98458-2_7

research assistant with my project documenting, ethnographically, the everyday realities of Syrian workers, rebels, and refugees in Beirut. To date, we have carried out over 30 months of combined participant observation, semi-structured interviews, focus group analysis, population surveys, life history collection, and image archiving amongst a small network of opposition-aligned Syrian workers in Beirut.

These men are referred to here as 'rebel-workers.' On the one hand, this is because all, though with varying degrees of enthusiasm, expressed anti-regime positions; some returned to protest and others later to fight. On the other hand, there was also an additional more macro hybridisation of these two identities: the economic conditions that increased reliance on worker remittance flows also resembles those same conditions that many scholars now suggest constituted an important material basis for the uprising itself (Azmeh 2014; Hinnebusch 2012; Matar 2012, Kadri 2016).

This chapter takes an initial step back from the current moment of refugee crisis instead to reveal the conditions through which Abdullah first left Syria and travelled to Beirut, but also carved out a means to participate in what he calls 'the revolution.' My aim is to add a drop of ethnographic colour to our more general understanding of the Syrian crisis and in so doing reveal how the crisis was navigated by migrant labourers in Lebanon. Through a single man's story, I hope to reveal something about how everyday practices of identity construction, resistance, and survival intersect with the overbearing realities of mass pauperisation, war, and uprising.

Abdullah was one of three brothers and two sisters. He stands at about 5 ft 11 inches. He wears his hair styled tightly into the sides, blended down into ever so carefully groomed 'designer stubble.' My research assistant typically sports relaxed athletic clothes, hooded jackets, jogging bottoms, and the like. But, despite the sporty look, his weight fluctuated endlessly and was the source of much anxiety. The size of his posterior often found itself the butt of other men's jokes.

Abdullah did indeed 'love the revolution.' Yet, his revolution had also long since transformed into a vicious civil conflict and proxy war. And at the time of writing, 'regime change' appears a long way off. With the regime looking set to remain, Abdullah's future is suspended between destruction across the border and ever-worsening socio-legal conditions in Lebanon. Hundreds and thousands of men just like him have come to board smugglers' boats.

In popular press narratives, Abdullah's revolution was another iteration in a wider series revolt known as the 'The Arab Spring.' This story typically begins with the self-immolation of a Tunisian Street vendor, Mohamed Bouazizi (Kraidy 2016: 23–52). Bouazizi's drastic protest—on 17 December 2010—was allegedly in response to the confiscation of his goods by a local police officer. Mass demonstrations followed with popular mobilisation spreading soon to Egypt. Syria followed in Egypt's wake. In fact, on 28 January 2011, echoing events in Tunisia, a man called Hassan Ali Akleh set himself ablaze in the northeastern Syrian town of Hasakeh (Yassin-Kassab and Al-Shami 2016: 35). But Akleh's act went unremarked (ibid.). Instead, the rupturing event of the Syrian uprising has been typically framed as the arrest and torture of 15 schoolboys in Dara'a (ibid.: 38). The Syrian authorities are said to have accused the boys of writing Arab Spring slogans on their school yard's walls (ibid.). In 2012, a proliferation of rebel militias appeared on the scene and by 2013 a brutal proxy war raged across Syria. Iranian and, later, Russian-backed forces sided with the al-Asad government; Gulf-sponsored extremists pledged their allegiance to various Islamist outfits. Those who fled the war zone found little security, and refugees living in neighbouring countries are now subject to numerous laws and edicts that limit freedom movement, gainful employment, and a dignified existence (Amnesty 2015).

It is with a view to this severe level of loss and devastation that Dala's insistence that Abdullah travel to Germany and begin a new life must first be read. Instead of precariousness, Dala imagines stability, instead of poverty she sees prosperity and in place of car bombs, peace.

Yet Abdullah's reluctance to leave Lebanon, and his expressed 'love of the revolution,' points toward the depth of his political transformation. Indeed, despite being initially physically separated from front-line mobilisation, my research assistant displayed all the trapping of a revolutionary awakening.[3] His transformation amounted to emergence of revolutionary subjectivity. In the broadest terms, 'revolutionary subjectivity' refers to the point at which any particular individual begins expressly to think of themselves as part of a broader collective force unified by a common goal. It is then imagined that this goal, if achieved, will bring about a radical transformation in any given socio-political order.[4] For Abdullah this goal was overthrowing the regime of Bashar al-Asad.

In what remains I will further describe the merging of 'rebel' and 'worker' identities through key moments in Abdullah's life between 2011 and 2016. I reveal in the process the contexts though which revolutionary commitments emerged and how it was the final threads of the al-Asad government's legitimacy snapped from sections of the population. I conclude that, prior to the uprising, labour migration to Lebanon transitioned from a choice evidencing *some* degree of consent to a coercive survivalist strategy. I conclude by noting how the recent imposition of the *kafala* labour sponsorship system in Lebanon represents yet another ratcheting-up of coercion. Thus, structural and physical violence have combined to ensure a steady stream of men and women with little choice for survival outside of the smugglers' boat.

Revolution from a Distance

It was March 2011 when Abdullah, who at that time was working in Beirut, first learned of anti-regime mobilisation occurring back home in Syria. In an instant, he became transfixed with Facebook, his apartment's satellite television, and, a little while later, WhatsApp messenger.[5]

A few months passed and the intensity of street organisation mounted, violence increased, and Abdullah made the decision that, during a break from university, he would take the arduous 30-hour bus journey back home to his village in Deir Ezzor.

In Lebanon, Abdullah developed his commitment to the uprising from a distance because, evidently, he lacked an opportunity to participate directly in street organisation. In many stories of the uprising, individuals point to their first experiences of participation and mobilisation as generative of a rebirth, making for tight bonds of 'togetherness' and 'collectivism' in opposition to the al-Asad government (e.g. Yassin-Kassab and Leila Al-Shami 2016: 57–77). However, Abdullah's political consciousness and the emergence of his revolutionary commitments preceded any participation in front-line activity. Intrigued by this, I asked him and other men how it was they came to be so political. Inevitably, I was pointed toward new communication technology. Without exception, *every* rebel-worker participant owned some manner of internet-enabled smartphone, and it was through this technology that art objects, local news stories, photographs, and videos shot on mobile cameras rapidly circulated. These items appeared valued in so far as they offered the men a seemingly 'less mediated' form of coverage from across borders. Powerful connections of solidarity formed between initial local organisers and men separated by geographic distance.

Indeed, in what Abdullah reflected upon as days of peaceful protest and youth organisation, he became something of an activist. However, when he would reminisce to me about those times, things did not always sound quite as 'peaceful' as he otherwise insisted. One of his favourite stories begins with him lounging around with mates in the Lebanese University's cafeteria. They were noisily discussing events allegedly taking place in Dara'a. Abdullah had already attended a few rapidly planned meetings on campus and was engaged in never-ending political discussions with fellow Syrians.

"Some of us were saying it will not be longer than three months and Bashar will fall [...] ok, some thought longer—but we all were convinced he was going," he said, when reflecting back on that time. In memories of 2011, it was typically understood that the coverage of the uprisings in Egypt and Tunisia was what fuelled a sense of excitement: could Syria be the next state to drive out its dictatorship?

Against this, Abdullah explained to me the emotional drive he felt to go back home or risk missing out on a transformative moment of Syrian history. Just as he was debating the necessity to go back and support the revolution, another group of whom he presumed were Harakat Amal-supporting students appeared to overhear their discussion. They shouted back a chain of insults.[6] "It was like Syria," he said.

What he means by 'like Syria' is that, even at a distance in Beirut, the relationship of Lebanese political forces was such that antagonisms flaring in his homeland could appear reproduced on the grounds of a foreign university campus.[7] Before these mounting confrontations, he had even been trying to organise an 'opposition solidarity march' through Dahieh.[8] However, after the cafeteria fight, his plan was soon abandoned.

Exams and the Future

Abdullah never graduated from college; he was expelled.

In the winter of 2014, my friend approached what would have been his penultimate round of examinations, but he decided against sitting the tests. Instead, he paid one of his peers to take the exams. Upon entering the hall, ID checks took place—the plot was revealed. It was, in hindsight, not the greatest of ideas, as his friend only bore a passing resemblance. Abdullah was dismissed from the university, his two and a half years of study amounted now to nothing. This was a real blow. Abdullah was the most intellectually gifted amongst his immediate kin. He scored the highest in his school exams back in Syria, and it was with these results in hand that he had decided to travel, in 2010, to Lebanon. He enrolled in the Social Sciences faculty at the Lebanese University.

His decision to travel abroad for work and study was made possible through his family's long-standing connection to seasonal work in Beirut. In fact, his elder brother Firas had already been working in construction in Beirut for some years, and their father had found employment in Lebanon intermittently during the late 1980s and 1990s. The advantage for poorer students studying in Beirut is that if they could secure cheap accommodation and a job they also might well begin to accumulate some cash for a future back in Syria.

Abdullah lived with Firas when he first arrived. At that time—while already having learned from his brother that conditions were not great—he nonetheless crossed into Lebanon with a vision of future of prosperity and a life of luxury. He told me how he saw only fast cars and plush apartments ahead. Unsurprisingly, Abdullah's first night living on a construction site was a somewhat unpleasant memory. But regardless of his first impressions, Abdullah did not want to disappoint his brother, who had even managed to wrangle him some work. He tried his best to work as a labourer, but he could not hack it: he quit after two weeks. "I hadn't gotten used to that type of work then," he later admitted. Abdullah was fortunate, he struck it lucky, quickly finding further employment working odd jobs in a sports nutrition supply shop in a central commercial district of Beirut: Hamra. When we first met in 2012, he was still working there, and meanwhile renting a spot in an apartment close to the shop and my own accommodation.

With regard to his eventual expulsion from the university, my friend was keen to stress that his punishment was draconian, especially considering that he was well known to the faculty as a hard-working, promising student. His grades stood significantly above the class average. When his fate was revealed, Abdullah found that he could not curry any favour amongst friendlier academic staff. In his later telling of the situation, he said he felt it all came down to the simple fact that sectarian politics had long infiltrated the Lebanese University. This was in view of the apparent the domination of Ḥarakat Amal around campus. Abdullah argues he was himself a 'known troublemaker,' especially in relation to his vocal support of the Syrian opposition.

Abdullah's decision to cheat emerges within a chain of identifiable and intensifying socio-economic pressures. His mother and sisters had become internally displaced in Syria, his elder brother with them. Firas was then stuck back home in Syria. He had been fighting with a Free Syrian Army (FSA) unit in Eastern Syria, having returned to Syria in 2013. When Firas learned their father had died in mid-2014 from a heart attack, he returned to his mother's side. He has not (yet) returned to combat. He became internally displaced with the rest of the family when the Islamic State crossed the Iraqi border in the summer of 2014.[9]

The family's farmland previously grew wheat but now lies fallow. As a consequence, Abdullah's $200 per month remittances have shifted from 'assistance' to 'lifeline.' He cobbled this money together by seemingly working every hour of the day. However, as a consequence of all this, he began missing classes, delaying his assignments, and finding himself unable to study for his summer 2014 examinations. Such was his preoccupation with the impossibility of studying and working that Abdullah wrote one of his research assignments on fellow rural-urban migrant worker students. All were united by the fact that they had once imagined they could combine an income and savings with a degree in Beirut. Most now faced an impossible task of precariously balancing these twin desires thanks to an increasingly war-torn Syria with attendant 'hyperinflation' (O'Brian 2013).

However, Abdullah had already invested much time in his degree, and with the little promises it held for a better future, as well as the weight of his mother's pride, he had to find a solution. That solution was cheating. The asset Abdullah might once have enjoyed, in building a future through his education while providing for his family through remittances, appeared now to be increasingly limited.

It was around a year later, after Abdullah's expulsion from the university, and on a rainy December evening in 2015 when my friend sat across from me in my apartment drinking Turkish beer. Despite the inclement weather, he could not resist the opportunity to sneak out of his home. He appeared to find some relief in explaining the complications newly married life was throwing up. These complications ranged from ever-present financial difficulties, his sense of total precariousness, and rural-urban cultural differences to his wife's apathy toward the revolution versus his determination to keep it alive.

I had attended Abdullah's autumn wedding some months earlier. Weddings are elsewhere a central and important ethnographic fixture, but when I began fieldwork in April 2012, there was little expectation I would have the opportunity to partake in one unless I were to travel somehow to

Syria. At that time, movement across the border from Lebanon to Syria remained a relatively straightforward and open affair. Indeed, the workers I first made acquaintance with, before I had met Abdullah, were still making regular trips back home, with some returning to join the protests and others later to fight. Many also returned to wed.

When I first 'entered the field,' I came to spend countless evenings hanging out with guys who live and work on construction sites dotted across central Beirut; these were evenings accompanied with tales of love, future brides, and imagined married life. With the uprising not yet significantly militarised, these migrant workers often still saw themselves as desirable, for they were making wages that—while poverty-inducing in Lebanon—were still comparatively high for Syria. True, it was not comparable to their parent's generation, and the on-site average of $450 per month might not sound like much, but it goes further across the border in Syria, especially if you manage to avoid rent by securing accommodation within a construction project. Moreover, these hard-won savings were still at this point hoped to materialise one day into future wedding ceremonies, dowries, businesses, or family homes.

One of the men I met on a construction site, Mohammed, was a student in Damascus University's journalism department. Mohammed had intended to work in Lebanon only for the summer. Through his cousin on the site, he had managed to secure accommodation on a central Beirut site while working the counter at a nearby pastry shop. Mohammed is from an impoverished rural Idlib background; his father is an out-of-work alcoholic, and his brothers are too young to work. He estimates he is making double what he would earn in Damascus for the same job.

Against the mounting conflict, Mohammed too—as with all the workers, refugees, and rebels I know—witnessed his planned future become fiction. He never returned to university. Instead, after eventually leaving for his village, he ended up fleeing with his family to Turkey. Presently his education is on hold; he works now at a clothes shop in a Turkish urban centre, not far from the border. Another of Mohammad's cousins, Bilal, a one-time roadside banana seller, also returned to Idlib in 2013, but he took a different path. In fact, Bilal remains in Idlib today, having completed military service he wanted to put his skills to use in the uprising. First, he joined an FSA brigade, then Jabhat al-Nusra, before, in 2015, abandoning the direct fighting altogether.[10] Today Bilal searches the wreckage of aerially bombarded buildings for bodies and survivors alongside other humanitarian organisations.

By contrast, men like Abdullah, who did not make an earlier return, now remain somewhat stuck in Lebanon, their entire lives uprooted in Beirut. The expected duration of residence moves from total uncertainty to an increasing likelihood of, and even necessity for, permanent settlement. So how exactly did Beirut, once a place of temporary and seasonal employment, become now a place for social reproduction? In other words, how is it that I came to attend the wedding of my research assistant?

A New Tradition

Abdullah's new wife, Dala, is from Idlib in Northern Syria. Dala is from a family of moderately wealthy shopkeepers, whereas my research assistant is from the more impoverished rural province of Deir Ezzor, in Eastern Syria. Dala, who is 23, is somewhat short, and she tends to wear a modern-style coloured hijab matched with bright tops. She is evidently intelligent and performing well at university; of late she has seemingly become an expert on the web of decrees, laws, and regulations governing those who attempt to gain illegal entrance to Europe. "Why does David Cameron say he'll only take 20,000 urgent case refugees?" she asked me at dinner one mid-November evening in 2015, "what exactly is an urgent case? All of Syria is an urgent case."

Abdullah's family's background is tribal and agricultural; Dala's background is urban and trade-orientated. Despite these evident differences in class and region, they had fallen for one another at university and, after a few months of courtship, announced their engagement. At that time, Abdullah acknowledged his betrothal would likely have proved impossible were it not for the upheaval generated by the Syrian uprising, for in the present state of war, displacement, and economic degeneration, marriage costs are significantly lower with parental control over partner choices seemingly weaker (The Syrian Observer 2015). There was nevertheless a round of initial protestations from Dala's father, but, eventually, he consented to the marriage, given that Abdullah was, at that time, a student in university and had, through construction work, a source of income.

Where the young couple's home regions of Idlib and Deir Ezzor share similarities is the fact they're both no longer controlled by the al-Asad government, but by Islamist militias. During the conflict, Idlib has exchanged hands many times, and, as of March 2015, it was successfully recaptured during an operation named 'Taḥrīr Idlib' [Liberate Idlib]. This operation was launched by a coalition of Sunni jihadist organisations known as 'Jaish al-Fatah' [the army of conquest]. Jaish al-Fatah's constituent outfits included the al-Qaida-aligned 'Jabhat al-Nusra' playing the most prominent role (Homsi 2015). Abdullah's village fell in June 2014 from relative isolation, to become territory of the Islamic State.

These occupations go some way to explain why the wedding was not carried out in Syria. However, travel to these regions remains, in fact, still technically possible, with at least one regular bus departing from central Beirut and ending its journey in the *de facto* capital of the Islamic State, Raqqa (Issa 2015). Even if the young couple were from a more tightly government-controlled area, their wedding still would likely have been carried out in exile. This is because—in addition to the physical violence of war—a further and interrelated formation of bureaucratic structural violence through the Lebanese labour sponsorship system has, since December 2015, acted to delimit movement across the Lebanese-Syrian border. I return to these limitations below, the point being here that with warfare accelerating in Syria, and the day-to-day violence of state institutions determining the flow of things in Lebanon, Abdullah finally decided that his wedding would have to take place in Beirut.

We had discussed the celebration and where to hold it many times. My friend changed his mind a lot. At first, he thought a small party at home would do, with only his closest friends invited, for these were, of course, frugal times. But as more individuals expressed a desire to attend, Abdullah felt compelled to switch gear and hold a larger affair. "There's a war though," I said on the phone after he made the decision, "and most of your guests are going to be refugees and workers like you. Surely they'd understand."

"My friends are not the problem," he answered back, "I need to show Dala's family that I'm not poor—that I'm a good man."

So, finally, he settled on an adequate but rather stripped down event space near Cola—a busy transport intersection to the south of Beirut. The space, on a veranda above an arghila café, did nonetheless provide ample space for dancing and socialising.

Abdullah's former housemates, Haytham, Adnan, and Mahmoud, greeted me at the door. The three are cousins from a village not far from Abdullah's. Shadi was also there, a friend made by Abdullah and Haytham at university, and from a larger city near the Iraqi border.

Haytham is tall, slim, and handsome, with dark eyes, set against well-shaped cheek bones. He studied with Abdullah at the Lebanese University, and the two remained friends for a prolonged period. However, at the time of writing, they are no longer on speaking terms. Despite for a time both working on the same large construction project, they now awkwardly avoid eye contact when passing. The cause of this fallout is money: shortly before the wedding, Abdullah insists he loaned Haytham $100; Haytham insists otherwise. "Huwa maslaḥji" [he's a self-interested person], Abdullah told me.

"Huwa kazzāb" [He's a liar], responded Haytham when I asked him about the fight. Haytham was once in a different economic position to the men with whom he shared an apartment in Sabra, a Palestinian camp in south Beirut. For a time he received, rather than sent, remittances: his studies were partially paid for thanks to his father's work in Amman. His rent in Sabra, in a two-room apartment shared with five workers, came in at just over $50 per month. With food costs kept low and minimal expenditure on luxuries, he was able to survive without much work. He would still occasionally take employment opportunities when they presented themselves, often through his kin and friendship network. As he began nearing the end of his degree, however, his father lost his job, and he had to take up more work in construction. Having now finished his degree, he is still working there today, faced with the seeming impossibility of finding employment relevant to his qualifications.

Another resident of the apartment, Adnan, installs motorway signage. He is shorter than the other men and sports 'designer stubble' and reflective aviator sunglasses. Adnan is the apartment's resident joker: a favourite of his is to shout, "Take your hand off my dick!" whenever the flat plunged into total darkness during frequent power cuts.

Mahmoud works with his uncle, Khaled, installing gypsum board in luxury apartment construction projects. He is the jokingly self-acknowledged 'housewife' in charge of cooking and cleaning. He is an amazing chef, reproducing for the men their favourites from village cuisine with massive amounts of rice, chicken, and stuffed vegetables. Everything is consumed sitting on the floor in a circle, with hands reaching into a central plate and water passed around the group from the same jug. Despite differences in age and status, there is no discernible division at the dinner table according to rank. That is, aside from children, who needed constantly reminding of the manners appropriate for collective eating, such as not grabbing at the food until everyone sits. These children appeared because, as the uprising degenerated further into war, they had been brought by men and women to the relative safety of Beirut. Whenever we were done eating, Shadi was always spared the duty of washing dishes, for that was already his job at a Lebanese upmarket restaurant. Instead, his main duty was to assist Mahmoud and me in cooking.

After exchanging greetings with the four men, I moved upstairs to join the wedding party. Immediately I noticed that the bride's side of the room was more heavily attended: this was likely down to the fact that nearly all of Dala's family, aside from one uncle, had long since transported their lives and assets to Beirut. Sitting on the groom's side, the majority of Abdullah's guests were young university students and Syrian migrant workers. I recognised some faces from the football teams with whom we had done battle during our regular Sunday evening matches.

The institution of what Abdullah insisted was a welcome 'new tradition' amongst young displaced worker-refugees in Beirut defrayed the cost of this well-attended celebration. Collectively, his closest kin and friends pooled together money to assist in the $700 venue hire, DJ, and refreshment costs. This pooling is done, of course, with the expectation that the gift will be returned when it is another's turn to wed.

"Back in Syria," Abdullah told me, some days after his own ceremony, "weddings might cost $5000 just for the celebration, ceremony, and the dowry." He stressed that some men were even prepared to drop an additional $1000 on the engagement party alone. By contrast, Abdullah's engagement party was a small gathering of friends in his shared apartment; he provided only soft drinks and cigarettes. He told me that the dowry by Dala's parents totalled just $600. Abdullah confirmed, "people can't ask for more" and, in a story that's reportedly become common throughout Syria, he said, "where would we get that money from these days?"

It is not so much the wedding itself that is the source of Abdullah's current predicament, but more a whole host of obligations and limitations that have mounted as the Syrian revolution, in which he once participated, has transitioned from its uprising phase into the bloody proxy war.

After the marriage, Abdullah moved out of his former home in Sabra with the aim of establishing a place for himself and Dala. The couple found a two-bedroom apartment on the edge of Bourj el-Barajneh, the Palestinian refugee camp. Due to its affordability, this camp, as with Sabra and Shatila, has become popular with Syrian worker-refugees. The newly-weds' rent totals $300 per month. The apartment—while conveniently located at a walking distance to some of Dala's family—came unfurnished and unequipped. Abdullah took out an in-shop loan from a nearby store: his debt was set at $1500 to outfit the new home. However, on top of these expenditures come the regular internet and mobile phone bills, electricity generator fees, and the need to maintain $200 per month remittances for his family in Syria.

At the time of writing, my friend is moving in and out of stable employment, but on average he brings home between $400 and $450 per month. Dala is working part time and generating around $350 per month. However, a broken phone, a sudden demand for increased remittances to Syria, or the loss of a job all risk pushing the couple into a state of precariousness with little options open aside from turning toward Dala's family connections.

A few months after the wedding, in early November 2015, we all went for dinner with the young couple at a restaurant along Beirut's coast. We all ordered chicken fajitas, a dish seemingly always popular with Syrian workers. Before our food arrived, we were smoking, drinking Pepsi, and discussing what's next for the young couple.

"Well, I've still not found a job," said Abdullah.

"You see!" interjected Dala, "Lebanon can't give him a future, just work, no future, low wages, high costs."

"Well, what should he do then, take a boat?" I asked.

"Yes," she replied. "My cousin's in Germany. I want him to go too—there's nothing here for him."

"But so many people have died crossing," I replied.

"But how many people have died in Syria?" Abdullah injected, "There's lots of pressure. What can I do? Stay here for nothing, go to the village and maybe someone will kill me, or get on a boat and maybe drown? I just don't want to leave and be so far from Syria; I want to go back to the village."

I was wrong to assume it was the risk to his life that was now the sole factor blocking my friend from relenting to his wife's pressure. This was not it. Instead, what pressed on his mind most was the thought of finally reaching Europe without a passport and being detained. Not knowing if he would be able to return to Syria, Abdullah did not want to disconnect from his friends who might remain in Beirut and thus further divorced from his imagined future back home in Deir Ezzor.

"See, there's no future here!" insisted Dala.

"What hope does he have in Europe?" I replied, "So many people can't get past the borders. What's going to happen to him then?"

But at that moment, we all looked up at a television hanging in the corner. Our eyes were drawn to scenes of bloodied people running from smoking buildings. A twin bomb blast carried out by Islamic State had, moments earlier, struck a popular market area in south Beirut. Forty-three people were killed and 200 wounded.

The bombs exploded just two streets away from the young couple's new apartment. And at that moment, Dala's insistence her husband set sail for Europe and forge them a new life seemed, for now, a whole lot less rash.

Revolutionary Subjectivity[11]

Men like Abdullah suddenly found themselves part and parcel of a collective alternative political force, with bonds of solidarity that stretched out across Syria and beyond. These bonds were made visible, as aforementioned, through online social media and satellite television feeds. His story above reveals an overwhelming sense of sheer excitement as to what *could be*. It is in these moments of excitement, collectivism, and effervescence that the barrier of fear between the people and the regime appeared to drop. The barrier of fear aside, what men also claimed to have felt fell away were many once taken-for-granted social boundaries between confessional groupings, genders, generations, and tribes. In short, as revolutionary subjectivity emerged, various other socio-cultural limitations were also claimed to have retracted.

Revolutionary subjectivity refers, then, to the point at which the individual in society begins to conceptualise herself as part of a broader social force, a force intent on radically reorganising the distribution of political and economic power in any given society. However, the emergence, materialisation, and subsequent degradation of this subjectivity is not some wholly political process, and the shape, texture, and depth of broader socio-cultural impacts that follow from radical transformations cannot be grasped in isolation from everyday life.

In orthodox Marxist theory, revolutionary subjectivity emerges also at the point at which a class transitions from acting as a class-in-itself—who share a common relationship with the means of production—to acting as a class-for-itself. When a class-for-itself politically mobilises, it becomes, for the first time, an agent and not merely a subject of history. For the working class under capitalism, this is the point at which workers move beyond day-to-day antagonisms with the owners of the means of production to become aware of themselves as a distinct class, that is, the proletariat who are structurally in opposition to the bourgeoisie.

For Marx (1990, 2008), a transformation in the mode of production results from a dialectical interplay between the objective and subjective conditions in any given society. It is this interplay that produces 'class consciousness.' In this sense, arguments purporting to identify the 'root causes of the Syrian uprising' would do well to follow the roots themselves, that is, to begin in the earth, at the base point of socio-economic reproduction and, in so doing, reveal how certain emerging antagonisms were endured, negotiated, or eventually resisted (Azmeh 2014; Matar 2012). Seen against the physical and structural violence, the Syrian uprising and the broader politico-economic structures that lay the foundations for that uprising function like over-determining frames through which men like Abdullah came to navigate their lives. Many of Abdullah's small everyday decisions, including his decision about where to marry or potentially to divorce, necessarily materialised against impersonal historical formations. However, in accounting for the journey to revolutionary commitment, we ought to take the emotional dimensions of an individual's revolutionary experience seriously.

In communicating dissent at immiserating conditions, a prominent role was afforded to new technology (Proudfoot 2016: 132–192). This technology, as is the case in Abdullah story, helped accelerate the collapse of the al-Asad's legitimacy in some quarters. But this must be balanced further against the fact there is something 'offline' about my research assistant's political journey. Abdullah is just one individual from a small farming village, similar to the thousands of other farming villages across Syria. It is precisely people like Abdullah who found themselves at the bottom rung of a process that looks very much like 'accumulation by dispossession.'

'Accumulation by dispossession' is a concept popularised by the geographer David Harvey (2005). Harvey—building on Marx's notion of 'primitive accumulation'—set out to identify how the neoliberal policy core, represented by financialisation, privatisation, the ending of redistributive measures, and the manipulation of crises, has resulted not in mutual prosperity but an ever-increasing flow of power and wealth to an ever-narrowing section of elites. These measures are at the heart of the International Monetary Fund's (IMF's) 'structural adjustment' conditions that must be met in return for a loan. Syria, however, unlike the more officially Western-orientated Arab states, has not been subjected 'directly' to these pressures; however, the IMF's spectral presence and influence can still be located in the ministries with regard to their fiscal and monetary policies carried out since the mid-2000s (Matar 2012).

These policies stand as a key foundation that intersects with all the various economic, environmental, and political triggers for the most recent round of Arab uprisings (Johnstone and Mazo 2011; Campante and Chor 2012; Kuhn 2012; Diwan 2013; Moore 2013; Joffé 2011; Ansani and Daniele 2012). Regardless of the considerable academic scholarship now devoted to deepening our understanding of these various catalysts, many mainstream media and popular analysis remain fixated on the role of 'sectarianism' in and of itself as generative or restrictive of political transformations in South West Asia and North Africa. This essentialist narrative has stultified much work on the Levant (Chit 2014). However, in the Syrian case, some scholars have instead described the multiple interweaving factors influencing the outbreak of this particular uprising (De Châtel 2014; Gleick 2014; Goulden 2011; de Elvira and Zintl 2014).

The Syria scholar, Raymond Hinnebusch, for example, has focused on what he calls 'authoritarian upgrading.' 'Upgrading' here refers to the process by which the al-Asad regime, through a combination of internal and external pressures, was forced to liberalise its economy and integrate itself into the world market. Throughout this integration, the regime maintained an anti-imperialist posture while keeping in place the repressive state apparatus (Hinnebusch 2012). It is evident that rural Syria was particularly hard hit by this 'upgrading'. What these reforms ended up doing was devastating social reproduction for rural Syrian citizens. Economic neglect and de-development turned out to be politically suicidal given that Syria's rural hinterlands and their agricultural towns and cities constitute the historical base of the Ba'th party's core (Kila 2013; Hinnebusch 2012; Perthes 2014).

It is not by coincidence that the Syrian countryside formed the area in which anti-government protests first flared and where at a later stage jihadi organisations could secure a ready recruiting pool of young volunteers composed of poor, out-of-work men. Places like Dara'a in Syria's fertile Hauran, for example, had previously benefited greatly from state assistance in agriculture, price-capping, and investment in irrigation systems, but in recent years the fallāḥīn [land workers] found life increasingly difficult (Hamade 2014).[12]

Between 2000 and 2010, the proportion of the Syrian population directly employed in agriculture declined from more than 33 per cent to 10 per cent; yet before the uprising an estimated 46 per cent of Syrians lived in rural areas, indicating a high degree of rural unemployment and underemployment (ibid.). This shock could, for some years, be warded off through the long-standing links between migration and remittance flows that many villages have maintained through work in Lebanon, Jordan, and the Gulf. However, from the 1990s onwards, these flows began to transform, no longer a source of 'cash injection,' and migration to urban centres became increasingly economically essential (Azmeh 2014).

These objective economic conditions are revealed in a context that gave rise, in part, to the pressures Abdullah faced in selling his labour for survival wages. These conditions led to the impossibility of relying on his family's land and his father's vegetable shop back home. Together this meant that his migration, his brothers, and the migration of many described below were part and parcel of a general trend of urbanisation. The Syrian countryside was thus increasingly stripped of its capacity to provide for the reproduction of human life. The fact that the fallāḥīn, as well as rural-urban workers, were often the first to rebel against these processes of dispossession should come, consequently, as little surprise (cf. Scott 1976).

A glimmer of revolution was thus able to find an appeal amongst rural young men, increasingly unable to generate enough money to fulfil a vast array of socio-culturally valued life roles. The denial of reforming these roles is key in the sense that individuals do not commit to political causes only through an act of sheer politico-economic calculation, but also because of the manner in which broader politico-economic conditions of exploitation intertwine with culturally defined principles and practices of daily life.

It is not for nothing that the most commonly cited example of accelerating prices amongst my network of informants was the bag of sugar. Consider, for example, the role of sugar in drinking sweet black tea. The exchange of tea is, as anyone who has visited Syria will attest, an essential component of hospitality such that to make sweet tea unaffordable is to deny a fundamental part of what it means to be a Syrian. It is possible certainly to take this observation a step further given that, for example, traditions of hospitality are not themselves isolated from other existing social relations of exploitation. Hospitality to guests is often only made possible thanks to the extraction of women's labour—either directly in the (male) host's household or through (female) wage labour on plantations elsewhere. But here my point is simply that the emergence of revolutionary subjectivity is always connected to a whole web of socio-cultural value denials. From this analytic perspective, determining economic triggers need not imply economic determinism, for there is no such thing as a bread riot.

But, faced with the absence of any serious alternative organisational and ideological force outside of the Islamism-liberalism nexus, those initial moments of populist antagonism, and any hint for alternative socio-economic structures which these antagonisms could have engendered, were always already ripe for subversion.

Conclusion: Labour Migration Pattern—From Consent to Coercion?

Before the intensification of the Syrian conflict, there existed a clear pattern of migration and return. Men undertook largely seasonal work and extended labour. There was little sign of permanent settlement and few signs of second-generation Syrian workers making good in Lebanon.

This pattern is specifically the phenomenon that the political sociologist, John Chalcraft, in his book *The Invisible Cage: Syrian Migrant Workers in Lebanon* (2009) set out to explain. His argument, drawing heavily on Gramsci, revolves around 'hegemonic incorporation.' This arrangement sees Syrian workers embedded "[…] within objectifying structures of accumulation by combinations of coercion and consent, repression, and choice" (ibid.: 3). The pattern of migration and return is not entirely determined by structural factors, notably the economic decline in rural areas, nor by the sheer agency of the migrant, who seeks fortunes abroad, but by multiple forms of agency and control. For Chalcraft, the subjectivity of the migrant is not wholly determined by structure, but those structures are still reinforced through everyday decisions.

What Abdullah's case suggests is that this interpretation of Syrian migrant labour flows has reached its limit. In the face of the war and economic disintegration of his homeland, whatever 'agency' Abdullah might once have enjoyed over his working life and his future has collapsed and is now wholly insignificant. Moreover, the pattern of travel and return was unravelling even before the uprising's initial outbreak thanks to the above outlined series of (intensified) liberalising economic reforms implemented in Syria since the mid-2000s.

The Lebanese state is also aware that it faces the possibility of more permanent settlement and has, since 2014, intensified the barrier (Janmyr 2016). Indeed, the extension and continuation of Syria's destruction have coincided with a whole host of legislative limitations that now severely inhibit the lives of Syrian labourers in Lebanon, producing in their wake immiserating conditions that risk handing more workers over to the likes of ISIS, or, otherwise, the smuggler's boat.

On 31 December 2014, the General Security Directorate of Lebanon issued a decree that stipulated that the entrance and residency of Syrians in Lebanon now fall under the discretion of both the Directorate and the Ministry of Social Affairs (Shoufi 2015). This ruling effectively nullified the long-standing free movement agreement that had existed between Beirut and Damascus. According to section 7 of the decree, Syrian nationals will only be permitted entrance into Lebanon if their purpose is "tourism, business visit, shopping, owner of real estate or tenant in Lebanon, study, transit, medical treatment or a visa application at a foreign embassy." Workers must obtain a permit from their employer as well as a letter of sponsorship from a Lebanese citizen. Employers must also pay a fee for every Syrian they hire, and all documents must be signed by a public notary. In sum, this marks the first time the *kafala* system has been extended to Syrian workers in Lebanon (Harbi 2014).[13]

A real-world warning regarding the Byzantine levels of bureaucracy that this new decree requires came when, just after the law was passed, Khaled, a 40-year-old gypsum board specialist I know who comes from one of Abdullah's neighbouring villages, was denied re-entry upon his return from Syria. Khaled had, several months earlier, hoped to re-start his family's farm. He was fed up with working in Beirut and wanted to return to his family, regardless of the difficulties that might entail. However, upon finding it was near impossible to make this desire a reality, he was compelled to return, only to discover on the border a newly required vast array of paperwork, passports, and letters needed to secure re-entry. In total, it took two months and much effort before he was back to Beirut.

The Lebanese government claims that these laws are designed to "protect Lebanese jobs" (Shoufi 2015). When arrangements were first announced, they were almost immediately opposed by Lebanon's major contracting and construction companies. Their main objection was that these laws risked interrupting their ready supply of cheap Syrian labour. This labour was cheap because it was foreign—aside from Palestinians, unskilled manual labour has almost always been entirely Syrian. These are not 'Lebanese jobs' but jobs for Syrians in Lebanon (Chalcraft 2009).

The Lebanese Contractors Syndicate of Public Work and Building estimated that, in 2014, 350,000 Syrians workers were distributed amongst 3400 companies (Shoufi 2015). The value of their represented companies is over $10 billion. According to the head of the syndicate, the cost of sponsoring a Syrian worker is around $2000 annually [and that's including health insurance, residence and work permits and notary contracts]. Whereas, he estimates the average wage for a labourer is $20 a day and

$30 a day for a foreperson. Among my primary research participants, the average monthly income was around $400–450. However, the International Labour Organisation estimates the situation is even worse, with the average Syrian wage in Lebanon coming in at $287 per month for men, which is 40 per cent less than the already largely notional national minimum wage of $448 per month. The Lebanese Minister of Labour recognised that these protestations were really about multi-million dollar businesses objecting to spending what amounted to only a small degree of their profit on legalising the status of their employees. The primary benefactor of the flow of workers into Lebanon remains, then, a small cluster of the elites.

Instead of 'protecting jobs,' the real effect of the *kafala* system is more accurately framed, perhaps, as monitoring and controlling the Syrian population and some sort of desire to decrease the likelihood of permanent settlement. This fact was close to being explicitly acknowledged when the Lebanese Minister for Social Affairs, Rachid Derbas, who, in response to the British Embassy's call that the labour laws be relaxed, replied: "…Lebanon is not a warehouse for people" (Issa 2015). However, in the same interview, he then went on to repeat the line that "changing the law is not possible, and it may not even be appropriate considering the high rate of Lebanese unemployment." Given that companies appear unwilling to sign the 'pledge of responsibility' and prepare permits for their staff, the result of the *kafala* system has been to suddenly transform sections of the Syrian population in Lebanon into highly precarious illegal workers, even more ripe for exploitation. Indeed, before the implementation of the law, nine per cent of Syrians were estimated to be illegally resident; by June 2014 some NGO estimated that figure to have hit 70 per cent (Janmyr 2016).

At the time of the decree's implementation, the warehousing company then employing Abdullah refused to sponsor its workers. Many of the Syrian labourers I know, especially those who live in areas popular with workers, now report the proliferation of private offices that offer to carry out labour sponsorship for Syrians but at the seemingly exorbitant fee of $600 (plus $200 processing). The costs of residence for an individual could potentially reach $1200. It appears, then, that the decree is also functioning to enable additional value grabs from the worker's pocket.

To draw this outline to a (temporary) conclusion: any element of consent that remained within the labour migration patterns has eroded, and it has eroded to the point that one of the few spaces remaining for 'choice' is whether Abdullah boards an illegal and dangerous boat to Europe or continues suffering in Lebanon. Syrian workers in Lebanon are caught tragically between physical violence at home and structural violence in Lebanon.

In one of our most recent conversations, my friend told me that he thankfully found a new job in construction, but that even here he cannot escape the call to board a boat: it is all his fellow workers talk about. The men are apparently not deterred by deaths and sea, nor the closing down of borders. I was not surprised to learn this, for how exactly can anyone return to Syria if their homes are destroyed, and economic life is disintegrated? But how can they remain in Lebanon if every day is marred by the fear arrest, deportation, and poverty?

Notes

1. The Lebanese University is the country's only public university. Syrians who enrol pay significantly lower fees than at the American University of Beirut (AUB) or the Lebanese American University of Beirut (LAU). At the faculty of Social Science, the enrolment fee is $700. While education would be cheaper still in the state-funded Damascus University, even before the uprising, men made the decision to study in Lebanon instead. This was because they saw a chance for (1) a better education and (2) the possibility of working alongside their study and generating savings that could then be re-invested in housing, marriages, business, and the like back in Syria.
2. The words used to describe events in Syria require careful elaboration. This elaboration develops throughout the text, but for now let me note that terms like 'revolution,' 'uprising,' 'civil war,' and 'proxy war' all contain partisan webs of association dividing those who align themselves with the al-Asad government or with the opposition.

   Analytically, I follow Thomassen's (2012) definition of political revolution as that which not only involves the *overthrow of the regime* but entails a popular movement of mass participation. Without mass participation, a drastic political change is less a revolution and more a coup d'etat. On an analytic level, given the high degree of splintering witnessed within the Syrian opposition, it seems accurate to refer to the first stages, from 2011 to 2012 as an 'uprising' before then transitioning into a *simultaneously* civil and proxy war. Civil because the conflict—despite the high presence of foreign forces—involved Syrians fighting Syrians but proxy given that this fighting is now also sustained by a high degree of imperialist and geopolitical interests.

Ethnographically the men in my research—who were all aligned with the opposition—understood the protests, armed uprising and (elements) of the war to be still part of a broader revolutionary process. The term they used was always thawra [revolution] and never intifada [uprising]. With the growth of internal opposition fighting, the entrance of the Islamic State, and the complete degradation of social and economic life, the term 'ḥarb ahlī-ya' [civil war] increased slightly in usage, but it was still not dominant in comparison to thawra.

For clarity's sake, when writing in a more analytic frame, I use the words 'uprising' and 'proxy war,' but when discussing the actions and ideas of informants, I use the term 'revolution'.

3. See Proudfoot (2017) on the use of awakening language in Syrian worker uprising narratives.
4. As a concept 'revolutionary subjectivity' is closely related to the Marxist notion of 'class consciousness', but differs in the sense that it describes more general *revolutionary dispositions* rather than merely 'class awareness' and acting in 'class interests.' Moreover, otherwise materially opposed groupings might share in these similar revolutionary dispositions (i.e. 'solidarity'), therefore 'revolutionary subjectivity' can spread through the traditional proletariat but can also be found amongst the *fallāḥīn* [land workers], rural-urban migrants, students, and intellectuals.
5. WhatsApp messenger became increasingly popular in Lebanon only after the more widespread take-up of the 3G network in 2012. The cost of sending an SMS and calling is prohibitively expensive. With WhatsApp one can send unlimited messaging and recorded audio clips provided one has a mobile device with either (1) Wi-Fi or (2) mobile internet.
6. Ḥarakat Amal is a political party typically explained to me by rebel-workers as being popular amongst Lebanon's Shia community as well as a party known for its support of the Syrian government.
7. The political division in Lebanese politics has been divided between '14 March' and '8 March' since 2005. Their dates refer to when parties within the alliances called for mass demonstrations in downtown Beirut in reaction to the assassination of the Prime Minister of Lebanon, Rafic al-Hariri, on 14 February 2005. March 8th called for a demonstration in support of al-Asad government, thanking the latter for its participation in ending the Lebanese civil war and supporting resistance movements to the Israeli occupation. The most significant membership has come from Maronite Christian-supported al-Tayyār al-Waṭanī al-Ḥurr (Free Patriotic Movement) as well as Shia-supported Hezbollah and Ḥarakat Amal. March 8th is therefore largely pro-Syrian government. March 8th are accused by their opponents of being proxies of the Iranian and Syrian governments.

March 14th is a coalition of parties composed mostly of the Sunni-supported 'tayyār al-mustaqbal' as well as the Maronite Christian, al-quwwāt al-lubnāniyya' and 'al-Katā'ib al-lubnāniyya.' They organised demonstrations against the al-Asad government, are anti-Syrian, and are accused by their opponents of being proxies funded by Saudi Arabia and guided by the United States.
8. The southern suburbs of Beirut and an area physically controlled by and understood to support Amal, Hezbollah, and the al-Asad government. This area also has a large stock of affordable housing and is therefore popular amongst Beirut's worker population, especially in the areas in, and directly surrounding the Palestinian camps.
9. The organisation was formally known as ISIS, the Islamic State in Iraq and Syria, or—ad-Dawla al-'Islāmiyyah fi Iraq wa ash-sham. This old name remains the source of the organisation's acronym in Arabic—'Da'ish' which continues to find in popular usage, though mostly amongst those who object to its existence. Indeed, Islamic State discourages its usage and has reportedly carried out corporal punishment against those found uttering it. Nonetheless, it is the term the individuals discussed in this paper use, and it will be deployed interchangeably with Islamic State, which also is often used clipped in the Arabic to 'Dawla' [State].
10. On 23 January 2012, Nuṣrah declared its formation with a video posted online. The group claimed responsibility for many of the suicide bombing operations during the early phases of the uprising as well as a number of strategic guerrilla attacks. Western governments including the United States and the United Kingdom have blacklisted *Nuṣrah* as a terrorist organisation due to its links with al-Qaida. In areas that fell under its control, such as districts in Aleppo, it seized bakeries and controls the distribution of food. It has also seen the implementation of Shari'a courts. During the uprising's opening stages, the Free Syrian Army lost a good number of recruits to Nuṣrah due to its reputation as a highly disciplined, well-financed, and powerful fighting force (Casey-Maslen 2014).
11. The arguments developed in this section of the paper are drawn from and further developed in my article, 'The Smell of Blood' (Proudfoot 2017). They are also further centralised in my book, *Revolution and Loss* (currently under editorial review).
12. The term 'fallāḥīn' [singular: fallah] is often directly translated to the English 'peasant.' This is, however, not quite accurate given that a 'peasant' generally implies that the worker does not own the land. In the Middle East, by contrast, sometimes the term is used for landless land workers, but it can also be applied to those who simultaneously own and work the land. For this reason, the more generic term 'land worker' is perhaps a more appropriate translation (Abufarha 2009: 29).

13. The *kafala* system is a labour sponsorship arrangement in which a citizen or a business pledges responsibilities for the migrant's legal and visa status. The system has been widely condemned by international organisations for generating a system where the employer or citizen is able to confiscate the migrant's passport and abuse their sponsees, who have little opportunity to pursue legal repercussions.

Bibliography

Abufarha, N. (2009). *The Making of a Human Bomb: An Ethnography of Palestinian Resistance*. Durham, NC: Duke University Press.

Amnesty. (2015). *Lebanon: New Entry Requirements for Syrians Likely to Block Would-Be Refugees*. Retrieved from https://www.amnesty.org/en/documents/document/?indexNumber=mde24%2F002%2F2015&language=en

Ansani, A., & Daniele, V. (2012). About a Revolution: The Economic Motivations of the Arab Spring. *International Journal of Development and Conflict, 2*(03), 1250013.

Azmeh, S. (2014). *The Uprising of the Marginalised: A Socio-Economic Perspective of the Syrian Uprising*. LSE Middle East Centre Paper Series, 06.

Campante, F. R., & Chor, D. (2012). Why Was the Arab World Poised for Revolution? Schooling, Economic Opportunities, and the Arab Spring. *The Journal of Economic Perspectives, 26*(2), 167–187.

Casey-Maslen, S. (2014). *The War Report: Armed Conflict in 2013*. Oxford: Oxford University Press.

Chalcraft, J. T. (2009). *The Invisible Cage: Syrian Migrant Workers in Lebanon*. Stanford, CA: Stanford General.

Chit, B. (2014). Sectarianism and the Arab Revolutions. *Socialist Review, 388*(February).

De Châtel, F. (2014). The Role of Drought and Climate Change in the Syrian Uprising: Untangling the Triggers of the Revolution. *Middle Eastern Studies, 50*(4), 521–535.

Diwan, I. (2013). *The Political Economy of the Arab Uprisings*. Boulder: Westview Press.

de Elvira, L. R., & Zintl, T. (2014). The End of the Baʿthist Social Contract in Bashar Al-Asad's Syria: Reading Sociopolitical Transformations Through Charities and Broader Benevolent Activism. *International Journal of Middle East Studies, 46*(02), 329–349.

Gleick, P. H. (2014). Water, Drought, Climate Change, and Conflict in Syria. *Weather, Climate, and Society, 6*(3), 331–340.

Goulden, R. (2011). Housing, Inequality, and Economic Change in Syria. *British Journal of Middle Eastern Studies, 38*(2), 187–202.

Hamade, K. (2014). *Lebanese and Syrian Agriculture and Rural Areas: What's After the Crisis?* Paper presented at the Lebanese Economic Association and Friedrich Naumann Foundation conference Beirut Crown Plaza Hotel.

Harbi, R. (2014). Push Back against Lebanon's Kafala System Gains Traction. *al-Akhbar*. Retrieved February 18, 2016, from http://english.al-akhbar.com/node/21806

Harvey, D. (2005). *The New Imperialism*. Oxford: Oxford University Press.

Hinnebusch, R. (2012). Syria: From 'Authoritarian Upgrading' to Revolution? *International Affairs*, *88*(1), 95–113. https://doi.org/10.1111/j.1468-2346.2012.01059.

Homsi, A. (2015). Idlib: Kaīfa Saqaṭat Al-Masīna Bīad Tanẓīm Al-Qāʿda. *al-Akhbar*. Retrieved February 18, 2016, from http://www.al-akhbar.com/node/229998

Issa, P. (2015). Taking the Beirut-to-Raqqa Bus. *The Daily Start*. Retrieved February 18, 2016, from http://www.dailystar.com.lb/News/Lebanon-News/2015/Oct-10/318372-taking-the-beirut-to-raqqa-bus.ashx

Janmyr, M. (2016). *The Legal Status of Syrian Refugees in Lebanon*. Working Paper. Beirut: IFI & AUB.

Joffé, G. (2011). The Arab Spring in North Africa: Origins and Prospects. *The Journal of North African Studies*, *16*(4), 507–532.

Johnstone, S., & Mazo, J. (2011). Global Warming and the Arab Spring. *Survival*, *53*(2), 11–17.

Kadri, A. (2016). *The Unmaking of Arab Socialism*. London: Anthem Press.

Kila, S. (2013). *Al-Thawra Al-Suriyya*. Beirut: Atlas Beirut.

Kraidy, M. M. (2016). *The Naked Blogger of Cairo: Creative Insurgency in the Arab World*. Cambridge: Harvard University Press.

Kuhn, R. (2012). On the Role of Human Development in the Arab Spring. *Population and Development Review*, *38*, 649–683.

Marx, K. (2008). *The Poverty of Philosophy*. New York: Cosimo, Inc.

Marx, K., & Engels, F. (1990). *Karl Marx, Frederick Engels: Collected Works* (Vol. 32). London: International Publishers.

Matar, L. (2012). The Socioeconomic Roots of the Syrian Uprising. *Middle East Institute Insight*, *58*(27 March).

Moore, P. (2013). The Bread Revolutions of 2011: Teaching Political Economies of the Middle East. *PS: Political Science & Politics*, *46*(02), 225–229.

O'Brian, M. (2013). What Syria Teaches Us About Hyperinflation *The Atlantic*. Retrieved August 19, 2016, from http://www.theatlantic.com/business/archive/2013/08/what-syria-teaches-us-about-hyperinflation/279184/

Perthes, V. (2014). *Syria Under Bashar Al-Asad: Modernisation and the Limits of Change*. London: Routledge.

Proudfoot, P. (2016). *The Living Dead: Revolutionary Subjectivity and Syrian Rebel-Workers in Beirut*. PhD thesis, The London School of Economics and Political Science (LSE).

Proudfoot, P. (2017). The Smell of Blood: Accumulation by Dispossession, Resistance and the Language of Populist Uprising in Syria. *City*, 1–20 (published online on 12 June 2017).

Scott, J. C. (1976). *The Moral Economy of the Peasant: Subsistence and Rebellion in Southeast Asia*. New Haven: Yale University Press.

Shoufi, E. (2015). A New Face for the Exploitation of Syrian Workers in Lebanon? *al-Akhbar*. Retrieved February 18, 2016, from http://english.al-akhbar.com/node/23883

The Syrian Observer. (2015). *Unpaid Dowry En Vogue in Syria's Besieged Areas*. Retrieved February 18, 2016, from http://syrianobserver.com/EN/Features/30224/Unpaid:Dowry_Vogue_Syria_Besieged_Areas

Thomassen, B. (2012). Notes Towards an Anthropology of Political Revolutions. *Comparative Studies in Society and History*, 54(03), 679–706.

Yassin-Kassab, R., & Al-Shami, L. (2016). *Burning Country: Syrians in Revolution and War*. London: Pluto Press.

PART III

The Politics of the Syrian Conflict

CHAPTER 8

Syria in the 'Resistance Front': Persistence Through Reconfiguration?

Aurora Sottimano

INTRODUCTION

The alliance between Syria and Iran, and the formation of the so-called axis of resistance, is one of the most fascinating and enduring examples of a regional alliance. It is a key pillar of Syrian foreign policy and a determining factor in the trajectory of the Syrian conflict.[1] To understand why secular Syria, the beating heart of Arabism, chose to align its foreign policy with the revolutionary Islamic Republic, we have to look back at the transformation in Syrian politics under Hafez al-Asad, when Syria was in the process of establishing its prowess in a turbulent region (as part of its strategy to confront the Israeli permanent aggression) and simultaneously confronting the unfolding of a domestic rebellion.

Formed in 1980 as a response to the direct challenges posed to Syria and Iran by Iraq, Israel, and the US, Syria's alliance with the Islamic Republic and later its protégée Hezbollah boosted Syria's regional position and contributed to its successful 'balancing' with international and regional powers. Concurrently, Syria continued to act as a swing state between Arab regional powers (Saudi Arabia, Egypt, and Iraq) in order to consolidate an Arab front[2] against the Zionist enemy. The alliance with Iran also served to legitimise the al-Asad government, domestically. Under

A. Sottimano (✉)
Leiden University, Leiden, The Netherlands

Bashar al-Asad, Syria embraced the 'resistance front' (*jabhat al-muqawama*) as a continuation of Hafez's domestic policy of *sumud* ('steadfastness'), with a renewed anti-imperialist stance against regional (Israel) and international (US) interference. This stance has been a key element of Syria's regional strategy and authoritarian upgrading.[3]

Since Syria is situated at the heart of a region traditionally penetrated by international powers and ravaged by armed conflicts, it comes as no surprise that the foreign policy of independent Syria often took priority over domestic concerns. This chapter does not rule out the power of systemic explanations: Syrian and Iranian behaviours have been in great part shaped by the exceptionally unstable regional arena within which these states operate, magnified by the context of a bipolar world and its demise. Syrian leaders have crafted foreign policy as a balancing strategy between rivals and enemies, centred on the regional role of Syria as champion of the Arab cause.[4] Regional power balancing and the survival of al-Asad regime required powerful regional friends like Iran and Hezbollah acting as deterrents, superpowers as international supporters, and Gulf monarchies as rich donors.

At a time when nationalist struggle, state building, and power consolidation coincided, Hafez al-Asad's balancing policies successfully addressed the contradiction between the revisionism rooted in the Pan-Arab identity of Syria—the liberation of Palestine and the unification of the Arab umma—and geopolitical realities, the division of the Arab front and the shift from a bipolar to a unipolar world, while consolidating the regime.[5] In the new regional and local context in which Bashar al-Asad operated in his first ten years in office—one in which Pan-Arabism was dead, non-state actors like Hezbollah emerged as powerful political agents, and a growing opposition of the disillusioned, embittered masses that directly challenged Arab autocrats—the al-Asad government confronted an ever-increasing need to sustain its internal support while facing its inability to either live up to its own legitimation claims or reform.

The onset of the Arab Spring has revealed a variety of complexities in the front. In this chapter, I argue that Syria's resistance discourse has shaped the Syrian foreign and domestic policies as well as the trajectory of the Syrian uprising in a decisive way. The al-Asad government and its allies have linked the repression of the uprising to their counter-hegemonic discourse: this strategy has allowed Syrian authorities to legitimise their use of a range of repressive measures against rebels, while Hezbollah gained greater strategic depth and Iran reinstated its 'regional alignment' strategy and influence. The adoption of the Western 'War on Terror' narrative marked a re-articulation of the Syrian nationalist discourse and foreign policy and the transformation of the 'resistance front' into a transnational counterinsurgency coalition. These developments demand a review of the ideological assumptions, capabilities, and persistence of the 'resistance front' while reassessing the connection between Syrian domestic and foreign policy.

Syria's 'Strategic Balance' with Israel

It is common wisdom that foreign policy imperatives dominated the policies of Hafez al-Asad. In search for a strategy to recover the Syrian Golan Heights, occupied by Israel during the 1967 war, as well as to reach a comprehensive settlement of the Palestine question—the twin goals of his foreign policy—Hafez al-Asad opted for functional cooperation with the existing Arab states which 'are with us in the struggle'.[6] Syria embarked in a 'double battle for development and liberation', which required an unconditional effort by all national forces for 'Syria's destiny'.[7] Syria's mission was to show 'steadfastness' in the face of Israel's military threat and the enemy's 'perpetual aggression'.[8]

After the 1979 Camp David Accords, which marked the end of the trilateral axis Damascus-Riyadh-Cairo and destroyed the Arab regional order of the 1970s, Syria embarked on a unilateral move to achieve a 'strategic balance' with Israel, which would enable it to withstand aggression and to negotiate a just settlement from a position of strength. Successful 'strategic balance' required the diversification of regional alliances and a shift from conventional warfare, which had been largely unsuccessful to the attainment of Syria's stated objectives (the recovery of the occupied Golan Heights and the liberation of Palestine) buttressed by Soviet support. Under the banner of Arabism, al-Asad defined the core component of his regional policy as mobilisation of all Arab resources for Syria's 'confrontational' mission.[9]

A string of momentous regional events followed the Camp David Accords and influenced the Syrian quest for strategic parity: the 1979 Iranian Revolution, the Iraq-Iran War, and the internationalisation of the Lebanese Civil War all contributed to the emergence of Syria as the leader of the camp opposed to Western influence in the region. al-Asad hailed the overthrow of Iran's conservative, pro-Western monarchy in 1979, which snapped the Tehran-Tel Aviv axis against Arab nationalism, as 'a huge gain for the Arabs'.[10] The birth of the Islamic Republic opened up new possibilities for Syria to establish its regional prowess by forging a defensive alliance with the new Iran, and with Hezbollah in the 1980s. The goal of this alliance was to build a credible deterrent posture, oppose common enemies—Israel, the Ba'athist government in Baghdad, and Arafat's Palestine Liberation Organisation whose strategy for a unified Palestine ran counter to Syria's bid for regional hegemony—while supporting common interests in Lebanon and against the US, and—for Syria—gaining leverage in its negotiations with Israel.[11]

Both partners provided invaluable support to one another in two consecutive crises: the Iran-Iraq War (1980–1988) and the 1982 Israeli invasion of Lebanon. Besides allowing the use of Syrian air bases, Syrian support for the Khomeini government prevented the creation of a united Arab front against Iran and helped al-Asad to undermine the rival Ba'athist government of Saddam Hussein. The Israeli invasion of Lebanon in June 1982 provided Syria and Iran with a new theatre for cooperation against their mutual foes. Between 1982 and 1985, Iran and Syria mobilised Lebanon's Shi'ites and waged an effective unconventional war that eventually drove out Israeli and Western forces from Syria's backyard. By establishing Hezbollah in 1982, the Islamic Republic opened a new Islamist front against Israel.[12] After a number of clashes in the early 1980s, Syria found in Hezbollah a militant proxy strong enough to ensure that Lebanon was unable to conclude a peace deal with Israel on its own.

The three years from 1982 to 1985 represented the height of Syrian reliance on Iran to undo the achievements of its enemies in Lebanon (the 17 May 1983 Israeli-Lebanese agreement, annulled in 1984, following the withdrawal of American troops) and to make a comeback in regional affairs as the most important player in Lebanese politics. Syria also managed to extract tangible economic benefits from Iran. In exchange for its assistance in stemming the Iraqi invasion, the Iranian authorities supplied Syria with cheap oil, and in 1982 the two countries signed a treaty of economic cooperation.[13] The 1989 Taif Accord, by which Syria was given tutelage over Lebanon, marked a triumph for al-Asad's regional and international balancing policy: the 'Syrian peace' in Lebanon was supported by Saudi Arabia and accepted by the US as a better alternative to anarchy.

Hafez al-Asad's Regional and International Balancing Strategy

The collapse of the Soviet Union prompted a revision of Syrian foreign policy to adapt to a unipolar world order. Saddam Hussein's invasion of Kuwait in 1990 gave Syrian leaders a chance to demonstrate to the US that Syria could advance American objectives in the region and provoked a storm in regional relations. To the Syrian (and Arab) public, who watched with astonishment as Syria, the proud beating heart of Arabism supported the US-led coalition to oust Iraqi forces from Kuwait,[14] al-Asad explained that Baghdad's aggression merely wasted Arab capabilities and resources in the struggle against Israel. He insisted that Syria was merely required to defend Saudi Arabia's international borders by the mandate of the Arab League: Syria's nationalist identity was not in question, nor was its alliance with Iran, which also condemned Iraq's aggression.

The main objective of Syrian foreign policy at this time was not to collude with the policies and interests of a pro-Western axis but rather to rehabilitate the Syrian-Saudi-Egyptian axis.[15] Syria's involvement in the Kuwait crisis and in US-brokered peace talks with Israel, its unchallenged control over Lebanon, its repositioning as a central actor in revitalised Damascus-Riyadh-Cairo axis, and its rehabilitation in the international community—all this was achieved without abandoning its alignment with both Iran and Hezbollah. Additionally, Syria and Iran signed a strategic accord in September 1991 and strengthened their alignment in response to the US policy of 'double containment' (designed simultaneously to isolate Iraq and Iran) and the Israeli security alliance with Turkey in 1996.[16]

Throughout the 1990s, while Hezbollah's military successes (e.g. in 1993 and 1996) raised its value as a card in peace negotiations and as a deterrent against Israel, al-Asad kept a close watch on Hezbollah's autonomy, which threatened to provoke Israeli retaliations against Syrian positions. By doing so, he demonstrated his investment in peace negotiations with Israel and his interest in controlling Lebanon rather than in supporting Hezbollah's agenda.[17] At the same time, closer relations with Hezbollah helped to improve relations with Iran. Thus, during this period, Syria was able to act as an intermediary between Tehran and Arab countries and a mediator between the West and Iran (e.g. during the hostage negotiations and the 'tanker war' in the Gulf waters during the 1980s).[18] In hindsight, two relations did not change over the three decades of Hafez's rule: the 'special relationship' with Iran and the antagonistic posture vis-à-vis Israel. The former was a key part of Hafez's deterrence strategy guaranteeing a regional balance of power and Syria's national interests, whilst the latter was a pillar of Syria's political culture: both were crucial to the survival of Hafez al-Asad's government.

Internationally, al-Asad's cooperation with the West—exemplified by Syrian participation in the 1991 US-led Gulf War coalition and the Madrid peace conference which developed from it and peace negotiations with Israel—ended in 2000 with the failure of peace negotiations with Israel and the US becoming an explicit threat to Syria.

Hafez al-Asad's Balancing of Domestic Threats

While Syria's ability to mobilise the symbols of Arabism gave al-Asad leverage over Iran, the Islamic Republic's religious authority made of Iran an indispensable ally during times of deep domestic crisis in Syria. From the very beginning of his rule, when al-Asad needed religious legitimacy as president of Syria, the Iranian-Lebanese cleric Musa al-Sadr affirmed the religious credibility of the al-Asad government with a *fatwa* which recognised the Alawi sect as a branch of Shi'ism.[19]

The support of Islamic authorities for the Syrian government became particularly important in the late 1970s, when al-Asad faced the major domestic challenge of an insurrection led by a radical faction of the Muslim Brotherhood. Syrian Islamic groups were outraged by Syria's involvement in negotiations with Israel, Syrian support for the Maronites in Lebanon against the Palestinians, and their exclusion from the government. The Syrian *Ikhwan* greeted the Iranian Revolution in 1979,[20] but the Iranian authorities ignored their appeal for support and publicly condoned al-Asad's violent suppression of the Hama revolt in February 1982. Iranian leaders maintained that, by forging close links with Jordan and Iraq while fighting the Syrian government that stood against Zionism—the common enemy of Islam—the Syrian *Ikhwan* had become a 'stooge of the West'.[21] In March 1982, a month after the Hama massacre, Iran and Syria signed a ten-year economic agreement and Asad agreed to cut off the Kirkuk oil pipeline to Banias, significantly damaging Iraq's ability to finance its war effort.

The relationship between the Hama massacre and al-Asad's decision to move closer to Iran is 'unmistakable'.[22] After 1982, the manipulation of religion remained an important element of Hafez's strategy to consolidate his religious and political power base, as shown by the development of Shi'a institutions in Syria, while the al-Asad government also forged links with foreign Sunni Islamist forces such as Hamas, Islamic Jihad, and the Jordanian Ikhwan.[23]

As mentioned earlier, the regional stance taken by the Syrian government was also a key element of its claim to legitimacy and its domestic security. Syria's alignment with Iran—one of the region's stronger powers and the only counterweight to Israel after Camp David—strengthened its 'confrontational' stand vis-à-vis Israel, rallying public opinion around the Syrian president and justifying the imposition of a strong security state and tight domestic control, which in turn ensured the survival of the al-Asad government.[24] Al-Asad himself recognised that losing domestic support over Syria's nationalist identity would be political suicide.[25] Similarly, Syria's alignment with Hezbollah also served to revive its 'steadfastness' message of nationalist defiance and regain popularity among the Syrian public, who had perceived Syrian military activities in Lebanon as directed against Palestinians.[26]

The focus on Lebanon's importance to Syria for political and military reasons tends to overshadow the domestic policy aspects of the Syria-Lebanese relations. After the Taif Accord, the Syrian *de facto* protectorate over Lebanon allowed Hafez al-Asad to play on two levels: the resistance to Israel and the lucrative reconstruction process led by Prime Minister Rafiq al-Hariri, thus awarding al-Hariri's political patron—Saudi Arabia—a stake in stabilising the country and also extracting profits for the Syrian elite.[27]

Yet the Syrian management of Lebanon was soon defined by another priority: following the death of Hafez's eldest son Basil in a car accident in 1994, the question of succession of the heir apparent, Bashar, dominated Syrian politics. The dynamic of succession required a close adherence to tested policies mobilising people's support[28] as well as the consolidation of a team of loyal supporters against a Sunni old guard, which Bashar perceived was resisting his rise. Thus, from the mid-1990s, the reconstruction agenda and the resistance strategy in Lebanon became part of a Syrian domestic power struggle between different wings of the al-Asad regime.[29] On taking responsibility for the Lebanon file from Vice President Abdel Halim Khaddam in 1998, Bashar aligned closely to Hezbollah, a process that continued during his rule.

Succession and Foreign Policy Under Bashar al-Asad

On taking power in July 2000, Bashar inherited from his father an experienced foreign policy team, including Farouk al-Sharaa, Foreign Minister from 1984 until 2006 and later Vice President in charge of foreign affairs, and Abdel Halim Khaddam, Vice President from 1984 to 2005, who ensured broad continuity in foreign policy orientation. A fierce nationalist political discourse remained the most important political tool for simultaneously defending geopolitical interests, governing regional relations, and legitimising domestic control. Yet Bashar's rise to power came at a time when Syria faced a series of regional challenges that pushed him to cross established thresholds.

First, the Israeli unilateral withdrawal from southern Lebanon in May 2000 brought Syria's role in the country into focus. Second, the failure of the Syrian-Israeli peace process and the military approach taken by the Bush administration after the 11 September 2001 attacks in the US interrupted the American-Syrian engagement and spelled the end of the tacit acceptance of Syria's regional stabilising role. But it was the 2003 Iraq War and its repercussions that redesigned the geopolitics of the region and complicated Bashar's efforts to consolidate his power. The two decade-old Syrian game of cautious balancing began to falter when Bashar took an opposing stance on the Iraq War in open conflict with the US, supported the Iraqi resistance by allowing movement of jihadist fighters to combat the US occupation in Iraq, and depicted his government as a bulwark of order against the chaos and sectarian conflict in Iraq.

Bashar's harsh ideological positioning against the Iraq War has often been criticised for leaving little room for the backstage diplomacy in which al-Asad senior excelled.[30] Far from an irrational defiance of US hegemony, Bashar's stance responded to both geopolitical and domestic security considerations. The fear that Syria might be next in line for US-led regime change and the prospect of being physically surrounded by enemies were the main regional determinants of Bashar's decision to oppose the war. The Syrian way to balance US threats was to raise the cost of any US attempt to implement further regime change and to strengthen its ties with Iran. In keeping the US embroiled in Iraq, Damascus and Tehran sought to pre-empt an offensive against themselves and to defend their interests in Iraq and the Levant. Moreover, the Syrian government successfully oriented Islamist activism towards targets associated with US imperialism and away from Syrian domestic issues.[31]

The real challenge for the young Syrian president was to balance Syria's position in an increasingly hostile environment without jeopardising his hold on power. As the implementation of promised economic reform—after riskier political and administration reforms were discarded—was opening new avenues for corruption rather than ensuring the announced transition to a 'social market economy', the Syrian authorities could not risk further to alienate public opinion and face a domestic constituency that identified strongly with the Iraqi insurgency.[32] Hence the vernacular of nationalism and solidarity against US imperialism swiftly replaced the debate over domestic reform. By championing the anti-imperialist position and giving asylum to a million Iraqi refugees, the Syrian president rode the antiwar sentiments of Syrian and Arab public opinion and harvested a windfall of political capital which helped him enhance his personal profile among the Syrian public, despite his failure to grant political concessions.[33] He chose to funnel this capital into support for his government which enabled him further to quell domestic dissent, overrule the more pro-Western policy advocated by powerful figures (including Abdel Halim Khaddam), and ultimately promote a concentration of power in the presidency.[34] Moreover, the display of domestic support conveyed the message that forceful regime change by foreign intervention was unacceptable to the Syrian public. Even the Syrian opposition would not accept regime change on a US tank.[35]

A Building Storm During Bashar al-Asad's Rule

In February 2005, the assassination of former Lebanese Prime Minister Rafiq al-Hariri, a powerful opponent of Syrian authority in Lebanon, marked a historical turning point in Syria's foreign relations. A wave of massive anti-Syrian demonstrations in Lebanon combined with international and regional pressure—with Saudi Arabia joining forces with France and the US—culminated in the expulsion of Syrian forces from Lebanon. Moreover, the issues of arm transfers to Hezbollah through Syrian territory, Syria's open border for Iraqi fighters, and its alliance with Iran, as well as the ongoing UN investigation into the assassination of al-Hariri—all contributed to Syria's inclusion in the 'axis of evil' as defined by US President Bush—an outcome which reversed years of cautious political balancing by al-Asad senior, who had carefully avoided a posture of open conflict with the US.[36] When the last Syrian troops left Lebanon, in April

2005, it appeared that Bashar had squandered the most important achievements of his father—control over Lebanon and the preeminent regional status of Syria—and the Syrian power system no longer controlled the external conditions of its stability.[37]

Meanwhile, a domestic storm was building up: following the defection of former Vice President Khaddam, who joined the accusation targeting the Syrian president directly of al-Hariri's murder, and the return of hundreds of thousands poor workers from Lebanon, for the first time Syrian public opinion was openly critical of the authorities' role in Lebanon, and the October 2005 'Damascus Declaration' called for peaceful regime change.[38]

Bashar used the internal fallout of the 'loss of Lebanon' crisis to crack down on internal critics of his government as accomplices of a US-promoted plot to rip the fabric of Arab societies apart, to assert control of the Ba'ath party during its June 2005 Congress, and to sideline domestic adversaries.[39] One of the major battles of 2005 was to regain Syrian public opinion: through increasingly frequent speeches, Bashar appealed to Arab, Syrian, and Islamic nationalism—a posture that strengthened the President's base of support and ultimately consolidated his hold on power in Damascus.[40]

To strengthen the political position of Syria in the region, regenerate the economy, and revive the networks of patronage damaged by Syria's retreat from Lebanon, Bashar al-Asad reshuffled Syria's foreign relations: Damascus sided with Iraq; improved relations with Turkey; shifted commercial interests towards China, Iran, and Turkey; sought to attract Arab investment inflows; and cooperated with Jordan over shared water resources. In this way, the Syrian government was also disarming an emerging Turkey-Israel-Jordan alliance which threatened further to isolate Syria, balancing Syria's growing dependence on Iran.[41] Concomitantly, a burgeoning alliance with Iran and Hezbollah allowed Syria to block the implementation of an American project aimed to install 'stability' in Iraq[42] and prompted re-engagement with Saudi Arabia. Despite Riyadh's anger over the assassination of Rafiq al-Hariri, Saudi Arabia helped Syria to patch up its relations with Lebanon and resume its role as a key intermediary between Iran and Sunni powers.[43] Bashar also opened up to Europe as both a partner in Syria's economic regeneration and a political shield against US hostility.

Syria in the 'Resistance Front'

In summer 2006, the purported 'divine victory' of Hezbollah—its ability to hold its ground although unable to thwart the extensive damage inflicted by Israel in the six-week war—stunned domestic and Arab public opinion and prompted a decisive shift in Syrian foreign policy. Against the background of the dissolution of the ever-elusive Arab solidarity, the rise of non-state actors, and the growing radicalisation of public opinion, Syria found a new centrality in regional affairs as the Arab state pillar of 'a new Middle East whose essence is resistance', which was composed of Hezbollah, Iran, and the Palestinian Hamas.[44] Like the existing Syrian-Iranian alignment, the 'resistance front' was neither a formalised military alliance nor a sectarian Shi'a coalition, but a partnership based on common enemies and a common rejection of Western hegemonic plans in the Middle East.

The 'resistance front' launched a strategic reorganisation of the regional system which gave Bashar both confidence and legitimacy. Going against decades of more prudent practice that had helped to mitigate security dilemmas, Syria allegedly started to integrate defence systems with its resistance partners.[45] The new collective logic of deterrence included Hezbollah's asymmetric guerrilla capability, Syria's arsenal of ballistic and chemically weaponised missiles, and Iran's military might—with the goals of increasing the potential costs of war to Israel and establishing 'a balance of forces that contributes to stability'.[46] After President Ahmadinejad's visit to Damascus in early 2006, Iran and Syria signed an agreement to expand military cooperation against what they called 'common threats'. Iran placed military advisors at key Syrian agencies, while Mohammad Nassif—the architect of Syria's 'Shiite' foreign policy under Hafez al-Asad—regained his key role in coordinating Syria and Hezbollah's positions.[47]

For embattled Syrian leaders operating in an increasingly dangerous regional political environment, having strong allies such as Hezbollah and Iran greatly outweighs the risks associated with deepening Syria's entanglement with them, as a weak Syria would 'stimulate Israel's appetite'.[48] Yet it remains unlikely that al-Asad senior would have gone so far in espousing so radical a position as the one conveyed by Bashar's harsh domestic policy speeches, in which he referred to Arab leaders as 'half men' while celebrating the victory of the resistance as a vindication of his own alignment with Hezbollah and Iran.[49] Diplomats and analysts who deplored Bashar's harsh tone failed to understand his need to pre-empt domestic destabilisation by publicly aligning his government with Syria's public opinion. The rise of strong non-state actors enjoying mass support and mounting popular anger radically changed the political context of the Syrian president's calculations. By embracing the resistance of 'heroic' Hezbollah, President al-Asad was once again simultaneously legitimising his government by siding with public opinion and reinforcing Syria's position in the international arena. In this way, Bashar defended Syria's pride and its militant identity, which is the legitimating glue between the al-Asad government and the Syrian people. In Syrian political discourse, Hezbollah's victory became a vindication of the 'steadfastness' strategy of al-Asad senior and a key achievement of Bashar's resistance posture.[50]

Contrary to expectations, Syria's association with the 'resistance front' did not limit its room for manoeuvre in foreign relations.[51] Syria's close relationship with Hezbollah renewed Damascus' influence in Beirut and gave Syria the chance to reassert its regional centrality to international actors. Syrian leaders portrayed the 2006 war as evidence of the cost of Syria's absence from Lebanon and sent the unequivocal message that only a strong government in Damascus would be able to keep control of Hezbollah and deliver peace in the face of growing disaffection of Arab public opinion.[52] Moreover, Syria maintained a working relationship with Saudi Arabia, which relentlessly sought Syria's cooperation in countering Iranian influence while it demonstrated its willingness to re-form the Arab front against Israel to an Arab public opinion which was overwhelmingly pro-resistance and sympathetic to Iran.[53] This shows that Syria's regional balancing policy was successful because of—not despite—its partnership in the front.

Similarly, Western powers swung between isolating and courting the allegedly weaker partner of the axis with the aim of breaking the alliance and ultimately weakening Iran. After Hezbollah's show of power in Lebanon, Western powers opted for the pragmatic policy of maintaining relations with the more approachable partner in the axis. That the al-Asad government derived leverage from maintaining this partnership was also visible in its mediation efforts between the various Iraqi factions, who were torn between Iran on one side and the US, Saudi Arabia, and Turkey on the other. The Syrian authorities have always been keen to be recognised as a key interlocutor in the regional and international diplomatic process—regardless of the outcome of such diplomatic activity—as this recognition provides an implicit security guarantee.

Partnership in the 'resistance front' was also the core of Bashar's self-legitimation strategy. For the young president, with no personal military or revolutionary credentials, continuity with the nationalist posture of his father and his association with victorious Hezbollah were central to his claim to rule the country of unabated 'steadfastness'. From 2003, when US pressure on Syria intensified, Bashar relied on Iran and Hezbollah to portray Western pressure aimed for Syria's withdrawal from Lebanon as international interference in Arab affairs. In 2005, Hezbollah preserved Syrian face, after the withdrawal of its forces from Lebanon, by staging mass 'thank you' demonstrations for the role Damascus had played in the country for 30 years.[54] The following year, Hezbollah's 'divine victory' won Syria popular support at the time of its greatest international isolation.[55] Iran and Hezbollah gave al-Asad outspoken praise for his support of the rejectionist front (*jabhat al-mumana'a*) and his refusal to submit to US-Israeli hegemonic plans in the region.[56] It was again Hezbollah who, with its show of force in Beirut during 2008, demonstrated the futility of the Western strategy of isolating Syria and broke the Western diplomatic boycott of Damascus.

It is therefore hardly surprising that, in contrast with the decades of skilful use of the 'Hezbollah card' by al-Asad senior, Bashar's public speeches were increasingly borrowed from Nasrallah's rhetorical repertoire and Syria was flooded by posters featuring the trinity Bashar, Nasrallah, and Hafez—who, according to a former regime insider, 'were he able to rise from the dead, would use these posters as fuel to burn his own son'.[57]

The 'Resistance Front' in the Syrian Uprising

Conventional accounts of the ongoing Syrian conflict tend to give priority to geopolitical drivers, often incorporating sectarian or ethnic identities as intervening variables: the competition for regional supremacy between Shi'a Iran and Sunni Saudi Arabia and their constellation of proxies dominate the analysis. Yet judged by their pre-2011 geopolitical policies, the strategies of regional actors involved in the Syrian tragedy are now 'a caricature': Tehran is assuming the role of protector of the Shi'as and engaging in an overtly sectarian policy, which it had hitherto tried to avoid.[58] Saudi Arabia's battle to contain Iranian influence by bankrolling moderate Sunni groups is likely to backfire: Riyadh has opened a front against Shi'a, Salafi Jihadists, and Muslim Brothers 'leaving it largely divorced from the

Islamist scene it aspires to lead'.[59] Moreover, a neorealist analysis of the anti-al-Asad coalition does not explain why the alignments one would expect under the balance of power theory—Saudi-Israeli, Saudi-Turkish, Turkish-Israeli—and the 'Sunni axis' premised on the sectarian understanding of patterns of regional policies have not thus far been realised.[60]

The uprising has remarkably transformed the resistance alliance as well, although not so much in geopolitical terms, apart from the defection of Hamas, which has left the 'axis of resistance' to Israel detached from every major Palestinian faction.[61] Hezbollah's direct involvement in the Syrian war with the rationale of preserving its power to fight Israel is weakening it while eroding its regional prestige.[62] Revolutionary Iran, once popular among the Syrian public, is now seen as an occupation force by opponents of the al-Asad regime.[63] Nevertheless, the 'resistance front' has remained 'the one element of Asad's upgrading which has shaped the tangent of the uprising in a decisive way'.[64] To explain the resilience of the alliance and its paradoxical trajectory—from a revisionist to a counterinsurgency force—we have to consider the ideological makeup of the region and struggles over domestic legitimation formulas.

Since the start of the uprising, Syria, Hezbollah, and Iran have adhered to the mobilisation and legitimating power of the narrative of resistance in which the conflict is a specific site of a broader struggle between 'the resistance' and a US-Israeli orchestrated plot backed by pro-Western Arab states. According to Iranian leaders, Syria's partnership in the front is the main reason for American hostility to al-Asad: the corollary is that all enemies of al-Asad are enemies of 'the resistance' and legitimate targets in an existential ideological zero-sum conflict. As Bashar proposed a programme of reform at the onset of the revolt and supports resistance movements against Israel, he has satisfied the two criteria that determine Hezbollah's position towards Arab governments.[65] Hence local rebels have no legitimate demands as 'what is being required of Syria is that it become a treasonous Arab regime'.[66]

From May 2013, as the conflict had descended into a multi-sided war by proxy and Nasrallah admitted the direct involvement of Hezbollah's fighters in Syria, the party's communication apparatus has invested time and effort in explaining to its Lebanese and Arab critics the changes in the 'resistance' strategy in the post-uprising regional order. In Hezbollah's political discourse, 'terrorists', '*takfiris*', and the Islamic State are a threat to the resistance and to the Lebanese nation, and they are strategically and discursively connected to the front's 'main enemies'—the Israeli state and the US government.[67] As the US started to launch airstrikes against jihadi positions in Syrian territories, the main enemies of the 'resistance front' are located within Syria. Hence the 'resistance front' involvement in the Syrian conflict is merely considered as an extension of the resistance campaign. The strategic significance of the front intervention in Syria rests on its responsibility to protect 'the geopolitical and strategic environment that Hezbollah requires for its continued operational integrity' rather than the expulsion of the Zionist occupiers.[68]

Hezbollah's conceptualisation of the Syrian conflict is revealing of the transformation of its politics from 'a politics of resistance to a politics of the resistance [axis] front'.[69] The strategic alliance is now a 'unity of military forces and military theaters'.[70] Attacks on Syrian targets are assaults on 'the entire resistance axis': thus, Hezbollah retaliated after Israel's Golan strike in January 2015 with an attack on the Shebaa Farms in occupied Lebanon. As the enemy threatens the strategic space of Hezbollah, its ultimate purpose has developed from the liberation of Israeli-occupied Arab territories to perpetual resistance against Israel and the West.[71] Like the Iranian Quds Force, which is its partner in Syria and Iraq, Hezbollah engages in extraterritorial operations and 'preventive self-defence' and appears to have extended its reach to Iraq and Yemen.[72]

The war on terrorism has prompted the al-Asad government to re-articulate its resistance discourse and deploy its authoritarian mechanism at the regional level. By adopting the rhetoric of the 'war on Islamic terror', the government gains legitimacy among domestic minorities and among international actors while justifying the crackdown on rebels. With this twist, the resistance strategy has gone full circle from a discourse of state building (Syria), liberation from oppression (Iran), and resistance to foreign occupation (Hezbollah), to a counterinsurgency discourse in which the 'resistance front' partners have become advocates of the status quo. The original resistance paradigm has turned into a blueprint for regional intervention: a reconfigured counterinsurgency alliance *de facto* grouping together the Hezbollah Islamic resistance, the Iranian Islamic Revolutionary Guard Corps, the Syrian Arab Army (or what remains of it after defections and losses), irregular Syrian groups, Iraqi militias, and other Iranian proxies.

Conclusion

Reflecting on Syria's alignment with its 'resistance front' partners—from the early days of the Syria-Iran alliance to the role of the front in the ongoing Syrian conflict—provides unique insights into the foreign policy and the domestic modus operandi of the Syrian government as well as the dynamics of the Syrian war.

Hafez al-Asad's alignment with Iran and Hezbollah helped the Syrian state to achieve its international objectives whilst deterring any opponent. Using a flexible balancing policy, Hafez handled the increasing complexities brought on by the Cold War and its demise and the evolution of the Arab-Israeli conflict without alienating the Ba'athist constituency of his government nor jeopardising his grip on power. In Hafez's time, when conventional wars, deterrent military strategy, and state-led development were pursued under the overarching discourse of nationalism, the objectives of state building, national security, and state consolidation conveniently coincided. Indeed, al-Asad senior excelled in making his government indispensable to various domestic and regional partners whilst cultivating a sense of national identification as a mechanism of controlled mobilisation.

Bashar rebranded his father's 'steadfastness' and embraced the 'resistance' as a shield from growing popular disenchantment with his reformist rhetoric. Yet a new regional political climate marked the turn of the millennium, with the US turning into an imminent regional threat, the rise of powerful non-state actors, a marked radicalisation of the embittered Arab masses, and a looming economic crisis. These developments threatened to destabilise the regional balance of power and exposed a deepening divide between Arab states and societies. On Hezbollah's coattails, Bashar chose to trade the 'plausible deniability' gained by his father's clever use of his regional alliances for a self-legitimation strategy and opted for deepening his engagement with the 'resistance front', whose influence had been rising through the three wars (Iraq, Lebanon, and Gaza) that marked the first decade of the millennium.

Analytically, this study suggests the need to reconsider the connection between foreign and domestic policy making and to focus on threats to state rulers, rather than threats to states as a unit, as a proper subject of analysis for understanding foreign policy alignments.[73] Using a flexible omni-balancing policy between threats and needs located in multiple environments (starting from the domestic), Hafez al-Asad successfully handled the increasing complexities brought on by the Cold War and its demise and the evolution of the Arab-Israeli conflict without jeopardising his grip on power. After 2005, when his son Bashar appeared to be losing his regional moorings and his government's survival was in question, Syrian authorities again deployed the time-tested omni-balancing strategy to prevent a perfect storm of alignment between domestic threats and international actors pushing for change. In 2011, Bashar al-Asad followed the old script and turned his internal crackdown into a regional/international issue, thus mobilising the 'resistance front' to save a key member of the alliance.

The Syrian uprising exposed the limitations of the long-established strategy of using foreign policy as a panacea for risky internal reform but also showed the lasting political instrumentality of a reconfigured 'resistance' stance. A crucial factor in the success and longevity of the 'resistance front' was the shared transnational identity of its partners as emerging anti-Western regional powers with a militant nationalist discourse, which enabled them to mobilise the potent supranational symbols of Arabism and Islam in support of common goals. The enduring appeal of a political culture of resistance in the conflict-ridden Middle Eastern region and the front partners' immediate, coherent, and well-defined perception of what was at stake for them in the Syrian uprising—in contrast with the poorly coordinated efforts, conflicting interests, and even violent infighting of the anti-Asad grouping—help to explain their remarkably unambiguous and consistent stance. The Syrian uprising and the 'War on Terror' prompted the front partners to re-articulate the original resistance paradigm, transforming the politics of resistance into the politics of the resistance partners and thus turning the front into a transnational counterinsurgency force, which deployed its authoritarian power mechanisms at the regional level. The authoritarian shift of 'the resistance' is unmistakable: for a large part of Arab public opinion, the reconfiguration of the 'resistance front' marks the epitaph of a once hugely popular 'resistance'.

To conclude, this analysis of Syria in the 'resistance front' suggests that the length and intractability of the ongoing war are in no small measure a result of the omni-balancing policies and legitimation strategies pursued by Syrian leaders in order to secure the Asad regime both internally and regionally. Hence the Syrian case shows the need to conceptualise the 'regime security' dilemma and the struggles over legitimation formulas of authoritarian states that are resistant to change yet in need of popular mobilisation to ensure regime survival.

Notes

1. While many players have been involved in the Syrian conflict over the last six years, adding further complexity to the war dynamic, this chapter focuses only on one group of actors, which is the al-Asad government and its allies.
2. The consolidation of an alliance of Arab states against Israel was a cornerstone of Hafez al-Asad foreign policy.
3. Like other authoritarian regimes, Syrian leaders have deployed a range of strategies to adjust to new global, regional, and domestic circumstances and fend off pressures for change. This process has been described as 'authoritarian upgrading'. See Steven Heydemann, "Upgrading Authoritarianism in the Arab World" (Brookings, 2007).
4. Anoushiravan Ehteshami and Raymond Hinnebusch. *Syria and Iran* (Routledge, 1997).
5. Ehteshami, 133.
6. "Texte intégral du Programme d'Action du Gouvernement présenté a l'Assemblée du Peuple le 18.2.1973", in *Rapport* 1972–1973, p. C75.
7. Mustafa Tlass, *Parole d'Asad* (Conseil, 1986), 154.
8. *Rapport 1973–1974*, p. A.1.
9. Volker Perthes, *The Political Economy of Syria under Asad* (Tauris, 1995).
10. Al-Asad's address to youth conference, Damascus, 7 November 1980: "Given the broad significance of this revolution and huge gains for us, the Arabs, from this revolution, is it not our duty to ask why was war launched against this revolution?" BBC/SWB/ME/6571/A4, 10 November 1980.
11. Jubin Goodarzi, *The Formative Years of the Syrian-Iranian Alliance*. PhD thesis, LSE, 2002.
12. Although officially established in 1985, Hezbollah was active militarily and politically since mid-1982 under the banner of the Islamic Resistance. See Norton, *Hizballah of Lebanon* (Council of Foreign Relations Press, 1999), 10–11.
13. Fred Lawson, "Les relationes syro-iranienne". In *La Syrie au Present*, edited by Baudoin Dupret, (Sindbad, 2007), 824.
14. Jubin Goodarzi, *Syria and Iran* (Tauris, 2006), xiii, 45.
15. Eberhard Kienle. *Contemporary Syria*. British Academic Press, 1994. Ghaidaa Hetou, "*Syria's Regional Alignment*". PhD thesis, University of New Jersey, 2014.
16. Michael Eisenstadt, "Arming for Peace? Syria's Elusive Quest for 'Strategic Parity", *Policy Paper* No. 31 (The Washington Institute for Near East, 1992).
17. Samii, Abbas. 'A stable structure on shifting sands: assessing the Hezbollah Iran Syria relationship. *Middle East Journal*, 62 no. 1 (2008). Bente Scheller, *The Wisdom of Syria's Waiting Game* (Hurst, 2013).

18. Goodarzi, *Syria and Iran*, 247.
19. Tine Gade "Sunni Islamists in Tripoli and the Asad regime 1966–2014", *Syria Studies* 7, no. 2 (2015), 33–34.
20. Hanna Batatu, Syria's Muslim Brethren, MEIP Reports 110 (1982) and the interview with Adnan Saad el-Din in *Al-Watan al-Arabi* n.270, 16–22 April 1982, quoted in Michel Seurat, *Etat de Barbarie* (Presse Universitaire de France, 2012), 135–136.
21. Conversation with Abolhassan Bani-Sadr, Versailles, France, December 1994. In Goodarzi, *Syria and Iran*, 300 (note 94).
22. Mark Haas, *The Clash of Ideologies* (Oxford University Press, 2012), 135.
23. Annabel Bottcher, "Official Sunni and Shi'i Islam in Syria". European University Institute, 2002.
24. Ehteshami, 102.
25. Scheller, 18.
26. Author's interviews with Syrians in Damascus (April 2010) and Beirut (during 2012, various dates).
27. Joseph Bahout. "The unraveling of Lebanon's Taif agreement". *Carnegie*. May 2016.
28. WikiLeaks cable 06DAMASCUS3998_a "Asad speech, on-the-ground realities".
29. Bahout (2016).
30. Author's interview with Michel Kilo, Damascus, March 2010.
31. Gade 2015, 51.
32. David Lesch. "The Evolution of Bashar al-Asad". *Middle East Policy Council* 17 no. 2, 2010.
33. Ibid.
34. See Joshua Landis' blog http://faculty-staff.ou.edu/L/Joshua.M.Landis-1/syriablog/2006/01/khaddam-damns-bashar-al-asad.htm.
35. Author's interviews with activists and opposition figures, Damascus, March 2010.
36. According to several Syrian opposition figures interviewed by the author, including Michel Kilo and Yassin Hajj Saleh (Damascus. April 2010) and Sadeq al-Azm (Beirut 2011).
37. See Scheller (2013) for a nuanced assessment of Bashar's policies in Lebanon.
38. Samir Aita. "Syria: what reforms while a storm is building?" *Arab Reform Brief*, 6 April 2006.
39. Lesch (2010).
40. See Aita (2006) and Lesch (2010).
41. Dan Diker and Pinchas Inbari, "Re-energizing a West Bank-Jordan Alliance", *Middle East Quarterly* Spring 2006, 29–36.

42. After the visit of Iranian President Mahmoud Ahmadinejad to Damascus in January 2006, the two countries formed several committees to deal with arm financing and military training. WikiLeaks cable 06 DAMASCUS1159_a "Syria-Iran relations flourishing".
43. Ibid.
44. Speech of President Asad, Syrian Journalists Union, 16 August 2006.
45. ICG (2010).
46. Ibid.
47. Author's interview with Omar Amiralay, Damascus, April 2010. See also WikiLeaks cable 06DAMASCUS642_a. "Syria's Iran policy".
48. ICG (2010).
49. Asad's Speech to the Syrian Journalists Union, 16 August 2006.
50. *Al-Thawra*, 5 April 2010.
51. ICG (2010).
52. Author's interviews with Syrians in Damascus, March 2010 and Beirut April 2012. See also *al-Thawra*, 16 August 2006 'Syrians will fight Israel in every part of the Golan just as Lebanese resistance fought you'.
53. Sonoko Sunayama. *Syria and Saudi Arabia* (Tauris, 2007), 220–221.
54. "Hezbollah Leads Huge Pro-Syrian Protest in Central Beirut", *The New York Times*, 8 March 2005.
55. Amal Saad Ghorayeb. "Understanding Hizbullah's support for the Asad Regime". *Conflicts Forum*, 2011.
56. Hasan Nasrallah speech, 11 November 2009.
57. Emile Hokayem. "Hizballah and Syria". *The Washington Quarterly*, 30 no. 2 (2007), 42.
58. Harling (2014).
59. Ibid.
60. Neorealist analyses are based on power balancing against threats, alliance making, security dilemmas, and hegemony seeking. For an assessment, see Hinnebusch *The International Politics of the Middle East*, Manchester University Press, 2015, ch. 10.
61. In January 2012 Hamas and its leader Khaled Meshaal abandoned its headquarters in Damascus, citing the al-Asad government's brutal crackdown on its people. The only Palestinian group remaining in al-Asad's Syria is Ahmed Jibril's PFLP-GC and Liwa al-Quds from the Handarat Refugee Camp in Aleppo City.
62. See Rola El-Husseini. "The Muslim World Is Turning on Hezbollah", *The National Interest*. April 2015. "Arab League Chief Urges Hezbollah to Stop Fighting in Syria." Reuters. 26 May 2013. International Crisis Group. "Hezbollah Syrian Conundrum". *Middle East Report* 175, 14 March 2017.
63. Author's interviews, Gaziantep, April 2015.

64. Hinnebusch (2015), 303.
65. Full interview of Hezbollah Secretary General Hassan Nasrallah with Al-Mayadeen TV, September 3, 2012.
66. ICG. "A precarious balancing act", Report 132 (2012).
67. Al-Manar, "Words by the Secretary General", 23 Sep 2014. See Viveka Bergh, *Hizbullah's Construction of National Identity*. PhD thesis, Uppsala University, 2015.
68. Ibid., Amal Saad. "From Classic to Post-Resistance: On Hezbollah's Transformation", *al-Akhbar*, 13 February 2015.
69. Ibid.
70. Saad (2015).
71. Hokayem (2007).
72. Saad (2015), ICG (2017).
73. David (1991).

Bibliography

Aita, S. (2006, April 6). *Syria: What Reforms While a Storm Is Building?* Arab Reform Brief.
Bahout, J. (2016, May). The Unraveling of Lebanon's Taif Agreement. *Carnegie*.
Batatu, H. (1982, November–December). *Syria's Muslim Brethren*. MERIP Reports 110.
Bergh, V. (2015). *Hizbullah's Construction of National Identity*. PhD thesis, Uppsala University.
Bottcher, A. (2002). *Official Sunni and Shi'i Islam in Syria*. San Domenico: European University Institute.
David, S. (1991). Explaining Third World Alignment. *World Politics, 43*(2), 233–256.
Dupret, B., Ghazzal, Z., Courbage, Y., & al-Dbyat, M. (Eds.). (2007). *La Syrie au Present*. Paris: Sindbad.
Ehteshami, A., & Hinnebusch, R. (1997). *Syria and Iran: Middle Powers in a Penetrated Regional System*. London: Routledge.
Eisenstadt, M. (1992). *Arming for Peace? Syria's Elusive Quest for 'Strategic Parity'*. The Washington Institute for Near East Policy, Policy Paper no. 31.
El-Husseini, R. (2015, April). The Muslim World Is Turning on Hezbollah. *The National Interest*.
Gade, T. (2015). Sunni Islamists in Tripoli and the Asad regime 1966–2014. *Syria Studies, 7*(2), 20–65.
Goodarzi, J. (2002). *The Formative Years of the Syrian-Iranian Alliance*. LSE thesis.
Goodarzi, J. (2006). *Syria and Iran: Diplomatic Alliance and Power Politics in the Middle East*. London: Tauris.

Haas, M. (2012). *The Clash of Ideologies: Middle Eastern Politics and American Security*. Oxford University Press.
Harling, P. (2014, January 14). The Arab World into the Unknown. *The Arabist*.
Hetou, G. (2014). *Syria's Regional Alignment*. PhD thesis, University of New Jersey.
Heydemann, S. (2007). *Upgrading Authoritarianism in the Arab World*. Saban Centre at the Brookings Institution.
Hinnebusch, R. (2015). *The International Politics of the Middle East*. Manchester University Press.
Hokayem, E. (2007). Hizballah and Syria: Outgrowing the Proxy Relationship. *The Washington Quarterly, 30*(2), 35–52.
International Crisis Group. (2010). *Drums of War: Israel and the "Axis of Resistance"*. Middle East Report 97.
International Crisis Group. (2012, November 22). *A Precarious Balancing Act: Lebanon and the Syrian Conflict*. Middle East Report 132.
International Crisis Group. (2017, March 14). *Hezbollah Syrian Conundrum*. Middle East Report 175.
Kienle, E. (1994). *Contemporary Syria: Liberalization between Cold War and Cold Peace*. London: British Academic Press.
Lesch, D. (2010). The Evolution of Bashar al-Asad. *Middle East Policy Council, 17*(2), 70–81.
Norton. (1999). *Hizballah of Lebanon*. New York: Council of Foreign Relations Press.
Perthes, V. (1995). *The Political Economic of Syria Under Asad*. London: Tauris.
Rapport sur l'économie Syrienne 1972–73, Damas OFA. 1973.
Saad, A. (2015, February 13). From Classic to Post-resistance: On Hezbollah's Transformation. *Al-Akhbar*.
Saad-Ghorayeb, A. (2011). Understanding Hizbullah's Support for the Asad Regime. *Conflicts Forum*.
Samii, A. (2008). A Stable Structure on Shifting Sands: Assessing the Hezbollah Iran Syria Relationship. *Middle East Journal, 62*(1), 32–53.
Scheller, B. (2013). *The Wisdom of Syria's Waiting Game: Syrian Foreign Policy Under the Assads*. London: Hurst.
Seurat, M. (2012). *Syrie: L'Etat de Barbarie*. Paris: Presses Universitaires de France.
Sunayama, S. (2007). *Syria and Saudi Arabia: Collaboration and Conflict in the Oil Era*. London: Tauris.
Tlass, M. (Ed.). (1986). *Paroles d'Assad*. Paris: Conseil.

PART IV

Sectoral Analysis

CHAPTER 9

The Political Economy of Public Health in Syria: Some Global and Regional Considerations

Kasturi Sen

INTRODUCTION

Until the early 1990s, Syria's economy was credited for its success in achieving national development goals in terms of promoting state-led industrialisation, securing relative self-sufficiency in food production, and creating job opportunities for the middle- and lower-income groups. The socioeconomic successes were underpinned by the nationalisation of banking and industry, controlling trade, capital accounts, foreign exchange, and land redistribution (Hinnebusch 1994; Matar 2016; Perthes 1994). Five-year national plans and centralised planning characterised the country's economic development—which aimed at supporting autonomy, like many countries that had emerged out of colonial rule. Policies emphasising import substitution and protection for local industry were endorsed to reduce dependency and ensure a degree of independence. Matar, among others, suggests that the Syrian state was viewed as a model for state capitalism, in the 1960s and 1970s, one which had tasked itself with supporting national development plans, on the one hand, and providing improved access to education, health care, and social support to the majority, on the

K. Sen (✉)
Wolfson College (CR), University of Oxford, Oxford, UK

other (Matar 2016). It is through this path of national development that Syria had aimed at shedding the legacy of colonial dependency. Politically however, Syria also viewed itself as a front-line state against Israel's aggressive expansionism in Palestine and the occupation of Syrian land (the Golan Heights in 1967), as well as remaining a constant threat to the whole region.

This chapter focuses on the commercialisation of the health sector in Syria as manifested by the EU-driven health sector modernisation programme (HSMP) ratified in 2003. The first section provides an overview of Syria's political economy before the conflict and sheds light on its health sector. The second addresses the impact of neoliberal policies on health services in low- and middle-income countries (LMICs) over the past three decades, whilst the remainder of the chapter addresses Syria's HSMP discussing some of the challenges it created both for the health sector and for its population. The concluding section sheds light on the additional risks on Syria's health sector posed by the current conflict.

Political Economy Background and the Health Sector

The approach to cautious economic reforms in Syria[1] from the 1990s onwards depended on a complex interplay of political alliances between the ruling elites, whose main constituency were the Alawites (a minority) and the majority Sunni bourgeoisie. The minority origins of the leaders of the ruling Ba'ath required the Ba'athist government to retain control over the development process to highlight its role in the distribution of benefits in welfare measures (health, education, and food subsidies in the main) and a desire to protect worker's rights (Hinnebusch 1994). While in theory welfare gains were made across the spectrum of classes, they were targeted at those most deprived in both rural and urban areas ultimately to strengthen the Ba'ath government's populist base. Over a period of three decades (1970–2010), this welfarist national development strategy was reflected in Syria's social indicators through rising levels of primary and secondary enrolments, higher literacy levels, improved life expectancy, and most of all, remarkable reductions in infant mortality rate (IMR) and maternal mortality rate (MMR) (United Nations Development Programme 2010). Nevertheless a combination of factors including economic, environmental, and political ones were to create challenges to this programme for a nationally driven capitalist development.

By the early 2000s, economic disparities between rural and urban areas and between those who owned capital and assets and those without widened, as market reforms began to take effect. These were compounded by a decline in oil revenues and a prolonged drought in the countryside particularly so in the wheat belt (IFAD 2009). Environmental factors together with market reforms and their effects eventually overwhelmed the country both economically and politically by the late 2000s (IRIN 2008; Matar 2016).

The shifts and changes in economic policy under the "social market economy" model created tensions already latent among sections of the urban population and the rural poor who were increasingly excluded from participating in economic activities in the 2000s (IRIN 2007a, 2008; Matar 2012; Thomas 2013). These shifts included a programme of disinvestment in public provision, the deregulation of sectors of the economy, and the privatisation of others. The acceptance of the new strategy was officially ratified at the 2005 Congress of the Ba'ath party (with contention) and formally adopted in the Tenth Five-Year Plan (2006–2010). The implementation of the "social market economy" however was underpinned by the neoliberal agenda, marked by its failure to address the growing economic disparities set apace by drought, inequalities, and discontent. These acted as major triggers for revolts in Syria and elsewhere in the region, where similar policies had been adopted, in most cases under pressure from the International Monetary Fund (IMF) and the World Bank.

Research on the impact of market-friendly policies on the health sector have been largely missing from the analysis of pre-conflict Syria, with the exception of a handful of studies based on secondary data and reports from international organisations (Galdo 2004; IRIN 2014; Matar 2012; Sen and Al-Faisal 2012). It was simply assumed as part of an unquestionable normative order to privatise facilities where state budgets were under stress, as in the case of Lebanon in the aftermath of civil war. But in the case of Syria, revenue stress apart, there was considerable pressure from the EU, a main trading partner for Syria, and the German Development Agency (GIZ)[2] to implement reforms as rapidly as possible (IRIN 2014; Sen and Al-Faisal 2012). Euphemistically called "reforms" of the public sector and of public provision, they were measures for administrative and economic transformations in order to ensure EU bilateral support. The rapid changes that followed in the health sector after 2003 had damaging consequences for a cross-section of society. They pushed small businesses such as affordable small health clinics which were run by general practitioners outside of the state sector to introduce charges for many health services for the population, hitherto free (IRIN 2008; Kassab and Lane 2011; Matar 2012).

Factors impacting Syria's economic downturn and triggering the leaning towards EU support[3] included declining oil revenues and a series of droughts in the late 1990s and early 2000s which affected general state income as well as agricultural output. The droughts were compounded by intensive groundwater usage and a pattern of land ownership which created insecurity and poverty, mostly for small tenant farmers in particular regions of the country. Despite attempts by the state to provide food subsidies to the worst affected areas during this period, it arrived too late to prevent impoverishment and mass outmigration to cities, notably to Damascus (IFAD 2009; IRIN 2007b).

Thus growing poverty induced by large-scale unemployment in both urban and rural areas was compounded by neoliberal economic policies which targeted the lifting of subsidies on essential food items in the late 2000s, among other measures. Unemployment in rural areas was also compounded by relatively high birth rate of three children and above per woman in the 1990s. A compressed demographic transition meant there were large number of young people, between 18 and 29 years especially males, over half of whom were unable to find jobs by 2008 (Abu-Ismail et al. 2010). Female participation rate in the labour force remained low (29 per cent) in 2007 and was concentrated in the services sector (UNDP 2010: 15). Economists highlighted the fact that there were up to 250,000 new entrants to the job market each year (before the conflict), yet only 140,000 vacancies were available in the formal sector. The majority of the unemployed youth and those who arrived from rural areas were relegated to working in the growing informal labour market in urban areas. The lax labour laws were unable to control the rapid expansion of the informal sector (Galdo 2004; International Labour Office 2010; El-Laithy et al. 2008). In 2005, the International Fund for Agricultural Development (IFAD) estimated that 30 per cent of Syrians were living in poverty, of which some 11.4 per cent lived below subsistence level, mostly in the agricultural areas of the northeast but also in the south of the capital Damascus. The official data claimed a much lower figure of 11.4 per cent (Abu-Ismail et al. 2010).

The new economic policies rooted in Investment Law No. 10 of 1991 were entrenched by 2003–2004, with its details enshrined in the Tenth Five-Year Plan of 2006–2010. The rhetoric was to promote a "vibrant economy" and to protect social welfare and jobs. However in reality the opposite took place. The "social market economy" was underpinned by cost-cutting across welfare sectors and the liberalisation of the banking and insurance sectors with a strong emphasis on macroeconomic stability. This resulted in the withdrawal of numerous subsidies for food, fuel, fertilisers, which the poor, especially in rural areas, depended upon, and liberalisation of trade, and an extensive programme for public and private partnerships (PPPs)[4] was implemented across sectors including health (Abu-Ismail and Mckinely 2005).

Foreign direct investment was mostly targeted at the so-called finance, insurance, and real estate (FIRE) sectors which involved unproductive and speculative types of activities with few social returns. In Syria, as in the rest of the Arab world, historically there was dearth of structural investment in productive sectors that could lead to job creation. In line with this, investment around FIRE supported a skewed growth, described as "jobless growth," that was a common outcome of new economic policies in most LMICs. They acted as a precursor to growing impoverishment and inequality across the world (Haddad 2011; Matar 2016).

The economic challenges facing Syria were compounded by ongoing conflicts in the region (Palestine, Iraq, and Lebanon) which created substantial numbers of refugees, many of whom came to Syria. By the time Syria began to experience its economic downturn in mid-2000s, for example, there were in excess of two million Iraqi refugees in Syria due to the allied invasion of Iraq. Among refugees, those who were able to withdraw capital out of Iraq bought property in Damascus at high cost, contributing to considerable inflation in property prices in the city and increases in the cost of rental accommodation for Syrians. Refugees from Iraq (and earlier from Palestine) were also entitled to free health care and education. But the pressure on services, from the latest wave of refugees into Syria, led to depreciation of the quality of health and educational services due to the sudden increase in demand. There was negligible support for Iraqi refugees in Syria either from donors or from the countries involved in the illegal invasion[5] (IRIN 2007a, b).

For many LMICs, market-led economic policies fractured state-led development process of the 1960s and 1970s, which had formed the basis for nascent welfare systems in India, China, and Brazil, among others. The welfare programmes however small had contributed towards some redistribution of resources and had a visible impact on social indicators such as the IMR and MMR, stagnant for decades under colonial rule (Qadeer et al. 2001; Yousef 2004).

For a number of countries in the MENA (Middle East and North Africa) region (Egypt, Syria, and Tunisia), the undermining of state-led development and the adoption of neoliberal policies overturned the social contract which had implicitly traded political participation with welfare provision (Abdel-Fadil et al. 2009). This inevitably generated volatility and created the space for Islamic movements to fill the gap. The void was created because market-led economic policies focused almost exclusively on economic growth at the expense of income distribution and social welfare. They were to act as a trigger to many of the protest movements in the late 2000s onwards throughout the region. As prices rose, wages remained stagnant and unemployment ensued, large sections of the population felt impoverished. The situation was compounded by the depletion of subsidies and the minimal social protections that had existed in many countries of the region prior to policies of macroeconomic adjustments.

In Syria, following the gradual withdrawal of the state from the social sector during the 1990s, Islamic charities were officially permitted to fill the gaps. In theory, these charities were supposed to undertake an administrative role for the efficient delivery of welfare services; however, this "administrative and technical function" had transformed into a political one by the mid-2000s when a combination of growing impoverishment and latent resentments against the government surfaced. Islamic groups were able to galvanise this discontent, especially among the rural and urban poor who were marginalised as a result of economic liberalisation (Thomas 2013). The secular Ba'athist state misallocated economic resources following the advice of the international financial institutions, while the Islamists had gained popularity in terms of reaching out to the Syrian poor (Al-Azmeh 2014).

The Impact of Neoliberal Policies on the Health Sector

Neoliberal policies throughout the world succeeded in usurping and transforming the notion of "the public" and of "society" into a collection of individual consumers and providers where health-care services were concerned. This phenomenon was common throughout the world and came to be known as the marketisation of health care. The MENA region experienced the restructuring of their health services in tandem with economic reforms and adjustments, more recently through two main processes.

The first includes countries that have experienced prolonged conflict, such as Lebanon, Iraq, and the Occupied Palestinian Territories (OPTs). In these cases, public health provision which once served a cross-section of the population was systematically undermined by conflict and replaced largely by a market-led health-care system. The war acted as trigger for private providers to fill the gaps. NGOs also picked up services but they were forced to accept those which were mostly not profitable encapsulating preventive care (vaccinations, antenatal care, mental health, services for people with disabilities, and care of the elderly). The need to make profit out of health services led to the creation of costly hospital-based tertiary care in Lebanon and increasingly so in the OPTs. In this neoliberal model, most often the different tiers of health care (primary, secondary, and tertiary care) are disconnected from each other making it irrational and expensive for patients.[6] Meanwhile NGOs, overstretched for resources, and overwhelmed by demand from the poorest segments of the population, who may not usually afford private hospital care, had to resort to charging nominal fees. Whilst Lebanon provides an important example of this model opportunistically established through war, its dominant characteristic may be described as a system of fee-paying, expensive high-tech hospitals, and a handful of public hospitals run by the Ministry of Health. A large number of hospitals are also underwritten by different political organisations, reflecting Lebanon's confessional political system.[7] The health-care system in Lebanon also includes a substantial NGO-led public health care. These provide as indicated earlier essential and basic health care and, more recently, emergency humanitarian services for Syrian refugees.

Syria, on the other hand, serves as an example for the second process, where a once strong public provider of free health services was transformed through EU-led reforms, prompting changes to the organisation and financing of health care long before conflict. This change shifted the burden of payment of health care from the state on to households and included the introduction of health-insurance schemes, PPPs, and user charges, all of which imposed pressure on household budgets. The change in health sector policy led to the subsidising of costlier hospital services (for newly established autonomous hospitals), with major investments, under the guise of PPPs. Such subsidies to private providers at the expense of a publicly financed and delivered care are a major feature of neoliberal reforms in health services throughout the world. Whilst out-of-pocket expenditure (OPE) always played a role in outpatient services and physician visits in

Syria, the market-led reforms meant people had to contribute also towards costly inpatient hospital services, which would otherwise have been free (Chen et al. 2012; IRIN 2007a).

The impact of commercialisation and privatisation on any country's health system is well documented for LMICs including those in Latin America, South Asia, and Africa (Kanji et al. 1991; Sen and Koivusalo 1998; Armada et al. 2001). Neoliberal economic policies on health services disproportionately affected those already poor, residing in rural areas and in the informal sector of urban areas. They also worsened the lives of vulnerable groups such as women, children, and the elderly, who often have the least resources to pay for rising costs and have greater health needs. The UNICEF Report, *Adjustment with a Human Face*, provides evidence of the impact of neoliberal economic policies on population health as early as 1987 with health data from countries affected by macroeconomic adjustment. The research revealed stark figures of growing malnourishment, child deaths, and declining health of mothers. Nearly all of the countries also faced increases in the cost of food and health care (UNICEF 1987).[8] The same laissez-faire policies were implemented in the MENA region from the 1990s onwards but remained poorly documented until very recently (Al-Azmeh 2014; IRIN 2007a; Matar 2016; Pfeifer 2014). Other than a handful of critical reports from UN agencies, including the International Labour Organization (ILO), the body of literature on economy and health policies in the MENA region under reforms have tended to reinforce the dominant neoliberal discourse. They have supported the rationale for marketisation and based them on arguments such as "poor performance" of the public sector, urging the need to increase output and "productivity" with a strong emphasis on growth (Bruck et al. 2007; Sukkar 2003). Such arguments however were already common parlance for countries such as India, Brazil, and South Africa, despite evidence of impoverishment and ill health which continues until today.

HEALTH SERVICES IN PRE-CONFLICT SYRIA

Historically, health services in Syria were centrally organised under the state with a command and control structure. There was strong emphasis on primary care, health promotion, and preventive activities (Galdo 2004; Khatib 2006; Sen and Al-Faisal 2013). Health services were financed either by public funds (state budget), private insurance, or out-of-pocket expenses (OPEs) which covered attendance in outpatient clinics and the cost of medication. State spending on health care (average $59.00 per capita in 2010) was derived from government revenues and administered by the Ministry of Finance.

The Syrian health sector was little studied due to the absence of consistent health data, a lack of research collaboration from outside the country, and a dearth of researchers trained in the analysis of health systems. These were compounded by the fact that analytical concepts relating to "health systems" analysis[9] were derived from the West whose tools were not easily applied to centrally planned economies. "Patient voice," for example, as an analytical tool to understand how well a health-care system responds to the patient need could not be applied to a country like Syria where health services were centrally organised. Despite these impediments, pre-conflict Syria witnessed positive health indicators, including declining IMR and MMR over more than three decades (1970–2010).

Table 9.1 also shows Syria experienced declines in IMR and MMR from 132 per 100,000 live births in 1970 to 14.0 in 2010 and in MMR from a high of 482 per 100,000 births in 1970 to 45.0 in 2010, despite a relatively low per capita spending ($59) and average income of $3900 in 2010. Until the recent conflict, Syria could thus credit itself with having among the best health indicators in the region; these included comprehensive vaccination coverage, improved living standards, greater citizens' awareness of health issues, and a reduction in illiteracy, especially among women (Galdo 2004; United Nations Development Programme 2010). There was also good access to clean water through improvements in infrastructure and a broad expansion of primary health care (PHC) (WHO Eastern Mediterranean Regional Office 2006). There was a strategic commitment amongst public professionals in Syria, to integrate health care at all levels: primary, secondary, and tertiary care to avoid fragmented provision. Syria was one of few countries in the region and among LMICs on

Table 9.1 Health indicators in Syria, 1970–2010

	1970	1993	2002	2003	2004	2010
IMR per 100,000 live births	132	33	24	18.1	17.1	14.0
Under-5 MR per 100,000 live births	164	44	29	20.2	19.3	16.0
MMR per 100,000 live births	482	107	71	65.4	58	45

Source: Health Indicators, Ministry of Health, Damascus (2010)

target to meet a majority of the Millennium Development Goals (MDGs) for IMR and MMR (Galdo 2004; United Nations Development Programme 2010).

Declining trends in MMR in Syria are also highlighted in Table 9.2 which compares Syria with countries at similar levels of economic development. The MMR indicators for Syria show considerable improvements, despite low state spending per capita and barely any donor input, in sharp contrast to those of Egypt and Jordan heavily dependent on donor support (World Health Organization and Eastern Mediterranean Regional Office 2006). To a large extent, these were achieved through a better informed population, improved levels of nutrition, good access to health services, and a relatively well-integrated health system, despite the predominance of organisational and operational verticality (Galdo 2004; Khatib 2006; Sen and Al-Faisal 2012).

Until its "modernisation" programme (HSMP) in 2003 (further elaborated below), Syria provided free health care to its citizens[10] with a ceiling for controlling charges that could be made by private providers (e.g. physician consultations, purchasing medicines, diagnostic tests). The right to comprehensive health care was guaranteed under the Constitution with coordination, management, and provision of services falling under the Ministry of Health (MOH) (Khatib 2006; Seifan 2011). The actual delivery of services took place through several ministries (Social Affairs, Education, Defence, and Local Administration) where those such as Defence and Education were better resourced than others creating a degree of systems segmentation. The largest number of beds in the country remained in the public sector (80 per cent) in 2000 although private providers increased their share of hospital beds by 41 per cent in the restructuring of health services between 2005 and 2010 (WHO 2011).

Table 9.2 MMR per 100,000 live births in Egypt, Jordan, and the Syrian Arab Republic

Year	Egypt	Syria	Jordan
1990	220 (130–350)	120 (52–290)	110 (64–210)
1995	150 (94–240)	77 (34–180)	95 (55–170)
2000	110 (69–180)	58 (26–130)	79 (46–140)
2005	90 (56–150)	50 (22–110)	66 (38–120)
2008	82 (51–130)	46 (20–100)	59 (35–100)

Source: Maternal Mortality 1990–2008—WHO, UNICEF–WB, MM estimation. Inter-Agency group

Responsibilities of the MOH included policy and strategy which were complemented by other ministries such as Finance, Education, Social Welfare, and Defence. The Ministry of Education, for example, was involved in school health, while several other ministries such as the Ministry of Defence provided exclusive health care of highest quality for its employees (Galdo 2004; Khatib 2006).

Estimations for the period immediately prior to conflict (2010) suggest more than two thirds of the population continued to use public health services for inpatient care. However for outpatient services, they had to pay a fee introduced by private providers under the HSMP. Patients used general practitioners (GP) services privately for consultations, diagnostics, and for the purchase of medicines (World Health Organization & Eastern Mediterranean Regional Office 2006). The distribution of expenditure on health services is outlined in Table 9.3.

The largest expenditure consisting of more than one third of the overall budget for health services (36 per cent) was allocated to the Ministry of Local Administration (MLA) for providing support services to all governorates, while a significant amount (26 per cent) was also allocated to the central MOH (Table 9.3). This was followed by the Ministry of Higher Education responsible for a number of teaching hospitals. The MOH retained strategic

Table 9.3 Public spending on health care in Syria in 2003

Ministry	Value ($ millions)	% of total public spending on health care
Ministry of Health (central administration, 4 hospitals)	137.72	25.71
Ministry of Local Administration (health care in 14 governorate)	192.86	36.00
Ministry of Higher Education (11 teaching hospitals)	103.84	19.39
Ministry of Social Affairs and Labour (1 general hospital)	5.03	0.94
Ministry of Defence (5 hospitals)	18.89	3.53
Ministry of Interior (health care for the police)	11.11	2.07
Other public institutions	66.16	12.35
Total	535.61	100.00

Source: Adapted from Dashdash et al. (2010), National Health Accounts for Syria, Ministry of Health and WHO, Damascus, Syria

and overarching responsibilities for health services in the country, despite its operational segmentation between different ministries. This profile shifted, however, with deepened commercialisation and privatisation. In part this was underpinned by the aspirations of a growing middle class, especially Syrian returnees from the Gulf States in the late 1990s (Khatib 2006; Sen and Al-Faisal 2012), who were exposed to high-tech health care. This influenced their negative attitudes towards Syria's public provision, which was viewed as a "service for the poor" (Khatib 2006; Hatem 2011).

OFFICIAL NARRATIVE OF THE HEALTH SECTOR'S MODERNISATION PROGRAMME (2003–2010)

During the period between 2003 and 2010, the Syrian state was engaged in the HSMP under the aegis of the European Commission (2003) and German Technical Cooperation (GTZ). The latter acted as the implementing agency for the EU. The HSMP was part of an EU bilateral aid cooperation agreement that encouraged the liberalisation of the Syrian economy in administrative and legal systems and in trade and small enterprise development (Dostal 2008; European Commission 2003; Khatib 2006; Ministry of Health Syria 2009). The publication of the WHO Commission on Macroeconomics and Health in 2001 (World Health Organisation 2001) contributed to liberalisation of the health sector in many LMICs under the influence of international financial organisations. The approach involved an impetus to increase a "stewardship" role (a non-service delivery) for the state and advocated a separation between financing a service and providing it (Ammar 2009; Bhutta 2001).

The Syrian HSMP was ratified in 2003, with a plan for implementation over a period of several years. The liberalisation of the economy by an EU-assisted programme was integral to the changes in the health sector. The whole liberalisation/programme was budgeted by the EU for 140 million euros with each phase of adjustment and reform implemented with extreme severity and speed as highlighted in the detailed documentation of the process by Jorge Dostal (Dostal 2008; Gaertner 2003; Khatib 2006; Schwefel 2003).

The aims of the modernisation programme were to:

- Improve the performance of hospitals
- Improve the management of the health sector

- Improve the quality of health services through accreditation
- Seek new methods of health financing, including user charges (Khatib 2006)

The HSMP was premised on the neoliberal view that restructuring financing was a key to improving the quality and efficiency of services. Reforms therefore involved the gradual withdrawal of direct state funding of services to be replaced by a combination of private and social insurance schemes (SHI). In this scenario, private providers in primary, secondary, and tertiary care increased through PPPs, a strategy commonly utilised in countries that have experienced similar reforms (Schwefel 2008; Sen and Sibai 2010). In theory, social insurance schemes act as payer and gatekeeper of this new PPP-led service structure. The aim was to reduce costs to the state and improve the quality and access to those services (The World Bank 2005; Zawaya 2010). However the reality was quite different as highlighted by the experiences of other countries of the region (Ammar 2009; Sen and Sibai 2010).

The HSMP in Syria already included PPPs in its early stages for non-clinical services (e.g. lab and diagnostics, contracted out to the private sector) but shifted in 2008 to also contracting out primary health care. Units were handed over to physicians and to NGOs, hospitals to specialist doctors, and medical supplies to private providers. These took place with active encouragement by the European Neighbourhood Program (Dostal 2008).

The process of the commercialisation of health care through the use of PPPs is a complex one, often due to operational factors such as the absence of clear criteria for managing contracts (e.g. quality assurance and cost) and due to the inexperience of public providers in running complex contractual arrangements. In the absence of effective regulation for determining standards of health-care delivery, matters were further compounded. For example any failure of the contracting-out process would be evident if there was a failure to ratify it or if there was a collapse of subcontracts, something which was increasingly common in the region (Gaffney et al. 1999; Khatta and Hussein 2011; Lagarde and Palmer 2009). But it would then be the responsibility of the state to accept liability and make amendments. Siddiqi who undertook a review of PPPs and contracting-out in the region noted that PPPs, among other reform-led interventions in Syria, remained in an experimental phase and their impact could not be clearly monitored (Siddiqi et al. 2006). This meant that the costs of these programmes to the state were also not calculated, but the programme remained operational.

However, despite such a problematic context in Syria and elsewhere in the region, donors continued to persuade the Ministries of Health, in this case the State Planning Commission and the Ministry of Health in Syria, to act as "stewards" and to complement this role with regulations in order to extend the programme for PPPs (European Commission 2003; Schwefel and Ministry of Health 2008).

User Fees

An integral part of the HSMP in Syria was the introduction of user fees and charges for hospital and health services (Schwefel and Ministry of Health 2008). In theory, poor people would be exempt from charges. User fees were being charged at MOH hospitals and health centres and in "autonomous" hospitals[11] after 2003. Fees for medicines and in private clinics were paid even prior to the introduction of more comprehensive charges. However, with no monitoring to assess the effects of charging, the populace at large was placed under an increasing pressure. Figure 9.1 highlights the exponential rise in OPEs against public expenditure between 1995 and 2009. Some suggest that changes to the financing of health care in Syria may have been the final straw that broke the camel's back since it increased burdens on poor households, already struggling from unemployment, high cost of living, and in particular the loss of food subsidies (Galdo 2004; IRIN 2008; Sen and Al-Faisal 2012).

The Impact of the Modernisation Programme on Syria's Health Sector

As mentioned earlier, the financing of health care prior to the aforementioned reforms in Syria was premised on universal access, free at the point of delivery. Even though the health system often provided greater choice and better quality of services for public sector employees, it retained free access for the majority of the population to primary, secondary, and tertiary care. For a small minority (less than one per cent of the population), private health insurance was used as an option to purchase private health care but which mostly addressed the needs of expatriates employed in international companies. The concept of health insurance was novel and not popular in Syria and in many other low- and middle-income countries (Hatem 2011; Prinja et al. 2012; Qadeer 2013).

GGHE vs. OPE Syria 1995-2009

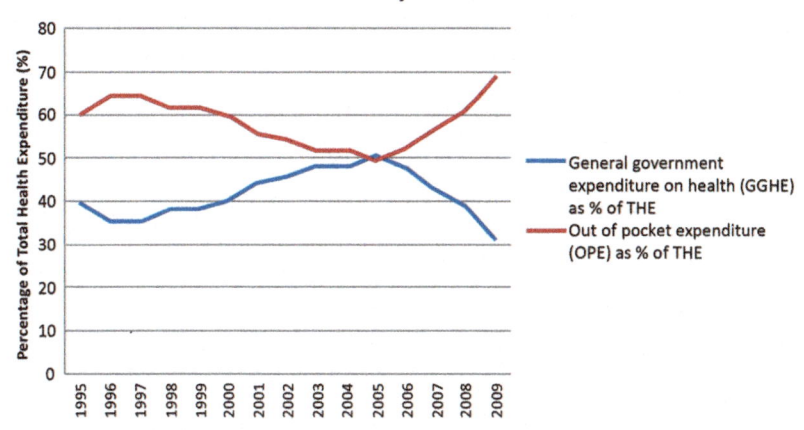

Fig. 9.1 Health expenditure trends: government health expenditure vs out-of-pocket expenditure. Source: compiled from National Health Accounts (2010), Ministry of Health, Syria, by C Van der Veer (IM), Belgium

A key feature of the changes to health financing in Syria following HSMP was the shifting from the existing mechanism (largely contribution-based for formal sector employees and subsidised for the poor and informal sector workers) to a new social insurance scheme (SHI). The feasibility of the scheme remains unknown even though it is popular in European countries where health insurance is a mandatory feature of their healthcare system. However exporting it to Syria, through the GIZ, may not have been appropriate since its effective functioning requires systematic documentation of medical and health records among other administrative functions. Due to the nature of the Syrian hospital system, these were either not available or of high quality, both essential for the proper working of the scheme. Overall the EU-led HSMP in Syria aimed at reducing public expenditure in health services, charging user fees, and supporting autonomous hospitals through PPPs and contacting out clinical and non-clinical services.

There also remained substantial and unresolved issues about the extent to which health services were to be controlled by private for-profit providers, an issue particularly relevant to nascent welfare states such as those in the MENA region (Al Nashif 2011). Empirical evidence from countries such as Lebanon, Egypt, and Jordan suggests that such commercial practices reduced access for those most in need of care (Elgazzarm et al. 2010). Despite widespread evidence to the contrary, the principle of user fees resurfaced in Syria, where the repercussions were already evident on households prior to the conflict.

Conclusion

The HSMP in Syria (2003–2008) included the introduction of user fees, insurance payments, and PPPs. These contradict the policies of universal access (free health care) enshrined in Syria's Constitution (Seifan 2011). They also created financial burdens for households. The increased life expectancy meant that patterns of disease were changing concurrently with the liberalisation of the health sector from communicable disease to long-term chronic conditions, which are usually costlier to treat. Whilst during the period of transition from a publicly funded system to an insurance-led one, there was some debate in Syria about the relevance of health insurance in a country where a large component of the labour force (45 per cent) was employed in the informal sector (and who remained without any protection). Some observers suggested that most Syrians had little understanding of the meaning of health insurance (Kassab and Lane 2011). The speed of change imposed from above caused hardship for the majority of the population and those who needed health care (Galdo 2004; IRIN 2008; Kassab and Lane 2011; Khatib 2006).

Current Crisis

The current conflict in Syria has had a devastating effect in terms of death, injury, and trauma on the one hand and health infrastructure and personnel on the other. By early 2016 there were estimates of some 450,000 deaths with three times that number injured (Syrian Centre for Policy Studies and United Nations Development Programme 2016). Much of the health-care system has been torn apart with more than half of qualified medical staff (notably physicians, lab workers, and nurses) fleeing the country, whilst others were killed while on duty. Diseases once eradicated, such as polio, typhoid, and cholera, re-emerged in parts of the country. The devastated state of water and sanitation has been a key factor in the spread of infectious disease (WHO 2014).

In such a chronic crisis, the reconstruction of the health sector will be a major challenge due to the lack of state funds and numerous political obstacles such as the ongoing challenges to state authority in different regions of the country. The negative experience of Lebanon shows clearly that there is never a greater need for a strong public provider, than in the aftermath of conflict. In Syria, there is need to plan for and avoid an even greater long-term health catastrophe through the ongoing process of privatisation. If however, the government chooses to continue to pursue further the path of commercialisation, there will be unbearable inequities in access to critical and essential health care with thousands of traumatised civilians who are in need (IRIN 2014; Jasarevic 2012).

As in the case of Iraq, the Syrian situation is compounded by economic sanctions[12] imposed since 1979 by the US and from 2011 by the EU and the Arab League. Intended to target the President of the Republic for "regime change" and dismantle the ruling Ba'ath party, the sanctions or measures are not ratified by the UN. Sanctions have had severe consequences for the population at large. They have prevented the repair of damaged utility generators (electricity and oil), affected drastically the value of the Syrian currency, and impacted the levels of employment when small businesses collapsed. Together with an escalation in the cost of basic essentials such as food, heating oil, and medicines, sanctions have created severe hardships for the population, yet raised little concern in the global policy community and experts of the region. Despite attempts by the government to remedy the situation through the provision of monthly food baskets, often those most in need could not be reached. Some prices have increased tenfolds since 2011, as shortages, plundering, and hoarding have taken hold. Sanctions have also contributed to an inability to treat those injured due to the lack of essential medicines and prosthesis and medicines for those with long-term chronic conditions for physical and mental health need (Al-Faisal et al. 2015; IRIN 2014; Jasarevic 2012; Nasser et al. 2013). Many Syrian have fled to neighbouring countries to access needed medicines, while the conflict also contributed to a reversing of many of the health gains of the past three decades. Life expectancy, for example, has been reduced by 15 years (from 74.9 to 55.6 years) between 2011 and 2016 (Syrian Centre for Policy Studies 2016).

The challenges facing the health sector in Syria have been worsened as a result of destruction, division, and the loss of medical personnel over the past six years. But the HSMP combined with the devastation caused to human resources and capital infrastructure from the current conflict poses serious challenges for the period of reconstruction and for the well-being of the population. The need for an integrated publicly led health-care system is of utmost relevance, an issue that needs to be addressed with vision and caution so that the health sector does not fall into the hands of those who profit from war and ill health, as has been the case for other countries in the region.

Acknowledgement The author would like to thank the editors for their painstaking comments.

Notes

1. There were two phases to reforms. The first from 1971 onwards was the programme of economic liberalisation ("Infitah Iqtisadi").The second starting in the late 1980s and consolidated between 2003 and 2008 for the health sector.
2. The German Development Cooperation (GTZ), official aid from Germany, was then renamed as GIZ in 2011 following a merger with other official development groups in Germany.
3. The ill-conceived and hurried policy measures failed to address rising unemployment and falling incomes but also speeded up a fast transition to full-scale liberalisation without checks and balances needed to regulate the market.
4. PPPs entail as it says a partnership whereby the private sector delivers certain tasks (running a school or a health service) but ownership and most significantly liability remains with the state.
5. Syria was the only country in the region implementing the temporary protection scheme (TPS) when the first wave of refugees arrived following the invasion. UNHCR and UNICEF reported in 2006 on Syria's openness and generosity; refer to UNHCR (2006), "Assessment on the Situation of Iraqi Refugees in Syria," p. 4.
6. In a public-led health-care system, primary health-care services act as gate keeper to refer people to secondary and tertiary care only if needed. Rarely do people go directly to hospital by referring themselves. In a disintegrated service, patients end up at a hospital first without referral.
7. Since 1999, the Ministry of Health in Lebanon made systematic efforts to reform the health system, owing to its high cost and inefficiencies.
8. See also Sen and Koivusalo 1998.
9. The analysis of "health systems" in vogue since the early 2000s was also rather inimical to centrally planned and delivered services.
10. The free health care did not include medicines which after consultations were usually the costliest items for patients. A detailed list of charges for health interventions by the private sector was provided by the Ministry of Health as guidelines to be followed (Sallouta et al. 2003).

11. Autonomous hospitals were allowed to manage themselves and charge patients as part of revenue raising.
12. Country-to-country measures which have not been ratified by the United Nations and hence illegal by international law. Its effects contravene among several inalienable rights, the right to health enshrined in the Economic Cultural and Social Rights.

Bibliography

Abdel-Fadil, M., et al. (2009). *Arab Human Development Report 2009 – Challenges to Human Security in the Arab Countries*. Beirut: United Nations Development Programme, Regional Bureau for Arab States.

Abu-Ismail, K., & Mckinely, T. (2005). *Macro Economic Policies for Poverty Reduction: Syria*. Damascus, Syria: UNDP.

Abu-Ismail, K., Abdel-Gadir, A., & El-Laithy, H. (2010). *Poverty and Inequality in Syria: Development Challenges(1997–2007)*. Damascus: UNDP.

Al Nashif, N. (2011). *Challenges in the Arab World – An ILO Response* (pp. 10–12). Geneva, Switzerland: International Labour Organisation.

Al-Azmeh, S. (2014). *The Uprising of the Marginalized*. London: LSE Middle East Centre.

Al-Faisal, W., Saleh, Y., & Sen, K. (2015). Syria: End Sanctions and Find a Political Solution to Peace. *The Lancet, 3*, (N/A). Retrieved January 8, 2015, from http://www.thelancet.com/pdfs/journals/langlo/PIIS2214-109X(15)00046-7.pdf

Ammar, W. (2009). *Health Beyond Politics: Beirut Beirut*. Lebanon: Lebanon, World Health Organisation and Ministry of Health.

Armada, F., Muntaner, C., & Navarro, V. (2001). Health and Social Security Reforms in Latin America: The Convergence of the WHO, the World Bank, and Transnational Corporations. *International Journal of Health Services, 4*(31), 729–768. Baywood Publishing Company, USA.

Bhutta, Z. A. (2001). Structural Adjustments and their Impacts on Health and Society: A perspective from Pakistan. *International Journal of Epidemiology, 30*, 712–716 Retrieved January 1, 2016, from http://ije.oxfordjournals.org/content/30/4/712.full.pdf+html

Bruck, T., Binzel, C., & Hendrich, L. (2007). *Evaluating Economic Reforms in Syria*. Berlin, Germany: Deutsche Institute Fur Wirtchafts Farschung.

Chen, M., Chen, W., & Zhao, Y. (2012). New evidence on financing equity in China's health care reform. *BMC Health Services Research, 12*(466), 1–13 Retrieved January 7, 2016, from http://www.biomedcentral.com/1472-6963/12/466

Dashdash et al. (2010). *National Health Accounts for Syria, Ministry of Health and WHO*. Syria: Damascus.

Dostal, J. M. (2008). *The European Union's Role in the Debate on Economic Reform in Syria*. In 58th Political Studies Association Annual Proceedings, Political Studies Association, ed., Swansea University, Wales: Political Studies Association.

Elgazzarm, H., Raadm, F., Arfa, C., Mataria, A., Salti, M., Chaaban, J., Isfahani, D. S., Fesharaki, S., & Majbouri, M. (2010). *Who pays? Out of Pocket Health Spending and Equity Implications in the Middle East and North Africa*. Washington, DC: The World Bank – HNP.

El-Laithy, H., Abu Ismail, K., & Hamdan, K. (2008). *Country Study: Poverty, Growth and Income Distribution in Lebanon*. New York: UNDP, Poverty Centre Country Study.

European Commission. (2003). *European Neighbourhood & Partnership Instrument, Syrian Arab Republic, Country Strategy Paper 2007–2013*. Brussels and Damascus.

Gaertner, R. (2003). *Public Private Partnership in Primary Health Care: Decision Paper: Towards a National Health Insurance System in Syria*. Syria: Ministry of Health.

Gaffney, D., Pollock, A. M., & Price, D. (1999). *The Politics of the Private Finance Initiative and the New. NHS, 39*.

Galdo, A. (2004). *Welfare in Mediterranean Countries: The Syrian Arab Republic*. Damascus, Syria: Formez, Caimed and Regione-Campagne.

Haddad, B. (2011). The Political Economy of Syria: Realities and Challenges. *Middle East Policy Council, XVIII*(2), 1–18.

Hatem, R. (2011). *The Expected Impact of the Introduction of the Social Health Insurance on the Syrian Public Hospital Management*. Greifswald, Germany: Ernst-Moritz-Arndt Universität Greifswald.

Hinnebusch, R. (1994). Liberalization in Syria: The Struggle for Political and Economic Rationality. In E. Kienle (Ed.), *Contemporary Syria: Liberalization Between Cold War and Cold Peace*. London: I.B. Tauris.

IFAD. (2009). *Rural Poverty in Syria: Rural Poverty Portal*. Rome: IFAD. 1-1-2016.

International Labour Office. (2010). *Gender Employment and the Informal Economy in Syria*. Policy Brief no. 8. 8, 2–6. 1-1-2010. Beirut, Lebanon. International Labour Organisation Regional Office. 1-9-2010.

IRIN. (2007a). *Economic Reforms Threaten Social Unrest*.

IRIN. (2007b). *Warning of Looming Crisis as Iraqi Refugee Influx Continues*.

IRIN. (2008). *Syria: Wealth Gap Widening as Inflation Hits the Poor*.

IRIN. (2014). *Syria's Health Care System Crumbling*.

Jasarevic, T. (2012, August 30). *Syria Humanitarian*. Geneva, Switzerland: World Health Organisation.

Kanji, N., Najmi, K., & Feroz, M. (1991). From Development to a Sustained Crisis: Structural Adjustment, Equity and Health. *Social Science and Medicine, 33*(9), 985–993. Elsevier, UK.

Kassab, D., & Lane, E. (2011). Healthy Business: Is There a Future for the Private Health Care Industry in Syria? *SYRIA TODAY Magazine* on line, Damascus, Syria.

Khatib, B. (2006). *Health Profile of Syria, 2006*. Indiana University School of Medicine, Department Public Health.

Khatta, M., & Hussein, S. A. C. (2011). *Women's Access to Social Protection in Syria*. London: Elsevier.

Lagarde, M., & Palmer, N. (2009). *The Impact of Contracting Out Health Outcomes and Use of Health Services in Low and Middle-income Countries [review]*. London: John Wiley & Sons.

Matar, L. (2012, March 27). *The Socio-economic Roots of the Syrian Uprising*. No. 58, 1–2. Singapore, Middle East Institute, National University of Singapore.

Matar, L. (2016). Economic Liberalization as an Irreversible Trend During the Bashar Regime: Socio Economic Fuel of the Syrian Crisis. In *The Political Economy of Investment in Syria* (pp. 107–135). Palgrave Macmillan.

Ministry of Health Syria. (2009). *Health Sector Modernization Program 2009*. Damascus, Syria.

Nasser, R., Mehchy, Z., & Abu Ismail, K. (2013). *Socio Economic Roots and Impact of Syrian Crisis*. Syrian Centre for Policy Studies, Damascus, Syria.

Perthes, V. (1994). The Stages of Economic and Political Liberalization. In E. Kienle (Ed.), *Contemporary Syria: Liberalization Between Cold War and Cold Peace*. London: I. B. Tauris.

Pfeifer, K. (2014). Neo Liberal Transformation and the Uprisings in Tunisia and Egypt. In R. Baharamitash & H. Esfahani (Eds.), *Reflections on the Political Economy of Change in the Middle East and North Africa* (pp. 1–40). UK: Palgrave.

Prinja, S., Kaur, M., & Kumar, R. (2012). Universal Health Insurance in India: Ensuring Equity, Quality and Efficiency. *Indian Journal of Community Medicine, 37*(3), 142–149. Retrieved January 1, 2016, from http://www.ijcm.org.in/text.asp?2012/37/3/142/99907

Qadeer, I. (2013). Universal Health Care The Trojan Horse of New Liberal Health Policies. *Social Change, 43*(149), 1–17. Retrieved January 1, 2015, from http://www.academia.edu/11401921/Universal_Health_Care_The_Trojan_Horse_of_Neoliberal_Policies_On_behalf_of_Council_for_Social_Development

Qadeer, I., Sen, K., & Nayar, K. R. (2001). Introduction. In *Public Health and the Poverty of Reforms*. New Delhi, India: Sage Publications.

Sallouta, R., Ali, R., & Sijani, N. (2003). *Medicine Prices, Availability and Component Costs in Syria*. Ministry of Health, Damascus, Syria.

Schwefel, D. (2003). *Improving National Health Accounts and Social Health Insurance in Syria: Some Assessments and Recommendations in a Modernized Framework – Final Report.* GTZ International Services, Berlin, SYR/AIDCO/2001/0215.

Schwefel, D. (2008). *Towards a National Health Insurance System in Syria.* Ministry of Health, Government of Syria, Berlin, AIDCO/2001/0215.

Schwefel, D., & Ministry of Health. (2008). *Health Sector Modernization Program: Towards a National Health Insurance System in Syria, 2003–2008.* GTZ, EPOS, Options, Berlin, Germany, SYR/AIDCO/2001/0215.

Seifan, S. (2011). *The Road to Economic Recovery in Syria.* St Andrews Centre for Syrian Studies.

Sen, K., & Al-Faisal, W. (2012). Syria: Neo Liberal Reforms in Health Sector Financing – Embedding Unequal Access? *Social Medicine, 6*(136), 146. Retrieved January 1, 2013, from http://www.socialmedicine.info/index.php/socialmedicine/article/view/572/1207

Sen, K., & Al-Faisal, W. (2013). Reforms and Emerging Non Communicable Disease: Challenges Facing a Conflict – Ridden Country; Syria. *International Journal of Health Planning and Management, 28*(3), 290–302. Retrieved January 1, 2015, from http://onlinelibrary.wiley.com/doi/10.1002/hpm.2193/abstract

Sen, K., & Koivusalo, M. (1998). Health Care Reforms and Developing Countries: A Critical Overview. *International Journal of Health Planning and Management, 13*(2), 199–215.

Sen, K., & Sibai, A. (2010). Health Care Financing and Delivery in the Context of Crisis: The Case of Lebanon. In J. P. Unger, P. Paepe, K. Sen, & W. Soors (Eds.), *International Health and Aid Policies: The Need for Alternatives* (Vol. 1, pp. 138–152). New York: Cambridge University Press.

Siddiqi, S., Masud, T. I., & Sabri, B. (2006). Contracting But Not Without Caution Experience with Outsourcing of Health Services in Eastern Mediterranean Region. *Bulletin of the World Health Organization, 84*(11), 867–875. Retrieved January 1, 2011, from http://apps.who.int/bookorders/anglais/detart1.jsp?sesslan=null&codlan=0&codcol=2&codcch=8411

Sukkar, N. (2003). *Syria: The Need to Reform Now!* (p. 33). Oxford: The Oxford Business Group.

Syrian Centre for Policy Studies. (2016). *Confronting Fragmentation: Impact of Syrian Crisis Report.* Damascus, Syria: UNDP.

The World Bank. (2005). *Syrian Investment Climate: Unlocking the Potential of the Private Sector.* Washington, DC: The World Bank.

Thomas, E. (2013). *Syria's Disabled Future.* Middle East Research and Information Project (MERIP). pp. 1–6. Retrieved January 7, 2016, from http://www.merip.org/mero/mero051413

UNHCR. (2006). *Assessment of the Situation of Iraqi Refugees in Syria.* Damascus, Syria: UNHCR, UNICEF & World Food Programme.

UNICEF (United Nations Int. Children's Fund). (1987). *Adjustment with a Human Face Vol. 1 and 2* (pp. 1–320). Oxford: Clarendon Press.
United Nations Development Programme. (2010). *Syrian Arab Republic: Third National MDGs Progress Report*. Damascus, Syria: United Nations Development Programme.
WHO. (2001). *Macro Economic Commission on Investing in Health for Economic Development*. Geneva: WHO.
WHO. (2011). *Syria: National Health Accounts: Health Metrics Network*. Geneva: WHO.
WHO. (2014). *World Health Organization: Syria Donor Update*. Damascus: WHO.
World Health Organization & Eastern Mediterranean Regional Office. (2006). *Health Systems Profile-Syria*. Cairo: WHO-EMRO.
Yousef, T. M. (2004). Development, Growth and Policy Reform in the Middle East and North Africa Since 1950. *Journal of Economic Perspectives, 18*(3), 91–116.
Zawaya. (2010). *Public Private Partnerships Play Dominant Role in Driving Sustainable Growth of Middle East Health Care Sector*. Dubai, United Arab Emirates: Zawya.

CHAPTER 10

The Political Economy of Thermidor in Syria: National and International Dimensions

Max Ajl

INTRODUCTION

Conventional narratives of the Syrian crisis trace a line of flight from neoliberal destatisation of the economy, the breaking of the historic link between the Syrian government and the peasantry, and then social and economic dislocation, opening the way to a proxy war upon Syria. This war occurred as outside forces—the US, the GCC states, and Turkey—encouraged the militarisation of the uprising and proceeded to arm, fund, and train forces internal and external to Syria, creating a zero-sum game within which armed conflict and rival claimants to sovereignty led to the destruction of much of the country.[1] The social hollowing out which created the internal basis for disillusionment with the government occurred through (1) rural impoverishment and (2) flight to urban and periurban slums. This chapter proposes to add several dimensions to this narrative. First, it situates the Ba'ath as the local manifestation of a much larger historical process, during which anti-systemic movements emerged throughout the globe. Amidst a global efflorescence of radicalism, Syrian intellectuals,

M. Ajl (✉)
Cornell University, Ithaca, NY, USA

© The Author(s) 2019
L. Matar, A. Kadri (eds.), *Syria: From National Independence to Proxy War*, https://doi.org/10.1007/978-3-319-98458-2_10

organisers, politicians, peasants, and workers found socialist and communist philosophies and utopias increasingly beguiling. Oppressed groups stepped onto the political stage and demanded a break with the traditional order. The post-1958 Syrian state is the product of that process. In order to understand the original state-society pact, analysts must break out of the box of the nation-state and "methodological nationalism" to see a global diffusion of ideas and aspirations.[2] But analysts must also understand the interplay between objective and quantifiable processes of social redistribution and the social struggle which compels such changes. To use Sandra Halperin's phrase, looking for such a causal factor means highlighting the "importance of social revolution for broad-based prosperity and democracy"—or certainly the first, prosperity, as the second, (political) democracy, does not apply to the Ba'ath governments.[3] In carrying out this analysis, one must keep in mind that "revolution" is a process which lies on a spectrum. Is-or-isn't-it-a-revolution is a less fruitful analytical enterprise than trying to assess the level of social mobilisation and to correlate it with the degree of social change, which may be important, even if it may fall short of full Jacobin-style destruction of the prevailing social order.[4]

In turn, to understand the process of Thermidor, or passive-revolution-in-reverse, through which non-state capital gradually regained power within Syria, this chapter adds to analyses which locate neoliberalisation amidst a pact between the budding state bourgeoisie and the old merchant classes.[5] It traces a multifaceted process through which the Israeli defeat of Arab nationalism in 1967 stalled or reversed the ascent of the radicals in Syria and elsewhere in the Arab region and induced a holding pattern, with the government of Syria oriented towards endurance, alongside an opening to foreign capital. Increasingly independent organisations of the lower classes became corporatist ones, less and less able to defend or deepen social gains. Private capital flourished in the commercial interstices of this system. As the lower classes' ability to defend their gains waned, private capital was increasingly able to set the political agenda.

On the global plane, this chapter traces a process through which the US moved to a system of "hot" capital flows in the wake of the 1973 so-called oil crisis. After that point, every national social formation became subject to one or another form of fiscal or currency-related pressure due to the breakdown of the Bretton Woods system and the "embedded liberalism" which went along with it.[6] In the Syrian iteration of that process, the sudden burgeoning of the Gulf States as centres of regional capitalism also meant a pressure of "dollarisation" on the Syrian economy. Post-1970 reforms and policies meant that this pressure found many points at which to alter the shape of the Syrian social formation—for example, land markets, tractor rental and ownership, and commerce.

Finally, this chapter traces this process through the early 2000s, as Syria entered a period of growth-without-development. The government, increasingly captured by the bourgeoisie, devoted fewer and fewer resources to rural development. Meanwhile the populist commitment to the peasantry waned amidst the resurgence of agrarian capitalism, with the state loosening its grip on certain sectors of rural production. Loans and pricing policies were increasingly oriented to the middle peasantry and larger. At the same time, industrial production was collapsing, eliminating a release valve for the social contradictions of the countryside—the absorption of rural unemployment. Finally, the drought, which began in 1999 and reached its desiccating apex in 2006–2008, shattered remaining rural livelihoods. However, this chapter adds to prevailing analyses of the drought a world-ecological angle, since the carbon dioxide emissions which produced that drought are global processes rooted in the production patterns of the global North. The following pages will also note continuing Syrian diversion of budgetary spending from investment to defence as not merely a phenomenon reducible to a self-explaining "Praetorian state" but rather as a Syrian response to global geopolitics and the US special relationship with Israel.

Putting Ba'athism and Revolution in World-Systemic Perspective

This chapter traces the ascendance of the Ba'ath and its early policies of agrarian transformation in a world-systemic lineage and conjuncture, identifying the philosophical mélange of right and left Ba'ath alike as part of a broader legacy of anti-systemic movements then sweeping the Arab world. In so doing it situates Ba'ath attempts at rural incorporation—a legacy that endured for decades—in their local and extra-local context.

When speaking of a "global revolution" or the rise of anti-systemic movements, this chapter refers not just to the simultaneous emergence in a great many countries of both nationalist and socialist movements aiming to seize the state and use its power to re-engineer the social class system. It also means something more grounded, specific, and concrete. That revolution meant, especially, the diffusion of specific ideas, a process through which early Syrian-Bolshevik alliances contributed "to a general

Syrian public consciousness that Soviet Russia was on the side of anti-imperialism and Syrian independence."[7] With socialism of various kinds increasingly a North Star for the various movements fighting for state power both in the Arab world and more broadly, nascent movements and intellectual clusters absorbed, debated, modified, and rejected some of these ideas. Communism and the Russian Revolution influenced both Michel Aflaq and Salah al-Din al-Bitar, with the former telling Patrick Seale that in his pre-Ba'ath days, "We were then Marxists with few reservations."[8] Meanwhile the Syrian Communist movement, which often pulled the Ba'ath leftward, was at the forefront of mass-based anti-imperialist movements, trade union organising, and the promotion of land reform in the countryside.[9] As early as 1951, 30–40 per cent of the population expressed pro-Soviet sentiments, in part due to the West's support for Israel, and the left-wing press inundated the public sphere with the theoreticians of leftist thought, to the point that "'half the intellectuals and even illiterates knew Marx and Lenin better than the leaders of Arab nationalism and Islam.'"[10] The Ba'ath itself was a far more fissiparous political movement in its early years than in its more sclerotic later ones. In the words of Fawwaz Traboulsi, "The tableau of Ba'ath was something different from the one you know now. It was a broad alliance that had everything in it, the Arab Spirit [Michel] Aflaq folks, the Algerian model people, and those supporters of armed struggle, as well as a large leftist bloc."[11] And the merger of Akram al-Hawrani's Arab Socialist Party (ASP) with the Ba'ath in 1952 added a strong pro-peasant strain. The ASP commanded a massive following of destitute peasants, creating a built-in pressure group within the party for rural redistribution. Later as the Ba'ath developed, "there was a strong statist and collectivist strain of romantic nationalism in [Aflaq's] thought: the nation and service to it were exalted above 'petty material' private interests."[12] At the same time, before the union with Egypt in the UAR, Afif al-Bizri, a "radical socialist," was the chief of staff of the army. In the estimation of one observer, "The socialist forces dominated the political scene in Syria just prior to the formation of the U.A.R."[13] Socialism along with unity and freedom was the Ba'ath's tri-faceted creed, with different elements of that trinity ascending and others descending depending on the moment and the broader tableau of political and social power.

By 1963, in Hinnebusch's estimation, "the military committee in alliance with young radical intellectuals … at the definitive Sixth National Congress, succeeded in fusing Marxism-Leninism to Arab nationalism in a new radicalised version of [Ba'ath] doctrine."[14] Ba'athism emerged as part of a global efflorescence of populist, socialist, and other anti-systemic movements encompassing the 1917–1973 wave of national revolts which went by various names, including the anticolonial movements or the emergence of the South.[15] What they had in common was the ambition for a national project. The precise nature of each project—the way the local population and political and intellectual leaders syncretised, modified, adulterated, or cynically deployed socialism locally—depended on the local contours of struggle, organisation, existing political parties, and arenas of economic disarray that would produce organic leadership.

The Early and Mid-Ba'athist Social Compact

From the 1950s onwards, local social movements and the political vehicles which sought to take those movements in hand and crystallise them in organisational form were omnipresent in Syria. Forces of socialism, communism, and left-wing Ba'athism were increasingly setting the agenda within Syria, echoing and reinforcing the global context of a rising wave of anti-systemic movements. From the mid-1950s to 1970, a series of coup d'états and nearly instant ripostes took place, with the ancien régime repeatedly and evanescently winning back power, only to see the Ba'ath again take and retake power. There were not merely tussles at the top but reflected active mobilisation from below. There were tremendous street demonstrations in 1962 against the right-wing coup d'état of 1961, and they demanded the application of the July 1961 Socialist Decrees. In December 1962, 22,000 teachers went on strike: "All schools were closed and a state of chaos spread over the country. The society was on the verge of insurrection."[16] The 1963 left-wing coup leaned heavily on peasants, workers, and students.[17] It was then that the Ba'ath again securely grabbed hold of social power, setting in motion a series of policies intended to tighten its relationship with the middle and lower peasantry, to deepen the agrarian restructuring and, as the decade bore on, simply to dispossess much of the country's bourgeoisie.

I here propose a rough typology of incorporation or enfoldment into the social pact. On the one hand, there is a populist-style model, which involves state distribution of public goods and for that reason continued reliance on state largesse for day-to-day survival. This model relies on a certain separation between the citizen and the producer, with subsistence secured through the intermediary of the state. On the other, there is incorporation through clientelism—in this case, the literal creation of a new class of middle peasants. Production is directly in the hand of the producer. The typology is uneven, given that reproduction is always production, but is intended to give a sense of who had direct control over the means of production and who relied more upon the state for their well-being. In the Syrian case, the former group, middle peasants, was indebted to the state and relied on it for guaranteed purchases, although the state also relied on it for the production of agricultural commodities which were central to social well-being and national-level economic planning and social management. Nevertheless, given that the middle peasants retained considerable agricultural land, and were also capitalist commodity producers, their insertion into the class structure also enabled differentiation in the Syrian countryside. Such continued class relationships would eventually lead to broader shifts in power.

The first Ba'athist agrarian reform, Law No. 161, was not the most austere. Passed on 27 September 1958, the law placed caps on landowners of 80 hectares of irrigated land and 300 hectares for rain-fed land. The law was meant to benefit 750,000 people, figuring five people per family—17 per cent of the overall population and 27 per cent of the rural population. The redistributed plots were to be 8 hectares of irrigated land, or 30 hectares of unirrigated land. The planners copied it from Egypt, where land types were far more uniform, especially within the Nile floodplain, and for that reason it flattened out the contours of Syrian land quality, which was far more varied than a simple bifurcation of irrigated/non-irrigated. In any case, it did not succeed—first of all due to the drought,[18] second due to a lack of skilled personnel to help implement it, and third, due to a high degree of landlord resistance. By the end of 1961, the government had expropriated 670,212 hectares and distributed just 148,400 hectares to merely 15,000 families. A 1961 revision moved the caps on land size markedly upwards to 200 hectares of irrigated land and 600 hectares of unirrigated land. However Law No. 88 of 1963 then shifted those limits sharply downwards, inaugurating the Ba'athist revolution in the countryside. Limits were lower, 15–45 hectares depending on the area or up to 200–300 hectares in areas with extremely low rainfall. By 1972, the government had expropriated 1.37 million hectares, with the great majority distributed and just 239,000 left undistributed.[19] Table 10.1 gives a certain sense of the successive reforms in the land laws:

The Ba'ath agrarian policies also allowed peasants farming on expropriated land to pay back the value of the land which the state had distributed

Table 10.1 Successive changes in the land laws, 1958–1963

Aspects of law	1958 law	Dawalibi's government, 20 Feb 1962, parliamentary revisions	Azmeh's government, 30 April 1962, revisions	23 June 1963, Ba'athist Revolution, March 1963, Law 88
I. Retention of land by landowners				
Irrigated	80	200	80	15–45 ha depending on area
Non-irrigated	300	600	300	80–200 ha dependent on rainfall
Non-irrigated in some areas	450	1200	450	Up to 300 ha in Northeast
II. Limits on gifts				
To wives	10 ha irrigated, 40 ha non-irrigated, to one wife	1/8th of land retained by owner, to all wives	10 ha irrigated, 40 ha non-irrigated, to all wives	8% of land allowed to landowner
To children	As above, 3 oldest children	As above (i.e. 1/8th), to *all* children	As above (i.e. 10 and 10) to all children	–
III. Payments to owners				
Length of payment period	40 years	10 years	(a) Compensations under LS 100,000, 10 years (b) Compensations over LS 100,00, 15 years	= 10 times avg. rent over 40 years
Annual interest	1.5%	2.5%	1.5%	1.5%
IV. Distributed land to peasants				
Irrigated land	10	10	8 ha	8 ha
Non-irrigated	30 ha	15 ha	30 ha (45 ha in some areas)	30–45 ha
V. Payments by peasants				
Length	40 years	Free	40 years	

(*continued*)

Table 10.1 (continued)

Aspects of law	1958 law	Dawalibi's government, 20 Feb 1962, parliamentary revisions	Azmeh's government, 30 April 1962, revisions	23 June 1963, Ba'athist Revolution, March 1963, Law 88
Cost	Full cost, including admin fees	Free	50% full cost, including admin fees	25% of value of land, sent to coops

Source: Ziad Keilany, "Land Reform in Syria," *Middle Eastern Studies* 16, no. 3 (1980): 214

to them through financing coops.[20] The state also implemented an array of other social policies, including populist policies: rural electrification and opening the universities in the countryside. From 1963 to 1977, the ratio of doctors to the population increased countrywide, except for Hasakeh in the Northeast. Nevertheless, doctors continued to concentrate in cities, despite programmes meant to countervail this trend. Teacher-student ratios also improved, showing a consistent attention to improving rural living conditions. There was an enormously egalitarian thrust to Ba'ath policies in the countryside.[21] However, that thrust was often at the *social-populist* rather than *productive* plane. Poorer people in the countryside were increasingly incorporated into the ruling pact, but only partially as meaningful contributors to increasing overall agricultural production, since a substantial sector of the rural population remained either landless or without sufficient land to fully support themselves. Nevertheless, the state supported them in other ways. They were beneficiaries of various channels of rent accruing to the state—both geopolitical rent, from the richer Arab countries, seeking to support Syria as a "frontline state" against Israel and other rents from increased oil revenue and guaranteed access to Soviet markets. These allowed the state to channel and redirect capital to various social sectors while also allowing space for a burgeoning private sector.

In addition to basic infrastructural investments, the Ba'athist state also expanded credit to the agricultural sector. From 1963 to 1966, the yearly average was 36.9 million Syrian pounds—although due to expropriations, time delays in setting land into production, and difficulties and exigencies of development planning during transitions, this period is not indicative of development priorities. From 1967 to 1970, that amount quadrupled to

143.2 million Syrian pounds.[22] During this second period, the agricultural sector also received 19.7 per cent of all credit which the state allotted.[23] Such numbers omit the class dimension of state support, sidestepping the fact that much of the credit during this period was flowing to the larger farmers. Nevertheless, while credit for productive investment went to those with larger resource endowments, long-term infrastructural investments were far more egalitarian, consistent with the state's attention to both the lower and middle classes in the countryside.

From 1970 to 1978, industrial output grew by 11.6 per cent a year.[24] GDP overall grew at 5.7 per cent per annum between 1960 and 1970, and 9 per cent between 1970 and 1979, with per capita income reaching $1030 by 1979.[25] Syria produced no capital goods and was therefore reliant on technology imports. Much of the industry was turnkey, essentially assembly plants. Still, import-substitution industrialisation (ISI) compared to the following period of economic liberalisation was relatively more productive.[26]

During this period the state also monopolised the purchase and sale of major agricultural commodities, such as cotton and wheat, thereby insulating the growers of those commodities from the vacillations and predations of the merchant class. This government policy in effect sharply restricted market operations, subjecting the production prices of crops—and therefore the social reproduction of farmers—entirely to the politics of state planning. For small farmers and large farmers alike, this could be a marked advantage. After the harvest, smaller farmers in the pre-reform period were compelled to sell to obtain cash for paying off debts they had accumulated during planting and gathering. Such pressure, combined with the opportunity for arbitrage provided by shifting prices, had previously afforded "the opportunity to warehouse keepers—the *khanjis* of Aleppo, the *bawaykiyyas* of Damascus, and the like in other towns—to buy grain at a cheap price and hold it in the expectation of considerable profit from a rise in its market value later in the year when stocks became low."[27] After the reform, this was no longer possible. Furthermore, credit itself was at least partially removed from the capitalist circuit. Through the extirpation of the merchant-arbitrage operations, more capital could stay in the productive circuit, allowing for agricultural investment amongst farmers and thereby theoretically allowing for increases in agricultural productivity, a fact which was borne out by post-1970 yield and overall production increases.[28] Furthermore, even for those farmers who more seldom had a surplus for investment, Ba'ath policies protected the small peasant from sudden immiseration, even lack of sufficient food to eat, which was precipitated by sharp manipulation and vacillation of prices by monopsonistic traders and hedgers. For smaller farmers, it seems almost certain that their lives had improved through this measure, even if by lesser degrees than for larger farmers.

Whatever would have been the destination of these policies cannot be known. But overall the trajectory from 1963 to 1967 was towards more rather than less radicalism, with the state bringing in communist ministers albeit in individual capacities, effectively legalising the Syrian Communist Party, defeating rightist deviations and countercoups, drawing closer to the Soviet Union, and decisively rejecting the nationalistic socialism of the earlier Ba'ath in favour of a far more Marxist-inflected model.[29] But political currents do not shift within isolated bodies, immune from larger geopolitical shifts, impulsions, and compulsions. This is the case for any and all populist or radical movements operating in the world system. For the Syrian Ba'ath, this emerged amidst the Arab Cold War, as Arab nationalist movements competed with one another for legitimacy both on the plane of internal social redistribution and external confrontation with Israel, vying for mass popular legitimacy.[30]

Early Stages of Thermidor: Confrontation with Israel and the Geopolitical Origins of the Ba'ath's Corrective Movement

Confrontation with Israel, a crucial means of internal legitimation for Arab states, could also be a mechanism for social regression and the ebb of the radical tide. In this way, the external realm also conditioned compromises and reversions and induced defeats. Narratives of teleological "corrective movements" do not account for this. Rather, corrective movement, or Thermidor, is a phenomenon which requires explanation and which demands the identification of mechanisms for governments' shifts to lesser rather than greater social redistribution. As Immanuel Wallerstein notes, it is important to remember the phenomenon of movements making "major compromises in terms of their long-run anti-systemic ideals" is a universal phenomenon and often the result of external intrusion, "directly and indirectly, political and militarily if necessary."[31] In this case, and more broadly, a major mechanism of social reversion in the Middle East has been Israeli military action—"When all the military defeats to which Arab formations have been subjected are considered, the Israeli factor alone … engrains a state of defeat."[32]

In 1967, the Syrian project suffered a blow sharp enough radically to reorient it—the Israeli defeat of the Arab armies in the 1967 war. In the words of the British Foreign Office, the consequence was that the "revolutionary Arabs" had been "completely deflated."[33] That, and the loss of Quneitra, "checked and gradually reversed the radicalisation of Syrian policies." A government which relied on nationalist legitimacy suffered gravely amidst poor performance on the military front, and the "lower priority it seemed to give to defense of the front than to the regime in Damascus, greatly diminished its nationality legitimacy."[34] Indeed, "the loss of Quneitra became a permanent reproach to the Ba'ath. The defeat demoralised the party's rank and file and, gravely weakening the radicals' leadership, provided the conditions for an intra-party challenge to them."[35] With the loss of legitimacy, there was a swelling of dissent and alternative contenders for leadership. Particularly, then-Defence Minister Hafez al-Asad led a faction which "sought to suspend the 'revolutionary struggle' because, in dividing Syrians and Arabs, it diverted them from their main enemy, Israel, and the 'main challenge of the phase,' recovery of the lost territories."[36]

This is an instance wherein Syria's insertion into an international state system overdetermined its internal course. Of course, describing any process of social change is "internal" is often to forget that purportedly national historical events are often part of a holistic development of much broader patterns of action, operating on multiplanar scales. And the Israeli defeat of Arab nationalism was not merely an Israeli policy but also a US policy, occurring with a US green light, reflecting US interests, and heralding a far tighter relationship between the US and Israel.[37] This moment illustrates precisely how the Israeli factor induced or certainly lubricated a shift in state policy, from building up overall productive capacity through radically redistributive policies, to justifying Thermidor on nationalist lines. Since the 1967 government could not—apparently—resist Israel and redistribute social power at home, the latter goal was sacrificed in favour of the former, with the Salah Jadid government the sacrificial animal for this conversion in state ideology and practice.

Thermidor and Petrodollars in Syria

This reversal in the Middle East was part of a longer shift in the historical pattern of post-World World II regional political management and global geo-economic planning. Thermidor was not a merely national phenomenon but was global, with the post-war surge of national liberation movements and post-colonial populist governments entering a prolonged twilight, and the hopes of global Fordism or global social democracy dashed amidst the decline of the 1917–1973 interlude of developmental states. After the Israeli "deflation" of the radical Arabs, the US broke apart the Bretton Woods system from 1971 to 1973, within which the dollar was pegged to gold reserves and other currencies traded at stable rates with the dollar. As Matias Vernengo notes, "US hegemony has increased in the post-Bretton Woods dollar system vis-à-vis the Gold-Dollar system of Bretton Woods, and that has been actively pursued by the US."[38] The result was that many governments had to abandon fixed exchange rates. Even states like Syria which sought to secure them were under heavy and inexorable pressure to unfix their exchange rates. The embedded liberalism of the post-war region in fact rested upon this system, and in its absence, there was increasing pressure on all states to abandon national welfare systems. The US could do as it wished in terms of monetary and fiscal policy and could then affect internal policies of other states to the extent that they permitted the de facto dollarisation of their economies or pegged their currencies to the dollar, thereby forgoing national fiscal sovereignty. States which sought to defend their currencies through capital controls could be an obstacle to this system.[39] The enormous flash flood of dollars, and the difficulty of defending capital controls amidst the enormous weight of regional dollarisation, eventually became another element of Thermidor in the region. This occurred through several mechanisms. First, Gulf-based Syrian expatriate capital accumulated dollar-based fortunes. Second, increasing business activities (mainly construction) in Saudi Arabia and Kuwait attracted Syrian migrant workers who sent remittances home in dollars. In 1980, remittances totalled $750 million, or five per cent of total GDP.[40] At the same time, both geopolitical rent and diasporic accumulation created a perverse incentive structure, as the Syrian state had to make fundamental choices about how to continue the process of state-directed development. Luring foreign capital meant assuring it a stable berth for growth.

This process took on its most stark form when the government opened the economy once again to foreign investments through Law No. 10 of 1991. The goal was to lure in diaspora and expatriate Syrian capital. Gross fixed capital formation was supposedly to receive a boost through private investment, which primarily went to short-term and non-productive types of ventures.[41] Although justified under the rubric of expecting the private sector to lead developmental or investment efforts, it is clear that private capitalists in North and South alike have preferred to leave the tasks of productive agricultural and industrial investment to the state or at the very least to rely on the state to create the fiscal scaffolding which enables such development. Private investment tails rather than leads state productive developmentalism. Thermidor, then, is also a process through which holders of private capital increasingly invest in such "ventures."

Rural Ba'athism: The Growth of Capitalist Middle Peasants (1963–2000)

During this period, the state sought to maintain its nationalist legitimacy by building up a domestic welfare state and constantly encouraging the growth of national production in agriculture and industry while also maintaining spaces within Syria for domestic accumulation. On the one hand, this meant price control for credits and inputs of all kinds, as the state engaged in price engineering to mould the class structure and productive activity in ways it deemed fit for survival. It kept prices of fuel for tractors and irrigation pumps low up to 1974, although it increased them again in 1975–1976, all the while staying below the standard world price. For fertilisers, prices stayed at a level between 65 and 95 per cent of world prices. As expressed in wheat, the prices of fertilisers declined 50 per cent from 1963 to 1976.[42] Furthermore, the government massively subsidised wheat producers. With the exception of the 1974–1976 period—when global wheat prices briefly spiked—the government paid prices well above border prices, or the equivalent price it would pay if it had to import wheat.[43] In 1973, for example, the government paid farmers 26 per cent above world market prices. In 1977–1978, US farmers received $85.58 per metric ton, while Syrian growers received $153.84. By 1981, per capita agricultural income increased 76 per cent over that of the 1960–1963 period, the price of electricity declined in real terms, and oil, bread, and sugar were all subsidised.[44]

At this level of granularity, the picture seems blurry. But other sources of information allow us to see a dual process. On the one hand, populist incorporation: the state taking pains to ensure the social reproduction of the peasantry, including the small peasantry, and even the landless. For the latter benefit as much as, if not more than, the former from food subsidies, rural electrification, and the spread of school and healthcare. On the other, after the initial Ba'thist land redistribution levelled out property ownership, rural differentiation continued. Indeed, the distribution of land is a crucial measure given land's centrality as a factor of production and an index of wealth in the countryside. Table 10.2 shows the distribution of land in the countryside in 1970 and 1981:

Several tendencies are clear in this statistical portrait. First, nearly a sixth of Syrian landholders had incredibly small plots of land in 1970 and 1981. If such plots were irrigated, they would be enough to live on, but generally this was not the case since those with such small parcels of land did not usually have access to credit to intensify their production through investment in irrigation technology. Second, as a result there is a massive drop in the number of farmers who are "mainly" occupied by agriculture, indicating a shift to relying on nonfarm labour to supplement agricultural incomes. The smaller peasant classes lacked sufficient social power to enforce, let alone deepen, the agrarian reform. There is a sharp gap between the black-letter law of property size caps and the actual distribution of rural property. Third, there is an important medium-size capitalist farming class in both years, in the size-band between six and fifty hectares (Table 10.2). It is generally stable between the two time periods—at least with respect to its overall size as a percentage of the rural property-holding

Table 10.2 The distribution of land in the countryside in 1970 and 1981

Size of holding	1970				1981			
	No. of holders	%	Area in ha	%	No. of holders	%	Area in ha	%
Smallest −1 ha	75,500	16.1	36,700	0.8	76,200	17.0	35,900	0.9
Small 1–6 ha	215,400	46.0	596,400	12.7	216,900	48.6	585,400	14.3
Medium 6–50 ha	165,300	35.3	2,563,900	54.8	143,600	32.2	2,118,200	52.0
Large 50 ha+[a]	12,500	2.6	1,477,500	31.6	9400	2.1	1,331,900	32.7
100 ha+	4300	0.9	957,100	20.5	3100	0.7	816,800	20.1
300 ha+	900	0.2	448,300	9.5	700	0.16	476,700	11.7
Total	468,000	100	4,674,600		446,200		4,071,400	100
Agricultural holders mainly occupied by agriculture	438,500	93.6			290,100	65.0		

Source: Volker Perthes, *The Political Economy of Syria Under Asad* (I.B.Tauris, 1997), 82

[a]The 50-hectare category is inclusive of the 100+ and 300+ hectare categories

population. Finally, there is also a large landholding agrarian bourgeoisie, clearly able to accumulate land and openly defy legal ceilings on land ownership. This process has been particularly pronounced in Syria's Northeast, which is not coincidentally the area's poorest. Proximity to political power has usually been the process through which state land was illegally privatised in the region, and the result has been the ability of "a small group to acquire enormous wealth at the expense of the peasant class, and it creates a new class of feudalists—including everything this word and the term 'class' involves," in the words of the head of the Ba'ath Party's peasant committee in Deir Ezzor in 1988.[45]

During this period, capital inflows enabled the state's Bonapartist role in the countryside as the state was situated above the various classes and claimed itself as the representative of all their interests. Under these circumstances, the National Peasants Union increasingly became a corporatist vehicle, with its leadership and thus its advocacy efforts and pressure more and more oriented towards the interests of the middle peasant. This reflected the state's need to control rural discontent and partially placate it while at the same time retaining capitalist property relations within a differentiated countryside. Thus, state policies at this point reflected this uneasy constellation of interests, with the state seeking to alchemise widely divergent class interests into a secure social pact. Given that the state was coordinating geopolitical rent inflows, it could postpone resolving irreconcilable social contradictions. By using seemingly exogenous resources—remittances and, later, oil proceeds and direct capital aid and grants from the larger oil-exporting nations—it was able through clientelist side-payments to bring together a populist coalition.

Given the mélange of state tendencies—corporatist, populist, but also state capitalist—the tableau is of government attempts to placate various classes in society while at the same time ensuring that they could not actually destabilise the social order. Land ownership is one index of this policy orientation. Another was the state's orientation to independent lower-class rural mobilisation. During this period, there was a parallel tamping down of insurgent peasant radicalism. The corporatist peasant unions had their radicalism tamed but their dynamism not entirely quelled. For example, in the pre-1970 period, there were many resolutions calling for agrarian reform, and in the latter period, none.[46] On the matter of credit, there was a 1965 demand to give cooperatives and small peasants priority access to credit. The government heeded this call. In 1970, peasants demanded that the state supply credit on the basis of sharecropping contracts and to grant it directly to the peasant rather than funnel it through the landowner. The government heeded this, as well. In 1977, there was a call for the Agricultural Co-operative Bank (ACB) to extend further credit to cooperatives in the second stabilisation zone. Infrastructural and extension services expanded, and by the 1980s, the state opened rural outlets for retailing basic fixed-price commodities.[47] This dynamic is the corporatisation of the initial Ba'athist radical rural orientation and its remoulding so as not to upset the basic capital endowments which the rural class structure reflected. But alongside corporatisation was a continued populist orientation.

From 1981 to 1994, the patterns were somewhat different (Table 10.3). For one thing, there was an increase in the number of people living on the land.

There is some shrinkage by 1994 of the largest landholders, likely due to inheritance. Other dynamics, however, had more force. The first is an increase in absolute landlessness in the countryside amidst both successive partition and repartition due to inheritance. Furthermore, many rural people were never able to take possession of land, relegated to being smaller tenants, agricultural day labourers, or sharecroppers. These patterns are geographically uneven. Landholdings smaller than one hectare continued to swell (see Table 10.3), again likely linked to demographic factors and inheritance. Nevertheless, the number of rural people attempting to live off parcels of land below subsistence size—in the absence of capital resources for intensification—continued to increase from 1981 to 1994. One may speculate that the trend magnified and sharpened from 1994 to 2010, especially given post-2000 privatisations of state land in the Northeast.[48]

Further Dynamics of Rural Capitalism

Other dynamics were also interacting with ongoing polarisation in land ownership, working in synergy to turn it into a source of accentuated class differentiation. For example, the expansion of petrodollars, linked to the post-1973 expansion of the Gulf as a node of regional accumulation, was undermining Syria's system of fixed exchange rates, inducing the de facto dollarisation of Syria.[49] Subsidies on irrigation and especially tractor fuel were not class-neutral in their effects. In 1985, tractors were 97.7 per cent privately owned. By 1990, the number of tractors reached 61,628 but with just 1.3 per cent non-privately-owned.[50, 51] As Batatu notes, "invest-

Table 10.3 The distribution of land in the countryside in 1981 and 1994

Size of holding	1981				1994			
	No. of individuals	%	Area (ha)	%	No. of individuals	%	Area (ha)	%
Smallest								
–1 ha	76,200	17.0	35,900	0.9	111,737	19.5	58,373.8	1.19
Small								
1–6 ha	216.900	48.6	585,400	14.3	265,327	46.3	729,097.2	15.5
Medium								
6–50 ha	143,600	32.2	2,118,200	52.0	184,472	32.2	2,822,156.9	60.2
Large								
50 ha+[a]	9400	2.1	1,331,900	32.7	11,657	1.9	1,077,818	22.9
100 ha+	3100	0.7	816,800	20.1	3042	0.53	365,626.9	7.8
300 ha+	700	0.16	476,700	11.7	350	0.06	169,366.7	3.6
Total	446,200	100	4,071,400	100	573193	100	4,687,446	100
Agricultural holders mainly occupied by agriculture	290,100	% of total 65.0			409,142	% of total 71.4		

Computed from 1981 and 1994 agricultural censuses

[a]The 50-hectare category is inclusive of the 100+ and 300+ hectare categories

ment in agricultural machines is one of the profitable opportunities deliberately left open for private capital by the government in its attempt to attract the new fortunes accumulated after 1973 and during the 1980s by Syrians working in the Gulf."[52] Indeed, to some extent Gulf-based capital allowed non-landowners to purchase machines and rent them out to those without sufficient capital to purchase their own, becoming another source of extraction from smaller farmers. Furthermore, given that at this early point channels for investment were restricted but farmland could be privately owned, the market became competitive and farmland itself became a lucrative investment with price increases per hectare far outpacing the rate of inflation.[53]

Another crucial mechanism for state-assisted rural differentiation was credit, again reflecting state policies and the priorities it accorded distinct social classes in its spending patterns. In this case, credit allocations reflected the mounting power of the rural capitalist class and the state's incorporation of that class as a crucial constituent of its ruling coalition. Furthermore, differences in interest rates between sectors offer insight into which sectors the state prioritised in terms of development and social support. Still, focusing merely on sectors allows for us to see how the state could ensure that agricultural credit was relatively cheap—lower than inflation and thus in effect a grant. From the mid-1970s to February 1981, for example, for smaller loans (below 50,000 Syrian pounds), the rate of interest was 5.5 per cent. For amounts larger than that, the rate of interest was 7.5 per cent.[54] By 1981—another important inflexion point, as the state was contending with an armed insurgency in which some of the petty bourgeoisie participated in some of its cities—the rate went below three per cent for smaller loans.[55] From 1981 onwards, rates from the Commercial Bank and Industrial Bank were between 7.5 and 9 per cent, and for industrialists after 1991, 9.5 to 10 per cent. Meanwhile, before 1981, coops could receive loans at a four per cent rate, while from 1981 to 1991, from two to six per cent, and from 1991 onwards, four to six per cent (depending on the amount).[56] Batatu notes that "agricultural credit was of most benefit to the growers of cotton. Other main beneficiaries were the investors in machinery and equipment, the growers of cereals, and in the mid-1980s the planters of fruit trees."[57] At the same time, while the credit *available* was flowing at preferential rates to the peasantry, it varied according to the state's macro policy and priorities in different periods. From 1967 to 1970, for example, as the radical Ba'ath was still dominating policy-making, credit to agriculture was 19.7 per cent of all credit, whereas from 1976 to 1980, as liberalisation began, it was just 5.4 per cent of all credit. By 1991–1994, it had rebounded to 11.6 per cent of credit, higher than previously but still lower than the share given during the initial radical phase.[58]

Here a shift in priorities is evident, reflecting the state's increasing proximity to and reliance upon its "business backbone," the Sunni urban sectors who profited from merchant and industrial activities (importantly in Aleppo and Damascus).[59] After 1982, this sector became increasingly powerful as the state offered privileges to big businessmen, including public sector projects, tariff walls, and tax exemptions. In the late 1980s, such projects further flourished, and state-private partnerships began to exert large influences on economic policy. The Guidance Committee was originally at the core of this shift in developmental priorities.[60] Such a shift in investment and state largesse also meant a relative neglect of the rural sector. From 1976 to 1994, state credit to agriculture as a percentage of total credit was below agriculture's contribution to either GDP or employment. Agriculture was not necessarily receiving adequate resources for reinvestment, as the state primarily was moving to market-based incentives. Anecdotal evidence suggests that credit provision was also a mechanism for agrarian differentiation: in 1980 the Minister of Economics stated that "Quite a lot of credit has been going to people with adequate finances." As Batatu observes, "the real problem lies in the fact that the Agricultural Cooperatives Bank still does not have enough resources to meet the needs of the peasants in the full," with some peasants continuing to pay rates of 30–40 per cent to usurers, who were the only providers of adequate rural credit.[61] Furthermore, it seems likely that those receiving credit with adequate finances were in fact diverting it to non-state loan markets, thereby undercutting the rates available on state-controlled flows and turning credit into a conduit for further rural differentiation.

In other ways, the government was also allowing further marketisation of Syrian agriculture. For example, in 1986 through Decree No. 10, the government had permitted shareholder companies to establish operations in the mixed sector with state permission and had to sell a stake of the enterprises to the state. These farms could produce whatever they wanted, sidestep price controls, and could trade imported goods to other public sector firms. They could also engage in currency transactions, allowing foreign investors to freely expatriate their money. And such monies, or profits, were not taxed until the seventh year after their first profitable year, creating considerable incentives for capitalist investment in agriculture, although by 1989 only 11 such farms had been founded due to the difficulties of securing land.[62]

Food Security and State Embedding Through Pricing Policy: Further Dynamics of Rural Capitalist Growth

Price-fixing policies have also been a major tool of government planning. Surveys of production expenses, procurement prices, and profit margins for some of the crops which take up most of Syria's arable land are below, for the years 1980, 1985, and 1990.

How these prices induced rural differentiation is not clear, given that post-1980 Syrian economic anthropology is generally sparse, with few studies indicating village-level outcomes of pricing policy, nor many surveys indicating production prices differentiated on a farm-size basis—the government appears to have set prices based on estimates, a common practice in regional agricultural planning. Still, some conclusions may be drawn about Ba'athist agricultural strategy from this period. First, one must note that in terms of social reproduction and social differentiation, in a semi-closed economy such as Syria's (absent massive crop smuggling, at least), world prices are not relevant to the producers themselves—although they may weigh on the calculations of state planners. Second, in 1980, wheat, sugar beet, and cotton producers were assured massive profit margins on their crops (see Table 10.4). Furthermore, barley was the *least* favoured of the major crops in 1980. Barley is traditionally a smallholder crop and is often but not always grown for subsistence. Wheat is far more predominant amongst richer and larger farms. Thus, when comparing periods, one can note a tendency towards social embedding, or a larger state attention through price policy, towards barley producers from 1980 to 1985 (Table 10.4). Perhaps this was linked to shorter-term considerations of the time, namely, the state's sudden shift in favour of the smaller-holder sector as it sought to shore up support amidst the Hama revolt.[63] But the remainder of agriculture suffered the state's neglect, despite rapid increases in procurement prices, as costs of production rose yet more rapidly. By 1990, this trend was reversed, with all crops assured a massive profit margin, meant to help the state achieve food security or self-subsistence in its targeted crops. Here state goals of conserving foreign exchange went hand in hand with goals of preserving and protecting its rural social

Table 10.4 Production expenses, procurement prices, and profit margins for selected crops

Crop	1980			1985			1990		
	Expenses	Price	Profit (%)	Expenses	Price	Profit (%)	Expenses	Price	Profit (%)
Durum wheat	62	80	29.0	123	138	12.2	469	850	81.2
Soft wheat	61	70	14.7	117	123	5.1	419	750	79.0
Non-irrigated barley	52	57	9.6	78	100	28.2	379	550	45.1
Sugar beet	16	22	37.5	29	31	6.9	91	125	37.4
Cotton	187	225	20.3	370	400	8.1	1167	1700	45.7

Source: Batatu, *Syria's Peasantry, the Descendants of Its Lesser Rural Notables, and Their Politics*, 50

base, especially amongst medium-size capitalist farms. Price policy meant the ensured social reproduction of a certain class of farmers and thus the entrenchment of social support for the government. But since capital endowments, mainly land, remained stable and there was a dearth of credit, the ability of smaller farmers to benefit from price engineering was limited.

The policy of state support for the medium- and larger-scale capitalist agricultural sector accelerated in the 1990s and 2000s, as the state devoted more and more investment to irrigation. This policy had several motivations. One was to ensure national self-sufficiency for cotton and cereals, as well as other strategic crops. Cotton was increasingly a fundamental part of Syria's rural, primary processing, and textile industries, while the government, for partially ideological reasons linked to policy priorities, wanted to ensure that the country produced what it consumed. Since from 1995 to 2000 prices were basically stable for inputs and outputs, the state chose to increase production by aiming for yield increases rather than using market-based incentives such as prices. However, stability with respect to how capital and profits *flow* between various agricultural sectors does not mean stability with respect to overall agricultural well-being or a stable class differentiation. There are few surveys on farmer income in modern Syria. A 2001 study showed that the quantity of cultivated land is correlated, albeit imperfectly, with expenditure and thus income. This 2001 survey found this correlation to be strongest amongst the smallest and largest landholders, with the middle peasants showing a murkier picture: in their sample those with farms smaller than one hectare almost uniformly belonged to the lowest expenditure classes, while those with land size above 50 hectares—large capitalist farms—uniformly belonged to three highest expenditure classes.[64] Because yield is higher on irrigated farms, the distribution of irrigated land is of particular importance for understanding social dynamics in the rural arena. However, survey data indicated that land inequality was nearly as pronounced for irrigated plots as in unirrigated ones, with 49 per cent of the holders operating merely 10 per cent of the irrigated land and 28 per cent of the holders operating 75 per cent of the irrigated land.[65]

Furthermore, according to the same 2001 survey, the larger farmers were also the ones who sold to state marketing boards and thus the ones who managed to grab for themselves the overwhelming portion of state producer subsidies. For cotton and wheat—both of which were highly subsidised—smaller farmers often sold nothing to the government, while larger farmers sold massive amounts.[66] For wheat, this is because agricultural families with smaller plots eat what they grow. Thus for wheat prices, support was highly regressive. Similarly, irrigation subsidies and credit from the Agricultural Co-operative Bank (ACB) continued to flow in a regressive manner, indicating that government policies were actively contributing to mounting rural differentiation. In one sense, this was tied to the stasis of land distribution efforts.

In the same survey, farmers reported that access to credit and land were the primary obstacles to greater agricultural production. Furthermore, other evidence has suggested that access to credit is decreasing. Credit is a means of stratification, thereby further reflecting the deterioration of the radical Ba'ath social compact and its move towards more support for the larger farmers and neglect of the smaller ones, never mind the landless or near-landless. The number of beneficiaries of ACB loans decreased by almost one-third from 1994 to 1999, while the overall number of borrowers went down from 749,703 in 1989 to 266,000 in 1999.[67] Loan size however increased, which was "suggestive of a movement toward larger farmers and/or toward better-endowed zones"—in either case, a move away from politically secured support for the smaller farmers and one towards political support for capitalist farming. Furthermore, Sarris suggests, "subsidies in the form of low lending rates and tolerance for defaults, encouraged by a system that does not make it incumbent on the lending bank to be self-reliant for resources, may have been gradually cornered by well-to-do farmers crowding out the poorer ones thereby reducing access to credit."[68] Information on ACB credit policies generally supports this hypothesis. For example, between 1990 and 1999, wheat's percentage of short-term loans was between 20 and 30 per cent of overall loans, decreasing relatively but not absolutely throughout the decade. Barley's percentage—a crop dominated by smallholders but theoretically susceptible to intensification—went from seven per cent of overall loans to about one per cent, declining in absolute and relative terms. Cotton went from 20 per cent to about one-third of overall short-term credit. Again, the sectoral and product-based differentiation of crops disallows definitive conclusions, but given correlations in Syria between growing cotton and wheat and larger plots, and barley on smaller plots, credit was almost certainly an element of differentiation as the smallholder sector was pushed close to the precipice, their production squeezed and starved of state support.[69]

Rural Immiseration in Syria and the Erosion of the Populist Pact

By the early 2000s, these processes were beginning to produce their penurious effects, as the state moved still further from its small farmer base. In part, this was the result of increasing policy orientation to capital-intense, irrigated farming. Furthermore, this process was linked to the ongoing process of state capture by the rural and urban bourgeoisie and the increasing sidelining of those elements within the Ba'ath who still adhered to earlier notions of redistribution, nationalism, and state-led growth, a process which accelerated as the decade bore on.[70]

The residual corporatist institutions, continuously weakened after the corrective movement, became more and more debilitated. The government saw workers' and peasants' unions as obstacles on the path to further economic reform. The government felt that private investment was the only way to grow—in a global geo-economic environment in which the fall of alternative poles of state and economic power had evaporated: "with the fall of Syria's Soviet patron and the 1990s peace process, external aid declined and the Ba'ath's nationalist policy now collided with the imperative to access inward investment as a substitute for aid."[71] Nationalism was the loser in this encounter. The administration, in turn, saw the old institutions as the repositories of that nationalism and "starved them of funds and attacked their powers of patronage."[72] With the hollowing out of the Ba'ath Party, including lower leaderships and all the integuments which bound it to the lower classes, the regime faced weakened "organised connection[s] to its constituency" and lessened "penetration of neighborhoods and villages."[73]

The weakening of vehicles for working-class representation and the diminishing relative weight of harder-line anti-liberalisation Ba'ath elements went hand in hand with increased poverty amongst Syria's poorer layers. In Idlib in 2001, for example, 80 per cent of the households had less than one hectare of land, and another 15 per cent owned between one and three hectares.[74] "This means that the minimum subsistence security provided by the land base is such that the social balance may be toppled with another round of subdivisions through inheritance."[75] At the same time, distributive—as opposed to productivist—populist policies were petering out. One crucial example is subsidised baked goods, for years a mainstay of the Syrian authoritarian-populist developmental pact and one which assured sovereignty of the state through the social security of its people. For example, the retail bread price in the US in 1977 was roughly 0.78 dollars a kilogram, whereas it was 0.14 dollars a kilogram in Syria at that time.[76] In 2001, however, if consumers had paid for bread based on open import prices, without tariffs or monopolies, they would have paid 10.51 Syrian pounds per kilogram, whereas under the subsidised price system, they paid 8.5 Syrian pounds per kilogram.[77] From 2005 to 2008, prices for baked goods increased over 60 per cent.[78] Clearly, benefits from subsidies were not merely decreasing on the consumer end with the state bearing less and less of the load of social production and well-being, but state resources were flowing more and more to the wealthier agrarian producers. At the same time, this was also a consequence of the state budget facing the world-systemic pressure of the 2005–2008 global food price inflation—a phenomenon which state institutions mediate, but not just as they please.

Social Consequences: Drought to Uprising

What were the consequences of these policies? In eight villages in Idlib, Hama, and Hasakah provinces in 2000, the percentage of immiserated groups amongst the total agricultural households reached 34–37 per cent.[79] Furthermore, the official statistics on agricultural households without land indicate that from 1981 to 1994, the number of landless rural households had doubled, from 11,224 to 22,860.[80] These rural people were concentrated in Raqqa, Deir Ezzor, and Hasakah. This number is in addition to leasers or sharecroppers farming less than two hectares, who numbered some 110,000.[81] There is reason to think these trends continued and heightened. Furthermore, poverty is concentrated in this segment of the rural population. Surveys found that in the early 2000s, 77 per cent of the poor in the countryside did not own land, but owned other assets, such as livestock—primarily, sheep, cattle, and poultry.[82] Thus, there was a massive sector of the Syrian marginal rural poor who relied on livestock for their well-being, particularly in the country's more arid Northeast—the centre of poverty. This was before the drought of 2008 but, it should be noted, after the drought of 1999, leaving a population perched on the precipice of absolute penury.

Many explanations of the drought focus on pre-drought agricultural de-development, or government policies focused on either (1) inadequate government response to the drought, (2) government policies favouring capitalist agriculture, or (3) government policies which encouraged irrigation, thereby aggravating the drought.[83] Although the government did respond inadequately to the drought, this occurred in the context of insufficient support for its emergency plans from the institutions of the global North. Likewise, government policies were in fact in place to rework irrigation patterns, but never received enough attention. Nevertheless, unsustainable irrigation patterns are evident across arid environments of the global South. Not every global South country saw a historic drought; nor has every global South country been at the centre of regional geopolitics. There is much less controversy over the government role in encouraging rural differentiation through malign neglect, everyday corruption, land counter-reforms, and other policies.[84] Nevertheless, it seems any government would have had trouble contending with the drought which swept Syria from 1999 to 2010.

This chapter adds here to dominant analyses focusing on the drought the world-ecological and geopolitical dimensions of drought and drought response in the Syrian context. Many analyses treat climate change and the government response to, in a non-comparative manner, a kind of "what-if" focused on questions of ethical responsibility for government policy, thereby immuring that policy and the limited manoeuvring room of global South states from the larger restrictive world-ecological context within which they operate. This method is in sharp contrast to how international covenants and conventions treat anthropogenic climate change. For example, in the convocations and assemblies which treat this problem, it is commonly understood and agreed that the global North countries bear the brunt of the responsibility for climate change. Controversy does not extend—at least at the level of analysis—to the responsibility of smaller countries such as Syria to anthropogenic climate change. The opposite is the case. Increasingly, analysts understand that the smaller and less-emitting countries are owed "climate debt" by the larger and richer ones. Furthermore, nearly all international climate change agreements share the departure point of common-but-differentiated responsibility—even if, in implementation, they inevitably water such initiatives down. Thus, in order to understand the drought, it is necessary to understand climate change as a world-ecological phenomenon, one which most countries are largely—although not entirely—encountering as an overwhelming force, with little, although some, agency with which to respond to the exigencies and emergencies climate change imposes.

It is against this background that one must interpret the drought which damaged Syria's agricultural system. The most extensive analysis notes that "the unusual severity and duration of the recent drought are likely attributable to human influence on the climate system," adding that "the drought was a visible and likely substantial contributing factor."[85] Thus, following De Châtel's injunction to avoid the "tendency to take certain events out of context and misinterpret or overstate their significance in relation to the current events unfolding in Syria," it seems overstated to suggest, as she does, that a focus on the global North-provoked ecological disaster of anthropogenic climate change "shifts the burden of responsibility for the devastation of Syria's natural resources away from the successive Syrian governments since the 1950s."[86] Rather, it is the opposite: the drought, which was the "worst 3-year drought in the instrumental record," occurred within the world-ecological context of global North-induced climate change. It is within that overall framework that the Syrian government was forced to respond.[87] If the legally established principles of common-but-differentiated responsibility and climate debt were applied to ethical accounting, it seems clear that focusing on the poor government response to the drought ought to be weighed against the global North's climate debt which it owes the Syrian government.

The consequences of the drought were large, with harvest failures and livestock mortalities cascading across the Syrian Northeast. From the drought's apex in 2007–2008 until 2010, 75 per cent of the households in that region endured a total failure of their crops, and herders had to sell their livestock, often at 60–70 per cent below cost—in effect, ceding their only important capital endowment.[88] The stock of animals went from 21 to 14–16 million. Wheat yields dropped by 47 per cent, barley yields dropped by 67 per cent, and in non-irrigated areas, wheat production descended by as much as 82 per cent as compared to the previous year.[89]

The country lost its emergency food stocks, and against the background of the global food price spikes of that year, households faced a food price inflation of some 20 per cent, further exacerbating the drought's effects.[90] The Syrian government launched an emergency appeal. Yet, "…according to WFP estimates, many more are in need of aid, but cannot be helped due to insufficient funding. The difficulties in obtaining adequate funding from international donors may be partly connected to the political tensions that still exist between Syria and the United States," once again a situation in which insufficient response to the drought is the outcome of regional and international geopolitics and is likely overdetermined by them rather than purely the output of putatively "internal" Syrian policy decisions.[91]

By 2009, child nutrition deprivation was endemic, with Deir Ezzor, Hasakeh, Raqqa, Aleppo, and Idlib comprising the most deprived governorates respectively—these were also the ones which saw the most exposure to the drought.[92] Furthermore, migration patterns wove together the social fabric of economic devastation in Syria's South and ecological devastation in the country's North. As the drought worsened, and in sync with pre-existing tendencies in population movements from 2004 to 2008, Northeastern sectors of the country almost certainly saw their poorer and unemployable layers migrate to urban centres, pressuring wages downwards.[93] By 2008–2009, large numbers had fled, especially to urban regions, periurban slums, and peripheral cities. All this in a context within which the government had largely abandoned its ISI policies, as "the bulk of investment activities during the Hafez and Bashar regimes were non-manufacturing types" and the "industrial investment needed to build the country's productive capacity and absorb the new entrants into the labour market was left to face its ill-fated deterioration."[94] As one observer noted in a dark augury, "It is therefore evident that the recent drought in the Northeast, especially if further protracted, is a risk to political stability in Syria, where water security problems are heavily linked to food security as well as to the state's ability to provide jobs for the population. The poor, unemployed and rootless masses in the slums of the cities are potentially susceptible to Islamism, the only serious opposition to the regime since the late 1970s."[95] We must add the caveat that "Islamism" is no organic component of the mindsets of the Syrian poor. Rather, it is spread through a network of Wahhabi mosques funded by the Saudi Arabian government, a key ally and instrument of the US in its politico-ideological war against anti-systemic and radical thought and practice. But such a prediction perfectly bore out the Syrian cataclysm as we know it today.

Conclusion

This chapter has sought to place Syrian development, both the radical redistributions of the early Ba'ath and the neo-Ba'ath and the counter-reforms of the later Ba'ath, as well as the 2000s era, in world-systemic context—the context of a history in which the global North reigns and is the overwhelming determinant of development outcomes. Indeed, this phenomenon is nowhere more pronounced than in the Middle East where Western arms trade, oil interests, and interventions are a matter of public record.

Rather than descriptive accounts of populism descending into neoliberalism, or a teleological account of marketisation, this chapter has tried to offer a causal account of development and redistributive processes, arguing that they are intimately tied to that nebulous, unquantifiable, but very choate force of organised social power. It was a dramatic rise of popular mobilisation which led to the Ba'ath redistributions of the 1960s, and it was a dramatic externally induced defeat of the hard left wing of the Ba'ath which led to a more right-wing government assuming power in 1970—the "corrective movement."

Moreover, it was in the context of hot capital flows and a burgeoning Gulf expatriate accumulation process that capitalism often re-entered the Syrian agricultural sector, with land, loans, and capital becoming massive mechanisms and indices of social differentiation. This chapter has also traced the political history of Ba'ath disembedding, following it through the process of, first, incorporation of the peasants into the social compact but at the same time the gradual blunting and eventual gutting of those forces' ability to defend if not advance on the early gains of the Ba'ath.

Finally, against nationally bounded accounts which focus on Syrian state agency in the context of drought prevention, this chapter has added a world-ecological dimension to the political ecology of drought, noting that it is only within and against the tableau of global North-induced anthropogenic climate change that we can begin to understand the roots of the Syrian crisis.

Notes

1. See, e.g. Amer Mohsen, "Syria: The 'comforting' narratives of the conflict," *Al Akhbar English*, May 22 2014, available at: http://english.al-akhbar.com/node/19880.
2. Andreas Wimmer and Nina Glick Schiller, "Methodological Nationalism, the Social Sciences, and the Study of Migration: An Essay in Historical Epistemology," *The International Migration Review* 37, no. 3 (2003): 576–610.

3. Sandra Halperin, *Re-Envisioning Global Development: A Horizontal Perspective* (Routledge, 2013), 11; Dietrich Rueschemeyer, Evelyn Huber Stephens, and John D. Stephens discuss the centrality of working-class struggle to achieving democracy: *Capitalist Development and Democracy* (University of Chicago Press, 1992).
4. See discussion in John Walton, *Reluctant Rebels: Comparative Studies of Revolution and Underdevelopment* (Columbia University Press, 1984), 171ff.
5. Bassam Haddad, *Business Networks in Syria: The Political Economy of Authoritarian Resilience* (Stanford University Press, 2011).
6. John Gerard Ruggie, "International Regimes, Transactions, and Change: Embedded Liberalism in the Postwar Economic Order," *International Organization* 36, no. 02 (1982): 379–415.
7. Garay Paul Menicucci, "The Russian Revolution and Popular Movement in Syria in the 1920s" (Ph.D., Georgetown University, 1994), 210.
8. Patrick Seale, *The Struggle for Syria: A Study of Post-War Arab Politics, 1945–1958* (Oxford University Press, 1965).
9. Menicucci, "The Russian Revolution and Popular Movement in Syria in the 1920s," 213–214.
10. Raymond A. Hinnebusch, *Authoritarian Power and State Formation in Ba'thist Syria: Army, Party, and Peasant* (Westview Press, 1990), 79.
11. Fadi A. Bardawil, *When All This Revolution Melts into Air: The Disenchantment of Levantine Marxist Intellectuals* (Columbia University, 2010), 101, fn16.
12. Hinnebusch, *Authoritarian Power and State Formation in Ba'thist Syria*, 89.
13. Safouh Akhrass, *Revolutionary Change and Modernization in the Arab World: A Case from Syria* (Atlas, 1972), 160–161.
14. Raymond Hinnebusch, *Syria: Revolution From Above* (Routledge, 2004), 46.
15. "Revolution and Liberation: 100 Years since the October Revolution, 50 Years since the Arusha Declaration," *Agrarian South: Journal of Political Economy* 6, no. 2 (August 1, 2017): vii–xi.
16. Akhrass, *Revolutionary Change and Modernization in the Arab World*, 171.
17. Ibid.
18. Ziad Keilany, "Land Reform in Syria," *Middle Eastern Studies* 16, no. 3 (1980): 209–224, 211.
19. Ibid., 212.
20. Raymond Hinnebusch, "The Ba'th's Agrarian Revolution (1963–2000), pp. 3–14, in Hinnebusch et al., "Agriculture and Reform in Syria," *Syria Studies* 3, no. 1 (December 16, 2013): 1–79.

21. Alasdair Drysdale, "The Regional Equalization of Health Care and Education in Syria since the Ba'thi Revolution," *International Journal of Middle East Studies* 13, no. 1 (1981): 93–111, 95.
22. Hanna Batatu, *Syria's Peasantry, the Descendants of Its Lesser Rural Notables, and Their Politics* (Princeton University Press, 2012), 56.
23. Ibid., 58.
24. David Waldner, *State Building and Late Development* (Cornell University Press, 1999), 19.
25. Ibid., 185.
26. Ali Kadri, *The Unmaking of Arab Socialism* (Anthem Press, 2016), 124–125.
27. Hanna Batatu, *Syria's Peasantry, the Descendants of Its Lesser Rural Notables, and Their Politics* (Princeton University Press, 2012), 47.
28. Ibid., 82.
29. Rami Ginat, "The Soviet Union and the Syrian Ba'th Regime: From Hesitation to Rapprochement," *Middle Eastern Studies* 36, no. 2 (2000): 150–171.
30. Malcolm H. Kerr, *The Arab Cold War: Gamal 'Abd Al-Nasir and His Rivals, 1958–1970* (Oxford University Press, 1971).
31. Immanuel Wallerstein, *The Politics of the World-Economy* (Cambridge University Press, 1984), 84; Michal Kalecki, *Essays on Developing Economies* (Humanities, 1979), 30–40. Wallerstein also writes, total autonomy is not at all possible, since strict autarky would mean a "major economic sacrifice" for the leading cadre—a particularly pertinent point in the case of what Kalecki called "intermediate regimes," with developmentalist projects but in a murky ideological grey zone between the capitalist and former communist countries.
32. Ali Kadri, *Arab Development Denied: Dynamics of Accumulation by Wars of Encroachment* (Anthem Press, 2015), 212.
33. Cited in Timothy Mitchell, *Carbon Democracy: Political Power in the Age of Oil* (Verso, 2011); Albert B. Wolf, "The Arab Street: Effects of the Six-Day War," *Middle East Policy* 22, no. 2 (June 1, 2015): 156–167.
34. Hinnebusch, *Authoritarian Power and State Formation in Ba'thist Syria*, 136.
35. Ibid., 136.
36. Ibid., 137.
37. Joe Stork, "Review," *Middle East Journal* 48, no. 3 (July 1, 1994): 553–556; Ali Kadri, *Arab Development Denied: Dynamics of Accumulation by Wars of Encroachment* (Anthem Press, 2015).
38. Matias Vernengo, "From Capital Controls to Dollarization: American Hegemony and the US Dollar," *Monetary Integration and Dollarization: No Panacea*, 2006, 245, 1.

39. Peter Gowan, *The Global Gamble: Washington's Faustian Bid for World Dominance* (Verso, 1999), 19ff.
40. Linda Matar, *The Political Economy of Investment in Syria* (Springer, 2016), 99. The inflationary and redistributive consequences of this for Syria are detailed below.
41. Ibid., 19ff, 99.
42. David Waldner, *State Building and Late Development* (Cornell University Press, 1999), 117.
43. In Harriet Friedmann, "The Political Economy of Food: The Rise and Fall of the Postwar International Food Order," *American Journal of Sociology*, 1982, S248–S286; the author explains the Soviet emergence into the world wheat market as the reason behind this spike.
44. Waldner, *State Building and Late Development*, 118–120.
45. Volker Perthes, *The Political Economy of Syria Under Asad* (I.B.Tauris, 1997), 89.
46. Hinnebusch, *Authoritarian Power and State Formation in Ba'thist Syria*, 208.
47. Ibid., 208.
48. Myriam Ababsa, "Contre-Réforme Agraire et Conflits Fonciers En Jazîra Syrienne (2000–2005)," *Revue Des Mondes Musulmans et de La Méditerranée*, no. 115–116 (2006): 211–230.
49. Matar, *The Political Economy of Investment in Syria*; Kadri, *Arab Development Denied*.
50. Batatu, *Syria's Peasantry, the Descendants of Its Lesser Rural Notables, and Their Politics*, 53; Volker Perthes, *The Political Economy of Syria Under Asad* (I.B.Tauris, 1997), 89.
51. Although the tractors are privately owned, they were heavily funded by the state. The mechanisation of agriculture in Syria during that period up until the 2000s was supported by the state through state banks and managed by the state through cooperatives. The state subsidised and provided loans to agrarian collectives in order to buy tractors to sell it to famers at subsidised prices, and thus they appear "private" in character but they are publicly funded and sponsored.
52. Batatu, *Syria's Peasantry*, 53.
53. Ibid., 53.
54. Batatu, *Syria's Peasantry, the Descendants of Its Lesser Rural Notables, and Their Politics*, 57.
55. Ibid., 57.
56. Ibid., 57.
57. Ibid., 57.
58. Ibid., 58.
59. Bassam Haddad, "The Syrian Regime's Business Backbone," *Middle East Report* 42, no. 262 (2012).

60. Bassam Haddad, *Business Networks in Syria: The Political Economy of Authoritarian Resilience* (Stanford University Press, 2011), 79ff.
61. Batatu, *Syria's Peasantry*, 58–59.
62. Hans Hopfinger, "Capitalist Agro-Business in a Socialist Country? Syria's New Shareholding Corporations as an Example," *British Society for Middle Eastern Studies. Bulletin* 17, no. 2 (1990): 162–170.
63. F. H. Lawson, "Social Bases for the Hamah Revolt," *MERIP Reports*, no. 110 (1982): 24–28; H. Batatu, "Syria's Muslim Brethren," *MERIP Reports*, no. 110 (1982): 12–36.
64. Alexander Sarris and Alessandro Corsi, "The Syrian Agricultural Producers: Structural and Distributional Features," in Ciro Fiorillo, Jacques Vercueil, and Food and Agriculture Organization of the United Nations, eds., *Syrian Agriculture at the Crossroads*, FAO Agricultural Policy and Economic Development Series 8 (Rome: Policy Assistance Division, Food and Agriculture Organization of the United Nations, 2003), 281–307, 298.
65. "Agriculture in Syria: Towards the Social Market" (World Bank, June 2008).
66. Sarris and Corsi, "Syrian Agricultural Producers," 302.
67. Alexander Sarris, *Agricultural Development Strategy for Syria* (FAO Project GCP/SYR/006/ITA, the National Agricultural Policy Center (NAPC), Damascus, 2001).
68. Ibid., 18.
69. Peter Wehrheim, *Taxation and Net Transfers to the Agricultural Sector*, Project GCP/SYR/006/ITA Assistance in Institutional Strengthening and Agricultural Policy (Damascus, Syria) December, 2001, 49. The problems of method are clear in the report's title: "sector." But the sector is an effect of the accounting and measuring devices which produce it—there is no reason to assume it is salient with respect to understanding the social origins or social outcomes of policies.
70. Jamal Barout, *The Past Decade in Syria: The Dialectical of Stagnation and Reform*, Doha, Qatar.
71. Hinnebusch, R., 2012: Syria: from 'authoritarian upgrading' to revolution? International Affairs, 88.1, 95–113, 97. Hinnebusch is one of the few scholars who consistently emphasises the world-historical factors underlying the gradual Ba'ath *infitah*.
72. Ibid., 99.
73. Ibid., 99.
74. N. Forni, "Land Tenure and Labour Relations. Chapter 12," *FAO Agricultural Policy and Economic Development Series (FAO)*, 2003, 330.
75. Ibid., 330.
76. USAID.

77. Michael Westlake, "The Economics of Strategic Crops. Chapter 6," *FAO Agricultural Policy and Economic Development Series (FAO)*, 2003; 147.
78. Syrian Statistical Yearbook, 2009.
79. M. A. Fadil et al., "Macroeconomic Policies for Poverty Reduction: The Case of Syria," *Damascus: UNDP*, 2007, 6.
80. Ibid., 7.
81. Ibid., 7.
82. Ibid., 7.
83. Francesca De Châtel, "The Role of Drought and Climate Change in the Syrian Uprising: Untangling the Triggers of the Revolution," *Middle Eastern Studies* 50, no. 4 (July 4, 2014): 521–535, https://doi.org/10.1080/00263206.2013.850076.
84. Ababsa, "Contre-Réforme Agraire et Conflits Fonciers En Jazîra Syrienne (2000–2005)"; Myriam Ababsa, "Crise agraire, crise foncière et sécheresse en Syrie (2000–2011)," *Maghreb – Machrek* No 215, no. 1 (July 15, 2013): 101–122.
85. Colin P. Kelley, *Recent and Future Drying of the Mediterranean Region: Anthropogenic Forcing, Natural Variability and Social Impacts* (Columbia University, 2014), 77, 81.
86. De Châtel, "The Role of Drought and Climate Change in the Syrian Uprising," 521–522.
87. Colin P. Kelley et al., "Climate Change in the Fertile Crescent and Implications of the Recent Syrian Drought," *Proceedings of the National Academy of Sciences*, March 2, 2015, 201421533, doi:10.1073/pnas.1421533112, 3241.
88. E. Erian, Bassem Katlan, and Ouldbdey Babah, "Drought Vulnerability in the Arab Region," *Special Case Study: Syria. Global Assessment Report on Disaster Risk Reduction. Geneva: United Nations International Strategy for Disaster Reduction*, 2010, http://www.preventionweb.net/english/hyogo/gar/2011/en/bgdocs/Erian_Katlan_%26_Babah_2010.pdf, 15.
89. Ibid., 7.
90. The mechanism for this inflation is not clear, given consumer subsidies for food and especially cereal products.
91. Hannu Juusola, "The Internal Dimension of Water Security: The Drought Crisis in The Northeastern Syria," *MARI L., Managing*, 2010, http://kms1.isn.ethz.ch/serviceengine/Files/ISN/124615/ichaptersection_singledocument/784e0ae7-0bd6-42d6-83f3-f2ca58edd42e/en/ch_1.pdf, 24.
92. UNICEF, *Multidimensional Poverty in Syria, A Comparative Research 2001, 2009*, June 2014, 27, 31.
93. Khalid Abu-Ismail, Ali Abdel-Gadir, and Heba El-Laithy, "Poverty and Inequality in Syria," accessed July 8, 2016, http://www.undp.org/con-

tent/dam/rbas/doc/poverty/BG_15_Poverty%20and%20Inequality%20 in%20Syria_FeB.pdf, 24–26.
94. Matar, *The Political Economy of Investment in Syria*, 128–129.
95. Hannu Juusola, "The Internal Dimension of Water Security: The Drought Crisis in The Northeastern Syria," *MARI L., Managing*, 2010, http://kms1.isn.ethz.ch/serviceengine/Files/ISN/124615/ichaptersection_singledocument/784e0ae7-0bd6-42d6-83f3-f2ca58edd42e/en/ch_1.pdf, 32.

Bibliography

Ababsa, M. (2006). Contre-Réforme Agraire et Conflits Fonciers En Jazîra Syrienne (2000–2005). *Revue Des Mondes Musulmans et de La Méditerranée*, no. 115–116, pp. 211–230.
Ababsa, M. (2013, July 15). Crise agraire, crise foncière et sécheresse en Syrie (2000–2011). *Maghreb – Machrek* No. 215, no. 1, pp. 101–22.
Abu-Ismail, K., Abdel-Gadir, A., & El-Laithy, H. *Poverty and Inequality in Syria*. Retrieved July 8, 2016., from http://www.undp.org/content/dam/rbas/doc/poverty/BG_15_Poverty%20and%20Inequality%20in%20Syria_FeB.pdf
Agriculture in Syria: Towards the Social Market. (2008, June). World Bank.
Akhrass, S. (1972). *Revolutionary Change and Modernization in the Arab World: A Case from Syria*. Atlas.
Bardawil, F. A. (2010). *When All This Revolution Melts into Air: The Disenchantment of Levantine Marxist Intellectuals*. Columbia University. Retrieved from http://gradworks.umi.com/34/47/3447836.html
Batatu, H. (1982). Syria's Muslim Brethren. Merip Reports, no. 110, pp. 12–36.
Batatu, H. (2012). *Syria's Peasantry, the Descendants of Its Lesser Rural Notables, and Their Politics*. Princeton University Press.
De Châtel, F. (2014, July 4). The Role of Drought and Climate Change in the Syrian Uprising: Untangling the Triggers of the Revolution. *Middle Eastern Studies*, 50(4), 521–535. https://doi.org/10.1080/00263206.2013.850076.
Drysdale, A. (1981). The Regional Equalization of Health Care and Education in Syria since the Ba'thi Revolution. *International Journal of Middle East Studies*, 13(01), 93–111.
Erian, E., Katlan, B., & Babah, O. (2010). *Drought Vulnerability in the Arab Region*. Special Case Study: Syria. Global Assessment Report on Disaster Risk Reduction. Geneva: United Nations International Strategy for Disaster Reduction. Retrieved from http://www.preventionweb.net/english/hyogo/gar/2011/en/bgdocs/Erian_Katlan_%26_Babah_2010.pdf
Fadil, M. A., Abu-Ismail, K., Roy, R., Ghonemy, R., Moustafa, A., Vernengo, M., El-Laithy, H., Islam, I., & Mckinley, T. (2007). *Macroeconomic Policies for Poverty Reduction: The Case of Syria*. Damascus: UNDP.

Fiorillo, C., Vercueil, J., & Food and Agriculture Organization of the United Nations (Eds.). (2003). *Syrian Agriculture at the Crossroads*. FAO Agricultural Policy and Economic Development Series 8. Rome: Policy Assistance Division, Food and Agriculture Organization of the United Nations.

Forni, N. (2003). *Land Tenure and Labour Relations*. Chapter 12. FAO Agricultural Policy and Economic Development Series (FAO).

Friedmann, H. (1982). The Political Economy of Food: The Rise and Fall of the Postwar International Food Order. *American Journal of Sociology*, S248–S286.

Ginat, R. (2000). The Soviet Union and the Syrian Ba'th Regime: From Hesitation to Rapprochement. *Middle Eastern Studies, 36*(2), 150–171.

Gowan, P. (1999). *The Global Gamble: Washington's Faustian Bid for World Dominance*. London and New York: Verso.

Haddad, B. (2011). *Business Networks in Syria: The Political Economy of Authoritarian Resilience*. Stanford University Press.

Haddad, B. (2012). *The Syrian Regime's Business Backbone*. Middle East Report 42, no. 262.

Halperin, S. (2013). *Re-Envisioning Global Development: A Horizontal Perspective*. Routledge.

Hinnebusch, R. (1990). *Authoritarian Power and State Formation in Ba'thist Syria: Army, Party, and Peasant*. Westview Press.

Hinnebusch, R. (2004). Professor of International Relations and Middle Politics Raymond, and Raymond Hinnebusch. *Syria: Revolution From Above*. Routledge.

Hinnebusch, R., El Hindi, A., Khaddam, M., & Ababsa, M. (2013, December 16). Agriculture and Reform in Syria. *Syria Studies, 3*(1), 1–79.

Hopfinger, H. (1990). Capitalist Agro-Business in a Socialist Country? Syria's New Shareholding Corporations as an Example. *British Society for Middle Eastern Studies. Bulletin, 17*(2), 162–170.

Juusola, H. (2010). The Internal Dimension of Water Security: The Drought Crisis in The Northeastern Syria. *MARI L., Managing*. Retrieved from http://kms1.isn.ethz.ch/serviceengine/Files/ISN/124615/ichaptersection_singledocument/784e0ae7-0bd6-42d6-83f3-f2ca58edd42e/en/ch_1.pdf

Kadri, A. (2015). *Arab Development Denied: Dynamics of Accumulation by Wars of Encroachment*. Anthem Press.

Kadri, A. (2016). *The Unmaking of Arab Socialism*. Anthem Press.

Kalecki, M. (1979). *Essays on Developing Economies*. Humanities.

Keilany, Z. (1980). Land Reform in Syria. *Middle Eastern Studies, 16*(3), 209–224.

Kelley, C. P. (2014). *Recent and Future Drying of the Mediterranean Region: Anthropogenic Forcing, Natural Variability and Social Impacts*. Columbia University. Retrieved from http://gradworks.umi.com/36/12/3612184.html

Kelley, C. P., Mohtadi, S., Cane, M. A., Seager, R., & Kushnir, Y. (2015, March 2). Climate Change in the Fertile Crescent and Implications of the Recent Syrian Drought. *Proceedings of the National Academy of Sciences*, 201421533. https://doi.org/10.1073/pnas.1421533112.

Kerr, M. H. (1971). *The Arab Cold War: Gamal 'Abd Al-Nasir and His Rivals, 1958–1970*. Oxford University Press.

Lawson, F. H. (1982). Social Bases for the Hamah Revolt. Merip Reports, no. 110, pp. 24–28.

Matar, L. (2016). *The Political Economy of Investment in Syria*. Springer.

Menicucci, G. P. (1994). *The Russian Revolution and Popular Movement in Syria in the 1920s*. Ph.D., Georgetown University. Retrieved from http://search.proquest.com.proxy.library.cornell.edu/pqdtglobal/docview/304107659/abstract/6508866DAC454B56PQ/59

Mitchell, T. (2011). *Carbon Democracy: Political Power in the Age of Oil*. Verso Books.

Perthes, V. (1997). *The Political Economy of Syria Under Asad*. I.B.Tauris.

Revolution and Liberation: 100 Years since the October Revolution, 50 Years since the Arusha Declaration. (2017, August 1). *Agrarian South: Journal of Political Economy*, 6(2), vii–xi. https://doi.org/10.1177/2277976017737902.

Rueschemeyer, D., Stephens, E. H., & Stephens, J. D. (1992). *Capitalist Development and Democracy*. University of Chicago Press.

Ruggie, J. G. (1982). International Regimes, Transactions, and Change: Embedded Liberalism in the Postwar Economic Order. *International Organization*, 36(02), 379–415.

Sarris, A. (2001). *Agricultural Development Strategy for Syria*. FAO Project GCP/SYR/006/ITA, the National Agricultural Policy Center (NAPC), Damascus.

Seale, P. (1965). *The Struggle for Syria: A Study of Post-War Arab Politics, 1945–1958*. Oxford University Press.

Stork, J. (1994, July 1). Untitled. *Middle East Journal*, 48(3), 553–556. https://doi.org/10.2307/4328733.

Vernengo, M. (2006). From Capital Controls to Dollarization: American Hegemony and the US Dollar. *Monetary Integration and Dollarization: No Panacea*, p. 245.

Waldner, D. (1999). *State Building and Late Development*. Cornell University Press.

Wallerstein, I. (1984). *The Politics of the World-Economy: The States, the Movements and the Civilizations*. Cambridge University Press.

Walton, J. (1984). *Reluctant Rebels: Comparative Studies of Revolution and Underdevelopment*. Columbia University Press.

Westlake, M. (2003). *The Economics of Strategic Crops*. Chapter 6. FAO Agricultural Policy and Economic Development Series (FAO).

Wimmer, A., & Schiller, N. G. (2003). Methodological Nationalism, the Social Sciences, and the Study of Migration: An Essay in Historical Epistemology. *The International Migration Review, 37*(3), 576–610.

Wolf, A. B. (June 1, 2015). The Arab Street: Effects of the Six-Day War. *Middle East Policy, 22*(2), 156–167. https://doi.org/10.1111/mepo.12135.

CHAPTER 11

Syria's Food Security: From Self-Sufficiency to Hunger as a Weapon

Myriam Ababsa

Self-sufficiency in food production has been a pillar of the Syrian economy from the days of the agrarian reform launched in 1958 until the neoliberal economic opening of the country in mid-2000s. After Turkey, Syria had the most productive agricultural sector of the Middle East. Agriculture was highly subsidised and counted for almost one-fourth of the gross domestic product (27 per cent of GDP in 2001, 18 per cent of GDP in 2010), employing 17 per cent of the working population (Wind and Dahi 2014; FAO/WFP 2016). Syria became self-sufficient in wheat production in 1991, thanks not only to its state irrigation projects but also to the multiplication of private wells, which were illegal wells, for the most part. In the Jazira, 80 per cent of irrigation depended on underground wells and rivers. The overuse of underground water resources led to a depletion of the water table and the death of historic rivers such as the Balikh, and the Khabour River which dried up in 2001 (Pecad 2008).

Syria was hit by a severe drought in 2006–2010. For the first time in its history, the country had to receive international aid and food supplies for one million farmers, herders, and their families. The drought accentuated the destruction of the agrarian sector, already weakened by the dismantling of the socialist structure. Even before the drought, between 2002

M. Ababsa (✉)
Institut Français du Proche-Orient, Amman, Jordan

© The Author(s) 2019
L. Matar, A. Kadri (eds.), *Syria: From National Independence to Proxy War*, https://doi.org/10.1007/978-3-319-98458-2_11

and 2008, Syria had lost 40 per cent of its agricultural workforce, because of mismanagement of water and land resources (Aita 2010). This was partly due to the implementation of the new agrarian Law 56 of 2004, which allowed landowners to terminate farming contracts. This law was highly contested as it is a highly capitalist, anti-socialist one that favoured landowners and thus constituted an element of agrarian counter-reform.

Since the war in Syria started in 2011, especially after the emergence of the Islamic State in 2013, food and water have become weapons and leverage to political change for the Bashar al-Asad government,[1] the Islamic State, and other armed groups. Access to food has been the main problem faced by the majority of Syrians, both in the state-controlled areas because of inflation and scarcity and within the besieged areas (19 in 2015), where people have been victims of food scarcity and war profiteers. UN Humanitarian food assistance has been mainly conveyed by the government until 2014, while Gulf charities have reached opposition-held areas from Turkey. People under the Islamic State are under awful pressure as wheat is lacking and smugglers cannot enter Raqqa or Deir Ezzor. Starvation has been a new threat in Syria (in Madaya and partially ISIS-controlled Yarmouk).

This chapter succinctly reviews the history of agriculture in Syria from the late 1950s until the present day (end 2016). It is structured in three sections. The first section discusses the government's historical aim of achieving self-sufficiency in food production starting in the late 1950s, showing that agrarian reform was later developed to serve the interests of the middle and large farmers. The second section briefly addresses the agrarian counter-reforms in 2000s and the impact of the drought in late 2000s. The third section presents how food has become a weapon since the war started in 2011. Looking at some of the besieged cities back in 2015 and 2016, it places the emphasis on survival and coping strategies.

The Socialist Objective of Promoting Food Self-Sufficiency

In 1958, during the United Arab Republic, Syria adopted Gamal Abdel Nasser's agrarian reform law, followed by additional legislation in 1963 and 1966. These laws offered the state the opportunity to manage rationally agricultural resources that had previously been plundered by absentee landowners. State farms were created and major irrigation projects implemented in order to attain self-sufficiency. Five-year plans had the objective to reach self-sufficiency. Food self-sufficiency was an aim for all socialist states in order to counter the West and to build their own legitimacy among former poor peasants and sharecroppers. The successive governments after March 1963 Ba'athist revolution used three interventionist methods to reach this aim: land reclamation (Euphrates Project), seeds improvement (of the Shami variety created by the International Center for Agricultural Research in Dry Areas, ICARDA, established in Aleppo in 1977[2]), and subsidies to fertilisers and fuel. However, in the context of economic opening which followed in the late 1980s, the concept of self-sufficiency changed in the Eighth Five-Year Plan (1996–2000) to food security, which focused on producing goods of relative advantage and exporting surpluses in order to cover the importation of goods not locally produced (El Hindi 2011: 46).

Self-Sufficiency Through Subsidies (A Costly Policy)

Agriculture was planned throughout Syria's history in order to reach self-sufficiency and boost exportation. Production was highly subsidised. The government subsidised all inputs (seeds, fertilisers, and fuel), was the sole buyer of wheat (except for high-quality wheat that were sold to private mills), and controlled all marketing channels during Syria's development trajectory. The General Establishment for Cereal Processing and Trade (HOBOOB) set the national price for wheat and managed 140 collection centres in the country through the General Company for Silos, Feed Mills and Seed Plants, two-thirds being in the Jazira. The storage capacity for crops was ten million tonnes, enough for two years consumption. It went down to four million tonnes, or ten months' worth of consumption. Two state-run companies were responsible for flour milling and baking: the General Company for Mills (GCM) and the General Company for Baking. In 2011, the government owned 26 mills and contracted 35 private millers (Ahmed 2016).

Table 11.1 shows the trend in production and yield of both wheat and barley during pre-conflict Syria. Yields of 2.5 tonnes of wheat per hectare were achieved in 2005 through the use of fertilisers, subsidised by the government. Additionally, a donum of wheat needed 50 kg of fertilisers (El Dahan 2016).[3]

In 2007, a farmer used to be paid by the government 11,300 Syrian Pound (SP) per tonne of durum wheat (Lançon 2011: 33), which was higher than wheat world prices. This subsidy to wheat accounted for

Table 11.1 Wheat and Barley production, surface and yield (1970–2011)

	1970	1980	1990	2000	2005	2010	2011
Wheat							
Surface thousands ha	1341	1449	1341	1679	1904	1599	1521
Production thousand tonnes	625	2226	2070	3106	4669	3083	3858
Yield in t/ha	0.5	1.5	1.5	1.9	2.5	1.9	2.5
Barley							
Surface thousands ha	1126	1210	2729	1317	1327	1527	1293
Production in thousand tonnes	235	1588	846	212	767	680	667
Yield in t/ha	0.2	1.3	0.3	0.2	0.5	0.4	0.5

Source: CBS 2013, *Agricultural Statistics, Time series 1970, 1980, 1990, 2000–2011*

nearly two per cent of GDP prior to 2011 (Ahmed 2016). As a result, bread was sold at a subsidised low price to the citizens, at 15 SP per bundle of 1.1 kg. In 2007, the government decided to reduce the share of durum wheat flour from 50 per cent to 25 per cent in the subsided integrated flour for bread making. It had a direct impact on domestic markets. As a consequence durum wheat consumption declined from 120 kg per capita in 2001 to 80 kg in 2007 (Lançon 2011: 26).

Nearly four million tonnes of wheat used to be produced yearly by Syria before the war. A total of 2.5 million were for internal consumption and 1.5 million tonnes were exported. Nearly half of the exportations were directed to northern African country members of the Great Arab Free Trade Agreement (GAFTA) (Algeria and Tunisia, where durum wheat is used for the production of semolina), a third to Italy (for the production of pasta), and the rest to neighbouring countries (Lançon 2011: 22). Other agricultural exports included cotton, sugar (over 150,000 tonnes in 2010), tomatoes (627,000 tonnes), potatoes (100,000 tonnes), fruit, olive oil, livestock, meat, and eggs.

Private Sector Production and Market

The public General Establishment for Fodder distributed minimum fodder rations. The private sector was allowed to trade in fodder both at home and abroad only after 1990 (El Hindi 2011). "The increasing soft wheat and durum production allowed the emergence of a private wheat based industry in Syria. Direct linkages between farmers and private mills are developing but remain marginal" (Lançon 2011: 29).

In 2010, agriculture contributed between 20 and 25 per cent of the country's GDP and was the main source of employment and income for 47 per cent of the population (MAAR 2010). In 2011, over 1.5 million hectares were cultivated with wheat and 1.3 million hectares with barley (Table 11.1). Winter wheat and barley were planted in December and January, for harvest in mid-May.

Syria's Bread Basket: The Jazira Region

Two-thirds of Syria's cereals (or three million tonnes) were produced in the Jazira region before 2011. The Jazira, a former pastoral area for nomadic and semi-nomadic tribes between the Euphrates and the Tigris, became the country's pioneering agricultural front in the 1950s. It is in this region that the great Euphrates and Khabour Project was implemented in the 1970s and where the main national hydrocarbon reserves were exploited after 1985. Before the conflict, the Jazira was a strategic region for Syria as it produced three-quarter of its hydrocarbons. Its population made up 17 per cent of Syria's overall population. However, it was also the region with the highest proportion of poor and the highest illiteracy rate. The Jazira hosted 58 per cent of Syria's poor population in 2004. This figure increased after the 2006 drought: the De Schutter report stated that poverty reached up to 80 per cent in 2010 (UNGA 2011).

This strategic zone was heavily controlled by successive Ba'athist governments that relied on medium-sized landowners from the semi-nomadic tribes of the valleys of the Euphrates, the Balikh, and the Khabour in order to carry out their development objectives (Batatu 1999). The 1958 land reform was only partially implemented in the North-East of Syria. Its limited application in the main zone of Syria's latifundia was due to technical obstacles—the absence of a land register, lack of staff, and the division of land between heirs—as well as political reasons (Petran 1972: 183). After 1963, the Ba'ath regime adopted a pragmatic policy towards the Jazira which consisted of promoting the emergence of a class of middle-sized tribal landowners who were loyal supporters of the party, while allowing the "feudal landowners" to keep the basis of their wealth.[4] In the middle valley of the Euphrates, large-scale landowners managed to retain up to 55 hectares of the most fertile land, located all along the valley, while leaving the semi-arid plateau lands to be expropriated and distributed.

Water Mismanagement

In the 1950s, Syria had more than eight million hectares of arable land. But because of improper irrigation techniques, huge surfaces have been salinised (in the Jazira). The irrigated area in Syria amounted to 1210 thousand hectares in 2000, which consumed 12 billion cubic metres of water with an average use of 10,000 cubic metres per hectare per year. It increased in 2004 to more than 1430 thousand hectares. Yet the area irrigated by modern techniques (sprinkler and drip) is two per cent of the total irrigated area in 2000 (Khaddam 2011: 63).

Much has been written about the devastating consequences the production of cotton had on the water reserves of the country (Khaddam 2011). The policy of high subsidisation of the cotton production consumed up to one-third of the country's water resources, salinised the soils because of the inefficient drainage system, and used considerable amounts of fertilisers. As mentioned, Syria became self-sufficient in wheat in 1991, thanks not only to its state irrigation projects but also to the multiplication of private wells. The number of private wells was estimated to have increased from around 135,089 in 1999 to over 213,335 in 2007[5] (NAPC 2010). Eighty per cent of irrigation in the Jazira depends on underground wells and rivers (94 per cent in the Hasakah governorate, 75 per cent in the Deir Ezzor governorate, and 50 per cent in the Raqqa governorate where the Euphrates Project was implemented with all its dams and canals). In 2005, due to groundwater depletion, a new law was issued forbidding new well drilling but it was not enforced. In 2007, Syria consumed 19.2 billion cubic metres of water which was 3.5 billion more than the amount of water replenished naturally, with the difference coming from groundwater and reservoirs, according to the Ministry of Irrigation.

The overuse of underground water resources led to a depletion of the water table and the death of historic rivers such as the Balikh, which dried up in middle of the 1990s, and the Khabour River which dried up in 2001 (Pecad 2008). From 60 cubic metres per second its flow decreased to zero and agriculture was carried on with 6 cubic metres per second of underground water. As a consequence of water table depletion, in 2008, some farmers preferred to rent fully vegetated irrigated wheat fields for the grazing of sheep at the high cost of $15 per donum, instead of harvesting them (Pecad 2008).

Agrarian Counter-Reforms and the Drought Effects in Late 2000s

Agrarian Relations: Law 56 of 2004

Between 2002 and 2008, Syria lost 40 per cent of its agricultural workforce, which dropped from 1.4 million to 800,000 (Aita 2010). Although workforce statistics had in the past shown wide fluctuations, in this case it appears to have partly been due to mismanagement of water and land resources and partly because of a new agrarian relation law. Promulgated on 29 December 2004, Law 56 allowed landowners to terminate, after three years, all tenancy contracts and replace them with temporary contracts. Applied as of December 2007, this law resulted in the expulsion of hundreds of tenants and workers, especially on the coast in Tartous and Latakia (Sarkis Fernández 2011).

In order to increase investment in the agricultural sector, landowners received the right to terminate tenants' contracts and expel them from the land they had been working on. The aim of the law was to "reach a more efficient agriculture for the wealth of the nation and better economic and social relations (*bi hadaf al istithmar al ardh bi sura saliha li tanmia al tharwa al qawmia wa iqama `alaqat iqtissadia wa ijtima`ia `adila*)" (paragraph 2, Law 56 of 2004). This complex law, containing 167 paragraphs, allowed landowners to terminate any contract, in exchange for meagre compensation, calculated with reference to the number of years tenants had spent working the land. According to paragraph 106, indemnities were calculated between 20 and 40 per cent of the land value (at 2 per cent of land value per years worked). Paragraphs 96 and 163 were contested. Paragraph 96 stipulates that the contract must be on paper and signed by a signature or a fingerprint, while paragraph 163 allows the cancellation of the contract without compensation if it was an oral contract. Most of the work in the greenhouses (where the displaced as the result of the drought coming from the Jazira had sought work) was based on informal oral contracts, *hissa*, which gave workers 20 per cent of the production's sales price (Sarkis Fernández 2011: 155).

Between 2006 and 2010, the total workers employed in the Jazira in agriculture dropped by 20 per cent, from 274,475 to 221,440, whilst in the Hasakah governorate, this drop was 30 per cent (from 110,335 to 77,547) (CBS 2011). These were striking drops as the demographic growth rate was high during that period. Another consequence of Law 56 was the increasing land speculation on agricultural land located at the edges of villages and cities. On the coast, near Banyas, peasants were expelled from the land they had built their houses on, planted trees on, and drilled wells: the land was sold at 20,000 to 30,000 SP per square metre. The fear was that this law would have the same consequences as Law 96 of 1992 in Egypt, which led to the expulsion of elderly and women farmers and accelerated the rural exodus to the cities (Bush 2002).

The ensuing protests were so big, as the communist party's online petitions describe, pushing President Bashar al-Asad to promulgate an amendment to Law 56 in 2006, allowing farmers to give oral proof of their former work, such as neighbours' testimonies. But this did not change the spirit of the law to allow landowners to expel farmers as they wished (Ababsa 2011, 2015).

The Effects of the Drought on Production and Livelihoods (2006–2010)

The years 2007–2009 were terribly dry years in the Middle East. Syria had to receive international aid and food supply for one million peasants living in the North Eastern provinces of Raqqa, Hasakah, and Deir Ezzor (the Jazira), the poorest region in Syria. Raqqa, Deir Ezzor, and Hasakah governorates accounted for 80 per cent of the country's total irrigated wheat acreage, or 680,000 hectares, producing in a good year (such as 2003–2004) roughly 2.7 million tonnes of irrigated wheat and 0.8 million tonnes of rainfed barley[6] (Pecad 2008). But in 2008 the production fell to 1.3 million tonnes, with no production in the Badia. The country's emergency cereals reserves had been used, but were not sufficient to cope with all the population's needs. According to the FAO Drought Appeal of 2008, up to 75 per cent of the Jazira farmers suffered total crop failure during the 2007–2008 planting season (FAO 2008). Wheat and barley yields dropped by 47 and 67 per cent, respectively, compared to the previous year during the same period. In the non-irrigated areas, production dropped by 82 per cent, and the barley harvest failed entirely.

In the 2008 and 2009 drought crisis, precipitation was reduced to a third of the normal amount. Many herders had to sell their livestock at 60 per cent below cost. As the fodder prices rose in January 2008 by 75 per cent, the flocks were reduced by a 50 per cent increase in animal mortality and a 70 per cent reduction in fertility rates (FAO 2008). Small farmers (less than 10 donums) and herders (less than 50 heads) were already vulnerable as their livelihoods depended on agriculture (Table 11.2).

Table 11.2 The evolution of cereals and legumes production 2004–2008

Cereals	2004	2006	2008
Wheat	4,537,000 t	4,931,500 t	2,139,000 t
Barley	527,200 t	1,202,400 t	261,000 t
Maize	210,200 t	159,000 t	281,300 t
Pulses			
Lentils	125,300 t	180,700 t	34,100 t
Chick peas	45,300 t	51,900 t	27,100 t
Dry broad beans	35,800 t	30,600 t	38,100 t

Source: Agriculture Yearbook 2009, table 14/4, www.cbssyr.org/yearbook/2009/chapter4-EN.htm

Tens of thousands of farmers fled to main cities' suburbs in search for informal jobs. In the Jazira, the source of two-thirds of Syria's cereals and cotton production, the consequences were dramatic. According to a report by the International Institute for Sustainable Development, between 160 and 220 villages were abandoned due to well dryness and harsh wind-blown sand that invaded the houses (Brown and Crawford 2009, DIS 2010). About 300,000 families were driven to Damascus, Aleppo, and other cities (OCHA 2009). The government launched an emergency programme in 2009 to reduce the consequences of the drought, but only a third of the requested $43 million dollars necessary were donated by the international community. As a consequence, the World Food Programme had to reduce food distribution to 200,000 persons in 2009, compared to 300,000 in 2008 (IRIN 2010).

The drought's consequences were exacerbated by the rise in fodder prices worldwide and by the government's decision to stop subsidising fuel in 2008. In January 2008, bread and fodder prices increased by 75 per cent. Fuel prices rose by 257 per cent (from 7 to 25 SP/litre). This had a strong impact on middle-sized farmers using motor pumps to extract water and run tractors. The situation got even worse for "middle" shepherds who used to drive water tanks to their flocks in order to graze anywhere in the Badia. The government created an Agriculture Support Fund to compensate for this price rise and allowed international agencies to distribute food to the poorest of the victims. Small herders and farmers had no choice but to sell all their meagre material and move to the cities looking for low-paid jobs in the informal sector and in plastic greenhouses in Dara'a region and the coast.

Worse than that, vegetable and fruit growers in dry northern Syria used polluted river water to irrigate their crops, which caused outbreaks of food poisoning among consumers. Experts pointed out that the problem stemmed from sewage and chemicals (chromium and lead) that were allowed to reach rivers in rural areas near Aleppo, Latakia, and Raqqa (ENS 2010).

Food as a Weapon and Hunger Policy in the Time of War (2011–2016)

During the civil war, more than 400,000 Syrians have been killed in fighting and bombing. A total of 4.8 million Syrians have crossed the borders to find refuge in neighbouring countries, and 9.4 million Syrians are in need of food assistance (FAO 2016). The agriculture sector has entered a vicious cycle, with farmers' rural migration to cities, destruction of the irrigation facilities, and increasing food needs. Farmers are lacking seeds and fuel and basic supplies to keep their flocks healthy. Wheat is used as a weapon to win allegiances. Bakeries are targeted. In besieged areas, between 400,000 and 1 million persons are victims of war profiteers. Some managed to organise food production, storage, and equal distribution. Until 2014, the UN Food Assistance was shipped to Latakia and distributed by the Syrian government. On 14 July 2014, the UN Security Council unanimously adopted UNSCR 2165 (UN News Centre 2014), authorising UN cross-border and cross-line delivery of humanitarian aid to conflict-affected populations without the government's approval.

Syria's Agricultural Geography During War

The new geography of Syria at war has also been a geography of food insecurity. The inhabitants of the region held by the government (Damascus, Latakia, Tartous, Sweida, Salamia) where the fighting is less intense have functional markets. Until July 2014 they were receiving most of UN World Food Programme's food assistance, shipped through Latakia. This distribution of food parcels along with the subvention of the bread at low price has attracted civilians from the opposition-held areas, as they were not able to afford the high food prices (Hudson 2014).

While wheat is produced in North and Northeast of Syria, the greatest demand is concentrated in the Western governorates of Damascus, Homs, and Hama. Syria's strategic wheat reserves amounted to 3.5 million tonnes. The majority of the 140 silos are in the Jazira, under Islamic State control. Only trained government employees have monitored and managed the storage, as it is a delicate task. Currently, only 22 of the 140 storage silos are operating (El Dahan 2016).

The main challenge for ensuring food security during times of war is not only to produce wheat in the context of fertiliser reduction, fuel scarcity, and fighting but also to transport it to markets. The areas under Islamic State's control are suffering greatly, especially Deir Ezzor where the government forces have been under siege for years. Although wheat is produced there, some of it is sold to Iraq and Turkey for double the price (El Dahan 2016).

Idlib, rural Aleppo, and Hasakah are witnessing the interruption of food supply to local markets due to periodic clashes between armed groups (FAO/WFP 2016). The main regions of agricultural production are at war: the Jazira (wheat), the Ghouta, the Al Ghab plain (vegetables), and Idlib (olives, wheat). In the Jazira, the Raqqa governorate is still producing, but under great constraints due to bombing and damaged irrigation infrastructure. North of Hama, fields of standing crops have been burned during fighting, turning a large part of Hama's population into being food insecure (FAO/WFP 2016). Less than half the agricultural land has been harvested in 2014/2015 and 2015/2016 cropping seasons, due to security reasons and lack of fuel and irrigation (FAO/WFP 2016).

The farmland and orchards of the Syrian coast and of Sweida have not been affected and continue to export fruit and vegetables to Iraq, Jordan, and Lebanon. Sweida has become the main agro-industry centre in the south of Syria, since the Jordanian borders closed due to fighting in Dara'a (Carnegie 2015).

Several UN agencies and the Crop and Food Security Assessment Mission (CFSAM) have estimated wheat production, showing better production in 2015, but with a deficit of nearly one million tonnes of wheat. But the major problem is transporting the crop from the Jazira and the North of the country to the consumption basins of Damascus and Aleppo. Roads are dangerous, need toll payments to opposition forces or to the Islamic State, and the transportation costs are therefore very high. Because of the war and the rise of the Islamic State, the major internal trade roads for wheat and barley have been cut between the Jazira and Aleppo (from Hasakah, Deir Ezzor, and Raqqa) and from Deir Ezzor to Damascus through Palmyra from May 2015 until May 2016. The desert road Raqqa-Ressafa-Salamia is also controlled by the Islamic State south of Raqqa.

The storage of crops also needs competence that neither the Islamic State nor the jihadist rebels possess. The producers have stockpiled wheat, because farmers were not able to transport it. This is a major threat to food sufficiency as they take the risk of losing the reserves to fungus or fighting.

In 2015, the Syrian government managed to buy only 450,000 tonnes of wheat, less than half the requested quantity needed to provide enough bread to government-held areas (El Dahan 2016). But it has tried to convince the farmers to sell to HOBOOB at $200 per tonne instead of $130 and promised to pay the crop within 24 hours to attract sellers (Hamlo 2015). This is due to the fact that farmers have transportation problem and are threatened by armed groups who want to stop them handing over to the authorities. Therefore some farmers prefer to sell for higher prices abroad or to brokers. For instance, in March 2015, IS allowed 185 trucks loaded with wheat from Qamishli to cross to government- controlled area (Hamlo 2015).

Additionally, the Islamic State has a problem in managing properly its silos. Therefore it allows engineers to go to Syrian government areas for training. In the words of Adam Vinaman Yao, the deputy representative of the FAO in Damascus: "often, when armed groups were able to keep control of wheat-related infrastructure, they would cut a deal with the regime: Workers could pass from one side to another to keep the production chain going". Agricultural experts in Islamic State-held Raqqa, for example, are allowed to come to Damascus for government training. "The militias are always interested to keep the expert because they know that the expert will take care of the system and keep it running" (Ciezadlo 2015).

New market roads have opened to Turkey for cotton, wheat, and olive oil, from rebel-held areas. As a consequence, Syrians must purchase olive oil on higher prices. Also, the private Syrian merchants import wheat from the Black Sea at $300 per tonne, which is cheaper than bringing wheat from Hasakah to Damascus ($310 in 2016) (FAO/WFP 2016). The very high internal transaction costs is due to a 25 per cent "tax" levied by armed groups controlling the roads.

Food insecurity concerns almost the third of the Syrian population. People are taking debts to buy food, as food prices are rising (FAO/WFP 2016). Inflation is rocketing, making food necessities such as wheat flour and rice very expensive and a key reason for food insecurity (FAO/WFP 2016).

The share of household expenditure on food has increased tremendously since the beginning of the crisis, at the expense of meeting other critical needs (FAO/WFP 2016). Families were found to be spending more than half of their incomes on food, and in some places such as Sweida, Aleppo, and Hama, this proportion is higher and has jumped to almost 80 per cent in Dara'a, one of the areas which witnessed some of the most intense fighting.

A majority of people were found to have a "poor" or "borderline" diet, based of bread, oil, sugar, and wild vegetables. Dietary diversity is somewhat better in the North-Western governorates of Idlib, Tartous, and Latakia, where households have some access to high-quality and vitamin-rich proteins and vegetables. People in the conflict-affected governorates of Deir Ezzor, Hasakah, Aleppo, and Hama have the worse food consumption indicators.

Additionally, social capital plays a major role. Families borrow from relatives and friends, a lucky few have family abroad. Few borrow from the banks. Nearly one in every three households is indebted. The purchase of food is the main reason for that debt.

Syria Agricultural Production Under War

In the context of war, Syrian farmers are trying their best to cultivate their land, using rudimentary technics. Some refugees are coming back from Turkey to sow their land in January for the winter crops, hoping to be able to harvest in May and June. But they face major difficulties to harvest in areas under control of the Islamic State. Some farmers displaced from Homs and Damascus went to farm villages in the fertile southern Hauran (villages of Tafas and Yadouda), whose inhabitants have fled to Zaatari camp in Jordan (Carnegie 2015).

Crops have been burned by the belligerents north of Homs and Hama. Besieged Syrians manage to cultivate as much as they can, taking risks to go to their fields or developing cultures within courtyards in cities and villages. Water is a major issue. New cisterns have been created, and when fuel is available, wells are being drilled and pumped.

According to the Syrian Ministry of Agriculture and Agrarian Reform, some 1.03 million hectares of wheat were planted between December 2015 and January 2016 (of which 430,000 were irrigated and 600,000 were rainfed), while 1.13 million hectares were planted with barley (of which 95 per cent were rainfed) (FAO/WFP 2016). But the productivity has been reduced due to the lack of fertilisers and of good seeds. The seeds produced in Syria are progressively losing their resistance to insects and

Table 11.3 Syria wheat, barley, and maize production (2010–2014)

	Average 2010–2014 (thousand tonnes)	2014	2015 estimate	Change 2014/2015 (%)
Wheat	2809	1865	2445	31
Barley	747	594	968	63
Maize	129	156	133	−15
Others	8	8	8	0
Total	3693	2623	3554	35

Source: FAO, GIEWS 2015 Country Cereal Balance Sheets

diseases (FAO/WFP 2016). Plus the usual rotation between cereals and pulse or legumes is neglected, and soil is at risk of losing its nutrients.

Table 11.3 presents wheat, barley, and maize production during war years. By 2015, famers were able to cope with the crisis and managed to increase total production by 35 per cent, as compared to 2014 (Table 11.3).

The area of land sown with wheat and barley during the 2015–2016 season stood at 2.16 million hectares, down from 2.38 million hectares the previous season and 3.125 million in 2010 (El Dahan 2016). As the prices of seeds, fertilisers, and fuel have hiked, farmers are forced to return to more traditional form of agriculture, with reduction of yield. The only solution for medium and large farmers is to drill new wells to irrigate new land, further using the aquifers. Farmers in rebel-held areas managed to harvest land in the Badia, drilling wells and pumping the underground water aquifers, despite a policy to forbid drilling, especially East of Salamia.

The chaos has led to the depletion of Syria's livestock. Some animals were smuggled to Iraq, Jordan, and Turkey, without proper vaccinations (which created a sanitary threat in these countries). From 15 million sheep and 2 million goats pre-war, only 60 per cent are left. The poultry sector, which was mainly private sector investment with significant exports of meat and eggs, has lost almost 70 per cent of its production according to Abdul Salam Ali, deputy minister of economy and foreign trade (Carnegie 2015).

Most preoccupying, the irrigation infrastructures built over the past 40 years have been damaged or stolen (motor pumps) and the fields in Hauran and the Jazira need to be decontaminated from landmines.

Hunger as a Weapon of War

During war, nothing escapes destruction. Farms, mills, and bakeries have been targets for the fighting subjugating powers, causing human hardships and misery. This started in August 2012, when aerial attacks hit 18 bakeries in Aleppo, the centre of opposition resistance then. "When the Free Syrian Army began to thrive in the regions of Idlib, Homs and Deir Ezzor, bakery bombings quickly followed. In the fall of 2014, the regime shifted its attention to the successful bread-making operation of the Islamic State, or Da'ish, bombing one outlet in the city of al-Raqqa" (Eng and Martinez 2016).

Additionally, the Aleppo wheat mills have been bombed, leaving functioning mills only in Damascus and Homs. The milling capacity therefore fell from 3.8 million tonnes before 2011 to around 2.8 million in 2015 (Carnegie 2015). In July 2016, Deir Ezzor inhabitants in the area controlled by the government were in major distress as only one single bakery was producing bread at a very high price (400 SP per kilo). The white flour was sold at 800 SP and a kilo of firewood was SP 250 (Mourad 2016). Running tap water is cut due to lack of power, so the inhabitants are drinking polluted water from a branch of the Euphrates (not from the river directly) or from salted wells, causing abdominal pains and diarrhoea. Water is sold at SP 1200 per barrel. In May 2016, in the area north of Latakia held by the rebels, only one bakery was functioning, and the price of a kilo of bread doubled from SP 100 to 200 (Ibrahim 2016). In August 2015, the kilo of bread was sold under 100 SP in the government-controlled areas (SP 60 in Damascus, SP 75 in Latakia), but was double in Raqqa controlled by the Islamic State (SP 200) and reached SP 800 in the Ghouta where fighting was high, to a maximum of 3500 in besieged Deir Ezzor (Table 11.4).

All warring parties are using food as a political tool to convince the population to stay loyal. The government is paying public sector salaries in areas no longer under its control, even in Dara'a and Raqqa. Subsidising of bread is not only the modus operandi of the socialist self-sufficiency ideology. It has been used during war as a political tool to win allegiance from the rebel-controlled areas where fighters have difficulties to distribute bread as bakeries are systematically bombed. While the price of kilogram of bread used to be SP 15 before the war, it increased to SP 35 in 2015 and is now ranging between SP 60 and 80. The Islamic State also uses the tool of bread to gain a foothold in towns and villages previously

Table 11.4 Bread prices by province in August 2015

City	Price (kg of bread) in Syrian Pounds
Deir Ezzor	3500
Ghouta	800
Dara'a	200
Raqqa	200
Aleppo	175
Homs	150
Suwayda	100
Hasakah	100
Tartous	75
Latakia	75
Damascus	60
Idlib	50

Source: http://syriadirect.org/news/syria-bread-prices-by-province/

held by other rebel groups (Eng and Martinez 2015). It is trying to reach its own self-sufficiency and is buying wheat at higher prices than the government.

Food Production in Besieged Areas and Coping Mechanisms

The UN estimated that in 2016, some 590,000 people lived in Syria's several besieged areas, without access to essential supplies (FAO/WFP 2016). In the besieged areas of Homs, residents have turned to makeshift survival strategies to circumvent the blockade (Al Jablawi 2016). Some citizens have managed courageously to break the blockade by producing food in the remaining rural areas or even within courtyards inside towns and villages. Not only is the food production remarkable, but even more, its distribution is done equally among the besieged population, under civilian control. This creates hope in the social resilience for the future.

In the government-controlled areas of Northern Homs, civilians have managed to produce and store wheat since Autumn 2015. The major local initiative is named "Our Bread from Our Land" project (*Khobzna min ardna*) and is supervised by Homs local council with the support of Syrian NGOs. This programme started in September 2015 at the initiative of the Homs Governorate Local Council with the support of the State of Qatar, through the Assistance Coordination Unit (ACU) (ACU 2015). It is a way to resist the blockade by the Syrian government imposed on the armed groups and which barred aid convoys from entering the area. Nearly 50 farmers sold 110 tonnes of wheat. The local council sold the bread at a lower price than the government. According to media activists, the price of a bag of bread decreased by 50 per cent. The local council gave loans to the farmers in exchange for pledges that they will not sell their yield outside the blockaded area (Al Jablawi 2016). Later in July 2016, the head of Homs local council reported to the journalists of *All4Syria* that he was facing major difficulties, as charity donations were not sufficient to continue to purchase anymore bread from Homs countryside.[7] The farmers preferred to store their own production, taking the risk of losing it.

The city of Darayya in the Western Damascus countryside was under siege for four years, between December 2012 and August 2016. Most of the 250,000 inhabitants left. The 10,000 left inside suffered awfully. The inhabitants cultivated every single piece of the remaining land, to grow wheat and vegetables (chards and spinach). The inhabitants also shared their food, and the local council oversaw the distribution of aid that reached the city (Al Jablawi 2016). The opposition forces managed to dig tunnels to convey food and medicine, as the al-Asad government seized the arable land in Eastern Ghouta. The population relied on charity and money transfers from displaced persons to their families via intermediaries. Residents managed to use organic waste to produce methane gas, to power generators. They installed wind turbines to charge energy storing batteries (Al Jablawi 2016).

Conclusion

Since the Syrian war started in 2011, especially after the emergence of the Islamic State in 2013, food and water became weapons and leverage to political change for the government, the local councils, and the Islamic State. The government is trying to maintain control over the wheat chain of production, as two-thirds of the wheat is produced in the Jazira and half is stored in the Raqqa governorate. In the meantime, the Islamic State is trying to reach its own food self-sufficiency. But in the context of high inflation, farmers prefer to sell their production illegally to Iraq and Turkey for double the price. The private sector manages to import wheat from the Black Sea countries at a cheaper price than from the Jazira due to a 25 per cent tax levied by the armed groups.

Food became the main preoccupation of a population subjected to inflation and scarcity. Gulf charities are distributing food from Turkey to the opposition-held areas. In besieged areas, the population is particularly suffering to feed itself as most are victims of war profiteers who take profit on the black market. Some manage to produce wheat (in the Ghouta). Paradoxically, in the areas under the Islamic State, especially in Deir Ezzor, the absence of black market is even worse for the population.

Notes

1. Bashar al-Asad became president of the Syrian Arab Republic in June 2000, after the death of his father, Hafez, who ruled from 1970 up until 2000.
2. ICARDA is a global research-for-development organization established with Rockefeller foundation support.
3. In Syria, farmers have used the unit donum for centuries. It corresponds to 0.1 hectares.
4. In this regard, an amendment to the land reform law was enforced in 1966 in order to protect recently irrigated lands from expropriation. This amendment was inspired by Ba'athist militants from Deir Ezzor, who were small and middle-sized landowners, anxious to oppose the cities' middle classes (Petran 1972: 183). Their aim was to control a region which was 92 per cent rural and whose 96 per cent of its inhabitants were illiterate and to create favourable conditions for the implementation of the great Euphrates and Khabour Project, by keeping a solid middle class.
5. In 2001, the cost of a 270-metre depth well was €16,000 in the Raqqa governorate, an investment that only tribe sheikhs and big landowner could afford.
6. A total of 1.7 million hectares of wheat are cultivated every year, of which 45 per cent is irrigated, mainly in the Jazira (Pecad 2008).
7. http://all4syria.info/Archive/331598

Bibliography

Ababsa, M. (2011). Agrarian Counter-Reform in Syria. In R. Hinnebusch (Ed.), *Agriculture and Reform in Syria*. Boulder: Lynne Rienner Publishers and University of St Andrews.

Ababsa, M. (2015). The End of a World: Drought and Agrarian Transformation in Northeast Syria (2007–2010). In R. Hinnebusch & T. Zintl (Eds.), *Syria: from Reform to Revolt* (Vol. 1, pp. 199–222). Syracuse, NY: Syracuse University Press.

Ahmed, G. (2016). *Syria Wheat Value Chain and Food Security*. Duke University, Policy Briefs, Minerva, p. 10.
Aita, S. (2010). *Hal hunak ishkália zirá'iya fi Súriya?* [Is There a Problem with Agriculture in Syria?]. Retrieved from http://annidaa.org/modules/news/article.php?storyid=3873
Al Jablawi, H. (2016, July 26). Syrians Rely on Ingenuity to Defy Hunger and Death. *News Deeply*, Syria. Retrieved from https://www.newsdeeply.com/syria/articles/2016/07/26/syrians-rely-on-ingenuity-to-defy-hunger-and-death
Assistance Coordination Unit (ACU). (2015, September 18). *The Project "Our Bread from Our Land" Buys 110 Tons of Wheat in the Northern Countryside of Homs*. Gaziantep: ACU.
Batatu, H. (1999). *Syria's Peasantry, the Descendants of Its Lesser Rural Notables, and Their Politics*. Princeton: Princeton University Press.
Brown, O., & Crawford, A. (2009). *Rising Temperatures, Rising Tensions: Climate Change and the Risk of Violent Conflict in the Middle East*. International Institute for Sustainable Development.
Bush, R. (Ed.). (2002). *Counter-Revolution in Egypt's Countryside: Land and Farmers in the Era of Economic Reform*. London and New York: Zed Books.
Carnegie. (2015). *Food Insecurity in War Torn Syria from Decades of Self-sufficiency to Food Dependence*. Retrieved from http://carnegieendowment.org/2015/06/04/food-insecurity-in-war-torn-syria-from-decades-of-self-sufficiency-to-food-dependence-pub-60320
Central Bureau of Statistics (CBS). (2011). *Syria Statistical Abstract*. Damascus: CBS.
Central Bureau of Statistics (CBS). (2013). *Agricultural Statistics, Time Series 1970, 1980, 1990, 2000–2011*.
Ciezadlo, A. (2015, December 18). The Most Unconventional Weapon in Syria: Wheat. *The Washington Post*.
DIS (Danish Immigration Service) & ACCORD (Austrian Center of Country of Origin and Asylum Research and Documentation). (2010). *Human Rights Issues Concerning Kurds in Syria*. http://www.nyidanmark.dk/NR/rdonlyres/FF03AB63-10A5-4467-A038-20FE46B74CE8/0/Syrienrapport2010pdf.pdf
El Dahan, M. (2016, April 26). Syrian Food Crisis Deepens as War Chokes Farming. *Reuters*. Retrieved from http://www.reuters.com/article/us-mideast-crisis-syria-wheat- idUSKCN0XN0G0
El Hindi, A. (2011). Syria's Agricultural Sector: Situation, Role, Challenges and Prospects. In R. Hinnebusch, A. El Hindi, M. Khaddam, & M. Ababsa (Eds.), *Agriculture and Reform in Syria*. Fife, Scotland: University of St Andrews Centre for Syrian Studies.

Eng, B., & Martinez, J. C. (2015). How Feeding Syrians Feeds the War. *Foreign Policy*, 11 February 2016. Retrieved from http://foreignpolicy.com/2016/02/11/syria-chemonics-assad-bread/

Eng, B., & Martinez, J. C. (2016). *Starvation, Submission and Survival. The Syrian War Through the Prism of Food*. Middle East Research and Information Project. MERIP 273.

ENS (Environment News Service). (2010). *Syria Drought Drags on, Rivers Polluted, Aid Funding Dries Up*. Retrieved from http://www.ens-newswire.com/ens/mar2010/2010-03-08-02.html

FAO. (2016). *Syria Food Production at All-time Low*. Retrieved from http://www.fao.org/news/story/en/item/452217/icode/

FAO, Drought Appeal. (2008). Retrieved from http://www.fao.org/emergencies/tce-appfund/tce-appeals/appeals/emergency-detail0/en/item/7857/icode/?uidf=6095

FAO/WFP. (2016, November 14). Special Report. FAO/WFP Crop and Food Security Assessment Mission to the Syrian Arab Republic.

Government of Syria, Ministry of Agriculture and Agrarian Reform. (2010). *National Programme for Food Security in the Syrian Arab Republic*.

Hamlo, K. (2015, 07/03). *Despites Incentives, Syrian Government Is Having Hard Time Purchasing Crops from Farmers*. The Arab Weekly, Issue 12, p. 16. Retrieved from http://www.thearabweekly.com/?id=983

Hudson, J. (2014, April 17). Exclusive: UN Docs Expose Assad's Starvation Campaign in Syria. *Foreign Policy*. Retrieved from http://foreignpolicy.com/2014/04/17/exclusive-u-n-docs-expose-assads-starvation-campaign-in-syria/

Ibrahim, A. (2016). *Double Prices for Bread in Latakia Countryside*. Retrieved from http://www.all4syria.info/Archive/317709

IRIN. (2010, September 9). *Syria Drought Pushing Millions into Poverty*. Retrieved from http://www.irinnews.org/report.aspx?reportid=90442

Khaddam, M. (2011). Syrian Agriculture Between Reality and Potential. In Raymond A. Hinnebusch (dir.), *Agriculture and Reform in Syria* (pp. 57–82). Boulder: Lynne Rienner Publishers and University of St Andrews.

Lançon, F. (2011). *Assessment of the Competitiveness of the Syrian Agriculture: An Application to Selected Representative Value Chains*. Syrian Arab Republic, Ministry of Agriculture and Agrarian Reform, National Agricultural Policy Center (NAPC), International Cooperation Center of Agricultural Research for Development- CIRAD.

Mourad, M. (2016). *Government areas in Deir ez-Zor: No Bread and Water*. Retrieved from http://www.all4syria.info/Archive/329855

NAPC. (2010). *National Agricultural Policy Centre (NAPC)*. Retrieved from http://www.syria-today.com/index.php/focus/5266-mining-the-deep

OCHA. (2009). *Syria Drought Response Plan*. Retrieved from http://www.un.org.sy/Syria_Drought_Response_Plan_2009.pdf

Pecad. (2008). *SYRIA: Wheat Production in 2008/09 Declines Owing to Season-Long Drought*. Retrieved from http://www.pecad.fas.usda.gov/highlights/2008/05/Syria_may2008.htm

Petran, T. (1972). *Syria: Nation of the Modern World*. London: Ernest Benn Ltd.

Sarkis Fernández, D. (2011). El contrato es la ley: estado, economía y políticas de la responsabilidad en la agricultura Siria. In I. T. Saborit (Ed.), *Antropología de la Responsabilidad* (pp. 151–183). A Coruña, Spain: Universidade da Coruña.

UN News Centre. (2014). *Security Council Renews Cross-border Aid Delivery to Syria for a Year*. Retrieved from http://www.un.org/apps/news/story.asp?NewsID=49632#.Weg7Vk0UnVg

UNGA. (2011). *Report of the Special Rapporteur on the Right to Food, Olivier De Schutter. Mission to the Syrian Arab Republic*. United Nations General Assembly.

Wind, E., & Dahi, O. (2014). *Syria's Agricultural Development. Current Realities and Historical Roots*. Fribourg University, Unpublished Paper. Retrieved from https://lettres.unifr.ch/fileadmin/Documentation/Departements/Sciences_historiques/Histoire_des_societes_modernes_et_contemporaines/Images/Recherche/WIND_and_DAHI_Agriculture_Syria_Fribourg_.pdf

CHAPTER 12

Conclusion: China's Role in Syria's National Security

Linda Matar and Ali Kadri

The reconstruction debate and its financing have come into prominence, especially c. mid-2017 after the Syrian government achieved significant military advances. A plethora of writings have focused on post-conflict projections, physical reconstruction, economic recovery and social rehabilitation (EIU 2017; Escobar 2017a; Lund 2017; Moubayed 2017; United Nations 2017). Doubtless, given the current stage of the Syrian conflict and the overwhelming level of physical devastation that so far ensued, the main questions that arise concern not only the fiscal means to finance reconstruction but also the infrastructural and capacity means needed to initiate it. It is also likely that the conflict will prove unstoppable in the foreseeable future, especially given the political rift between the

L. Matar (✉)
National University of Singapore, Singapore, Singapore
e-mail: linda@nus.edu.sg

A. Kadri (✉)
London School of Economics (LSE), London, UK

National University of Singapore, Singapore, Singapore
e-mail: a.kadri@lse.ac.uk

© The Author(s) 2019
L. Matar, A. Kadri (eds.), *Syria: From National Independence to Proxy War*, https://doi.org/10.1007/978-3-319-98458-2_12

international powers. The war has acquired its own momentum. In this final chapter, we argue reconstruction in times of prolonged conflict—that is, the Syrian case—should address the interface between reconstruction and national security. We insist on this inflexion because we believe imperialist aggression will continue to target Syria. We also pay a special attention to the role that China can play in reinstating Syria's national security. Our colleagues at the National University of Singapore who are knowledgeable in Mandarin were generous enough to help us access Chinese resources.[1] We gathered the Chinese perspective concerning Syrian reconstruction. Interestingly, and as will be demonstrated below, many references reveal that China is keen on supporting and financing Syria's economic revival, physical reconstruction, and social reintegration.

The mainstream narrative recommends Western-funded reconstruction should sidestep the Syrian government and target territorial areas that lie outside the government control (Heydemann 2017; Itani and Schneider 2017). The rationale is that official channels for financing reconstruction will boost the al-Asad regime's authoritarian rule and enrich its cronies. Furthermore, Western funders should reach out to the local administrative groups in opposition areas. The aim is to entrench decentralisation by empowering the local communities or military groups outside of the state's reach. The mainstream embellishes its language with rhetoric reminiscent of the Paris commune, such as local councils or communities. This vocabulary gives the impression that the opposition in Syria is a genuine grassroots democracy.

The very phrase "the al-Asad regime" personalises the state. It reduces the state to its head. The mainstream narrative dismisses how the Syrian state currently faces an existential threat, given the hegemonic imperialist assault led by the US and its allies. In fact, the establishment of decentralised rule across Syria's territory would weaken national security, allowing external forces to prolong their intervention in Syria. Decentralised governance would also reinforce social divisions based on sectarian and ethnic schisms. It would relegate citizenship to tribe-like social forms. In short, it would endow the current de facto partition with de jure legitimacy. Shattered security and disintegrated zones occupied by various externally funded military groups will cement the institutional structures for permanent instability and conflict.

Contrary to the Western-influenced mainstream narrative, we argue in this chapter that reconstruction efforts should bolster the Syrian state's resilience capacity, irrespective of who helms it. The point of reconstruction, whether now or at the conflict's end, is to enable the state to restore its legitimate sovereignty over the country's territory. In previous publications, we posited Syria is witnessing an imperialist assault, which necessitates the formation of unusual coalitions to deter Western-backed reactionary groups (Kadri 2012; Matar and Kadri 2015).

State consolidation and centralised rule are crucial to re-establish national security and to mitigate external interventions in Syria's internal affairs. Chinese authors argue that Syrian reconstruction involves not only economic but also security reconstruction (Li 2018). Because it is highly unlikely that US-led imperialism will ever halt its expansion, stances on Syria should be nationalist and anti-imperialist. Internal disputes between local forces, whether they be regarding enhancing political participation or the wresting of state power altogether, should be postponed until the national liberation of Syria is complete. This viewpoint is endorsed by Syrian nationalists opposed to any Western intervention in Syria. A prominent Syrian scholar, Mounir Hemesh, asserts Syria's need for reconstruction should not be exploited to open doors for Western intervention and influence. He explains assumptions about inadequate national resources and inefficiencies of the public sector to carry out the task of economic and social restoration are false (Hemesh 2014: 7). He further argues: "the safest way to secure financial resources for development and reconstruction … is to resort to an independent developmental strategy that relies on available national resources and on financial contributions and investments from Syria's allies. This is the only way Syria can preserve its national sovereignty and dignity" (Hemesh 2014: 19).

As regards Syria's allies, China, the rising economic powerhouse, has the strategic interest and capacity to assist in the task. Given China is a strong advocate of a sovereign Syrian state, it is in the mutual interest of both countries for China to intervene early on. China can afford to support the reconstruction of the physical and social infrastructure in the government-controlled and recently liberated areas. Immediate and active reconstruction efforts can bring back relative stability across Syria's territory. A stable Syria is key to safe strategic crossroads between Asia, Europe and Africa, serving China's Belt and Road Initiative (BRI).

Reconstruction can foster economic and political relations between China and Syria and promote mutual benefit. Syria can gain from Chinese finance and experience in infrastructural development and capacity building (Zhang 2017a). Suffering from deficient productive resources, Syria can also benefit from Chinese machinery and equipment by engaging

Chinese small and medium enterprises (SMEs). Accordingly, the Syrian government has repeatedly conveyed that Chinese, as well as Russian and Iranian, deals are prioritised when settling reconstruction contracts (SCMP 2017). In turn, China can move its industries and enterprises to Syria, releasing part of its overcapacity while creating new markets for the consumption of its goods in Syria and other neighbouring Middle Eastern countries (Li 2018: 84-87). However, it should be noted that such effort cannot build national security if it sacrifices the Syrian state capacity to rebuild. Iraq's rebuilding experience after 1991, under the embargo, is proof that national capacities can be successfully redeployed in reconstruction. China's overcapacity problematic should not be solved by supplanting what remains of Syria's capacity.

Unlike Western countries and international financial organisations dominated by the US and Europe that impose a set of structural adjustment reforms on host economies as conditions to providing loans, aid, investments and trade agreements, China does not intervene in local affairs. It respects the sovereignty of developing states to act upon their policies (Escobar 2017b). It is this relative autonomy over policy that drives developing economies, including Syria, to "look East" rather than West. China insists that its involvement in the Syrian reconstruction and other countries' infrastructural development should be based on BRI's three main principles—joint discussion, joint venture, and joint benefit—that can be facilitated via consistent collaboration between China and the host economies (Li 2018).

Learning from the Iraq case after the 2003 US invasion, one should note that if the current imperialist attack on Syria succeeds in dissolving the state, no durable peace will prevail. Iraq's experience of prolonged political instability, eroded security and cheapened social value and national capabilities may be replicated in Syria (Kadri 2012). Additionally, the Arab region's reconstruction experience, especially in Iraq and Lebanon, exemplifies a history of reconstruction efforts which fostered state deconstruction and weakened society's national identity, because they failed to bolster a central government that places the rights of the individual above the rights of the sect. The crystallisation of individual and communal rights in a rationalised state structure is an *a priori* condition for overall security. So far, in the Arab context, reconstruction efforts have been measures to promote the objectives of imperialism in setting the background for continued war and/or the dissolution of the development achievements that would have otherwise buttressed the future security of the state and society (Kadri 2017).

In fact, Syrians are aware of the dire implications of Western influence in the Arab region. In December 2017, Damascus University and Mother Syria Assembly (MSA) organised a conference, entitled "Towards a national economic vision for the future Syria." Syrian academics and researchers discussed national strategies to place Syria on a self-reliant and independent path in pursuing economic renewal while confronting internal and external challenges. Syrian academics emphasised the potential role of the state despite diminished resources and ongoing international sanctions (MSA 2017).

Syria's allies, Russia and Iran, continue to support the Syrian government in its war. China has also supported Syria during the course of the conflict. Politically, it has intervened several times in the United Nations Security Council in favour of Syria. Alongside Russia, it blocked bids by Western powers that condemned the Syrian government over the alleged use of chemical weapons and vetoed other resolutions that could have opened avenues for a military invasion of Syria. As a strong supporter of Syria's sovereignty and territorial integrity, China stated the Syrian issue should be solved via political not military means (Gao 2017; Ministry of Foreign Affairs of the People's Republic of China 2017a; Yang 2017). It assigned a special envoy for Syria whose role is to encourage mediation efforts between all parties to resolve the conflict through diplomacy (Sina 2018). Its Foreign Minister, Mr. Wang Yi, has been vocal about China's keenness to support Syria during his meetings with various key Syrian diplomatic figures, assuring that China sticks to its long-standing position calling for fostering stability in Syria (Gao 2017; Ministry of Foreign Affairs of the People's Republic of China 2017b). China believes that the real safety zone in Syria should be one that secures the core status of all Syrians in the political settlement process (Li 2018; Yang 2017).

China has expressed interest in contributing to Syria's reconstruction. It is interested in expanding its gigantic outward investment project, the New Silk Road, to the Arab region. A special legal commission was created in Beijing by the Syrian Embassy in China, the China-Arab Exchange Association, and the Beijing-based Shijing law firm. The commission was established to provide Chinese companies with legal advice on issues pertaining to business and investment in Syria. A corresponding document on the formation of the commission was signed on 4 July 2017, confirming that China seriously intends to conduct business in Syria (Sputnik International 2017).

Historically, China has been particularly interested in the oil-rich Middle East, which has attracted infrastructure investment in its energy sector. Syria, however, is important not because it holds large oil reserves, but because of its proximity to Arab Gulf oil. According to Chinese sources, Syria's strategic position makes it an important node in the ancient Silk Road. For that reason, Syria's stability may contribute to the future success of the Belt and Road Initiative (BRI) in the Middle East (Ministry of Commerce of the People's Republic of China 2017; Liu 2017; Zhang 2017b). Previous Chinese investments in risky or conflict-affected countries signify that China does not shy away from committing to long-term investment in politically unstable environments. Actually, China stands as Africa's "single largest funder and builder of infrastructure" (EIU 2016). Syria is no exception, especially since geography makes it an important stop along China's One Belt One Road (OBOR).

The section below presents a summary of the economic and social repercussions of the brutally protracted conflict. This is followed by a summary of China's actual and planned involvement in Syria's restoration since the outbreak of the crisis. For China's outward investment in Syria to be socially and economically effective, it needs to be tied to a national plan ensuring reconstruction and infrastructural policies re-enshrine the nation's security. The concluding section addresses this issue.

War Implications

Seven years of war paired with Western sanctions, territorial disintegration and destruction of infrastructure and urban systems have aggravated the disintegration of Syria's economy and society. Worse of all, the loss of life and the exodus of refugees have created an irreparable gap in Syria's human capacities.

Since the start of the war in 2011, secondary sources have had to estimate statistical figures since both the Syrian Central Bank and the Central Bureau of Statistics have not generated new national data—a way in which the war has also denied Syrian ability even to know and represent its own national production. A World Bank Report, issued in mid-2017, estimated the cumulative losses in GDP during the war years to be four times 2010 GDP, or $226 bn (World Bank 2017). In real terms, GDP declined by 61 per cent in 2015 as compared to 2011—non-oil GDP contracted by 52 per cent, while the oil component shrank by more than 90 per cent following the plunge in oil production due to the government's lack of control of the oil fields in Syria's Northeast (World Bank 2017: 54). The study quantified physical damage across eight governorates, estimating that in the housing sector, 8 per cent has been destroyed and 23 per cent partially destroyed. In the medical and education sectors, almost half of the facilities were partially damaged, while 16 per cent and 10 per cent, respectively, suffered from complete destruction (World Bank 2017).

With the crippling of industry and agriculture amid physical destruction, tightening sanctions and continuous shortages in supply of fuel and raw materials, an informal economy has thrived—based on looting, smuggling and contraband. The Syrian Ministry of Industry estimated the destruction in the industrial sector, private and public, at more than SYP one trillion. Since the conflict's start, more than half of the manufacturing companies in the public sector have stopped operations (The Syria Report 2016). More critically, the country's foreign exchange reserves dropped to $1 bn in 2015, down from $21 bn before the conflict (IMF 2016: 28). This can hardly finance one month of imports.

In response to the acute shortfall in oil and tax revenues, the government has cut down on capital spending. Current expenditures, however, remained steady. As the government relied on concessionary loans from its allies, public debt increased from 30 per cent in 2010 to 150 per cent of GDP in 2015 (World Bank 2017: 63). It may be that the resilience of the al-Asad government is not only related to military Russian backing but also to indirect Chinese financial backing through Chinese provision of credit lines to Iran (The New Arab 2017). Government economic measures over the last seven years aimed at restoring normalcy to economic life have fallen short of their targets, though, as resources have shifted gears to satisfy the war effort and the finances needed to buttress it.

The conflict's social consequences have been catastrophic. With 5.3 million registered refugees according to UNHCR and another 6.6 million forcibly displaced inside the country, Syria holds the world's largest number of IDPs (UN 2016–2017). War and territorial divisions have disrupted economic life and reduced people's mobility, pushing total unemployment to 52.9 per cent in 2015—with youth unemployment rising to 78 per cent (World Bank 2017: 68; UN 2016).

The combination of war and sanction-induced supply shortages, the rising import to export ratios, the sharp depreciation of the Syrian pound and the lifting of government subsidies on essential items starting in mid-2014 have pushed up food prices. The price of the essential commodity basket increased 487 per cent by the end of 2016 as compared to 2012

(World Bank 2017: 74). According to the Syrian Centre for Policy Research, more than two-thirds of Syrians are living in extreme poverty, unable to afford essential food and non-food commodities. Another 35 per cent of the population are trapped in abject poverty and relied on "in-kind food assistance" (SCPR 2016: 8). Obviously, the areas most affected by continuous fighting such as Raqqa, Idlib and Deir ez-Zor exhibit the highest poverty rates (IMF 2016; SCPR 2016). Other estimates reveal nearly seven million Syrians can be classified as food insecure (FAO 2016). As families struggle to afford their daily living needs, child labour has risen and more than two million children have left schools (IMF 2016). Simply put, Syria's human capital stock has been devastated. The above empirics, however, only provide a snapshot of the calamity of the Syrian conflict.

The Syrian government has announced its plans to start limited reconstruction in the areas under its control (SANA 2018). With the help of its allies, it is repairing power stations that were destroyed during the war. Starting in 2016, Russian and Iranian companies were granted reconstruction contracts in various sectors including oil, infrastructural and telecom sectors, based on production and profit-sharing with Syrian parties. Russia signed contracts worth 850 mn euros in order to rebuild infrastructure, while Iran also signed accords worth a few hundred million euros to repair power grids (Straits Times 2017). The potential projects will be executed under the aegis of the state and are aimed at reconstructing the public sector.

CHINESE OUTWARD INVESTMENT PLANS IN CONFLICT SYRIA

The stubborn contradictions of the external players that have intervened in the Syrian war since 2011 have added to the crisis's complexity. The recent developments in the field have shifted the balance of power in favour of the al-Asad government and its allies, Russia, Iran and a still shy but rising China. But this does not undercut the need for a conclusion to the conflict, be it by a clear-cut military victory or by an international consensus that commits to ending war finances and installing a political settlement that bridges the political differences among all warring factions.

As mentioned earlier, Syria has sought its allies' help in wartime reconstruction. Russia and Iran are financially constrained and cannot shoulder the weighty reconstruction bill. However, the excess productive capacity and financial wherewithal of China allows it to play a key role in this endeavour even amid Syria's strife. Chinese investment in politically unstable African countries, such as Kenya and Tanzania, signifies that China will not baulk at investing in risky economies, especially when it invests for political as well as long-term economic benefits. In this regard, China can play a constructive role in Syria's reconstruction and get the economy and society back in shape.

It is only logical to note that China has a geostrategic interest in securitising the Syrian state, because the fall of Syria signifies its loss to the Western orbit. Such an outcome would weaken China and its allies and shift the global power structure considerably in favour of the US and its allies. Since China has supported a sovereign and centralised state in Syria, its immediate intervention in Syria's reconstruction would serve its interests. This in turn would solidify the rule of the Syrian state over the territory and strengthen Syria's sovereignty. Financial outlays provided in the context of economic and physical refurbishment could play a crucial role in bolstering Syria's autonomy, independence and territorial integration. That is so irrespective of who is at the head of that state.

Chinese political intervention in Syria is not confined to backing the Syrian government at the UNSC. It goes a step further to include military training and cooperation to the Syrian army. The Chinese Defense Ministry announced the Chinese military is ready to strengthen its cooperation with its Syrian counterparts (Global Times 2016). In August 2016, a Chinese military delegation including the rear admiral, Mr. Guan Youfei, and other Chinese advisors visited Syria to train soldiers to use weapons and materiel purchased from China. Mr. Guan, who heads the Office for International Military Cooperation under the Central Military Commission, stated China's People's Liberation Army Navy (PLAN) is willing to cooperate with Syria's military and deliver the necessary personnel training in weapons that are supplied by China (SCMP 2017). Beijing is keen to enhance not only government-to-government but also military-to-military cooperation (Global Times 2016; AP 2016). Although China has emphasised that it has no intention to send troops to Syria, as such a decision would work against its foreign policy that opposes external armed intervention in domestic conflicts, it discretely deployed troops to Syria around mid-2017. The Chinese official narrative behind this manoeuvre was that their personnel provided the necessary training and offered advice on health issues and other logistics to the Syrian army (Middle East Eye 2017). Nevertheless, this development signifies China—to a relative degree—is emplaced on Syrian lands.

Since the crisis's outbreak, China has supported Syria by providing humanitarian aid and pledges for potential investment and reconstruction projects. According to Chinese state media, China gave 1000 tons of rice to Syrian citizens as part of its BRI's humanitarian plan (CGTN 2017). In 2015, the Chinese government provided 100 mn yuan (around $16 mn) worth of humanitarian assistance to Syria and its neighbours, Jordan and Lebanon, that have hosted large numbers of Syrian refugees (Sina 2015). In the first half of 2017, China and Syria signed three agreements worth more than $40 million to aid the internally displaced and the returning refugees in need of water, food, shelter and medical services (Gao 2017). Additionally, the Chinese government gave $1 mn to the International Red Cross Society in May 2017 to help internally displaced Syrians (Xinhua 2017).

From a business perspective, the Chinese company Pacific Century CyberWorks (PCCW) was contracted in 2014 in the telecoms sector to improve the landline connectivity in the governorate of Hasakeh. PCCW has been active in Syria since 2012 as it was the main provider of internet traffic in Syria, along with Türk Telecom and Telecom Italia, which, according to the Syria Report, have possibly stopped their operations during the conflict (The Syria Report 2014). In 2015, Huawei, one of China's largest telecommunication equipment makers, inked an agreement to counsel the Syrian government on the national strategy for the development of Syria's IT and telecom sector (Daily Beast 2015). The Huawei deal is not new to Syria. The Chinese company had previously signed a $20 mn arrangement in 2011 to supply equipment to the Syrian telecom sector (The Syria Report 2011). Additionally, representatives from the Tebian Electric Apparatus (TBEA), a Chinese company that provides renewable energy solutions and power transformers to power plants, met with Syrian officials in 2016. The aim of the meeting is to supply the Aleppo Thermal Plant with gas turbines to enable it to resume production (The Syria Report 2016). All these deals signal intense Chinese corporate interest in doing business in Syria. The Chinese ambassador to Syria, Mr. Qi Qianjin, recently expressed that China is prepared to play a greater role in rebuilding and reconstructing Syria as the war gradually subsides. This will help in promoting security, peace and hope for Syria's residents (SCMP 2018). Additionally, Mr. Qin Yong, Vice President of the China-Arab Exchange Association, advised Chinese companies to survey and assess cities like Damascus, Homs, Tartous and Latakia—sites marked by favourable conditions for carrying out reconstruction plans (Sina 2017).

Chinese interest in conducting business in Syria is not new. Before the conflict, China had concentrated investments in Syria's oil and gas sector.

Companies like China Petrochemical Corporation and China National Petroleum Corporation had invested in Syria's hydrocarbon sector but suspended their operations in 2013 (Belt and Road 2018). Chinese companies also owned shares in a few local oil-producing companies, such as Al Furat Petroleum Company, Syria-Sino Al Kawkab Oil Company, Oudeh Petroleum Company and Dijla Petroleum Company (The Syria Report 2018). However most of these companies decommissioned their operations after the loss of government control over the East and Northeast parts of the country.

From an OBOR perspective, Syria represents an important hub and transit point. Because of its geostrategic position, Syria provides a route to the Mediterranean through which Beijing can transport goods and passengers to Europe. Syria can also play a key role in the transportation corridors in the Levant—the Iraq-Iran-Syria corridor—along OBOR's eventual route (Escobar 2017a). Syria was a key point on ancient trade routes. Damascus flourished or foundered according to the vicissitudes and cyclical upturns and downturns of long-distance trade. The battles for Damascus in the fifteenth century blocked the flows through the old Silk Road and precipitated a crisis, which led to the great crisis of the Eastern world, just as Europe was making inroads through its conquest of the seas, in preparation for the rise of capitalism (Kadri 2016). Palmyra, an important stop on the old Silk Road, hosted the caravans of traders that came from the East, carrying silks, spices and art crafts. Before the conflict, Syria held the Silk Road festival annually to signify the key role that it played in the Silk Road as a centrepoint between the East and the West (Simmons 2009). Syria's relation with China is nearly as old as recorded history. A Chinese proverb says China sees with both eyes, while the world is blind, except for Syria and Mesopotamia that see with one eye. Syria was the only culture outside the middle heavenly kingdom that achieved the latter's respect (al-Alawi 2009). However, at the current stage, the real relevance of Syria to China is its strategic importance. The power play on Syrian territory is an imperialist power play. The victors of that war may make or break the OBOR.

The official narrative behind the activation of the New Silk Road is that China aims to strengthen economic partnerships among countries along the Belt and Road Initiative, providing them with long-term credit on concessional terms. Various financial institutions, including the Asian Infrastructure Investment Bank (AIIB) with capital of $100 billion, half of which comes from China, and the Chinese Silk Road Fund with capital of $40 billion, are responsible for financing OBOR projects (Gosh 2017).

China currently has in its storehouses more than $3 trillion in foreign exchange. It is both blessing and burden, being both a huge store of financial wealth and also held in US-denominated dollars. As the US holds the power to devalue the dollar and as Chinese excess capacity must be mobilised, China must lighten the tension by putting to use these dollars to expand its markets. By quickly investing this financial wealth in physical assets abroad, China partially rids itself from servitude to US capital. Unlike the Gulf states which are merely money rich, China can back its financial entrepreneurship abroad with credit and the utilisation of its own industrial resources (Kadri 2018). On 29 November 2017, the Chinese foreign ministry spokesperson, Mr. Geng Shuang, stated China is motivated to engage in Syria and other Middle East countries, explaining:

> Too many people in the Middle East are suffering at the brutal hands of terrorists … We support countries in the region in exploring a development path suited to their national conditions and are ready to share governance experience and jointly build the Belt and Road and promote peace and stability through common development. (Gao 2017)

Within this context, China would not hesitate to contribute to Syria's reconstruction and pave the way for reviving political stability in Syria (Ministry of Foreign Affairs of the People's Republic of China 2017b). In various press conferences and interviews, the Chinese Foreign Minister, Mr. Wang, has voiced China's intentions to defend Syria's territorial reintegration in order to reinstate the country's sovereignty (Ministry of Foreign Affairs of the People's Republic of China 2017a). After all, from the Chinese viewpoint, Syria's stability may guarantee the successful business operation of OBOR across the Middle East.

More recently, a series of networking events were held in 2017 with the express purpose of drawing closer relations and collaborations between Chinese and Syrian investors. The Syria Day Expo, held in Beijing in July 2017, was a collaborative effort between the China-Arab Exchange Association and Syrian Embassy. The meeting attracted 1000 representatives from Chinese enterprises who are eager to do business in Syria (SANA 2017; Belt and Road 2018). The Chinese business delegations have been active in seeking out not only business tenders in areas of reconstruction but also the formulation of bilateral trade deals needed for the successful operation of China's Belt and Road Initiative. The Syrian and Chinese governments have discussed their intention to open up direct air flights in order to promote trade and commercial exchanges between the two countries that will in turn facilitate Chinese companies' involvement in Syria's reconstruction (Syria Times 2017).

In August 2017, the 59th Damascus International Fair brought together Chinese, Russian and Iranian businesses (Garrie 2017). As a result of the great emphasis placed on Syrian reconstruction, over 30 Chinese firms, including China Energy Engineering Group and China Construction Fifth Engineering Division Corp., Ltd., visited Syria in 2017. They have examined with interest projects in the infrastructure sector (roads, airports, houses, bridges, hospitals) and have plans to rebuild electricity, energy and communication networks (Bai 2017; Zhang 2017b). In July 2017, China has also announced its plans to invest $2 bn in an industrial park to attract around 150 Chinese companies to Syria and provide 40,000 employment opportunities (Escobar 2017a). The industrial park can serve as a potential implementation and production centre for China's BRI in the region. In early 2018 one of the Chinese multinational manufacturing companies that produces heavy machinery, SANY, also visited Damascus. Representatives from SANY met with Syrian officials to discuss investment opportunities, particularly in areas of manufacturing (The Syria Report 2018). One may conclude that China's accent on industrial investment in Syria may go further than merely infrastructure and oil and can be another building block towards accelerating Syria's economic revitalisation.

The Syrian geopolitical environment will remain fragile, presenting challenges to comprehensive restoration efforts (Zhang 2017a). The commencement of these projects will no doubt face hurdles given the general absence of overall security, a weak business environment and financial difficulties. And it is for this reason that we have argued that financial and physical reconstruction in time of war should mainly bolster the state's resilience against external threats. Moreover, the Western-imposed sanctions, which disrupted the functioning of Syria's institutions, impede the settling of business deals in either US dollars or the Euro. One way to overcome the latter financial hurdle is for both countries to settle their deals and trade in the Renminbi (RMB), which is definitively under negotiation by both parties.

Chinese and other forms of infrastructural investment need to be woven into the Syrian government's reconstruction policy. The latter cannot be isolated from the nation's development trajectory. It ought to be subordinate to a broader national plan that aims at placing the country on a path of economic and social revival. This national plan should ensure that the government is sovereign over its policies and that infrastructural refurbishment preserves Syria's national security.

Concluding Remarks

Recent imperialist history in the Arab region can be viewed, in many ways, through the prism of the invasion and occupation of Iraq. This disaster cascades across the country, continuing to wreck the Iraqi state and its population. The US creed of targeting sovereign or semi-sovereign states for deconstruction in this region is amply evident, as we may see from Iraq. This is what lies in store for Syria. However, since the invasion and occupation of Iraq, global power balances have changed. We now have serious competitors such as China, alongside Russia's presence on the ground in Syria. Both states have Syria's integrity in mind. The chance is there for Syria to cultivate. It has already gained ground. But the choice of policy now will have a bearing on cementing its future shape as a state. Fighting its war of independence and reconstruction must march hand in hand. They cannot and ought not be separated, at least without weakening each other. These are reinforcing pillars of the state. However, reconstruction in times of war must be part of a suite of macro policies. The macroeconomic policies under war conditions are about allocating resources to the home and national fronts. Reconstruction can strengthen the home front effort by laying down the infrastructural foundation that tallies with the demands of the social superstructure.

National security buttresses state legitimacy over its territory and mitigates the regressive repercussions of the war on Syria. As argued earlier, decentralisation reforms and/or territorial disintegration would pave the way for a protracted and prolonged conflict. Through decentralisation, US-sponsored external forces would cement their sordid and catastrophic intervention. We have also postulated that the Arab region's reconstruction experience, as exemplified by the cases of Lebanon and Iraq, reveals that since reconstruction did not foster the nation's security, the result was state debilitation and denuded sovereignty.

However, if one were to compare the reconstruction or development experience in the Arab region to that in East Asia, the latter experience reveals that national policies since the 1960s have focused on reinforcing security over policy and territory (Jomo 2001). East Asian states have exercised a certain level of autonomous decision-making when pursuing structural transformation that enabled them to outmanoeuvre the dictate of neoliberalism. They have jointly embarked upon economic transformation while nurturing their security priorities. Stronger security structures enabled East Asian states to underwrite long-term investment. Also, we ought not to forget that infrastructural investment was people-centred, with priority given to the health and education sectors, and as such the whole development experience exhibited a class dimension (Kadri 2018; Patnaik 2016).

As Arab states (neo)liberalised, they allocated resources away from social and national security apparatuses. They allowed neoliberalism to congeal in the form of national-level policies. Resources, including security resources, were channelled upward towards the narrow group in society whose economic ties tended to the West. The Arab states squandered their autonomy as they cleaved economic objectives from security concerns. As these states became vulnerable and ruled by a class with wealth based abroad, the potential for internal collapse became palpable. As we have discussed in the introduction to this volume, collapse and state destruction is a favoured outcome to US-led imperialism. War to imperialism is the US's economic lifeline. That is why constructing independent national plans must be delinked from the imperialist centre (Ajl 2018a, b).

Against this backdrop of encompassing violence, Syrian reconstruction must learn from its past and from its region. Syria rebuilt its economy in the post-colonial days through socially grounded and embedded independent policies. It regulated the channels that funnel wealth abroad—the trade and capital accounts—and internally financed its economic expansion. It also laid out developmental architectures using social rather than capitalist accounting, the latter with a short-term horizon and the former with a long-term horizon. The long-term social payoff offset the short-term economic costs. Throughout this radical transformation, especially in the 1960s and early 1970s, it maintained a close collaboration between the civilian and military sectors to ensure its national defences.

At the time of writing, no effort is being spared to split Syrians on sectarian and ethnic bases. The bugles of the mainstream have all reduced a Syrian national belonging to identities whose basic political function is to destroy Syria. The existence of the state is not an option Syrians can forego. It is a necessary and primary form of social organisation and platform for political expression. That is the case not because there is some inherent yearning to be patriotic or to idolise the state. The state is the organ which distributes resources and incomes. These are the material foundation of the share of value obtained by the working class. As such, the state serves a material function. It delivers welfare and social security, a fortiori through national security, which grows by the degree of its independence from imperialism. A state with a modicum of sovereignty is anathema to imperialism, because imperialist accumulation requires the destruction and depopulation of dependent states. That is why to rebuild a strong state is to rebuild the national unity of Syrians. Reconstructing the broken spirits of Syrians is the foremost task. Such labour, the labour of history, concerns the rights of working people as they crystallise in the state and its institutions. This is the task now before us.

Note

1. Special thanks are due to Ms. Teo Sze Lynn Fiona, Mr. Tan Yong Kang Jasper, and Mr. Koh Kelvin.

Bibliography

Ajl, M. (2018a). Delinking, Food Sovereignty, and Populist Agronomy: Notes on an Intellectual History of the Peasant Path in the Global South. *Review of African Political Economy, 45*(155), 64–84.

Ajl, M. (2018b, May 29). Auto-centered Development and Indigenous Technics: Slaheddine el-Amami and Tunisian Delinking. *The Journal of Peasant Studies.*

Al-Alawi, H. (2009). *Al-ʿAmal al-Kamila.* Damascus: Dar Almada.

AP. (2016, August 18). Chinese Admiral Visits Syria in Show of Support. *Associated Press News.*

Bai Tiantian. (2017, September 25). 叙利亚驻华大使:中国企业将优先获得参与叙重建的机会 [Syrian Ambassador to China: China Enterprises Will Be Given Priority in Syrian Reconstruction Opportunities]. *Huanqiu online.* Retrieved December 22, 2017, from http://world.huanqiu.com/exclusive/2017-09/11279054.html

Belt and Road. (2018). *Syria Economic Profile.* Retrieved January 22, 2018, from http://beltandroad.hktdc.com/en/country-profiles/syria

CGTN. (2017, November 21). *China Delivers Food Aid to Syria Under the Belt and Road Initiative.* Retrieved December 20, 2017, from https://news.cgtn.com/news/3263544d78637a6333566d54/share_p.html

Daily Beast. (2015, October 27). China Looks at Syria, Sees $$$. *Daily Beast.* Retrieved January 22, 2018, from http://thebea.st/1kKdWNr?source=email&via=desktop

Economist Intelligence Unit (EIU). (2016). *One Belt, One Road, An Economic Roadmap.* London: EIU.

Economist Intelligence Unit (EIU). (2017, September). *Syria Country Report.* London: EIU.

Escobar, P. (2017a, July 13). The New Silk Road Will Go Through Syria. *Asia Times*.

Escobar, P. (2017b). The Belt and Road Initiative: China's Answer to Globalisation? *Third World Resurgence, 319/320*(Mar/Apr), 10–11.

FAO. (2016, November 15). Food Production in Syria at All-Time Low. Retrieved June 10, 2017, from http://www.fao.org/emergencies/fao-in-action/stories/stories-detail/en/c/453428/

Gao, C. (2017, November 30). Why China Wants Syria in Its New Belt and Road. *The Diplomat*. Retrieved December 3, 2017, from https://thediplomat.com/2017/11/why-china-wants-syria-in-its-new-belt-and-road/

Garrie, A. (2017, August 19). Damascus International Fair Signals Syria's Revival. *Global Research*.

Global Times. (2016, August 18). China Boosts Syria Support. *Global Times*. Retrieved December 17, 2017, from http://www.globaltimes.cn/content/1001150.shtml

Gosh, J. (2017, June 10). One Belt, One Road, One Grand Design? *IDEAs Blogs*.

Hemesh, M. (2014). *A National Model for Development and Reconstruction*. Economic Files. Damascus: Syrian Economic Society. Retrieved from http://www.mafhoum.com/syr/articles_14/2014-6.pdf

Heydemann, S. (2017, August 24). Rules for Reconstruction in Syria. *Brookings Institution*.

IMF. (2016). *Syria's Conflict Economy*. IMF Working Paper, WP/16/123.

Itani, F., & Schneider, T. (2017). *Rebuilding Syria. Localized Revitalization Strategy*. Washington, DC: Atlantic Council.

Jomo, K. S. (2001). *Southeast Asia's Industrialisation*. Palgrave Macmillan.

Kadri, A. (2012). *The Political Economy of the Syrian Crisis*. Working Papers in Technology Governance and Economic Dynamics (Number 46), The Other Canon Foundation, Norway.

Kadri, A. (2016). Islam and Capitalism: Military Routs, Not Formal Institutions. In E. Reinert et al. (Eds.), *Handbook of Alternative Theories of Economic Development*. Cheltenham: Elgar Publishing Limited.

Kadri, A. (2017, April 19). *Imperialist Reconstruction or Depopulation in Syria and Iraq*. IDEAs Featured Articles.

Kadri, A. (2018). *The Cordon Sanitaire: A Single Law Governing Development in East Asia and the Arab World*. Basingstoke: Palgrave Macmillan.

Li, S. (2018, March). "一带一路"对接叙利亚战后重建：时势评估与前景展望 ["The Belt and Road" Initiative and Post-War Reconstruction in Syria: Assessments and Outlooks]. *Arab World Studies*.

Liu, B. (2017, February 16). 参与叙利亚重建 有利于推动"一带一路"建设 [Participation in Syrian Reconstruction is Conducive Towards One Belt One Road]. *21 Century Financial News*. Retrieved November 18, 2017, from http://epaper.21jingji.com/html/2017-02/16/content_56214.htm

Lund, A. (2017, March 8). Rebuilding Syria's Rubble as the Cannons Roar. *IRIN*.
Matar, L., & Kadri, A. (2015). Investment and Neoliberalism in Syria. In A. Kadri (Ed.), *Development Challenges and Solutions After the Arab Spring*. Basingstoke: Palgrave Macmillan.
Middle East Eye. (2017, August 9). The Dragon and the Lion: China's Growing Ties with Syria. *Middle East Eye*.
Ministry of Commerce of the People's Republic of China. (2017, November 9). 一带一路框架下中资企业如何走进中东. [How Will Chinese-Funded Enterprises Enter the Middle East Under the Auspices of One Belt One Road?]. Retrieved November 17, 2017, from http://cafiec.mofcom.gov.cn/article/zjsj/201711/20171102668097.shtml
Ministry of Foreign Affairs of the People's Republic of China. (2017a, April 13). 王毅就叙利亚局势阐述中方立场. [Wang Yi, on China's Position on Syria]. Retrieved November 18, 2017, from http://www.fmprc.gov.cn/web/zyxw/t1453414.shtml
Ministry of Foreign Affairs of the People's Republic of China. (2017b, November 24). 王毅:反恐、对话、重建是新阶段解决叙利亚问题的三个着力点 [Wang Yi: Anti-terrorism, Dialogue and Reconstruction Are the Three Key Foci in Syria's New Phase]. Retrieved December 12, 2017, from http://www.fmprc.gov.cn/web/zyxw/t1513697.shtml
Mother Syria Assembly (MSA). (2017, December 12). MSA 1st Economic Conference: National Economic Vision for Future Syria. *MSA News*.
Moubayed, S. (2017, February 6). When the Guns Go Silent, Who Foots the Bill? China Is Ready. *Asia Times*.
Patnaik, P. (2016, December 8). Developing "Infrastructure". *MR online*.
SANA. (2017, July 10). Syrian Day Held in Beijing to Promote Damascus International Fair. *SANA News*.
SANA. (2018, January 9). Khamis: New Stage of Rebuilding Aleppo Province Started. *SANA News*.
Simmons, G. (2009, October 31). Waypoint on the Old Silk Road. *The National*.
Sina. (2015, October 16). 中国向叙利亚等国提供1亿元人民币人道主义援助 [China Provides 100 Million RMB Humanitarian Assistance to Syria and Other Countries]. *Sina News*. Retrieved March 10, 2017, from http://mil.news.sina.com.cn/2015-10-16/1651841392.html
Sina. (2017, May 9). 叙利亚邀请中国参与叙重建 承诺给予优先权 [Syria Invites China to Participate in Syria Reconstruction]. *Sina News*. Retrieved February 20, 2018, from http://mil.news.sina.com.cn/china/2017-05-09/doc-ifyeycfp9399627.shtml
Sina. (2018, February 1). 俄媒:中国参与叙利亚全国对话大会 大国角色不断凸显 [China's Special Envoy to Syria Attended the Syrian National Dialogue Conference, Highlighting China's Prominent Role in Syria's Reconstruction]. *Sina News*. Retrieved February 20, 2018, from https://news.sina.cn/gn/2018-02-01/detail-ifyreuzn1055300.d.html

South China Morning Post (SCMP). (2017, April 7). China's Role in Syria's Endless Civil War. *SCMP*. Retrieved March 1, 2018, from http://www.scmp.com/news/china/diplomacy-defence/article/2085779/backgrounder-chinas-role-syrias-endless-civil-war

South China Morning Post (SCMP). (2018, February 12). China to Step Up Aid to Syria as War Winds Down. *SCMP*. Retrieved March 1, 2018, from http://www.scmp.com/news/china/diplomacy-defence/article/2133064/china-step-aid-syria-war-winds-down

Sputnik International. (2017, July 11). China Sends a Strong Signal About Its Geopolitical Interests in Syria. *Sputnik International.*

Straits Times. (2017, December 25). China Eyes Role in Rebuilding of War-Torn Syria. *The Straits Times.*

Syria Times. (2017, February 23). China's Participation in Reconstruction in Syria Discussed. *The Syria Times*. Retrieved December 2, 2017, from http://syriatimes.sy/index.php/economy/29294-china-s-participation-in-reconstruction-in-syria-discussed

Syrian Centre for Policy Research (SCPR). (2016). Confronting Fragmentation: Impact of the *Syrian Crisis Report*. UNDP Country Office in Syria.

The New Arab. (2017, September 16). China Provides $10 Billion Credit Line to Iran. *The New Arab*. Retrieved December 10, 2017, from https://www.alaraby.co.uk/english/news/2017/9/16/china-provides-10-billion-credit-line-to-iran

The Syria Report. (2011, April 14). STE Contracts Huawei for Cable Network. *The Syria Report.*

The Syria Report. (2014, June 16). China's PCCW Awarded Telecom Services Contract. *The Syria Report.*

The Syria Report. (2016, September 27). Chinese Company Eying Aleppo Power Plant Contract. *The Syria Report.*

The Syria Report. (2018, January 30). Chinese Companies Starting to Look for Opportunities in Syria. *The Syria Report.*

United Nations. (2016–2017). *Survey of Economic and Social Developments in the Arab Region 2016–2017: (Summary)*. Beirut: United Nations Economic and Social Commission for Western Asia.

United Nations. (2016). *Syria at War*. Beirut: United Nations Economic and Social Commission for Western Asia.

United Nations. (2017). *Fiscal Policy Considerations for Post War Reconstruction in Iraq, Syria, Yemen and Libya*. Beirut: United Nations Economic and Social Commission for Western Asia.

World Bank. (2017). *The Toll of War: The Economic and Social Consequences of the Conflict in Syria*. Washington D.C.: World Bank Group.

Xinhua. (2017, November 1). 记中国向叙利亚流离失所者提供人道主义援助 [China's Provision of Humanitarian Aid to Syrian Displaced Persons]. *Xinhua.*

Retrieved January 12, 2018, from http://www.xinhuanet.com/2017-11/01/c_1121886956.htm
Yang, Y. (2017, September 23). Chinese FM Meets Syrian Deputy Prime Minister. *Xinhua*. Retrieved December 20, 2017, from http://www.xinhuanet.com/english/2017-09/23/c_136630865.htm
Zhang, B. (2017a, November 22). 中国参与叙利亚重建:优势与挑战 [Chinese Participation in Syria's Rebuilding: Advantages and Challenges]. *The Contemporary World*.
Zhang, J. (2017b, December 21). 中国斥巨资参与叙利亚重建 港媒:中企迎绝佳机会 [China Has Heavily Invested in Syrian Construction. Hong Kong Media: Chinese Enterprises Welcome Good Opportunities]. *Sina News*. Retrieved December 22, 2017, from http://news.sina.com.cn/o/2017-12-21/doc-ifypxrpp3152421.shtml

Index[1]

A
Ababsa, Myriam, 22, 23, 254
Abboud, Samer, 42, 43, 48, 110n2
Abdel-Malek, Anouar, 7
Aflaq, Michel, 212
Aggression, 6, 8, 161, 163, 165
  imperialist aggression, 1, 7, 9, 270
Agrarian
  agrarian counter reforms, 23, 248, 253–256
  agrarian reforms, 214, 222, 223, 247, 248
Agriculture
  production, 119
  sector, 256
  self-sufficiency, 247–264
Ajl, Max, 22, 23, 283
Aleppo, 38, 41, 42, 44, 63, 74, 76, 79, 82, 86, 109, 122, 155n10, 217, 227, 235, 249, 255–257, 259, 261
Alliance, 18, 19, 21, 22, 56, 59, 61–63, 65, 68, 78, 83, 86, 110, 154n7, 161, 163–165, 169–172, 174–177, 178n2, 180n60, 186, 211, 212, 271
  cross-class alliance, 32
Aoyama, Hiroyuki, 18, 74, 77, 79, 80, 83, 85–88
Arab
  Arab formations, 218
  Arab nationalism, 22, 33, 60, 61, 77, 89, 164, 210, 212, 219
  Arab region, 24, 210, 272, 273, 282
  Arab Socialist Party, 212
  Arab Spring, 4, 6, 17, 30, 72, 87, 135, 162
  Arab world, 54, 58, 189, 212
al-Asad, Bashar, 3, 7, 16, 21, 30, 34–36, 38, 40, 41, 46, 48, 71, 72, 87, 88, 135, 136, 141, 147, 148, 153n2, 154–155n7, 155n8, 162, 168–170, 177, 178n1, 248, 254, 263, 264n1, 270, 275, 276

---

[1] Note: Page numbers followed by 'n' refer to notes.

A

al-Asad, Hafez, 1, 16, 18, 19, 21, 32–33, 39, 40, 57–63, 65, 71, 81–87, 89, 161–167, 171–176, 178n2, 178n10, 219
Autonomous, 76, 104, 110, 191, 198, 199, 203n11, 282
Autonomy, 76, 110, 165, 185, 238n31, 277, 283
  autonomy over policy, 272

B

Ba'ath, 4, 6, 22, 32, 34, 40, 59, 78–85, 87–89, 117, 170, 186, 187, 201, 209–214, 216–219, 223, 226, 230–232, 236, 240n71, 251
Barley, 228, 229, 231, 234, 249–251, 254, 255, 257, 259, 260
Barout, Jamal, 105
Bretton Woods, 22, 210, 220

C

Camp David Accords, 57, 65, 163
Capital
  capital accumulation, 19, 109
  capital relation, 11
  financial capital, 12, 19
  national capital, 3
  US-led financial capital, 6, 7
Capitalism, 6, 7, 11, 34, 40, 60, 61, 74, 146, 185, 210, 211, 224–228, 236, 279
Centralised economic planning, 97
China
  Belt and Road Initiative, 271, 274, 279, 280
  One Belt One Road, 274
Class
  class relationship, 2, 214
  class struggle, 4, 6, 7, 15

financial class, 3, 7, 9
imperialist class, 6, 13
merchant class, 33, 210, 217
neoliberal class, 2
social class, 19, 74, 76, 86, 211, 226
US-led capital class, 12
working class, 2, 4–6, 12, 22, 102, 103, 105, 115, 146, 232, 237n3, 283
Conditions
  objective conditions, 4, 15, 108, 115
  subjective conditions, 4, 147
Conflict, 1, 6, 9, 11, 15–18, 20–22, 29–50, 55–59, 63, 64, 66, 68, 72, 79, 80, 88–90, 96, 97, 102, 109–110, 115–130, 134, 140, 141, 150, 153n2, 161, 162, 168, 169, 173–177, 178n1, 186, 188, 189, 191, 193, 195, 200, 201, 209, 251, 269–271, 273–282
Consumption, 3, 19, 23, 35, 42, 102, 106, 108, 109, 111n7, 125, 249, 250, 257, 259
Credit, 3, 9, 12, 100, 104, 105, 107, 108, 185, 193, 216, 217, 221–224, 226, 227, 229–231, 275, 279, 280

D

Damascus, 8, 19, 38, 41, 42, 47, 58, 63, 74, 76, 79, 82, 86, 109, 129, 140, 151, 168, 170–173, 180n42, 180n61, 188, 189, 217, 219, 227, 255–259, 261–263, 278, 279, 281
Decree Number 66 of 2012, 8
Deir Ezzor, 23, 41, 122, 129, 136, 141, 145, 223, 232, 235, 248, 252, 254, 257, 259, 261, 262, 264, 264n4

Democracy, 6, 9, 40, 73, 77–80, 85, 88, 210, 220, 237n3, 270
Drought, 23, 35, 41, 118, 120, 187, 188, 211, 214, 232–236, 247, 248, 251, 253–256

E
Economic
  economic and social policies, 2
  economic development, 2, 97, 99, 110n2, 130, 185, 194
  economic history, 1
  economic liberalisation, 19, 33, 59–62, 68, 104, 111n7, 190, 202n1, 217
  economic model, 2
  economic reforms, 3, 4, 34, 78–80, 95, 96, 115–116, 150, 169, 186, 190, 231
  economic revival, 270
Expenditure, 99–101, 121–126, 130n5, 130n7, 143, 144, 195, 198, 199, 229, 230, 258, 275

F
Fertiliser, 23, 119, 120, 189, 221, 249, 252, 257, 259, 260
Financial
  financial capital, 12, 19
  financial class, 3, 7, 9
  financial institutions, 279
  financial sector, 12, 103
Five-year plan, 97, 185, 248
Food
  food as a weapon, 256–263
  food insecurity, 256, 258
  food production, 23, 185, 247, 248, 256, 262
  food security, 15, 21, 22, 228–231, 235, 247–264
  food supplies, 23, 247, 254, 257
Food and Agriculture Organization (FAO), 247, 254, 256–260, 262, 276

G
GDP per capita, 97
German Development Agency (GIZ), 187, 199, 202n2
Global imbalance, 6, 10–11
Golan Heights, 72, 163, 186
Gross domestic product (GDP), 3, 23, 96–102, 107, 118–121, 123–126, 130n1, 217, 220, 227, 247, 250, 251, 274, 275

H
Haddad, Bassam, 34, 189
Hama, 19, 37, 41, 44, 58, 59, 66, 74, 79, 82, 86, 166, 167, 171, 174, 180n61, 228, 232, 256, 257, 259
Hasaka, 122, 129, 232, 252–254, 257, 258
al-Hawrani, Akram, 212
Health
  health sector, 21, 22, 121, 186–193, 196–202, 202n1
  health sector modernisation programme (HSMP), 21, 22, 186, 194–201
  health services, 21, 22, 117, 121, 186, 188, 190–199, 202n4
  public health, 121, 185–202
Hemesh, Mounir, 1, 96–98, 109, 111n3, 271
Hinnebusch, Raymond, 17, 32–36, 41, 58, 61, 83, 109, 134, 148, 185, 186, 212, 240n71

I

Idlib, 66, 122, 129, 140, 141, 232, 235, 257, 259, 262, 276
Ikhwan, 33, 166
Imperialism
  class of imperialism, 6
  cordon sanitaire of imperialism, 2
  US-led imperialism, 6, 8, 9, 13, 15, 271, 283
Income, 3, 4, 61, 96, 102, 108, 109, 118, 120, 121, 128, 129, 139, 141, 152, 188, 193, 202n3, 217, 221, 222, 229, 251, 259, 283
  income disparity, 102–103
  income distribution, 19, 96, 190
  income gap, 98, 117
  income inequality, 4, 101, 103
Industry, 4, 5, 9, 11, 106, 185, 217, 221, 229, 250, 275
Inflation, 4, 19, 98, 99, 101, 105, 106, 108, 189, 226, 232, 235, 241n90, 248, 258, 263, 264
Insurgency, 42, 45, 169, 226
Interest rate, 103–105, 226
International Centre for Agricultural Research in Dry Areas (ICARDA), 249, 264n2
International Monetary Fund (IMF), 5, 96, 99, 100, 104, 107, 109, 147, 187, 275, 276
  Article IV Consultation Report, 99
Investment
  private investment, 98–100, 102, 119, 220, 221, 231
  public investment, 98–100, 107, 117, 124
Iran, 21, 23, 33, 45, 56, 58–60, 64, 72, 161–176, 273, 275, 276
Iraq, 7, 24, 31, 32, 34, 48, 49, 53, 54, 58, 59, 65, 66, 82, 117, 127, 161, 165, 166, 168, 170, 175, 176, 189, 191, 201, 257, 260, 263, 272, 282
Iraq War, 168
Irrigation, 36, 109, 118, 119, 148, 221, 222, 224, 229, 230, 233, 247, 248, 252, 256, 257, 260
Islamic State (IS), 23, 56, 72, 139, 142, 145, 154n2, 155n9, 174, 248, 257–259, 261, 263, 264
Islamic State of Iraq and Syria (ISIS), 11, 12, 47–49, 56, 63, 65–67, 155n9
Israel, 2, 21, 23, 33, 34, 53, 57, 59, 60, 65, 71, 72, 116, 161–167, 171, 172, 174, 175, 178n2, 180n52, 211, 212, 216, 218–219

J

Jazîra, 247, 249, 251–255, 257, 260, 263, 264n6
Jihadist, 7, 30, 43–46, 48–50, 67, 89, 141, 168, 173, 258

K

Kadri, Ali, 3, 23, 95–97, 99, 104, 107, 108, 110, 111n7, 134, 271, 272, 279, 280, 283
Kienle, Eberhard, 18, 58, 60, 65, 67

L

Labour
  labour demand, 3
  labour history, 6
  labour market, 3, 120, 126, 188, 235
Law
  Law No. 10 of 1991, 188, 220
  Law No. 10 of 2016, 8

Lebanon, 20, 22, 24, 31, 33, 58, 59, 64, 65, 71, 72, 74, 127, 133–153, 153n1, 154n5, 154n6, 164–170, 172, 173, 175, 176, 179n37, 187, 189, 191, 199, 201, 202n7, 257, 272, 278, 282
Lenin, Vladimir, 4, 212
Liberalisation, 19, 96, 97, 101, 105–107, 109, 120, 189, 196, 200, 202n3, 210, 227

M
Macroeconomic, 17, 19, 95–110, 118, 189, 190, 192
Madrid peace conference, 166
Manufacturing, 19, 100–102, 106, 109, 118–120, 130n1, 275, 281
Market, 2, 3, 19, 20, 35, 59, 67, 97, 101, 103, 105–107, 109, 110n2, 119, 120, 122–125, 146, 148, 187, 188, 202n3, 211, 216, 217, 221, 226, 227, 239n43, 249–251, 256–258, 264, 280
Marx, Karl, 30, 147
Matar, Linda, 3, 19, 20, 23, 97, 98, 100, 106–108, 110, 134, 147, 185–189, 192, 271
Mesopotamia, 279
Military, 2, 10, 32, 38, 39, 44, 45, 47, 49, 55, 57, 58, 60, 66, 76–82, 84, 85, 87, 117, 122–126, 130n7, 140, 163, 165, 167, 168, 171, 173, 175, 176, 180n42, 212, 218, 219, 269, 270, 273, 275–277, 283
Mobilisation
  mass mobilisation, 40
  regime mobilisation, 41, 42
Muslim Brotherhood, 39, 41, 117, 166

N
Nasser, Gamal Abdel, 248
National
  national capital, 3
  national defence, 2, 283
  national identity, 177, 272
  national liberation, 15, 219, 271
  national plan, 185, 274, 281–283
  national policies, 282
  national resources, 271
  national security, 2, 9, 23, 24, 176, 269–284
  national sovereignty, 88, 271
  national unity, 18, 88, 284
Nationalism
  Arab nationalism, 22, 33, 60, 61, 77, 89, 164, 210, 212, 219
  Syrian nationalism, 77
Neoliberal
  neoliberal policies, 5, 116, 117, 119, 121, 122, 147, 186, 190–192
  neoliberal reforms, 1, 15, 21, 103, 118, 191
Neoliberalism, 2, 5, 21, 36, 89, 236, 283
al-Nusra Front, 72

O
Opposition, 31–34, 36, 38–40, 42–47, 49, 56, 66, 68, 72, 85, 88, 136, 138, 146, 153–154n2, 162, 169, 179n35, 179n36, 235, 257, 261, 263, 270

P
Partition, 224, 270
  partition of Syria's territory, 110, 270, 271

Path dependency, 30, 36, 45, 49, 109
Patnaik, Prabat, 283
Peasant, 33, 35, 36, 59, 61, 62, 117, 155n12, 210, 212–214, 218, 222–224, 227, 229, 231, 236, 249, 254
  capitalist middle peasants, 221–224
Policy
  fiscal, 98–104, 125–126, 220
  foreign, 15, 21, 33, 34, 56, 67, 161–163, 165, 168–169, 171, 176, 177, 277
  monetary, 103–105, 108, 109, 147
  neoliberal, 5, 116, 117, 119, 121, 122, 147, 186, 190–192
Political economy, 6, 21, 68n1, 185–202, 209–236
Poverty, 3, 98, 103, 108, 116, 121–122, 128–129, 135, 153, 188, 232, 233, 251, 276
Price, 2, 3, 12, 19, 98, 102, 103, 105, 108, 117–120, 122–124, 128, 149, 189, 190, 201, 217, 218, 221, 226–230, 232, 235, 239n51, 249, 250, 253–258, 260–263, 275
Production, 2–4, 6, 11, 23, 60, 74, 98, 100, 101, 106, 109, 116–120, 122–124, 146, 147, 211, 214, 216, 217, 221, 222, 228–232, 234, 247, 249–260, 262, 263, 274, 276, 278, 281
Proxy war, 11, 17, 18, 36–45, 134, 135, 144, 153–154n2, 209

R

Raqqa, 11, 23, 66, 122, 129, 142, 232, 235, 248, 252, 254, 256–258, 261–263, 264n5, 276
Rebels, 15, 63, 134, 135, 140, 149, 162, 174, 175, 258, 261, 262

Reconstruction, 8, 23, 24, 72, 110, 167, 200, 201, 269–274, 276–278, 280–283
Reform, 1–5, 20, 30, 33, 35, 38–40, 78, 80, 87, 88, 96, 98–100, 104, 105, 107, 117, 118, 148, 162, 169, 174, 177, 187, 191, 192, 196–198, 202n1, 202n7, 211, 212, 214, 217, 251, 264n4, 272, 282
Refugee, 11, 41, 89, 116, 127, 134, 135, 140–142, 144, 169, 189, 191, 202n5, 259, 274, 275, 278
  refugee crisis, 134
Regime, 4, 7, 9, 19, 32–50, 50n1, 55, 56, 58–62, 65, 68, 73, 77, 78, 80, 81, 83, 85–87, 129, 134, 135, 146, 148, 162, 167–170, 173, 174, 177, 178n3, 213, 219, 231, 235, 251, 258, 261, 270
  regime formation, 46–48
Resistance front, 21, 161–177
  axis of resistance, 161, 174
Resource, 2, 7, 16, 17, 19, 23, 35, 45–47, 49, 55, 56, 61, 62, 67, 95, 97, 99–101, 106–108, 110, 116, 120–122, 124–126, 128, 163, 165, 170, 189–192, 194, 201, 211, 217, 223, 224, 227, 230, 232, 234, 247, 248, 252, 253, 270, 271, 273, 275, 280, 282, 283
  resource allocation, 3, 96, 97, 103, 126
Revolution
  revolutionary awakening, 135
  revolutionary subjectivity, 133–153
  revolution from a distance, 136–137
Russell, Bertrand, 6, 15
Russia, 3, 10, 23, 45, 56, 72, 89, 212, 273, 276, 282

S

Saudi Arabia, 53, 56, 155n7, 161, 164, 165, 167, 169, 170, 172, 173, 220
Seale, Patrick, 18, 53–55, 57, 65, 71, 72, 79, 80, 212, 237n8
Sect, 32, 40, 46, 74–76, 78, 82, 89, 166, 272
Sectarian, 4, 6, 8, 19, 33, 35, 39–43, 46–48, 64, 73, 74, 78, 83, 86, 89, 138, 168, 171, 173, 174, 270, 283
Sector
  informal, 62, 102, 103, 108, 120, 188, 192, 199, 200, 255
  private, 2, 3, 20, 60, 96, 99, 101, 102, 104–106, 108, 109, 110n2, 111n7, 119, 121, 197, 202n4, 202n10, 216, 220, 250–251, 260, 263
  public, 2, 47, 59, 62, 97, 98, 107, 111n7, 117, 187, 192, 194, 198, 227, 261, 271, 275, 276
Security, 2, 32, 33, 35, 37–39, 41–44, 46, 47, 49, 67, 84, 87, 97, 106, 117, 127, 128, 135, 165, 167, 168, 171, 172, 176, 228–232, 235, 247–264, 269–284
Seifan, Samir, 97, 98, 101, 102, 106, 111n5, 111n6, 194, 200
Sen, Kasturi, 21, 22, 185
Shock therapy, 3, 20, 96
Social
  social class, 86, 211, 226
  social cleavage, 18, 19, 71–90
  social compact, 213–218, 230, 236
  social contradiction, 211, 223
  social movement, 18, 29, 36–37, 213
  social redistribution, 210, 218
  social struggle, 210

Socialism, 1, 2, 81, 104, 212, 213, 218
Social market economy, 97, 100, 110n2, 169, 187, 189
Sottimano, Aurora, 21, 161
Sovereignty, 2, 9, 89, 104, 107, 110, 116, 119, 209, 220, 232, 271–273, 277, 280, 282, 284
  national sovereignty, 88
State
  security state, 167
  sovereign state, 232, 277, 282
  state consolidation, 176, 271
  state failure, 30, 31, 45–49
Strategic, 16, 24, 54, 55, 80, 155n10, 163, 165, 171, 175, 193, 195, 229, 251, 256, 271, 274, 279
  strategic balance, 163–164
Structure, 8, 15–24, 29–31, 36, 41, 43, 49, 54, 66, 83, 117, 120, 123, 124, 150, 192, 214, 220, 221, 224, 247, 248, 270, 272, 277, 283
Struggle for Syria, 18, 53, 54, 71, 72
Struggle for the Middle East, 71
Subsidy, 19, 124–126, 249
Syria
  Syria Central Bank, 99, 106, 274
  Syria Central Bureau of Statistics, 97, 100, 106, 116, 118, 121, 274
  Syrian Center for Policy Research (SCPR), 20, 115
  Syrian conflict, 6, 15, 17, 18, 21, 29–31, 56, 72, 90, 115–130, 150, 161, 173, 175, 176, 178n1, 269, 276
  Syrian Economic Society, 96, 100, 104
  Syrian Prime Ministry, 8
  The Syria Report, 101, 275, 278, 279, 281

Syria State Planning Commission, 97, 100, 101, 104, 198
uprising, 21, 30, 49, 95, 129, 135, 141, 147, 162, 173–175, 177

T

Taif Accord, 164, 167
Tax, 34, 46, 97, 98, 100–102, 108, 111n5, 115, 126, 227, 258, 263, 275
Thermidor, 22, 209–236

U

Unemployment, 3, 98, 102, 117, 120, 126, 148, 188, 190, 198, 202n3, 211, 275
United Arab Republic (UAR), 53, 55, 65, 77, 79, 80, 212, 248

V

Value
  value of human lives, 12
  value of the commodity, 12
  value relations, 5, 7
  war as value relationship, 12–15
Violence, 5, 31, 37, 38, 42–46, 49, 50, 56, 64, 122, 126–129, 136, 142, 147, 153, 283

W

Wage, 4, 11, 49, 98, 102–103, 105, 108, 120–122, 124, 140, 145, 149, 151, 152, 164, 190, 235
Wang Yi, 273
War
  anti-colonial war, 1
  civil war, 29, 31, 43, 65, 153–154n2, 187, 256
  imperialist war, 7, 12–13
  new war, 50, 122
  proxy war, 36–45, 134, 135, 144, 153–154n2, 209
  war zone, 2, 135
Water
  water mismanagement, 23, 120, 248, 252, 253
  water reserves, 252
  water resources, 120, 170, 247, 252
West, 6, 19, 34, 48, 56, 60, 65, 66, 89, 165, 166, 175, 193, 249, 272, 283
Wheat, 139, 187, 217, 221, 228–231, 234, 239n43, 247–252, 254–264
World Bank (WB), 5, 96–99, 105, 111n4, 187, 197, 240n65, 274, 275
World Trade Organisation (WTO), 5

Z

al-Za'im, Husni, 55

Printed by Printforce, the Netherlands